THE WORLDS
OF
ROMAN WOMEN

A LATIN READER

THE WORLDS
OF
ROMAN WOMEN

A LATIN READER

ANN RAIA

CECELIA LUSCHNIG

JUDITH LYNN SEBESTA

THE FOCUS CLASSICAL LIBRARY
Series Editors • James Clauss and Stephen Esposito

Aristophanes: Acharnians • Jeffrey Henderson • 1992 • 1-58510-087-0
Aristophanes: The Birds • Jeffrey Henderson • 1999 • 0-941051-87-0
Aristophanes: Clouds • Jeffrey Henderson • 1992 • 0-941051-24-2
Aristophanes: Frogs • Henderson • 2008 • 978-1-58510-308-9
Aristophanes: Lysistrata • Jeffrey Henderson • 1988 • 0-941051-02-1
Aristophanes: Three Comedies: Acharnians, Lysistrata, Clouds • Jeffrey Henderson • 1997 • 0-941051-58-7
Euripides: The Bacchae • Stephen Esposito • 1998 • 0-941051-42-0
Euripides: Four Plays: Medea, Hippolytus, Heracles, Bacchae • Stephen Esposito, ed. • 2003 • 1-58510-048-X
Euripides: Hecuba • Robin Mitchell-Boyask • 2006 • 1-58510-148-6
Euripides: Heracles • Michael R. Halleran • 1988 • 0-941051-01-3
Euripides: Hippolytus • Michael R. Halleran • 2001 • 0-941051-86-2
Euripides: Medea • Anthony Podlecki • 2005, Revised • 0-941051-10-2
Euripides: The Trojan Women • Diskin Clay • 2005 • 1-58510-111-7
Golden Verses: Poetry of the Augustan Age • Paul T. Alessi • 2003 • 1-58510-064-1
Golden Prose in the Age of Augustus • Paul T. Alessi • 2004 • 1-58510-125-7
Hesiod: Theogony • Richard Caldwell • 1987 • 0-941051-00-5
Hesiod: Theogony & Works and Days • Stephanie Nelson • 2009 • 978-1-58510-288-4
The Homeric Hymns • Susan Shelmerdine • 1995 • 1-58510-019-6
Ovid: Metamorphoses • Z. Philip Ambrose • 2004 • 1-58510-103-6
Plautus: Captivi, Amphitryon, Casina, Pseudolus • David Christenson • 2008 • 978-1-58510-155-9
Sophocles: Antigone • Ruby Blondell • 1998 • 0-941051-25-0
Sophocles: Electra • Hanna M. Roisman • 2008 • 978-1-58510-281-5
Sophocles: King Oidipous • Ruby Blondell • 2002 • 1-58510-060-9
Sophocles: Oidipous at Colonus • Ruby Blondell • 2003 Revised • 1-58510-065-X
Sophocles: Philoktetes • Seth Schein • 2003 • 1-58510-086-2
Sophocles: The Theban Plays • Ruby Blondell • 2002 • 1-58510-037-4
Terence: Brothers (Adelphoe) • Charles Mercier • 1998 • 0-941051-72-2 [VHS • 0-941051-73-0]
Vergil: The Aeneid • Richard Caldwell • 2004 • 1-58510-077-3

TABLE OF CONTENTS

PREFACE

When we began our Latin studies, the lives of Roman women (save for the likes of a scandalous Clodia) were of little interest to classicists, few of whom ventured to ask "What were the women doing?" Today we are the beneficiaries of the work of feminist scholars who have produced valuable collections and analyses of sources in translation on the social history of ancient women, such as Fantham et al., *Women in the Classical World*, and Lefkowitz and Fant, *Women's Life in Greece and Rome*. A most welcome addition is the 2002 publication of ancient women's texts in Latin and English translation, *Women Writing Latin* I, edited by Churchill, Brown, and Jeffrey. In addition, classicists and their students can now access a growing corpus of English and Latin texts, images, papers, and syllabi on the Internet (*Corpus Scriptorum Latinorum, Diotima, Latin Library, Perseus, Stoa, VRoma*). However, research reveals few Latin text with English commentaries in print about women: Balme and Morwood's *On the Margin* treats women briefly, in the non-elite group of slaves and foreigners.

We saw a need for an anthology of readings about women that was directed to the intermediate stage of Latin learning, the transition from adapted Latin to the original that proves so difficult for both student and teacher. The present work offers a collection of unadapted Latin texts solely by or about women — elite, non-elite, slave, freed, free — that indicate the range of activities, concerns, and social roles of women in ancient Rome. In our effort to find and represent women of all ranks and status, we searched both words and images and every genre of literature from the third century BCE to the second century CE, including authors not normally read in undergraduate courses, such as Valerius Maximus and Aulus Gellius. We found women everywhere, playing as children and as adults making contributions to the family, to the workplace, to the arts and crafts, and to social and civic affairs; their presence in all areas of Roman life, often barely discernible but always significant, inspired our title, *The Worlds of Roman Women*.

This book is designed to be used as a course text or supplementary reader by college and secondary school students who have completed a basic introduction to Latin grammar, syntax, and vocabulary. Since our primary goal is to encourage intermediate Latin students to read extensively and through reading to develop confidence in their ability to translate and understand the language, we have provided extensive glosses and notes facing each selection, for ease of reading. The vocabulary at the end of the book is intended to provide forms and meanings for words appearing in the text that are not explained in the glosses. We presume that students will be able to recognize commonly found constructions (ablative absolute, indirect speech, purpose and result clauses) but may have difficulty identifying other subjunctive uses (relative clauses of characteristic, various conditional clauses); these uses are explained in the notes, which also provide brief translation hints where necessary; observations on word order and figures of speech; literary, historical and biographical information; and other material to assist understanding.

The Latin selections are divided into "worlds." Each world is introduced by an essay that provides a context for the Latin passages and summarizes the key ideas and major issues that affect women's lives in that particular world. Each text is prefaced by a brief introduction providing information about the author and selection and, where appropriate, identifying the woman. Images were selected to illustrate the worlds and to offer the reader less familiar depictions of Roman women. The indices contain a profile of authors arranged alphabetically and a chronological list of the women who appear in the text, keyed to the author, work, and the world she appears in. A select bibliography of recommended works is provided to aid student project research and further exploration.

This anthology was created by three women who received their doctorates in the third quarter of the twentieth century. Living in three time zones, we collaborated across the continent almost solely through e-mail and conference calls: Ann Raia in Rye, New York, Cecelia Luschnig in Moscow, Idaho, Judith Lynn Sebesta in Vermillion, South Dakota. We each teach courses dealing with Roman women: Ann Raia's "Roman Women: *Puella, Matrona, Meretrix*" syllabus is on-line at *Diotima;* Cecelia Luschnig's advanced Latin course resulted in the creation of the text-commentary website *De Feminis Romanis* at *Diotima;* Judith Sebesta's "Women in Antiquity" syllabus is on-line at *Diotima*. Ann Raia earned her Ph.D. at Fordham University and has taught Latin, Greek, classics in translation, and Honors courses at The College of New Rochelle since 1964. Cecelia Luschnig's Ph.D. is from the University of Cincinnati; she began teaching in 1965 and has taught Latin, Greek, word origins, and classical literature at the University of Cincinnati, Ohio University, the University of Washington, and the University of Idaho. Judith Lynn Sebesta earned her Ph.D. at Stanford University and has taught Latin, Greek, classical humanities and Honors courses at the University of South Dakota since 1972.

We acknowledge and thank Barbara McManus, *femina docta et amica,* for her innumerable generous contributions to this work as consultant on feminist scholarship, source for images of women, and exacting first reader. We are most grateful to our reviewers, particularly Professor Ortwin Knorr, whose careful reading and expertise led to many improvements in this edition; all errors that remain, of course, are our own. We thank William A. Whitaker for permission to export his on-line program *Words* as a basis for our vocabulary. We are grateful to Prentice Clark, our editorial assistant, for her patient technical expertise. In addition, Ann Raia wishes to thank The College of New Rochelle's School of Arts and Sciences for the 2004 faculty development grant that provided resources for the production of this manuscript; her students in "Roman Women" for their enthusiasm and feedback; and her sister, Rose DeVita, for help in developing the vocabulary section. Cecelia Luschnig would like to thank first Lance Luschnig for helping with the images and putting up with a lot; Dona Black, for drawings that have inspired a new project; Hannah Etherton, interlibrary loan librarian at the University of Idaho and former Latin student; Richard Naskali, director *emeritus* of the University of Idaho Arboretum. Judith Lynn Sebesta wishes to thank her Latin teacher, Dorothea Sparks, for inspiring her with a love of Latin; her undergraduate professors, Edwin Bassett, John Hawthorne, and Nancy Helmbold, and her graduate professors, Antony Raubitschek and Lionel Pearson for their teaching and mentoring; and Larissa Bonfante and John Bodel, for their NEH summer seminars filled with insights upon life in the classical world.

LIST OF ABBREVIATIONS

(1) = 1st conjugation verb
A&G = Allen & Greenough's *Grammar*
AA = *Ars Amatoria*
abl. = ablative
abl. abs. = ablative absolute
acc. = accusative
adj. = adjective
adv. = adverb
AUC = *Ab Urbe Condita*
BG = *de Bello Gallico*
c. = common gender
C. = Gaius
ca. = *circa*
CLE = *Carmina Latina Epigraphica*
CIL = *Corpus Inscriptionum Latinarum*
Cn. = Gnaeus
comp. = comparative
conj. = conjunction
d. = died
D. = Decimus
dat. = dative
de Arch. = *de Architectura*
depon. = deponent
ed. = edition
ed(s). = editor(s)
e.g. = *exempli gratia* (for example)
El. = *Elegiae*
Ep. = *Epistulae, Epigrammata*
et al. = *et alii* (and others)
f. = feminine
fl. = *floruit* (flourished)
frag. = fragment
freq. = frequentative
gen. = genitive
Gk. = Greek
i.e. = *id est* (that is)

ILS = *Inscriptiones Latinae Selectae*
imperf. = imperfect (tense)
indecl. = indeclinable
infin. = infinitive
interj. = interjection
interrog. = interrogative
l. = *liberta/libertus* (freedwoman/freedman)
L. = Lucius
lit. = literally
loc. = locative
m. = masculine
M. = Marcus
m/f. = masculine or feminine
n. = neuter, noun
NA = *Noctes Atticae*
n.d. = no date
NH = *Naturalis Historia*
nom. = nominative
OLD = *Oxford Latin Dictionary*
P. = Publius
perf. = perfect (tense)
pl. = plural
Praef. = *Praefatio* (Preface)
prep. = preposition
pron. = pronoun
Q. = Quintus
rel. = relative
Sat. = *Saturae, Satyricon*
s. = singular
sing. = singular
subj. = subjunctive
super. = superlative
T. = Titus
v. = verb
voc. = vocative
vol(s). = volume(s)

INTRODUCTION

In 1965, M. I. Finley wrote an essay entitled "The Silent Women of Rome," in which he outlined the problems facing those who investigate the lives of Roman women, since women appear only in sources written by Roman men, who focused mainly on feminine sexual (im)morality. Even Roman women's epitaphs were written by men and were framed to reflect men's ideals of women's behavior. In the words of Suzanne Dixon, "the dominant *voice* and *gaze* of ancient art and writings is male, elite, Italian, middle-aged and citizen Roman" (2001: 21). However, while ancient literary sources on women have not changed, attitudes and approaches have. Since 1965, Finley's picture has been extensively revised by the new theoretical frameworks and methodological approaches introduced by feminist classical scholars. These have radically and permanently altered the way we study not only women but also other groups who have been marginalized and stereotyped by the predominately elite male authors of Roman literature.

Classics is by nature an interdisciplinary field. While originally concentrating on the Latin and Greek texts, classicists find relevant everything that comes from or pertains to the ancient world, from the minutest object of the material culture to the grandest monument; from the most meager fragment of a lost work to the most magnificent epic. Until recently, the methodologies of other disciplines were little used by classics professionals. Now, however, feminism, itself a multidisciplinary enterprise, has given Latin and Greek scholarship a whole new direction that is bringing to light and restoring the silenced populations of classical antiquity. In her book *Classics and Feminism: Gendering the Classics*, Barbara McManus describes the influence that feminism has had on classical scholarship in America since the special issue of *Arethusa* on ancient women (6.1, 1973) and the publication of Sarah Pomeroy's paradigm-shifting social history of Greek and Roman women, *Goddesses, Whores, Wives, and Slaves* (1975). McManus identifies the following six new methodological principles established by these two works:

1. "groups of women (not 'Woman') must be studied in the specific context of socioeconomic class, culture, and time period";

2. "sources must also be differentiated and interpreted with due respect for their individual codes, conventions, and biases";

3. "the most fruitful approach to studying ancient women will employ multiple viewpoints" and be collaborative in nature;

4. "feminist scholarship will be interested in women *qua* women, not as a vehicle for the exploration of masculine ideology…nor as a category to think with";

5. "feminist perspective is not monolithic but can encompass considerable diversity; in fact, respectful dialogue and debate open the most productive path to knowledge";

6. "[feminism] requires an interest in theory, in conjecture, in 'the discernment of patterns, inter-relationships, and chains of causality' rather than the mere accumulation of 'facts'" (1997: excerpted from 18-19).

These principles have enabled classical scholars to move beyond the confines of traditional philology and encouraged us to take a new look at both the textual and non-textual evidence (such as coins, art, architecture, epitaphs) in the light of feminist and other theoretical approaches. The Roman literary canon remains, of course, a primary source, but new approaches give unexpected insights into Roman women's lives. In her article "Women as *Same* and *Other* in Classical Roman Elite," Judith Hallett argues that the Roman literary canon conceptualizes the elite Roman woman in ways that are persistent if not always consistent, even within the work of the same author: she was *Other*, not-male, possessed of different talents, therefore often seen as lesser; she was also *Same*, displaying male virtues associated with her elite male kin and entering the public arena as an active participant (1989). In the literary canon women are defined in opposition to men, which differentiates and devalues both women and their activities, placing them outside the norm and presenting them as alien or at best exotic. However, they are also identified with the male kin of their class and thus praised or criticized for demonstrating qualities and talents that are prized in men and for taking the lead in male spheres such as politics. Sometimes, indeed, class trumps gender in Roman society.

Feminist scholars have moved beyond the canon to other sources of evidence (e.g., legal texts, letters, inscriptions, epitaphs, paintings, sculpture, architecture) to show how frequently actual practice across the classes contradicted or at least tempered the ideology of sex polarity. Following their example, we now ask broader, deeper, and more focused questions about Roman women's lives, search in non-traditional sources of information, frame our answers with qualification, acknowledging the limits of our evidence in regard to time period, class, speaker, audience, and genre. In addition, reading ancient texts in translation gives an incomplete notion of their content. Feminist scholars, by attending to word selection and syntax as well as author bias and audience expectation, have demonstrated anew that language is not transparent, that it communicates traditions, attitudes, and conventions. Within each of the worlds presented here, readers will see some of the tensions and paradoxes that are so characteristic of the ancient Roman presentation of women.

While reading these texts, it is well to remember Suzanne Dixon's warning: "we should be wary of accepting specific information about specific women at face value. Understanding *genre* means being alert to the gaps and biases which keep certain women out of some texts and to the rules determining which aspects of their lives will be highlighted in others" (2001: 25). The selections in this book are drawn from many different types of sources, each with its own conventions of genre and preoccupations. Excerpts from comedy and satire capture the exaggerated stereotypes and male biases that are the product of social and sexual anxieties about women. Scholarly or technical works aim at objectivity, but by relying on the lore of the past rather than developing and testing new hypotheses they reinforce cultural stereotypes. In addition, Roman literature frequently employs *exempla* (examples) to illustrate the virtues and vices of specific women and men as well as the wider implications of their behavior and its consequences of reward or punishment. These texts were commonly used in the education of citizens, particularly statesmen and orators, who were made to memorize them in school and were encouraged to use them in speeches, letters, and conversation. Suetonius relates that the emperor Augustus had the habit of sending excerpts from his readings (*praecepta et exempla*) to provincial governors, military officers, and family members, to remind them of their duties (*Vita Aug.*

89). This way of looking at the world was bound to create a certain degree of black-and-white thinking, moral petrifaction rather than clarity. As a result, women, when they cannot speak for themselves, often appear in one of two extremes, as either impossibly virtuous or uncommonly vicious. For instance, Livy's Lucretia gives as her reason for suicide that she does not want some later woman using her as a precedent for escaping punishment for unchaste behavior (*AUC* 1.59). On the other hand, Tullia, the wife of Tarquinius Superbus, seeks to justify her bloody kin-murders aimed at securing the kingship for her husband by pointing to Tanaquil's success in making two men king, her husband and her son-in-law (see the World of the State). The use of women as *exempla* leads to their being seen not as individuals but rather in terms of the roles they fill in society. Therefore Roman women are celebrated as wives and mothers who reflect well on their noble ancestors and kinsmen, or they are censured for behavior that brings public disgrace upon their families through impropriety, ambition, or pursuit of luxury.

Women are at a disadvantage in Roman history, since the cultural goal for them was invisibility and silence. Ancient Roman historians often simply omit them and focus instead solely or primarily on leading men, a strategy that Livy adopted in regard to Claudia Quinta (see the World of the State). Dixon observes that "those women who are mentioned by Appian, Livy or Tacitus typically perform very restricted roles, either demonstrating a general principle, or throwing light on the character of a leading male, rather than advancing the narrative in their own right" (2001: 20). Another strategy was to present women as a theme or trope without regard for their human subjectivity. For example, women figure prominently in several ways in the first book of Livy's history: as victims of rape (and thus as catalysts for male action), as improper actors in the affairs of the state, and as metaphors for the male citizen body. Acts of violence against women, narrated from the perspective of an Augustan male, are interpreted as a stage toward an ultimately positive outcome, just as Rome's destruction of nations through war and subsequent assimilation is presented as creating universal concord (Arietti 1997). The rape of Rhea Silvia is seen as leading to the birth of Romulus, founder of Rome; the rape of the Sabine women is a means for the continuance of Rome through the offspring born of this rape and subsequent marriage to Roman men; the rape of Lucretia precipitates the overthrow of the monarchy and the creation of the Roman Republic. Sandra Joshel (1992a) notes that in Livy's stories of early Rome the female body becomes a metaphor for the private territory of the Roman male: Sextus Tarquinius conquers the chastity of Lucretia and thus invades the home of her husband Collatinus; by besieging and conquering Collatinus' home, Sextus has reduced Collatinus, and by implication the Roman males, to the status of a conquered people.

Another aspect of Latin literature arises from the fact that it was produced primarily by men. In poetry, however, there are several possible exceptions to what Habinek refers to as "the institutionalization of literature as a written, professional, elite enterprise, which constitutes itself as a male enterprise and situates women accordingly" (1998: 123). The poetry assembled here offers several individualized portrayals of women, perhaps because a few women actually speak and some male poets attempt to understand the feminine perspective. Ovid praises and encourages his step-daughter Perilla, a talented poet who was silenced by his exile (*Tristia* 3.7). Sulpicia gives voice to her love affair and proclaims herself not the passive beloved but a poet in her own right. Martial commends a fellow-poet, another woman named Sulpicia, for her passionate treatment of married love. Finally, a woman perhaps named Terentia left a memorial to herself as well when she composed a farewell to her brother and had it carved on a pyramid in Egypt. In prose, Seneca gives a moving portrait of his mother's virtues and details the bravery of an unnamed maternal aunt.

Our text includes less commonly read literary sources such as letters, honorary inscriptions, tomb epitaphs, and eulogies which, while they convey traditional cultural values and societal expectations that cut across class, also depict individual women. Other than a few letters excavated from the fort at Vindolanda in Britain, no actual letters from Roman women have survived. However, Nepos quotes the letters of Cornelia, the mother of the Gracchi, which some scholars believe may well be authentic. Sometimes letters written by men give insight into women's lives: Cicero's letters reveal that his wife Terentia capably managed his affairs in his absence; Pliny's letters testify that his wife's aunt educated her niece, his wife Calpurnia, so well that not only was she dedicated to him but she was eager to continue her studies in order to share his life fully.

Literature has had a privileged position in past classical studies, but feminist scholarship has turned to visual sources to fill out the picture of women's lives. Natalie Kampen examined women's self-representation on funerary monuments in Ostia to discover that "for women as for men in the Roman world, gender experience changed from one social level to the next, even though the dominant and visible ideologies of the first, second and third centuries were aristocratic and patriarchal" (1981: 75). Sandra Joshel (1992b) closely studied occupational inscriptions in Rome to form a picture of the non-elite workers of the empire (see the World of Work). Unfortunately, in a textbook of this sort it is impossible to provide the visual evidence that would illuminate the words we offer. However, we will briefly mention here two significant topics that merit further exploration: the presence of women in physical space in ancient Rome, and the meaning of artistic representations of Roman women.

Since concepts of gender affect how a society organizes itself, it is not surprising that such concepts also determine how physical space, whether private or public, is organized and used. Greek and Roman societies gendered their private physical space so differently that Cornelius Nepos thought it necessary to preface his biographies of famous men with an explanation:

> There are many things that are proper according to our customs that are thought unseemly by the Greeks. For who of the Romans is made ashamed by bringing his wife to a banquet? Or whose *materfamilias* does not hold chief place in the house and carries on her duties in the middle of a crowd? The case is quite different in Greece. For a wife is not brought into a banquet unless the guests are close relations, nor does she sit anywhere except in the innermost part of the house, which is called "the women's quarters" and no one goes into there unless very closely related to her. (*Praef.* 6-7).

Nepos' words indicate that the Roman *atrium* house was not organized along lines of gender. A Greek wife was restricted to those rooms reserved for her and the other women, slave or free, of the household. All rooms, however, were equally accessible to the Roman *matrona*, even when guests and clients were present. That a public room such as the *atrium* was ungendered is underscored by the presence in such a room of portrait busts and statues of female ancestors along with those of male ancestors.

While most public spaces were open to Roman women, save for those times when a space hosted a group of men engaged in a political activity, such as a *comitium* (assembly) or jury, honorific space seems to have been restricted almost exclusively to men down to the late Republic, in that we know of very few statues erected in honor of a woman (e.g., Cloelia and Cornelia, mother of the Gracchi). Though Caesar and Augustus were the first to place portrait statues of women in public places, these continued to be less common than those of men, and often the female figure was more symbolic than representational. For example, on the frieze of the Temple of Peace built by Vespasian in 75 CE, women are shown engaged in the production of cloth. Since spinning and weaving were traditional occupations of the *matrona,* which earned her the epithet *lanifica* and became a sign of her conjugal fidelity, chastity, and dedication to her family, the frieze has been interpreted as a visual *exemplum* underscoring Flavian legislation for moral reform. On the *Ara Pacis* (Augustus' Altar of Peace), the first state monument that depicts real women and children, Livia and Octavia, Augustus' wife and sister, are placed significantly near the female personifications of Roma and Italia or Tellus. These feminine figures, whether real or abstract personifications, promoted Augustus' social program by representing the importance of motherhood, family life, and marital loyalty.

From the time of Augustus, we have evidence of women commissioning monuments and art. Livia became a patron of the arts both in Rome and in the provinces. As early as 35 BCE Augustus granted unique public honors to both his wife Livia and his sister Octavia, giving them control over their own wealth, erecting public statues of them, and extending to their persons *sacrosanctitas*, the privilege of inviolability possessed by the plebeian tribunes. Livia used her wealth to build several temples that represented virtues particular to women; she built the *Aedes Concordiae* in honor of her harmonious marriage. Through her own and her husband's efforts, Livia was made an *exemplum*. Other wealthy women all over the empire imitated Livia's public and domestic behaviors. In the mid-first century CE Eumachia constructed in the forum of Pompeii a building with a *porticus* dedicated to *Concordia Augusta,* with lavishly carved marble entrance panels that echo the acanthus relief decoration on the *Ara Pacis*. The guild of cloth-makers, dyers, and launderers placed a statue of Eumachia in the courtyard of the building which she had financed for them.

Beginning with Livia, official state images of empresses became models for elite women, freedwomen and women of the lower social classes. Diana Kleiner has pointed out that the figure of Livia, more than any other female figure on the *Ara Pacis*, is presented as "the ideal Roman woman…the model for the family group portraits that became the norm for the sepulchral commemorations of freedwomen in the age of Augustus" (1996: 38-39). In the early Principate, tombstones show freedwomen proudly dressed as *matronae*, sometimes with Livia's hairstyle, set beside husbands wearing the toga — poses and clothing that proclaimed their status as Roman citizens. It is more difficult, however, to interpret funerary depictions of *matronae* in the late first century and early second century CE in which women appear in various states of undress, ranging from a tunic slipping off one shoulder to complete frontal nudity. Why would a respectable *matrona*, whose goal was to be chaste and modest, allow herself to be portrayed in this way? One possible explanation is that these statues, despite the elaborate hairstyles and portrait heads, were viewed symbolically rather than realistically, as appropriations of the positive qualities of the goddess Venus, following in the private sphere the lead of official statues portraying empresses with the attributes of various goddesses. To represent a deceased woman as a partially nude Venus was to suggest that she was an exemplary *matrona* or *mater*, worthy of being compared to Venus, who was worshipped by *matronae* in several cults, among them *Venus Verticordia* (Venus who directs the heart away from lust to chastity) and *Venus Obsequens* (Venus the obedient). The nudity of Venus was a "costume" that women could put on their statues to suggest their beauty, fertility, and "the ideals of cultivation and refinement represented by the perfect physique of the goddess" (D'Ambra, 2000: 102).

Sometimes visual evidence enables us to make connections that are invisible in the literary remains. A Roman doll found on the Via Valeria in Tivoli gives us a glimpse of the way that state images of women of the imperial court touched even the lives of young girls playing in their homes. This fully jointed, anatomically correct ivory doll wears a gold necklace, bracelets, and anklets and bears the unmistakable features and hairstyle of the empress Julia Domna (170-217 CE). One can imagine a little Roman girl dreaming of great possibilities as she played with this doll.

Through the efforts of feminist classical scholars and those taking an expansive theoretical approach alongside their more traditional colleagues, Roman women's voices are beginning to be heard today, both metaphorically and literally, from a wide diversity of sources and over a long span of time. This book joins in that enterprise of discovery and understanding by inviting a wider audience to hear these voices *in Latin* and to see Roman women of different ages and classes in a variety of settings and relationships.

Replica of the statue of Eumachia in the building she constructed for the fullers' guild in the Forum in Pompeii. Photo courtesy of *The VRoma Project*.

PART ONE
THE WORLD OF CHILDHOOD

A child's life in the ancient world hung by a thread. Death lurked everywhere, from difficulties of birthing, exposure, disease, or hard work. It is only in the last three or four hundred years that the idea of childhood has become a distinct category, central to our social and political lives, though recent scholarship reveals that the Romans had a real recognition of children and their development (Rawson: 2003). Children in general, whether in literary or artistic works, are drawn as diminutive adults, though in the Empire we begin to see more childlike portraits. This is not to say, of course, that children were not important: among the elite, sons were needed to carry on the family name and to see that the family tomb and cult were kept up; in poorer families, sons were expected to become workers and to make sure that the parents were cared for in old age. The value of a daughter was in her future marriage, through which political and economic alliances were forged among elite families, adding to the prestige of the family. Daughters were more likely than sons to be separated from the family: they could be exposed or sold. Many girls were reared and loved, as we see clearly in the tender feelings expressed in the epitaphs and in Pliny's letter about Minicia's death. Nonetheless, as happens even now, a family might be too poor to feed another mouth.

At birth a child was placed on the floor by the midwife for inspection. This was the first peril. The father (*paterfamilias*) or the parents together decided whether the child was to be reared. The *Laws of the Twelve Tables* required that healthy boys be reared, but only a first daughter. Deformed or sickly infants of either gender might not be taken up (Table IV.1. "A dreadfully deformed child shall be quickly killed"), nor those whose paternity was suspected. The birth of a healthy child was cause for joyous celebration. The front door was decked with laurel leaves, symbolic of Apollo's protection and a sign for friends to gather to congratulate the father; the mother was cared for in the birthing room by the midwife, sometimes also by her own mother and perhaps other female relatives. When the infant was eight days old, a gathering of family, friends, and neighbors was held both to acknowledge the birth and to celebrate the purification of mother and child (*dies lustricus*). Within thirty days the child was registered at the temple of Saturn. A boy had a special naming ceremony on the ninth day, at which time he was given the *toga praetexta* (a toga with a broad purple border) and the *bulla* (a protective talisman of metal or leather) to wear until he reached puberty. A girl's name was her father's *gens* name in the feminine (e.g. *Tullia*, affectionately called by the diminutive *Tulliola*, was the daughter of M. *Tullius* Cicero), and some women have a second name besides the *gens* name as, for example, *Minicia Marcella* (see Pliny the Younger *Ep.* 5.1.3; the second name is known from her epitaph).

Young children were in the care of their mother (*materfamilias*); upper class children were often raised and given early schooling at home by nurses and pedagogues. Sometimes a strict and upright older relation oversaw the rearing of children in manners, morals, and early education (see Tacitus, *Dialogus* in the World of Family). When she reached twelve, the age of menarche and the minimum legal age of marriage, a girl was considered grown. Her betrothal or marriage, the family's goal for her, was her coming-of-age ceremony. A girl from an elite family would probably be married by the age of fifteen, unless she had been dedicated to a religious cult such as the Vestal Virgins. Girls might be married to much older men, as was Calpurnia to Pliny (see the World of Learning). Pliny describes the charming thirteen-year-old Minicia as already betrothed. The early marriage of girls, before they were physically developed, is one factor that accounts for the high rate of death in childbirth and the frequency of miscarriage (see Pliny the Younger, *Ep.*8.10 in the World of the Body).

Child labor was a significant element in the Roman economy. Children of the poorer and slave classes started their working lives early. The little that is known of them frequently comes from their funerary inscriptions. Girls, usually slaves or freedwomen, often appear as entertainers (like Eucharis), dancers, singers, interlude artists, or mimes. Others are depicted as salespersons in the markets and are documented in literature, papyri, and on monuments as weavers, maids, dressers, and attendants. On the farm, little girls tended animals and gathered fruit. Slave children were at work by the age of ten and sometimes as early as five (there is even a young acrobat whose death at eighteen months is recorded). Whatever their class, children were prepared for adulthood early in life, though many did not reach it.

Short though childhood was, it was not all strict discipline. In Roman sculpture we see elite children with their pets, including birds, dogs, and goats. Girls playing ball and ring-toss and boys running with hoops, kicking balls, and riding in go-carts are depicted in reliefs. Naevius' poem reflects such a scene, though the girl is flirting rather than actually tossing the ball. Such works of art and literature give evidence of children playing with groups of friends, not solely in a family setting. Girls are also shown playing music, dancing, and reading and writing. Little in Roman literature is specifically about children, but the pieces in this section reveal something of a girl's life: Naevius' charmer making a game of flirting; Pliny's Minicia, a perfect budding young woman, friendly, respectful, and subdued, like the unnamed *puella casta* in the epitaph; Eucharis, an accomplished child actress and singer. The letter and the epitaphs poignantly remind us of the brevity of life in the pre-modern world. Aulus Gellius' description of the choice of Vestal priestesses illustrates an option open to very few freeborn children; their election brought prestige to their families and themselves, for Vestals were among the most honored and influential women in the state.

CLE 1518: Funerary Inscription, CIL 6.40

In this inscription, which was found in Rome and is of uncertain date, the stone, rather than a grieving relative or master, "speaks" to the passers-by, praising the deceased for those qualities prized in a young girl: chastity and goodness. The stone is dedicated to a 6 year old girl whose name, Evodia Cypara, betrays her foreign origins. The inscription is in hendecasyllabic meter.

> SUM CASTAE CINERUM LAPIS PUELLAE
> CUSTOS. ME RELEGENS PIUS VIATOR,
> HUIUS COGNITA SI TIBI FUISSET
> VIRTUS, LACHRYMULIS TUIS RIGARES.

Notes to Funerary Inscription, *CLE* 1518:

1   **sum**: the subject is the stone, the inscription itself. **castus**, -a, -um *innocent, pure*. **cinis**, -eris m. *ashes*. **lapis**, -idis m. *stone*; *gravestone*.

2   **custos**, -odis m/f. *one who/that which protects, guards*. **me = lapidem**, object of **rigares**. **relego**, -ere, -legi, -lectum *read, go through*. **viator**, -oris m. *traveler* with **relegens** and **pius**.

3   **huius = castae puellae**; genitive with **virtus**. **si**: translate before **huius virtus**; a contrary-to-fact condition in mixed time with the subjunctives (**cognita fuisset** and **rigares**).

4   **lacrimula**, -ae f. *little tear* (diminutive for affection, pathos, or emphasis). **rigo** (1) *water, moisten*.

Notes to Funerary Inscription, *ILS* 5213:

1   **Eucharis**' name means "very graceful or beautiful" in Greek. **l.** is the abbreviation for
        liberta. **doctus**, -a, -um *learned*. **eruditus**, -a, -um *well-instructed, accomplished*. **omnes
        artes**: accusative of respect with adjectives, **docta, erudita**, "in." **heus!** (interjection) *Alas!*
        oculo errante: addressed to one glancing at the stone and to the traveller as well. **leti domus**:
        the tomb was often referred to the final "home," in the plural here because it stands among
        many others. **morare**: imperative singular of the deponent verb **moror** (1) *delay, stop, pause*.
        Epitaphs often requested the traveler to stop to read the *inscription* (**titulus**, -i m.). **gressus**, -us
        m. *step*. **perlego**, -ere, -legi, -lectum *read through to the end*. **nata**, -ae f. *daughter* (<perfect
        participle of **nascor**).

5   **reliquiae**, -arum f. pl. *remains*. **conloco**/colloco (1) *place* (themselves) *down, settle down*.
        viridis aetas *a green age*; a vegetal metaphor for the life-cycle which is continued in the
        word **floreret**. **cum**: circumstantial clause (with subjunctive verb). **crescente** modifies **aevo**.
        aevum, -i n. *age, lifetime*. **conscendo**, -ere, -scendi, -scensum *climb to the top, rise to* (+ acc.).
        propero (1) *hasten, hurry*. **denego** (1) *deny, refuse*. **ultra** (adv.) *further, beyond*.

10   **docta [eram]**. **modo** (adv.) *only recently*. **ludus**, -i m. *performance, show*; pl. *festival of
        public games*. **decoro** (1) *add beauty, grace, glory,* or *honor to*. **Graeca** modifies **scaena**.
        scaena, -ae f. (< Gk. *skene*) *stage*. **appareo**, -ere, -ui, -itum *be seen, appear*. **en** (interjection)
        observe! behold! **cinis**, -eris m. *ashes*. **Parcae**, -arum f. pl. *The Fates*. There were four Roman
        goddesses of Fate: Parca (whose name was often used for the group in general), Nona, Decuma,
        and Morta. The Fates are **infestae** (*hostile*) because they have caused Eucharis' death in her
        youth. **deposierunt**, de-: an alternate perfect form for **posui** was **posivi** which in poetry was
        contracted to **posii**. **carmen**, -inis n. *chant, song; poem*. The word is another pun, referring
        both to the funeral dirge and to this poetic inscription.

15   **studium patronae**: objective genitive. **decus**, -oris n. *esteem, distinction, glory*. **sileo**, -ere, -ui
        be silent, be voiceless. **amburo**, -ere, -ussi, -ustum *burn, consume by fire*. **letum**, -i n. *death*.
        taceo, -ere, -ui, -itum *say nothing, fall silent*. **reliqui...diem**: the tragic theme of children
        dying before their parents is common in children's epitaphs. **fletus**, -us m. *weeping, tears*.
        genitor, -oris m. *father*; pl. *parents*. **antecedo**, -ere, -cessi, -cessum *go before, go on ahead,
        precede*. **genitus**, -a, -um *born* (perfect passive participle of **gigno**). **septeni**, -ae, -a (adj. pl.)
        seven, seven times.

20   **tenebrae**, -arum f. pl. *darkness*. **Dis**, Ditis m. *Pluto*, the divine king of the Underworld. **rogo
        ut**: jussive noun clause or indirect command, with the subjunctive.

        Epitaphs often end with the suggestion that the traveler pray for the earth to lie lightly
on the deceased: **Terra sit tibi levis.**

ILS 5213: Funerary Inscription for Eucharis, CIL 6.10096

This 1st century BCE epitaph is written in verse, a medium appropriate for an inscription that commemorates a girl "learned in all the arts." As is common in epitaphs, it is written in the first person. Readers are perhaps expected to believe that Eucharis herself wrote these verses as a last example of her erudition and poetic skill. Though Eucharis' father erected it to mark his love for his young daughter, the epitaph also prominently features the devotion Eucharis displayed towards her *patrona* (benefactor). The importance of the *patrona* is shown by the fact that her name, Licinia, formed part of Eucharis' name, as was customary for a freed slave. The epitaph nowhere names Eucharis' parents. The meter is iambic senarius (*in six feet*), the most common verse for dialogue in drama, both comedy and tragedy, and frequently employed in inscriptions.

Eucharis Liciniae l. docta erudita omnes artes virgo vixit an. XIIII.

Heus! oculo errante qui aspicis leti domus
morare gressum et titulum nostrum perlege,
amor parentis quem dedit natae suae,
5   ubi se reliquiae conlocarent corporis.
Hic viridis aetas cum floreret artibus
crescente et aevo gloriam conscenderet,
properavit hora tristis fatalis mea
et denegavit ultra vitae spiritum.
10   Docta erudita paene Musarum manu,
quae modo nobilium ludos decoravi choro
et Graeca in scaena prima populo apparui.
En hoc in tumulo cinerem nostri corporis
infestae Parcae deposierunt carmine.
15   Studium patronae, cura, amor, laudes, decus
silent ambusto corpore et leto tacent.
Reliqui fletum nata genitori meo
et antecessi, genita post, leti diem.
Bis hic septeni mecum natales dies
20   tenebris tenentur Ditis aeterna domu.
Rogo, ut discedens terram mihi dicas levem.

Notes to Pliny, *Ep.* 5.16 (Sections 1–4):

C. Plinius Marcellino Suo S.: letter salutation: the name of the sender in the nominative, the addressee in the dative (often with **suo** or **suae**), and the abbreviation **S.** or **S. D.**: *salutem* (or *salutem dicit*). The identity of Marcellinus is in doubt. He may be Aefulanus Marcellinus, the recipient of letter 8.23, also relating to a death.

1   **tristis**, -e *sad*. **Fundanus**, -i m. C. Minicius Fundanus, a friend of Pliny who became consul and later proconsul of Asia. He was a student of philosophy and a friend of Plutarch. **filia minore defuncta**: abl. of cause with **tristissimus**. **defungor**, -i, -functus/a sum *finish, die*. **qua puella**: abl. of comparison, translate "than." Latin often begins a sentence with a relative pronoun or adjective to connect the new thought to the previous one. See below (6). **festivus**, -a, -um *lively, jolly, jovial*. **non modo...sed** *not only...but (also/even)*. **prope** (adv.) *nearly, practically*.

2   **nondum** *not yet*. **impleo**, -ere, -evi, -etum *fill, complete*. **anilis**, -e (cf. **senilis**) *of/suitable to an old woman*. **matronalis**, -e *of or suitable to a matrona*. **verecundia, -ae** f. *modesty, bashfulness, shyness*.

3   **ut** *how*. **cervix**, -icis f. *neck, shoulders* (often in pl.). **inhaereo**, -ere, -haesi, -haesum *hang on, cling to*. **complector**, -i, complexus/a sum *embrace*. **nutrix**, -icis f. *nurse, nanny*. **paedagogus**, -i m. *personal slave* who accompanied a child, *minder*. **praeceptor**, -oris m. *teacher*. She would have had private tutors for grammar school. Some of the philosophers of this time, notably Musonius Rufus and perhaps Plutarch, favored equal education for women. **pro** *for*. **diligo**, -ere, -lexi, -lectum *cherish, love, prize*. **lectito** (1) frequentative of **lego**, *read* (a frequentative is a verb derived usually from the supine stem of another verb to show intensity or repetition of action), thus *read often, eagerly*, or *assiduously*. **parce** (adv.) *sparingly*. **custodite** (adv.) *cautiously, with reserve*. **ludo**, -ere, lusi, lusum *play, frolic*. **qua... qua...qua**: ablative; anaphora – repetition for emotional effect. **illa**: nominative, referring to Fundanus' daughter, whose name is not given, but would have been Minicia after her father's *nomen*, and, since she is the younger daughter, she might be called Minicia Minor. Because of the custom of naming girls from their father's *gens* name (cf. *Tullia, Julia, Cornelia*), there is no need to mention her name, although a second name (*Marcella*) is known from her epitaph. Her urn and epitaph were found in the family tomb (*ILS* 1030): **D. M. Miniciae Marcellae Fundani f(iliae). v(ixit) a(nnos) xii m(enses) xi d(ies) vii. D.M.** = Dis Manibus (*to the dear departed*, lit. "to the divine shades"). It is common to include months and even days when a very young person dies. There is a slight discrepancy between her age (not quite thirteen) and the age Pliny ascribes to her. **temperantia**, -ae f. *self-control, discretion*. **constantia**, -ae f. *perseverance, firmness*. **novissimus**: superlative of **novus**, -a, -um *new, fresh, recent*, in the superlative: *most recent, last*. **valetudo**, -tudinis f. *health*, often *ill-health*.

4   **obsequor**, -i, -secutus/a sum *comply, yield/submit to* (+ dat.). **adhortor** (1, depon.) *encourage*. **destitutam** < destituo, -ere, -ui, -utum *forsake, defraud*. **viribus** < vis. **corporis viribus vigore animi**: notice the word order which is thought of as forming an X (or *chi*), called *chiasmus*:

corporis   **X**   vigore
    viribus   animi .

C. Plinius Caecilius Secundus (minor), *Epistulae* 5.16

In this letter (dated to the first decade of the 2nd century CE), Pliny the Younger writes to a friend about the tragic death of a young girl, the daughter of Fundanus. Pliny shows great affection for this modest, mature, brave girl who took such joy in living and learning. Already at thirteen she displayed the virtues admired in grown women and was engaged to a fine young man (*egregius iuvenis*, 6). He offers a lively picture of a young woman in the contentment of her family life, studying, playing, socializing with adults, then falling ill and dying. Pliny is sensitive to a father's sorrow, admonishing Marcellinus not to underestimate the father's loss and grief.

C. PLINIUS MARCELLINO SUO S.

(1) Tristissimus haec tibi scribo, Fundani nostri filia minore defuncta. Qua puella nihil umquam festivius amabilius, nec modo longiore vita sed prope immortalitate dignius vidi. (2) Nondum annos xiiii [quattuordecim] impleverat, et iam illi anilis prudentia, matronalis gravitas erat et tamen suavitas puellaris cum virginali verecundia. (3) Ut illa patris cervicibus inhaerebat! ut nos amicos paternos et amanter et modeste complectebatur! ut nutrices, ut paedagogos, ut praeceptores pro suo quemque officio diligebat! quam studiose, quam intellegenter lectitabat! ut parce custoditeque ludebat! Qua illa temperantia, qua patientia, qua etiam constantia novissimam valetudinem tulit! (4) Medicis obsequebatur, sororem patrem adhortabatur ipsamque se destitutam corporis viribus vigore animi sustinebat.

Notes to Pliny, *Ep.* 5.16 (Sections 5–11):

5   **duro** (1) *make hard, harden, persevere, hold out.* **hic** refers to **vigor animi** (in 4). **illi**: dative of reference (translate *for*) referring to young Minicia. **usque ad** *right up to.* **spatium**, -i n. *extent, length.* **infractus** < **infringo** *break, weaken.* **quo = ut eo**: here introducing a relative clause of result.

6   **funus**, -eris n. *death.* **indignius** *more cruel* (with abl. of comparison). **destino** (1) *assign; engage, betroth.* **egregius**, -a, -um *outstanding.* **nuptiae**, -arum f. pl. *wedding.* **vocati [sumus]**: i.e. the invitations had already been sent out. **quod**: Latin sentences often begin with a relative pronoun; translate "and this." **maeror**, -oris m. *grief, mourning.*

7   **exprimo**, -ere, -pressi, -pressum *squeeze out, express.* **acceperim** < **accipio** (ad + capio: note vowel reduction after a prefix in compound verbs). What use of the subjunctive does **quantum** introduce? Notice how the word order, **quantum animo vulnus**, shows his grief overwhelming his spirit. **ut multa luctuosa**: **ut** with **multa**, *how.* **multa luctuosa** object of **invenit**. **luctuosus**, -a, -um *causing sorrow, distressing.* **praecipio** (**prae + capio**), -ere, -cepi, -ceptum *take beforehand, figure out beforehand, direct.* **margaritum**, -i n. *pearl.* **vestes margarita gemmas**: asyndeton, lack of conjunctions. **quod**: the antecedent is **hoc**. **fuerat erogaturus**: "he had been about to spend"; future active periphrastic. **erogo** (1) *pay out, expend.* **tus**, turis n. *frankincense* (an aromatic gum used in funeral rites, religious ceremonies and in medicine). **unguentum**, -i n. *ointment.* **tus et unguenta et odores**: an example of polysyndeton, overuse of conjunctions. The first three items were bought for a joyous event; the latter three are bought later for her burial. **impendo**, -ere, -pendi, -pensum *pay out, disburse.*

8   **eruditus**, -a, -um *educated.* **ut qui...dediderit**: relative clause of characteristic implying cause ("since he is the kind of person who"). **ab ineunte aetate** *from early youth.* **ineo**, -ire, -ii/ivi, -itum *enter, go/come in.* **aspernor** (1, depon.) *reject, disdain.* **expulsis virtutibus**: ablative absolute. **pietatis est totus**: **totus** with the genitive indicates the involvement of the subject; **pietas**, -atis f. here refers to *fatherly affection* or *devotion.*

9   **ignosco**, -ere, -novi, -notum *forgive, make allowances for.* **ignosces...cogitaveris**: future more vivid condition. **refero**, -ferre, -tuli, -latum *recall, reproduce.* **exscribo**, -ere, -scripsi, -scriptum *make a perfect copy of.*

10   **proinde** (adv.) *therefore, consequently.* **si quas**: "After **si, nisi, num,** and **ne, 'ali-'** goes on holiday" (i.e., **quis, quid** instead of **aliquis** after these particles). **memento**: imperative of **memini** *remember.* **solacium**, -i n. *comfort.* **castigatorius**, -a, -um *full of reproach/reproof, censorious.* Since Fundanus was a Stoic, Marcellinus might have expected him to bear his grief without show of emotion. **mollis**, -e *gentle, soft.*

11   **ut...sic** *just as...so*; a simile comparing grief to an open wound. **crudus**, -a, um *bleeding, raw.* **medens**, -entis m. *doctor.* **reformido** (1) *shun, draw back from in fear.* **ultro** (adv.) *of one's own will, voluntarily.* **mox** (adv.) *soon, later on.* **admotus**, -a, -um *approach, apply* (as medicines). **vale**: the typical formula for closing a letter.

C. Plinius Caecilius Secundus (minor), *Epistulae* 5.16 (continued)

(5) Duravit hic illi usque ad extremum, nec aut spatio valetudinis aut metu mortis infractus est, quo plures gravioresque nobis causas relinqueret et desiderii et doloris.

(6) O triste plane acerbumque funus! o morte ipsa mortis tempus indignius! iam destinata erat egregio iuveni, iam electus nuptiarum dies, iam nos vocati. Quod gaudium quo maerore mutatum est!

(7) Non possum exprimere verbis quantum animo vulnus acceperim, cum audivi Fundanum ipsum--ut multa luctuosa dolor invenit-- praecipientem, quod in vestes margarita gemmas fuerat erogaturus, hoc in tus et unguenta et odores impenderetur.

(8) Est quidem ille eruditus et sapiens, ut qui se ab ineunte aetate altioribus studiis artibusque dediderit; sed nunc omnia, quae audiit saepe quae dixit, aspernatur expulsisque virtutibus aliis pietatis est totus.

(9) Ignosces, laudabis etiam, si cogitaveris quid amiserit. Amisit enim filiam, quae non minus mores eius quam os vultumque referebat, totumque patrem mira similitudine exscripserat.

 (10) Proinde si quas ad eum de dolore tam iusto litteras mittes, memento adhibere solacium non quasi castigatorium et nimis forte, sed molle et humanum. Quod ut facilius admittat, multum faciet medii temporis spatium.

(11) Ut enim crudum adhuc vulnus medentium manus reformidat, deinde patitur atque ultro requirit, sic recens animi dolor consolationes reicit ac refugit, mox desiderat et clementer admotis acquiescit. Vale.

Notes to Gellius, *Noctes Atticae* 1.12 (Introduction–Section 8):

Introduction: **ritus**, -us m. *usage, rite, habit* **caeremonia**, -ae f. *sacred rite*. **religio**, -onis f. *obligation, duty, pledge, observance*. **capiatur, incipiat**: subjunctives in an indirect question. **Quo... iure esse incipiat**: esse + abl. of quality *belong to*; **incipio**, -ere, -cepi, -ceptum *begin*. **statim** (adv.) *immediately*; **ius**, iuris n. *legal status*; **simul ac/atque** *as soon as*. **quodque** *and the fact that*. **Labeo**: M. Antistius Labeo, a well-respected Roman jurist who died about 10 CE. He is said to be the author of 400 volumes which survive only in fragments. **heres**, heredis m/f. *heir, heiress; a successor*. Gaius, in Book 4 of his *Institutes*, discusses the rules for passing down property and the family *sacra*; females could inherit through a will the family property, but not the family *sacra*, which were the property of the *paterfamilias*. The *Lex Voconia* (169 BCE) forbade senators from willing their property to a woman, but the law had lost force by the 1st century CE. Vestals had the privilege of making wills that named females as their heirs. **intestatus**, -a, -um *without an heir, intestate, without witnesses*. Only daughters (not sisters, cousins, etc) could inherit wealth from an intestate father. However, Vestals were not permitted to claim the property of an intestate *paterfamilias*, nor could anyone be the heir of a Vestal who died without a will, as her property passed to the public treasury (Labeo's *Commentaries on the 12 Tables*).

1   **qui** *those who*. **nego** (1) *say* (that + indirect statement) *not*. **fas** n. (only in nom. and acc.) with **est**: *(it is) lawful, sanctioned, permitted*. **item** (adv.) *likewise*.

2   **patrimus**, -a, -um *of one who has a father living*. **matrimus**, -a, -um *of one who has a mother living*.

3   **debilis**, -e *weak, disabled* **-ve**: enclitic conjunction, *or*. **deminuta** < **deminuo**, -ere, -ui, -utum *diminish, weaken*. **labes**, -is f. *fall, defect*. **insignita** < **insignio**, -ire, -ivi, -itum *mark*.

4   **etiamsi** *even if, although*. **avus**, -i m. *grandfather*. **potestas**, -tatis f. *power, authority*. **ambo**, -ae, -o *both*.

5   **servio**, -ire, -ivi, -itum *be enslaved, be in service*, with **servitutem**, cognate acc. (internal object). **negotium**, -i n. *business*. **versor** (1, depon.) *engage in*.

6   **sacerdotium**, -i n. *priesthood, sacred office*. **excusatio**, -onis f. *excuse*. **mereor**, mereri, meritus/a sum. *deserve, be entitled to*. **aiunt** < **aio**, defective verb *say yes, affirm*. **flamen**, -inis m. *priest, flamen, sacrificial priest*: in Rome there were fifteen *flamines*, each associated with the cult of one god. **augur**, -is m. f. *diviner, seer*. **quindecimviri sacris faciundis**: one of the major colleges of Roman priests, custodians of the Sibylline books and supervisors of the foreign cults in Rome. (Originally the number of these priests was two; see Livy 5.13.6.) **quindecemvirum** and **septemvirum** are archaic genitive plurals; translate as *one of the fifteen men/one of the seven men*. **septemviri epulones**: another of the colleges of priests, in charge of the banquet of Jove (**epulum Jovis**). **Salius**, -i m. one of the *Salii* (< **salire** *to dance*): in Rome they were part of the cult of Mars. Like the Vestals they had to have both parents living.

7   **sponsa**, -ae f. *betrothed woman*. **vacatio**, -onis f. *exemption, dispensation*. **tribuo**, -ere, -ui, -utum *confer, give*. **tubicen**, -inis m. *trumpeter*. **soleo**, -ere, -itus/a sum *be accustomed*.

8   **Capito Ateius**: C. Ateius Capito, a Roman legal scholar of early imperial times, known for the conservatism of his legal opinions, well-respected in his own day, but soon considered obsolete. He specialized in sacral and pontifical law.

Aulus Gellius, *Noctes Atticae* 1.12

Gellius, an encyclopedist of the 2nd century CE, describes the selection of Vestal Virgins. We learn the names of his sources, the ages and legal or familial status of the girls selected, the location to which they were taken and the words of the ritual, but nothing about the girls themselves, their lives and duties. Other sources record that the kings Numa and Servius established a priesthood of six Vestals whose duty was to tend Vesta's sacred fire and remain chaste, on pain of death by being buried alive. In his *Life of Numa* Plutarch writes:

> The strict observance of chastity for the holy virgins was established by the king [Numa] at thirty years, during which, for the first ten years, they learn what they need to know, in the next they perform what they have learned, and in the third they are themselves the teachers of others. After this time if she wishes, a Vestal is permitted to marry and after putting aside her priestly service to take up a new style of life. Only a few are said to have welcomed this freedom, and those who did were not happy. . . . Numa bestowed great honors on them, including the right to make a will even while their father was alive and to handle their other affairs without a guardian, as if they were mothers of three children. The *fasces* are carried before them when they go out, and if they happen to pass a man being led to his execution, his life will be spared. (9.5-10)

1.12. *Virgo Vestae quid aetatis et ex quali familia et quo ritu quibusque caerimoniis ac religionibus ac quo nomine a pontifice maximo capiatur et quo statim iure esse incipiat, simul atque capta est; quodque, ut Labeo dicit, nec intestato cuiquam nec eius intestatae quisquam iure heres est.*

(1) Qui de virgine capienda scripserunt, quorum diligentissime scripsit Labeo Antistius, minorem quam annos sex, maiorem quam annos decem natam negaverunt capi fas esse; (2) item quae non sit patrima et matrima; (3) item quae lingua debili sensuve aurium deminuta aliave qua corporis labe insignita sit; (4) item quae ipsa aut cuius pater emancipatus sit, etiamsi vivo patre in avi potestate sit; (5) item cuius parentes alter ambove servitutem servierunt aut in negotiis sordidis versantur.

(6) Sed et eam, cuius soror ad id sacerdotium lecta est, excusationem mereri aiunt; item cuius pater flamen aut augur aut quindecimvirum sacris faciundis aut septemvirum epulonum aut Salius est. (7) Sponsae quoque pontificis et tubicinis sacrorum filiae vacatio a sacerdotio isto tribui solet. (8) Praeterea Capito Ateius scriptum reliquit neque eius legendam filiam, qui domicilium in Italia non haberet, et excusandam eius, qui liberos tres haberet.

Notes to Gellius, *Noctes Atticae* 1.12 (Sections 9–19):

9   **atrium Vestae**: an area east of the Forum Romanum including the temple and grove of Vesta and the Vestals' house. **emancipatio**, -onis f. *the releasing of a person from* **patria potestas**. **minutio capitis** *loss of the rights of a citizen*. One loses the rights of a citizen by being sold into slavery or entering a disreputable profession (gladiator, prostitute). **adipiscor**, -i, adeptus/a sum *acquire, attain*. **litterae**, -arum f. pl. *records, literature*. **ex(s)to**, -are, ex(s) titi *be extant, exist, be found*. **Numa**: Numa Pompilius, second king of Rome. **esse captam**: infinitive in indirect statement.

11   **lex Papia**: laws are named after the magistrate proposing them. **caveo**, -ere, cavi, cautum *beware, guard against*. **ius cavet ut =** a legal phrase, *the law provides that*. **arbitratus**, -us m. *decision, discretion*. **sortitio**, -onis f. *act of choosing by lot*; subject of **ducta erit**. **contio**, -onis f. *assembly*. **nunc** (adv.) *now, today*; Gellius explains that in his day a Vestal could be chosen without the lottery (**sortitio**) required by the *lex Papia*. **honestus**, -a, -um *respectable*. Patrician status was not a requirement for Vestals, though most of them came from senatorial families. **locus**, -i m. *place, station*. **nascor**, -i, natus/a sum *be born*. **cuius**: objective gen. with **ratio**, referring to the Vestal-to-be; the antecedent is **filiam**. **dumtaxat** (adv.) *as long as, provided that, at least* (+ subjunctive). **salvis...observationibus**: abl. absolute, *with the religious requirements being preserved*. **salvus**, -a, -um *safe, unharmed*. **ratio haberi** *consideration be given to, regard be paid to*, + objective gen.: **cuius**. **gratia**, -ae f. *exemption, dispensation* (*from* + gen.).

13   **propterea...quia** (or **quod**) *because, for this reason...that*. **prendo** (= **prehendo**), -ere, prendi, prensum *take hold of, grasp*. **veluti** (also **velut**) *just as, like*. **Fabii Pictoris**: Quintus Fabius Pictor, senator and historian, who wrote a history of Rome in Greek to bring Roman traditions to the Hellenic world. **sacerdos**, -dotis m/f. *priestess, priest*. **Quae...faciat**: relative clause of purpose, "who is to..." **siet**: ancient form of **sit** (subjunctive of **est**). **Quirites**, -ium m. pl. the Roman citizens; used in speeches, solemn ceremonies or appeals. The term was thought to derive from the Sabine town of Cures. Addressed to soldiers, it is insulting because Quirites refers to civil life rather than war. **uti = ut** with **ita**: "as...so." **quae** *one who*. **lege**: abl. of quality. **Amata**: *Beloved*, said to be the name of the first Vestal.

15   **plerique**, -aeque, -aque *most, very many*. **Diales** were the *flamines* assigned to Jupiter. **L. Sulla**: Lucius Cornelius Sulla (138-78 BCE) General, Dictator, Consul. **rerum gestarum**: Res Gestae, *Exploits*, the title of many autobiographies. **M. Cato**: Marcus Porcius Cato, the famous Censor, farmer, orator, and writer. **de Lusitanis**: a speech Cato gave against Servius Galba who as praetor in 151 BCE massacred the Lusitanians (inhabitants of modern day Portugal) who were suing for peace. Cato's prosecution came to nought, as Galba was elected consul for 144. **deficio**, -ere, -feci, -fectum *revolt, desert*. **augurium**, -i n. *augury, art of interpreting omens*.

18   **praeterea** (adv.) *in addition, besides*. **intestae quisquam**: understand **est heres**. **bona**, -orum n. pl. *goods*. **redigo**, -ere, -egi, -actum *bring back, collect, take up*. **id quo iure fiat**: indirect question. **quaeritur**: *is missing, is not available*. **inter capiendum** *at the point of being "taken."* **appello** (1) *call, name*. **trado**, -ere, tradidi, traditum *pass on, hand down, transmit*.

Aulus Gellius, *Noctes Atticae* 1.12 (continued)

(9) Virgo autem Vestalis, simul est capta atque in atrium Vestae deducta et pontificibus tradita est, eo statim tempore sine emancipatione ac sine capitis minutione e patris potestate exit et ius testamenti faciundi adipiscitur. (10) De more autem rituque capiundae virginis litterae quidem antiquiores non extant, nisi, quae capta prima est, a Numa rege esse captam.

(11) Sed Papiam legem invenimus, qua cavetur, ut pontificis maximi arbitratu virgines e populo viginti legantur sortitioque in contione ex eo numero fiat et, cuius virginis ducta erit, ut eam pontifex maximus capiat eaque Vestae fiat. (12) Sed ea sortitio ex lege Papia non necessaria nunc videri solet. Nam si quis honesto loco natus adeat pontificem maximum atque offerat ad sacerdotium filiam suam, cuius dumtaxat salvis religionum observationibus ratio haberi possit, gratia Papiae legis per senatum fit.

(13) "Capi" autem virgo propterea dici videtur, quia pontificis maximi manu prensa ab eo parente, in cuius potestate est, veluti bello capta abducitur. (14) In libro primo Fabii Pictoris, quae verba pontificem maximum dicere oporteat, cum virginem capiat, scriptum est. Ea verba haec sunt: "Sacerdotem Vestalem, quae sacra faciat, quae ius siet sacerdotem Vestalem facere pro populo Romano Quiritibus, uti quae optima lege fuit, ita te, Amata, capio."

(15) Plerique autem "capi" virginem solam debere dici putant. Sed flamines quoque Diales, item pontifices et augures "capi" dicebantur. (16) L. Sulla *Rerum Gestarum* libro secundo ita scripsit: "P. Cornelius, cui primum cognomen Sullae impositum est, flamen Dialis captus." (17) M. Cato *de Lusitanis*, cum Servium Galbam accusavit: "Tamen dicunt deficere voluisse. Ego me nunc volo ius pontificium optime scire; iamne ea causa pontifex capiar? si volo augurium optime tenere, ecquis me ob eam rem augurem capiat?"

(18) Praeterea in *Commentariis* Labeonis, quae ad duodecim tabulas composuit, ita scriptum est: "Virgo Vestalis neque heres est cuiquam intestato, neque intestatae quisquam, sed bona eius in publicum redigi aiunt. Id quo iure fiat, quaeritur." (19) "Amata" inter capiendum a pontifice maximo appellatur, quoniam, quae prima capta est, hoc fuisse nomen traditum est.

Gnaeus Naevius, Fragment from a comedy 74.9

In this fragment from a comedy (believed by some to be from the *Tarentilla*, "Young Woman of Tarentum"), Naevius (a 3rd century BCE poet of epic and drama) describes a flirtatious girl in a circle of other young people. She is animated and vivacious, with the imagination to make everyone in the circle feel different and special. The comparison to a group of children playing ball suggests that boys and girls may have played together. The meter is trochaic septenarius (*in seven feet*) catalectic (the last foot is only one syllable).

<blockquote>

Quasi pila

playing
in choro ludens datatim dat se et communem facit.
Alii adnutat, alii adnictat, alium amat, alium tenet.
Alibi manus est occupata, alii pervellit pedem;
5   anulum dat alii spectandum, a labris alium invocat,
cum alio cantat, at tamen alii suo dat digito litteras.

</blockquote>

Notes to Naevius, Fragment 74.9:

1   **pila**, -ae f. *ball*. The form is ablative with **ludens**.

2   **chorus**, -i m. *performance of a dance, band* (of companions, compared to the performers of a chorus). **se dare** *to devote oneself, offer oneself*. **ludo**, -ere, lusi, lusum *play*; + abl. *play with*. **datatim** (adv.) *giving in turn*. **communis**, -e *available*.

3   **alius**, -a, -ud *other, one, another*; **alius ... alius** *one ... another*; **alii**: dat. **adnuto** (1) *nod to/at*. **adnicto** (1) *wink at*.

4   **alibi** (adv.) *elsewhere*. **occupatus**, -a, -um *taken up, busy*. **pervello**,-ere, -i *pinch, excite, pull, tweak*. Another reading is *percellit*, "strike"; but this word is used of more violent actions than playing footsie.

5   **anulus**, -i m. *ring*. **labrum**, -i n. *lip*. (Imagine "air kisses.")

PART TWO
THE WORLD OF LEARNING

The literary sources for the World of Learning mainly concern the upper classes and so limit our full understanding of girls' and women's learning, whether for the work force or for marriage and child rearing. Our evidence comes from some of the leading scholars and men of letters of their day (Quintilian, Suetonius, Pliny) and equally celebrated poets (Ovid, Martial, Juvenal) as well as one woman of poetic achievement (Sulpicia), all from the first century BCE to the second century CE.

For Roman girls and boys the first teachers were their parents. Mothers particularly were praised for imparting elegance of language to their children (see Cicero and Quintilian), because it was believed that women, having fewer outside influences to corrupt their ears and tongues than men did, retained the virtue of old-fashioned speech (and anything from the good old days had the Romans' approbation). Because of this early home-schooling Quintilian is in favor of both parents being as well educated as possible. This is why nurses were disparaged by the more censorious writers: who better than a well brought up mother to be her child's nurse and first teacher?

Both Ovid and Augustus were interested in their daughters' education. Augustus made sure that his daughter and granddaughters learned wool-working, perhaps because, as father of his country (*pater patriae*), he wanted to be seen instilling the traditional values in his own family. Ovid encouraged his step-daughter, whom he calls *doctissima*, to write poetry. Family histories and archives were passed on from parent to child; we learn from Tacitus, for example, that Agrippina Minor wrote a memoir about her mother which he used as a source for his portrait of Agrippina Maior (*Annales* 4.53).

After the first years, wealthier families hired or bought private tutors for their children. Even if these were engaged primarily for the boys, it is clear that girls also participated in the lessons (as was the case of Minicia in Pliny's letter; see the World of Childhood). Other parents sent their children to "public" schools, some of which were co-educational. They were public in that they were outside the home, but they were neither free, state-sponsored, nor compulsory. Parents paid fees to the schoolmasters and some communities took up subscriptions to bring in a teacher. For example, Pliny writes (*Ep.* 4.13) of endowing a school in his home town, Comum.

Primary schools (*ludi*), under a *magister* or *litterator*, taught the basics: reading, writing, and functional arithmetic, including an elaborate system of finger calculation for managing money (see Horace *Ars poetica* 325-30). Schooling was practical and learning took place by rote. Once letters and syllables were mastered, examples were copied out on waxed tablets and memorized as moral lessons; later, passages were memorized for literary and rhetorical tropes, because it was the mark of an educated person to quote from memory. Beatings were a time-honored memory enhancer, as Horace attests: he never forgot what *plagosus Orbilius* ("Orbilius of the many floggings") dictated to him (*Ep.* 2.1.70). On the other hand some teachers of a more tender disposition must have dangled the carrot instead of brandishing the stick: Horace is also the source of the still-effective strategy of giving treats to children to motivate them to learn ("ut pueris olim dant crustula blandi / doctores, elementa velint ut discere prima," *Sat.* 1.1.25-26).

Secondary school (*schola*), in the charge of a *grammaticus*, concentrated on literature, especially poetry, writing, and public speaking, as well as the study of Greek, if it had not already been taken up in the earlier grades or learned at home. Epic poetry was at the heart of literary studies. Some of these primary and secondary schools, at least in imperial Rome, were attended by boys and girls together. The exact ages for the different levels are unclear, but it seems that *schola* started around eleven or twelve. Several poems of Martial allude to the poetry read in school (*Ep.* 1.35; 3.69); *Ep.* 8.3.16 gives evidence that there were classes of mixed gender when he observes that the bombastic schoolmaster bellowing out the lines incurs the hatred of maiden and boy alike ("et grandis virgo bonusque puer"). Some young women advanced far in their appreciation of literature and in their poetic abilities. Catullus writes of a woman whom he calls "Sapphica puella Musa doctior" ("more learned than Sappho's Muse," 35.16). Besides Ovid's Perilla, we know of two women named Sulpicia who were accomplished poets, one who claims to have taught Roman women to compete with the Greeks in composing lyric poetry (see "Sulpicia's complaint" in this unit; see the World of Flirtation for the other). Pliny's young wife, an orphan, was conscientiously educated by her aunt at least to the level reached at *schola*. Not only does she learn his speeches by heart and set his poems to music, but when they are apart she consoles herself with his books as he does with her letters, which he admires for their charming style (6.7).

For more advanced learning young men went to study with rhetoricians, philosophers, and sometimes even mathematicians. Advanced study was not usually pursued by women. Women who undertook higher education privately and flaunted their knowledge, as did the learned woman in Juvenal's famous satire (VI, esp. 434-56), were objects of mockery. On the other hand, the influential Roman philosopher and teacher Musonius Rufus of the first century CE, whose pupils included many prominent citizens as well as the philosopher Epictetus, believed that daughters should receive the same education as sons and that women should also study philosophy. The existence of women poets and stylists, including Hortensia (see Quintilian), an orator in her own right, and women who were patrons of the arts attests to a high level of education for some well-to-do Roman women in the late Republic and early Empire.

This was the learning of the upper classes and the literary elite, inheritors of an education that fitted them for the lives they were to lead as members of their class in society. But what of the majority of citizens, immigrants, and slaves, living in cities, towns, and rural lands, who lacked the resources of the upper classes? Two imperial endowments provided for the sustenance and training of poor and orphaned girls, called the *puellae Faustinianae*, the first named after Faustina, the wife of Antoninus Pius, and the second after her daughter Faustina, the wife of Marcus Aurelius, in whose memory they were founded. These girls were also given a dowry to help them marry. There must have been a high rate of functional numeracy and literacy for anyone engaged in business, labor, or the crafts. A certain degree of learning was required to read the inscriptions and signs that were everywhere, whether announcing employment or advertising rooms to let, to write graffiti or put up signs for one's own business, and to make sure one was not cheated in the market or by one's employer or landlord. As one of the freedmen attending Trimalchio's feast says with some pride, "I didn't study geometry, literary theory, or other such gobbledygook, but I can read the letters carved on stones, and I can figure the percentages of interest to the penny. . ." (Petronius, *Satyricon* 58.7).

From Roman Egypt many apprenticeship documents relating to the artisan and working classes have survived on papyrus (see the World of Work for some of the many crafts and types of work practiced by women). From the literary evidence we know of some slave children attending school with their masters' children and rising in the world. Freed women and men had the greatest chance for advancement in means and status, but for the artisan and working classes and for slaves in general there was little or no choice in career or opportunity for upward mobility.

Tombstone of a ten-year-old Roman girl named Avita from the eastern provinces; the inscription is in Greek. She is shown reading, with a bookstand and scroll displayed prominently beside her. Photo courtesy of the British Museum ©Copyright The Trustees of the British Museum.

Notes to Pliny, *Ep.* 4.19 (Sentences 1-5):

Calpurniae Hispullae Suae S.: the formula for the salutation of a letter: the name of the sender in the nominative, the addressee in the dative (often with **suae** or **suo**), and the abbreviation **S.** (or **S. D.**), *salutem* (or *salutem dicit*), "says hello." Calpurnia Hispulla is the aunt of Pliny's wife Calpurnia. She is one of over forty women either mentioned by name or identifiable from context in Pliny's letters.

1   **cum**: introduces a causal clause with the subjunctive, *since*. **pietas**, -tatis f. *family affection* and *loyalty*. **fratrem**: refers to the late father of Pliny's wife. **amantissimum tui**: like other adjectives, present participles may have comparatives and superlatives. **tui**: objective gen. (the use of the genitive as an object of a verb, adjective, or noun expressing feeling). **par**, paris (adj.) *equal*. **caritas**, -tatis f. *dearness, affection for, love*. **diligo**, -ere, -lexi, lectum *value, esteem, love*. **ut** *as*. **nec** (non) **tantum...verum etiam** (~ non modum...sed etiam) *not only...but also*. **amita**, -ae f. *aunt* (on one's father's side; an aunt on one's mother's side is **matertera**). **affectus**, -us m. *mood, fondness for*. **repraesento** (1) *exhibit, bring back into the present*. **maximo tibi gaudio**: double dative – dat. of purpose with dat. of reference, that is, "a cause of the greatest joy to you." **gaudium**, -i n. *joy*. **fore = futurum esse**. **dignus**, -a, -um *worthy* (of) + abl.: predicate adj. with **eam** understood as subject of **evadere**. She is described as worthy of three family members. Notice the anaphora (repetition) and asyndeton (lack of conjunctions). **avus**, -i m. *grandfather*. Calpurnia's grandfather was Calpurnius Fabatus, a native of Comum, Pliny's hometown (see 8.10 in the World of the Body). **evado**, -ere, -si, sum *turn out, come out*.

2   **acumen**, -minis n. *sharpness, keenness*. **frugalitas**, -tatis f. *thriftiness, economy*. With **est** and these two nouns, understand **ei**, dat. of possession. **castitas**, -tatis f. *purity*. **indicium**, -i n. *evidence, sign*. **accedit his** *there is added to these, in addition*. **litterarum, mei**: objective gen. with **studium** and **caritate** respectively. **concipio**, -ere, -cepi, -ceptum *take up, adopt*. **libellus**, -i m. (diminutive of **liber** *book*) *little book, writing*. **lectito** (1) (freq. of **lego**) *read eagerly*. **edisco**, -ere, -didici *learn by heart*.

3   **qua**: with **sollicitudine**. **illa**: nom. with **afficitur**. **sollicitudo**, -inis f. *anxiety*; notice the word order, as if she is overcome by her anxiety. **ago**, -ere, egi, actum *do* (of various activities), *plead* (a case). **acturus**: understand **esse**. **afficio**, -ere, -feci, -fectum *treat, affect*. **dispono**, -ere, -posui, -positum *place here and there, arrange, post*. **qui nuntient**: relative clause of purpose; understand **eos** as object of **disponit** and antecedent of **qui**. **assensus**, -us m. *agreement, approbation*. **clamor**, -oris m. *loud noise, applause, acclaim* (also a *hostile cry*). **excito** (1) *bring out, raise, rouse*. **eventus**, -i m. *occurrence, outcome*. **tulerim**: perfect subjunctive of **fero**. **si quando** *if ever*. **recito** (1) *read aloud, recite*. **eadem** refers to Calpurnia. **in proximo** *in the next room*. **discerno**, -ere, -crevi, -cretum *separate, set apart*. **velum**, -i n. *sail, veil, curtain*. **sedeo**, -ere, sedi, sessum *sit*. **avidus**, -a, -um *eager, greedy*. **auris**, -is f. *ear*. **excipio**, -ere, -cepi, -ceptum *take up, catch, receive*.

4   **versus**, -us m. *line of verse*. The writing of verse was a hobby among the elite. Pliny refers to his verse in several of his letters. From 4.14 it is clear that some of them were on the naughty side. **formo** (1) *set to music*; below (in 7) *train, educate*. **cithara**, -ae f. *lute, cithara* (> "guitar"). **artifex**, -icis m/f. *artist*.

5   **in dies** *daily, as the days proceed*. **concordia**, -ae f. *harmony, union*. **paulatim** (adv.) *little by little*. **occido**, -ere, -cidi, -casum *fall, die, be lost*. **senesco**, -ere, senui *grow old*.

C. Plinius Caecilius Secundus (minor), *Epistulae* 4.19

What happens to a young Roman woman in her teens once she leaves the care of her family and moves into the home of her husband and into his circle? In the case of Calpurnia, Pliny's young wife, she continued her education, which prepared her well for life with a man like Pliny who took great pride in his literary accomplishments. She had been brought up by her aunt and clearly had an appreciation for literature and the arts. In this selection Pliny writes to Calpurnia Hispulla, his wife's aunt, in gratitude for his harmonious life married to her niece. Calpurnia, Pliny's second or third (and final) wife, was much younger than he, but they seem to have had an affectionate relationship (see also *Ep*.7.5). He must have been close to forty when he married Calpurnia, who was probably not yet out of her early teens. Despite the age disparity, she was a devoted and active participant in their life together, emotionally and intellectually. Sherwin-White in his commentary writes, "This letter is often condemned as intolerable by modern standards, but it reveals our great ignorance of Roman married life of which it gives us a rare glimpse."

C. PLINIUS CALPURNIAE HISPULLAE SUAE S.

(1) Cum sis pietatis exemplum fratremque optimum et amantissimum tui pari caritate dilexeris, filiamque eius ut tuam diligas, nec tantum amitae ei affectum verum etiam patris amissi repraesentes, non dubito maximo tibi gaudio fore cum cognoveris dignam patre dignam te dignam avo evadere.

(2) Summum est acumen summa frugalitas; amat me, quod castitatis indicium est. Accedit his studium litterarum, quod ex mei caritate concepit. Meos libellos habet lectitat ediscit etiam.

(3) Qua illa sollicitudine cum videor acturus, quanto cum egi gaudio afficitur! Disponit qui nuntient sibi quem assensum quos clamores excitarim, quem eventum iudicii tulerim. Eadem, si quando recito, in proximo discreta velo sedet, laudesque nostras avidissimis auribus excipit.

(4) Versus quidem meos cantat etiam formatque cithara non artifice aliquo docente, sed amore qui magister est optimus. (5) His ex causis in spem certissimam adducor, perpetuam nobis maioremque in dies futuram esse concordiam. Non enim aetatem meam aut corpus, quae paulatim occidunt ac senescunt, sed gloriam diligit.

continued onto 27

Notes to Pliny, *Ep.* 4.19 (Sentences 6-8):

6   **decet**, -ere, -uit (impersonal) *it becomes, it behooves, it is fitting.* **educo** (1) *bring up, rear.* **praeceptum**, -i n. *precept, rule, direction.* **instituo**, -ere, -ui, -utum *teach, educate.* **in tuo contubernio** *in your tent-companionship, in living together with you.* **viderit** and **consueverit**: subjunctives in relative clauses of characteristic; the subject is **quae**. **denique** (adv.) *finally, in short.* **ex tua praedicatione** *from what you said about me.* **consuesco**, -ere, -suevi, suetum *become accustomed, form a habit.*

7   **vereor**, -eri, -itus/a sum *revere, respect.* **statim** (adv.) *at once, immediately.* **formare, laudare, ominari**: infinitives with **solebas**. **ominor** (1, depon.) *predict, prognosticate*; that is, to predict that I would become. **talem...talis...qualis** *such...as*; **talem** in agreement with **me**.

8   **certatim** (adv.) *earnestly, eagerly, competitively.* The competitive spirit is seldom far from Pliny's mind: here he suggests that he and his wife are vying to thank her aunt for each other. **gratias ago** + dat. *thank.* **invicem** (adv.) *for each other.* **eligo**, -ere, -legi, -lectum *select, pick out, choose.* **vale**: the typical formula for closing a letter. There is no need for the writer to add his/her name because it is already at the top. **valeo**, -ere, valui, valitum *be well*; as a greeting, *farewell.*

Notes to Martial, *Epigrammata* 3.69 (Lines 5-8):

5   **haec** = my verses. **nequam** (indecl. adj.) *good for nothing, worthless* (with **iuvenes**). **iuvenis**, -is m. *youth, young man.* **facilis**, -e *easy, agreeable, compliant.*

6   **senior**, -oris m. comparative of **senex**, senis m. *elder, old man, graybeard.* **torqueo**, -ere, torsi, tortum *twist, put on the rack, torment.* **legat**: jussive subjunctive ("let...").

7   **venerandus**, -a, -um *respectable, venerable.*

8   Notice that both girls and boys are studying the verses of Cosconius.

C. Plinius Caecilius Secundus (minor), *Epistulae* 4.19 (continued)

(6) Nec aliud decet tuis manibus educatam, tuis praeceptis institutam, quae nihil in contubernio tuo viderit, nisi sanctum honestumque, quae denique amare me ex tua praedicatione consueverit. (7) Nam cum matrem meam parentis loco vererere, me a pueritia statim formare laudare, talemque qualis nunc uxori meae videor, ominari solebas. (8) Certatim ergo tibi gratias agimus, ego quod illam mihi, illa quod me sibi dederis, quasi invicem elegeris. Vale.

Martial, *Epigrammata* 3.69.5-8

What did nice girls read at school? Not Martial's epigrams. In this poem Martial compares his own verses to those of a certain Cosconius. Martial's are not suitable for the classroom, but they attract a more lively and diverse audience, including "easy" girls. The implication, however, is that Cosconius' poetry is tame enough to be textbook reading for boys and girls (here briefly glimpsed at school), or perhaps for reading with one's aunt, à la Calpurnia. We know that Pliny and Martial were acquainted and that the poet had written an epigram in Pliny's honor (9.19); Pliny returned the compliment by giving him a going-away present when he left Rome and by writing a letter (3.21) on the occasion of Martial's death. The meter is elegiac couplet.

5   Haec igitur nequam iuvenes facilesque puellae,
      Haec senior, sed quem torquet amica, legat.
   At tua, Cosconi, venerandaque sanctaque verba
      A pueris debent virginibusque legi.

Notes to Ovid, *Tristia* 3.7 (Lines 1-25):

1   **vado**, -ere *go, go quickly, rush, walk.* **saluto** (1) *greet, wish well, call on*; **salutatum**: supine, used after verbs of motion to express purpose. **subito** (adv.) *quickly, unexpectedly, suddenly.* **peraro** (1) *plough, traverse the sea, inscribe with a stylus on a wax tablet*; this richly metaphoric verb modifies **littera**. **invenio**, -ire, -veni, -ventum *come upon, find, discover.* **Pieris**, Pieridis f. *Muse* (daughter of King Pieros, a Macedonian).

5   **scierit**: from the alternate form of the perfect **scii**. **nec mora [est]** *without delay.* **quidve** = **quid** + **-ve**; **-ve** *or*: from the same root as **vel**, it attaches to the end of the word it must be translated before. **quid** *why.* **venias, agam**: subjunctives in indirect question. **quid** is the object of **agam**. **vivere, reverti, cogere**: infinitives in indirect statement after **dices**; the subject is **me**. **sic ut** + subjunctive: *in such a way that.* **nolim**: < **nolo**, nolle, nolui *wish not.* **longa**: scansion shows that this is an ablative, modifying **mora**. **levo** (1) *relieve, lessen, ease*; with **levata** supply **esse**. **noceo**, -ere, nocui, nocitum + dat *harm, hurt*; **nocuere**: a contracted form of **nocuerunt**. **revertor**, reverti, reversus/a sum *revert, return, turn back.*

10   **aptus**, -a, -um *suitable, joined together.* **cogo**, -ere, coegi, coactum *gather together, collect, compel, force.* **alternus**, -a, -um, *alternating*; the reference is to elegiac poetry, where hexameter verse alternates with pentameter. **pes**, pedis m. *foot, (here of verses) meter.* **communis**, -e *common* (in the sense of *shared*), *familiar.* **ecquid** (adv.): translate "at all." **inhaereo**, -ere, inhaesi, inhaesum + dat *cling to.* **patrius**, -a, -um *father's, hereditary.* **cano**, -ere, cecini *sing, recite.* **fatum**: Ovid is talking about Perilla's *destiny*, or her particular *alotted life*, and not "the Fates." **natura**: subject of **dedit** in l. 14. **pudicus**, -a, -um *pure, chaste, decent.* **dos**, dotis f. *dowry; gift, talent.* **ingenium**, -i n. *character, ability, genius.*

15   **hoc**: scans long; refers to **ingenium** in l. 14. **Pegasis**, -idis *of Pegasus*, the mythical winged horse born of the blood of Medusa, and associated with poetic inspiration. **deduxi**: from **deduco**, a compound of **duco**, *bring down, escort*; with **primus** (idiom) "I was the first to..." **ne** = **ut** + **non** followed by the subjunctive: a purpose construction. **fecundus**, -a, -um *abundant, fruitful.* **vena** , -ae f. *vein; water-course*; here used as a metaphor for *talent*. **pereo**, -ire, -ii, -itum *be lost, perish, be wasted.* **aspicio**, -ere, aspexi, aspectum *notice, catch sight of.* **tener**, -era, -erum *young, tender*; modifies **annis**. **comes**, -itis m/f. *companion, partner, attendant.* **pectus**, -oris n. *heart, mind.*

20   **vates**, -is m/f. *bard, poet, priest.* **Lesbius**, -a, -um *of the Greek island of Lesbos*; used almost always to refer to the poet *Sappho*. **ne**: introduces the subjunctive after verbs of fearing. **retardo** (1) *check, detain.* **casus**, -us m. *falling down, event, circumstance, disaster.* **iners**, -ertis *timid, inactive.* **licet**, -ere, licuit, licitum est (impersonal) *it is permitted, lawful.* **tua... nostra**: understand **carmina**.

25   **praebeo**, -ere, -ui, -itum *offer, show.* **factis modo** modifies **versibus**; translate "just composed."

Publius Ovidius Naso, *Tristia* 3.7

This epistolary poem, written from Ovid's exile in about 10 CE, is addressed to Perilla, thought by many to be Ovid's step-daughter by his third wife, a member of the Fabian family. It serves as evidence that some upper-class Roman males, despite cultural biases against women in general, found it possible to display their high regard for their daughters (see also Cicero's expressions of affection for his daughter Tullia in various letters to Atticus and his family). Ovid pictures his step-daughter sitting at home beside her mother or reading or writing at her desk when his message arrives. Although nothing remains of her work and we do not have certain evidence of her life, Ovid, her instructor in the arts, praises her poetic talents and her learning, calling her *doctissima*, and encourages her not to fear to take up writing poetry once again, as long as it is fit for respectable women to read. The meter is elegiac couplet.

> Vade salutatum, subito perarata, Perillam,
> > littera, sermonis fida ministra mei.
> Aut illam invenies dulci cum matre sedentem,
> > aut inter libros Pieridasque suas.
> 5 Quicquid aget, cum te scierit venisse, relinquet,
> > nec mora, quid venias quidve, requiret, agam.
> Vivere me dices, sed sic, ut vivere nolim,
> > nec mala tam longa nostra levata mora:
> et tamen ad Musas, quamvis nocuere, reverti,
> 10 aptaque in alternos cogere verba pedes.
> "Tu quoque" dic "studiis communibus ecquid inhaeres,
> > doctaque non patrio carmina more canis?
> Nam tibi cum fatis mores natura pudicos
> > et raras dotes ingeniumque dedit.
> 15 Hoc ego Pegasidas deduxi primus ad undas,
> > ne male fecundae vena periret aquae;
> primus id aspexi teneris in virginis annis,
> > utque pater natae duxque comesque fui.
> Ergo si remanent ignes tibi pectoris idem,
> 20 sola tuum vates Lesbia vincet opus.
> Sed vereor, ne te mea nunc fortuna retardet,
> > postque meos casus sit tibi pectus iners.
> Dum licuit, tua saepe mihi, tibi nostra legebam;
> > saepe tui iudex, saepe magister eram:
> 25 aut ego praebebam factis modo versibus aures,

Notes to Ovid, *Tristia* 3.7 (Lines 26-54):

26   **cesso** (1) *do nothing, be idle.* **causa**: predicate nominative. **rubor, -oris** m. *redness, blush*; understand **tui** with **ruboris** (i.e., she is ashamed because of her idleness). **exemplo** *by/from* (my) *example*. **laedo, -ere**, laesi, laesum *wound, hurt, offend*; contracted form of **laeserunt**. **poena, -ae** f. *punishment, penalty*. **fatum, -i** n. *fate, misfortune, destiny*. **sequor**, sequi, secutus/a sum *follow*; **secuta sis**: potential subjunctive, following **forsitan**, with the idea of fear implied, i.e., "Perhaps...you (thought/feared) you also would follow." **pone = depone**: the simple form is used for the compound form, probably for the sake of alliteration. **tantummodo** (adv.) *only*.

30   **neve** (conj.) *and not, nor*; continues the negative command introduced by **tantummodo**. **discat. desidia, -ae** f. *idleness, apathy*. **in** + acc. *to, towards*. **sacra, -orum** n. pl. *sacred rites, worship, religion*. **decens, -entis** *comely, seemly*. **facies, -ei** f. *appearance, looks, face*. **vitio** (1) *spoil, corrupt*. **ruga, -ae** f. *wrinkle, crease*. **antiquus, -a, -um** *old, illustrious*; scansion shows that it modifies **fronte**. **senilis, -e** *of an old person*.

35   **inicio, -ere**, ineci, iectum *lay on, put on*. **formae**: dative with a compound verb. **damnosus, -a, -um** *ruinous, harmful*. **quae**: refers to **senectus**. **strepitus, -us** m. *sound, clatter*. **passus, -us** m. *step*. **non faciente**: a phrase modifying **passu**, with **strepitus** as its direct object. **cum** + indicative = *at the time when*; in a temporal clause **cum** takes the indicative if it expresses time only. **doleo, -ere**, -ui, -itum *grieve, lament, be in pain*. **speculum, -i** n. *mirror*. **mendax, -acis** (adj.) *lying*. **queror**, queri, questus/a sum *complain*; **querere** is an alternate form of the 2nd s. future. **sunt tibi**: dative of possession. **opes, -um** f. pl. *wealth, resources*. **modicus, -a, -um** *moderate, modest, slight*. **cum** + subjunctive: *although*, in a simple concessive clause.

40   **sed**: translate first. **fingo, -ere**, finxi, fictum *imagine, suppose*; introduces the indirect statement with **opes** understood as its subject. **census, -us** m. *registered property, wealth*. **nempe** (adv.) *surely*. **dat**: the subject is **fortuna**; the object is **id**. **quicumque**, quaecumque, quodcumque: relative pronoun, *whoever at all, whatever at all*; the antecedent is **id**. **libet, -ere**, libuit, libitum + dat. (impersonal verb) *it pleases*; understand **ei**, in reference to **fortuna**. **Irus, -i** m. the beggar in Odysseus' house at Ithaca; used generically to mean a poor man. **Croesus, -i** m. the King of Lydia, considered the wealthiest man ever; used generically to mean a rich man. **singula ne referam**: the phrase means "in sum, in short" (literally a purpose clause, "in order that I not give the details"). **exceptis...bonis**: ablative absolute.

45   **en** (interj.) *observe! behold!* **cum** + subjunctive: *although*. **adimo, -ere**, -emi, -emptum *remove by physical force, take away, confiscate*. **comitor** (1, depon.) *be attended by*. **fruor**, frui, fructus/a sum + abl. *enjoy the company of*. **Caesar, -aris** m.: originally this name signified the dictator Julius, then it became the title for the Julio-Claudian emperors; Ovid uses it as a flattering reference to Augustus, Caesar's nephew and adopted heir. **iuris...nihil**: partitive genitive. **quilibet**, quaelibet, quodlibet: indefinite pronoun, *anyone at all*. **saevus, -a, -um** *cruel, savage*. **finio, -ire**, -ivi, -itum *finish, end, limit*. **ensis, -is** m. *sword*.

50   **me...extincto**: ablative absolute. **superstes, -itis** *surviving*. **dum**: conj. + indicative, *while, as long as*. **victrix, -icis** f. *victorious, triumphant*. **domo, -are**, -ui, -itum *conquer, tame*. **Martius, -a, -um** *of* or *belonging to Mars*. **maneo, -ere**, -si, -sum *await, be in store for* (+ acc.). **usus, -us** m. *use, experience*. **qui**, quae, quod: relative pronoun, *who*; the antecedent of **quam** is **tu**. **qua** (adv.) *as far as, where*. **usque** (adv.) *all the way to, right up to*. **rogus, -i** m. *funeral pyre*.

Publius Ovidius Naso, *Tristia* 3.7 (continued)

aut, ubi cessares, causa ruboris eram.
Forsitan exemplo, quia me laesere libelli,
　　tu quoque sis poenae fata secuta meae.
Pone, Perilla, metum. Tantummodo femina nulla
30　　neve vir a scriptis discat amare tuis.
Ergo desidiae remove, doctissima, causas,
　　inque bonas artes et tua sacra redi.
Ista decens facies longis vitiabitur annis,
　　rugaque in antiqua fronte senilis erit,
35　　inicietque manum formae damnosa senectus,
　　quae strepitus passu non faciente uenit.
Cumque aliquis dicet "fuit haec formosa" dolebis,
　　et speculum mendax esse querere tuum.
Sunt tibi opes modicae, cum sis dignissima magnis:
40　　finge sed inmensis censibus esse pares,
nempe dat id quodcumque libet fortuna rapitque,
　　Irus et est subito, qui modo Croesus erat.
Singula ne referam, nil non mortale tenemus
　　pectoris exceptis ingeniique bonis.
45　　En ego, cum caream patria vobisque domoque,
　　raptaque sint, adimi quae potuere mihi,
ingenio tamen ipse meo comitorque fruorque:
　　Caesar in hoc potuit iuris habere nihil.
Quilibet hanc saevo vitam mihi finiat ense,
50　　me tamen extincto fama superstes erit,
dumque suis victrix omnem de montibus orbem
　　prospiciet domitum Martia Roma, legar.
Tu quoque, quam studii maneat felicior usus,
　　effuge venturos, qua potes, usque rogos!"

Notes to Suetonius, *Vita Divi Augusti* 64 (Sections 2-3):

2   **filiam**: Augustus' daughter, Julia, was exiled for adultery by her father and died of starvation after her last husband, Tiberius, cut off her stipend. **neptis**, -is f. *granddaughter*: Julia and Agrippina Maior. **instituo**, -ere, -ui, -utum *instruct, educate*. **lanificium**, -i n. *working in wool*. **assuefacio**, -ere, -feci, -factum *accustom, habituate*. **veto** (1) *forbid*. **propalam** (adv.) *openly, publicly*. **diurnus**, -a, -um *of the day, daily*. **commentarius**, -i m. *notebook, public record*; Augustus kept an account of the events that took place in his household. **referretur**: after **quod** in relative clause of characteristic (< **refero** *repeat*). **extraneus**, -i m. *stranger*. **coetus**, -us m. *coming together, encounter, company*; **coetu**: abl. of separation . **adeo** (adv.) *so far, to such an extent*; with **ut** introducing a result clause. **decorus**, -a, -um *well-mannered, suitable*. **iuvenis**, -is m. *young man, youth*. **quondam** (adv.) *once*. **parum** (adv.) *not enough*. **facio**, -ere, feci, factum *do, act, conduct oneself*. **quod**: with the subjunctive introduces a clause that gives a reason that is not the writer's or speaker's own, "because, to Augustus' mind,..." **Baiae**, -arum f. pl. *Baiae*, a high-class vacation spot on the Bay of Naples. **salutatum**: supine with **venisset**, "to greet," "to call on."

3   **nepos**, -otis m. *grandson*: Gaius and Lucius, both of whom died under suspicious circumstances. **nato** (1) *swim*. **rudimentum**, -i n. *first lessons, early training*. **per se** *personally*. **plerumque** (adv.) *for the most part*. **nihil aeque quam ut**: "nothing as much as that." **elaboro** (1) *take pains over*. **imitor** (1, depon.) *copy, imitate*. **chirographum**, -i n. (< Greek) *handwriting*; this may refer to a script Augustus developed for encrypting confidential letters.

Notes to Quintilian, *Institutiones* 1.1 (Paragraphs 4, 6):

4.1   **ante omnia** *first of all, above all*. **sit**: jussive subjunctive, "let" with **ne**. **sermo**, -onis m. *speech, conversation*. **vitiosus**, -a, -um *full of grammatical errors*. **nutrix**, -icis f. *nurse*. **Chrysippus**: the philosopher Chrysippus (280-207 BCE), co-founder of the Stoic school. **opto** (1) *choose, prefer*. **quantum res pateretur**: translate "as far as possible."

2   **mores**, morum m. pl. *morals*. **his**: i.e., the nurses. **haud dubie** *without a doubt*. **prior**, prius (comparative adj.) *more important*. **ratio**, -onis f. *attention, consideration*. **recte** (adv.) *properly*.

6.1   **quam plurimum** *as much as possible*. **eruditio**, -onis f. *education, learning*. **eruditionis**: partitive genitive with plurimum. **optaverim**: potential subjunctive.

2   **contulisse** < **confero**, -ferre, -tuli, -latum *convey, contribute*. **accipio**, -cipere, -cepi, -ceptum *hear, read, learn through tradition*. **posteri**, -orum m. pl. *posterity*. **trado**, -ere, -didi, -ditum *hand down, pass down*. **C. filia**: "daughter of Gaius." **reddo**, -ere, -didi,-ditum *imitate, reflect*. **oratio...habita** *a speech delivered*. **Q. filiae**: "daughter of Quintus" (genitive). **apud triumviros**: "before the tribunal of the triumvirs"; the triumvirs, Octavian, Antony, and Lepidus, were bent on raising money by taxing the women. The content of Hortensia's speech is recorded in a Greek version by the historian Appian (*Civil Wars* 4. 32-4). **in sexus honorem**: "as a compliment to her sex."

Gaius Suetonius Tranquillus, *Vita Divi Augusti* 64.2-3

It is harder to picture the daughter and granddaughters of Augustus working at their wool than Ovid's daughter with her books. The educational methods of Augustus left something to be desired, judging from the tragic life and death of his female progeny. The elder Julia, whose insistence on maintaining her sexual autonomy incurred the cruel rage of her father, learned more than wool-working from her early home-schooling. Macrobius speaks of her love of literature, which may account for her brilliant wit later in life (*Saturnalia* 2.5.2). This first-century CE account of Augustus' life shows the emperor's contrasting ideals of education for females and males.

(2) Filiam et neptes ita instituit, ut etiam lanificio assuefaceret vetaretque loqui aut agere quicquam nisi propalam et quod in diurnos commentarios referretur; extraneorum quidem coetu adeo prohibuit, ut L. Vinicio, claro decoroque iuveni, scripserit quondam parum modeste fecisse eum, quod filiam suam Baias salutatum venisset.

(3) Nepotes et litteras et natare aliaque rudimenta per se plerumque docuit, ac nihil aeque elaboravit quam ut imitarentur chirographum suum.

Marcus Fabius Quintilianus, *Institutiones* 1.1: Paragraphs 4, 6

Quintilian sets forth a practical rationale for educating upper-class women in the opening of his first-century CE book on oratory: as *materfamilias*, she is the young boy's first model for proper language learning. Unlike that of the *paterfamilias*, who spends little time with his young children and whose speech is affected by many different people and environments, her speech may have a natural elegance of diction and purity that can enhance their son's rhetorical abilities even before his formal education begins. Quintilian supports the traditional expectation that women take full responsibility for their young children's upbringing and warns against the deleterious effect of the low-class speech of slaves. In this passage he singles out three women to praise for their excellent Latin: Cornelia, mother of the Gracchi; Laelia, daughter of Gaius Laelius Sapiens; and Hortensia, an orator herself and the daughter of Quintus Hortensius, Cicero's rival for first place in Roman oratory.

4 (1) Ante omnia ne sit vitiosus sermo nutricibus: quas, si fieri posset, sapientes Chrysippus optavit, certe quantum res pateretur optimas eligi voluit. (2) Et morum quidem in his haud dubie prior ratio est, recte tamen etiam loquantur.

6 (1) In parentibus vero quam plurimum esse eruditionis optaverim. (2) Nec de patribus tantum loquor: nam Gracchorum eloquentiae multum contulisse accepimus Corneliam matrem, cuius doctissimus sermo in posteros quoque est epistulis traditus, et Laelia C. filia reddidisse in loquendo paternam elegantiam dicitur, et Hortensiae Q. filiae oratio apud triumviros habita legitur non tantum in sexus honorem.

Notes to Juvenal, *Satura* 6 (Lines 434-456):

434   **gravior**, -ius (comparative adj.): i.e., worse than women criticized in previous passages. **coepi**, -isse, coeptum (perfect, with present meaning) *begin*; she (**illa**) starts her harangue before sitting. **discumbo**, -ere, -cubui, -cubitus *recline* (at dinner).

435   **pereo**, -ire, perii, -itum (**periturus**, -a, -um: future active participle) *die, perish.* **ignosco**, -ere, -novi, -notum + dat. *pardon, make allowances for*; naturally, she takes the side of the woman (Dido). **Elissa** = Dido. **committo**, -ere, -misi, -missum *pit against, match* (as in the arena). **vates**, -is m. *sage, poet.* **inde** (adv.) *then.* **Maro**, Maronis m. Publius Vergilius Maro, Vergil (70 B.C.E. - 19 CE), author of *Eclogues, Georgics, Aeneid.* **trutina**, -ae f. *scale, balance.* **cedo**, -ere, cessi, cessum *yield, give way.* **grammaticus**, -i m. *teacher of literature.* **turba**, -ae f. *crowd, throng.* **taceo**, -ere, -ui, -itum *fall silent, be speechless.* **causidicus**, -i m. *pleader, advocate.* **praeco**, -onis m. *auctioneer.*

441   **tot** (indecl. adj.) *so many.* **pariter** (adv.) *equally, at the same time as.* **pelvis**, -is f. *basin.* **tintinnabulum**, -i n. *a bell.* **dicas**: potential subjunctive in second person, impersonal. **pulso** (1) *beat, bang*; during an eclipse loud noises were made to scare off the evil spirits and bring back the moon (or sun). **tuba**, -ae f. *trumpet.* **aes**, aeris n. *copper, bronze*; **aera** pl. *cymbals.* **fatigo** (1) *tire, wear down*; jussive subjunctive. **una**: here, [*she*] *alone.* **laboro** (1) *labor, be in difficulty* or *danger*; i.e., in eclipse. **succurro**, -rere, -ri, -sum + dat. *help.* **finis**, -is m. *end, limit.* **sapiens**, -entis m/f. *philosopher.* **et**: adverbial *even* (to a philosopher excess even of virtue becomes a vice).

445   **quae** [*she*] *who.* **nimis** (adv.) *too, excessively.* **facundus**, -a, -um *fluent, eloquent.* **crure medio** *the middle of the leg*; **crus**, cruris n. *leg, shin.* **tenus** (prep. + abl.) *all the way up to*; < **tenus** n. *stretched cord.* **tunica**, -ae f. *tunic*; men's tunics were knee length while women's were worn down to the feet. **succingo**, -ere, -cinxi, -cinctum *tuck up, gird up.* **Silvanus**, -i m. *Silvanus*, a rustic god to whom farmers sacrificed: **Sylvano mulieres non licet sacrificare** (according to the *Scholia*, or marginal notes, found in some of the manuscripts). **quadrans**, -antis m. *¼ of an* **as**, *the smallest Roman coin.* **lavo**, -are/-ere, lavi, lautum *wash, bathe* (passive); **quadrante lavari**: *bathe in the quarter-as baths, go to the cheapest public bath*, restricted to men (women had to pay twice as much). **habeat**: this and the following subjunctives are hortatory (or jussive); usually **ne** in the negative, occasionally in poets **non**. **tibi quae iuncta**: "who [is] joined (in marriage) to you." **dicendi genus**: *style of speaking*, as taught by the rhetoric teachers; object of **habeat**. **curvus**, -a, -um *rounded, tortuous.* **sermo rotatus** *rounded speech*, or *speech flourished like a weapon* (a military metaphor).

450   **torqueo**, -ere, torsi, tortum *twist, bend.* **enthymema**, -atis n. (< Greek) *enthymeme, an argument based on the syllogism* (see Quint. *Inst.* 5.14.1-4.). **et** (adv.) *also.* **odi hanc ego**: notice the belligerent word order, with the woman surrounded by the hostile male. **repeto**, -ere, -ivi/-ii, -itum *return to, seek to recover.* **volvo**, -ere, volvi, volutum *roll* or *unroll* (as a scroll), *reel off, recite, turn over* (in the mind). **Palaemo**, -onis m. Remmius Palaemon, a Roman grammarian of the time of Tiberius and Claudius. **servata...lege et ratione**: ablative absolute. **ratio**, -onis f. *manner, structure, rule* (i.e., she never makes a mistake in grammar). **ignotus**, -a, -um *unknown.* **tenet** = **tenet memoria** "knows by heart"; **antiquaria** is the subject. **antiquarius**/-a m/f. *antiquarian, classicist*; in apposition to the subject.

455   **nec curanda viris**: "and things not cared about by men." **opicus**, -a, -um *stupid, uncultured.* **castigo** (1) *correct, find the faults in.* **soloecismus**, -i m. *solecism, misuse of language.* **liceat**: jussive subjunctive ("let") < **licet** *it is permitted* + dat. **maritus**, -i m. *husband.*

Marcus Junius Juvenalis, *Satura* 6.434-56

What man wants to be out-talked, corrected, or outsmarted by a woman? This passage (written about 116 CE) brings into focus the intellectual woman, an object of male sniping and ridicule from time immemorial. The creator of this example of the type, the satirist Juvenal, attacks all the vices of his age from political corruption through lewd and lascivious behavior. While he deplores the diversity of Rome's imperial population, conspicuous consumption, and the degenerate lives of the nobles, his favorite topic is the wickedness of women. Barbara Gold writes that in Satire 6 Juvenal may have been more concerned with "Roman male inadequacies" than with women, who would then be only an "accidental target" (1998: 382). Juvenal's language impresses upon us the mannishness of the educated woman: her presumption in pitting the poets against each other like gladiators (436); her manner of dress, worship, and personal hygiene (446-7); and her strategic use of language as a weapon (449-50). The meter is dactylic hexameter.

Illa tamen gravior, quae cum discumbere coepit

435 laudat Vergilium, periturae ignoscit Elissae,

committit vates et comparat, inde Maronem

atque alia parte in trutina suspendit Homerum.

cedunt grammatici, vincuntur rhetores, omnis

turba tacet, nec causidicus nec praeco loquetur,

440 altera nec mulier. verborum tanta cadit vis,

tot pariter pelves ac tintinnabula dicas

pulsari. iam nemo tubas, nemo aera fatiget:

una laboranti poterit succurrere Lunae.

inponit finem sapiens et rebus honestis;

445 nam quae docta nimis cupit et facunda videri

crure tenus medio tunicas succingere debet,

caedere Silvano porcum, quadrante lavari.

non habeat matrona, tibi quae iuncta recumbit,

dicendi genus, aut curvum sermone rotato

450 torqueat enthymema, nec historias sciat omnes,

sed quaedam ex libris et non intellegat. odi

hanc ego quae repetit volvitque Palaemonis artem

servata semper lege et ratione loquendi

ignotosque mihi tenet antiquaria versus

455 nec curanda viris opicae castiget amicae

verba: soloecismum liceat fecisse marito.

Sulpicia, *Conquestio* 7-11

If an educated woman gets the chance to speak for herself, she fares better than Juvenal's straw woman of the infamous Satire 6 who bores everyone by weighing Homer against Vergil. This extract is from a poem attributed to Sulpicia (*Epigrammata Bobiensia* 37.7-11), chosen because in it she establishes her claim as a woman poet giving a voice to women. However, the text is difficult and the authorship not above suspicion. Who is this Sulpicia? Is this a poem by Sulpicia, the wife of Calenus, whom Martial honors in his two poems (*Ep.* 10.35 in the World of Marriage; *Ep.* 10.38) about a contemporary female poet who celebrates her love for her husband in erotic lyrics? Or could this be the work of a third Sulpicia, a medieval fabrication, or a forgery from late antiquity?

Sulpicia begins her poem by addressing the Muse with an appeal for help in writing a serious poem (about Domitian's expulsion of the philosophers from Rome) in dactylic hexameters, the meter of epic and satire. In the lines below the poet refers to her earlier work, which featured salty, sexy verses addressed to her husband, a genre which she is abandoning.

> cetera quin etiam quondam quae milia lusi
> primaque Romanas docui contendere Graiis
> et salibus variare novis, constanter omitto
> 10   teque quibus princeps et facundissima calles
> aggredior: precibus descende clientis et audi.

Notes to Sulpicia, *Conquestio*:

7   **cetera milia**: object of **omitto** (9). She refers here to her earlier poetry, which seems to have been fairly prolific. **quin etiam** *yes and*, *and furthermore*. **quondam** *once*. **quae**: object of **lusi**. ludo, -ere, lusi, lusum *play*, *amuse oneself with* (as in writing light verse).

8   **prima docui** (idiom): "I was the first to..." **contendo**, -ere, -tendi, -tentus *stretch*, *contend*, *vie with*. **Graius**, -a, -um *Greek*.

9   **sal**, salis m. *salt*, *wit*. **constanter** (adv.) *without change*, *with equanimity*.

   omitto, -ere, -misi, -missum *leave off*, *give up*.

10   **te**: the Muse Calliope. **quibus**: refers to hexameter verses, "[in the meter] in which"; the form is ablative of respect. **princeps**, -cipis *holding first place*, *foremost*. **facundus**, -a, -um *eloquent*. **calleo**, -ere *be experienced*, *be skillful*.

11   **aggredior**, -i, -gressus/a sum *approach*, *apply to*. **prex**, -is f. *prayer*. **descendo**, -ere, -scendi, -scensum *come down* [in answer to]. **cliens**, -entis m/f. *client*, *dependant*: the recipient of patronage.

PART THREE
THE WORLD OF MARRIAGE

It is difficult to distinguish actual women's voices in the readings for this unit, dating from the second century BCE to the early second century CE and including letters, funerary inscriptions, anecdotes, and biographies. Two funerary inscriptions are written as words spoken by the deceased women to passers-by, but it is very unlikely that the women themselves wrote them, although they probably would have agreed with the thoughts expressed. Pliny's polished phrases in speaking of his wife Calpurnia indicate that he intended his letters to be published, but that does not necessarily make the feelings they express less sincere. Sources such as these, which present the male view of what a woman should or should not be, helped reinforce the behavioral ideal of a Roman woman and encouraged her to think that by conforming to this view, she, too, might gain some renown.

In western societies today, marriage is generally a condition that is authorized by civil authority and frequently involves a religious ceremony as well. Many would agree that marriage is a union undertaken by two individuals for their mutual happiness, which may include the procreation of children. Roman marriage was somewhat different. The traditional Roman view, that the purpose of marriage was the procreation of children, is reflected in the poem about Claudia Rufina, in the *Laudatio Turiae*, and in the funerary inscription for Claudia. The state, however, required no legal ceremony before a priest or government official. Rather, the Roman marriage ceremony was primarily a social rite with economic overtones; it was witnessed by family and friends and often accompanied by a sacrifice to the gods (usually of a pig). A marriage contract including stipulations for the disposition of the bride's dowry in case of divorce or widowhood would be drawn up, approved by the couple's family, and signed by the spouses.

The state did, however, establish several conditions necessary for a marriage to be legal (*iustae nuptiae*, or *iustum conubium*). For example, the state required that both bride and groom be Roman citizens or belong to a group such as the Latini that had the right (*conubium*) to contract marriage with a Roman citizen. Bride and groom also had to have as individuals the right of *conubium*. For example, they had to be old enough to be physically capable of consummating a marriage. Social rank was also important. The Twelve Tables originally barred marriage between patricians and plebeians, though this prohibition was abolished in 445 BCE. The Augustan laws regulating marriage (18 BCE and 9 CE) kept senators and their descendants from marrying freed slaves, persons engaged in trades deemed *infamis* (e.g. actors, mimes, prostitutes), or women convicted of adultery.

How did marriage affect a woman in terms of her status and property rights? It depended upon whether she married *cum manu* or *sine manu* (with or without *manus*: literally, "hand," signifying authority). If she married *sine manu*, she remained under the *potestas* of her father, who controlled her and her property. If she married *cum manu*, she still legally had the status of a child, but she was now under the power of her husband. In either case, she had no legal control over her property so long as her father or husband was alive. There were several ways to establish a marriage *cum manu*. A religious ceremony, *confarreatio*, was prescribed for those holding religious office for life, such as the *flamines* and *flaminicae*. A husband might "buy" his wife (*coemptio*) and acquire *manus* over her. Or, if husband and wife lived together without her absence overnight for one year (*usus*), he could acquire *manus*. She could prevent this, however, if she spent three consecutive nights away from their home each year. By the end of the Republic marriage *cum manu* was uncommon, due perhaps to the increasing independence and wealth of women.

Parents or guardians negotiated the first marriage of young women of the upper classes. If the groom was young, or a mature man still under his father's *potestas*, his parents, too, were involved. However, a lower-class young orphan, a middle-aged *libertina*, or a widow might have considerable latitude in contracting her marriage due to her circumstances. For those individuals possessing *conubium*, the free consent and intent of both parties was also required, though in the case of a young girl such a stipulation may not have had much effect.

We are better informed about the ceremonies that accompanied marriage for a member of the upper classes, among whom the consent and intent might be announced publicly at a betrothal ceremony, which usually took place at an early age. At that time or later, a marriage ceremony would be held. The bride took off her *toga praetexta* and dressed in a white tunic (*tunica recta*). Her hair was parted by a special spear, was braided into six locks (*seni crines*), and tied up with white woolen fillets (*vittae*). She wore a flame-colored veil (*flammeum*) over her head and yellow shoes (*socci*) on her feet. The family and guests gathered in her house to hear both parties assent to their marriage, after which the matron of honor (*pronuba*) joined their right hands, symbolizing their union. After a meal, three young boys escorted the bride to her new house, where she was carried over the threshold by her husband to prevent her from stumbling (a bad omen). To what extent the lower classes followed these ceremonies doubtless depended upon their finances and circumstances.

Just as marriage was brought about by the consent and intent of the parties involved, so divorce occurred when either or both withdrew their consent and intent. No divorce decree had to be granted by the state. All that remained to be done was to carry out the terms of the marriage contract regarding the disposition of the dowry. Children legally belonged to their father and usually resided in his household after a divorce.

To judge from inscriptions, concubinage (*concubinatus* or "bed-fellowship") was a common substitute for marriage, used by those who did not possess the right of *conubium*. All ranks of society made use of *concubinatus*, from *libertini* to the highest ranks of society: Antonia Caenis, a freedwoman of a member of the imperial family, was the concubine of the emperor Vespasian for a long period of time until her death.

Slaves, because they were property, could not legally marry anyone, even another slave. However, they could enter into a recognized "living together" called *contubernium* (see the epitaph of Hygia in the World of Work). *Contubernium* was a term borrowed from the military, where it indicated a "tent group" that shared sleeping arrangements and food. Aurelia Philematium and her husband L. Aurelius Hermia began their life together as *contubernales*. Varro suggests that the privilege of *contubernium* be offered to *vilici* (farm managers) as a motivator and reward for hard work. Columella (see the World of Work) advises that the female *contubernalis* be rewarded for bearing a certain number of children:

he recommends that a woman who bore three sons should be exempted from work, while a woman who has borne more (presumably only sons) be given her freedom. Yet any of her children born while she was a slave remained the property of her owner, who could and often did sell them. In fact, even when children were not sold off, slave mothers could not expect to rear their own children.

Given that many marriages, particularly first marriages, were arranged for the couple and were prompted by political and economic concerns, especially among the upper classes, it is as impossible to know how happy these marriages were as it is to define what a "happy marriage" is. Certainly, less than happy couples existed: in the selection from Plautus, Menaechmus is deservedly hen-pecked by his wife. The happiness of a couple, however, is celebrated on many epitaphs by the formulaic phrase *sine querella* ("we lived together without disagreement"), and in some instances this statement was as true then as it is for married couples today. The *Laudatio Turiae*, the selections on Sulpicia, Domitia Decidiana, Antonia, and Pliny's Calpurnia, are evidence that love or at least affection could exist between spouses. A number of texts (the *Laudatio Turiae*, Tertia Aemilia, Turia, Sulpicia) offer evidence of the loyalty of wives under difficult emotional and political circumstances. When their husbands committed suicide in political protest or were ordered to do so, some wives chose to die with them (see the selection on Porcia) and thus gained renown for their devotion. Equally indicative of a personally satisfying union, however, is the epitaph to the unknown *carissima coniunx*, so deeply mourned by her husband. No doubt most Roman wives would have been content with such a tribute to their marriage.

Notes to Martial, *Epigrammata* 10.35 (Lines 1-21):

1   **Sulpicia**, -ae f. Sulpicia, a poet of the first century CE, the wife of Calenus. **legant**: jussive (or hortatory) subjunctive. **uni**: dative; **unus** is one of nine adjectives that show gen. in -**ius** and dat. in -**i**. Here the adjective refers to a woman married only once who came to be honored with the epithet **univira**. **placeo**, -ere, -ui, itum + dat *please, satisfy*. **maritus**, -i m. *husband*. **nupta**, -ae f. *bride*.

5   **haec** refers to Sulpicia. **Colchis**, -idos Colchian, i.e., Medea. **adsero**, -ere, -ui, -sertum *claim* (as her subject), *appropriate*. **furor**, -oris m. *rage*. **dirus**, -a, -um *dreadful*; the epithet is "transferred" from **prandium** to **Thyestae**. **prandium**, -i n. *lunch*. **refero**, -ferre, rettuli, relatum *bring back, report*. **Thyestes**, -ae m. Thyestes, whose brother Atreus tricked him into eating the stewed bodies of his own children. **Scylla**, -ae f. There were two mythological figures with this name: a man-eating sea-monster living in the straits of Messina, and a Megarean princess who betrayed her father Nisus for love. Martial refers to the second Scylla, one in a list of mythical perpetrators of crimes against family members. **Byblis**, -idis f. Byblis, daughter of Miletus, who fell in love with her brother. **castus**, -a, -um *chaste, pure*. **probus**, -a, -um *good, virtuous*. **lusus**, -us m. *play, sport, act of playfulness*. **deliciae**, -arum f. pl. *delight, enjoyment*. **facetiae**, -arum f. pl. *joke, clever activity*.

10   **cuius** = **Sulpiciae**. **qui** with subjunctive here amounts to a general condition: "whoever," "if anyone would." **carmen**, -inis n. *song, poem*. **aestimo** (1) *appraise, value*; **aestimarit** = **aestimaverit**. **nullam** refers to Sulpicia. **nequior**: compararative of **nequam** (adj.) *naughty, mischievous* (in a playful sense). **sanctus**, -a, -um *innocent, virtuous*. **talis**, -e *such, of such a kind*; **tales** modifies **iocos**. **Egeria**, -ae f. Egeria, a Roman goddess associated with water, wife and adviser of Numa. She was worshiped with Diana and with the Camenae, water-goddesses who came to be identified with the Muses. **iocus**, -i m. *joke, sport*; Egeria advised Numa about setting up the sacred laws and priestly orders. **udus**, -a, -um *wet, moist, damp*. **Numa**: Numa Pompilius, the second king of Rome. **crediderim**: potential subjunctive. **antrum**, -i n. *cave, grotto*.

15   **hac condiscipula** and **hac magistra**: ablatives absolute; **hac** refers to Sulpicia. **condiscipulus**, -i m. & **condiscipula**, -ae f. *school-mate, fellow student*. **magistra**, -ae f. *teacher*. The suggestion that Sappho, the most famous woman of the ancient Greek world, could have learned from Sulpicia is striking. **esses**: the apodosis (conclusion) of a contrary-to-fact condition with the ablative absolute serving as the conditional (or "if") clause. **doctus**, -a, -um *learned, skilled*. **pudicus**, -a, -um *chaste, virtuous*. **Sappho**, -us f. Sappho, lyric poet of Lesbos of the 6th century BCE, admired throughout antiquity for the beautiful sound of her poetry, but a frequent subject of lurid stories about her private life. **tecum** is addressed to Sappho. **pariter** (adv.) *equally*. **simul** (adv.) *together, at the same time*. **visam** refers to Sulpicia. **durus**, -a, -um *hard, harsh, pitiless* (of lovers who are "hard-to-get"). **Phaon**, -onis m. Phaon, a youth of Lesbos with whom Sappho is said (falsely) to have fallen in love and over whom she is said (falsely) to have killed herself when he did not return her love. **amaret**: subjunctive in the apodosis (conclusion) of a contrary-to-fact condition. **frustra** (adv.) *in vain*. **Tonans**, -antis m. the *Thunderer*, one of Jupiter's cult-titles. **uxor...puella** is in apposition with **ea**.

21   **eripio**, -ere, -ui, -reptum *snatch away*. **erepto Caleno**: ablative absolute. **viveret**: imperfect subjunctive in a contrary to fact condition, as above. Like Porcia (see Valerius Maximus 4.6.5. in this unit), she would not have wanted to survive her husband.

Marcus Valerius Martialis, *Epigrammata* 10.35

In this poem and in 10.38, Martial celebrates the life and poetry of Sulpicia and her fifteen years of married love with Calenus. It seems from the one fragment of her verse that survives, as well as from references to her by Martial and several writers of the 4th and 5th centuries CE, that her poems were sexually explicit. We are accustomed to thinking of the Roman matron as stern and upright — at best, her husband's helpmate and companion, mother of his children, but hardly as a sexual innovator. This Sulpicia, the sexy *matrona*, is someone new and surprising for us. Martial recommends her verse to both women and men to keep their married life fresh. The meter is hendecasyllabic.

Omnes Sulpiciam legant puellae,
uni quae cupiunt viro placere;
omnes Sulpiciam legant mariti,
uni qui cupiunt placere nuptae.
5   non haec Colchidos adserit furorem
diri prandia nec refert Thyestae;
Scyllam, Byblida nec fuisse credit:
sed castos docet et probos amores,
lusus, delicias facetiasque.
10   cuius carmina qui bene aestimarit,
nullam dixerit esse nequiorem,
nullam dixerit esse sanctiorem.
tales Egeriae iocos fuisse
udo crediderim Numae sub antro.
15   Hac condiscipula vel hac magistra
esses doctior et pudica, Sappho:
sed tecum pariter simulque visam
durus Sulpiciam Phaon amaret.
frustra: namque ea nec Tonantis uxor
20   nec Bacchi nec Apollinis puella
erepto sibi viveret Caleno.

Notes to Funerary Inscription, *ILS* 8393, *Laudatio Turiae* (excerpts):

For ease of reference, we will refer to the woman described in this inscription as Turia, though her actual name is not known. The inscription itself is in a very fragmentary state, with many words or parts of words missing. The Latin text presented here (from Herman Dessau's *Inscriptiones Latinae Selectae*) is based on restorations of possible words, which we have not indicated in order to facilitate translation. We have added line numbers to make it easier to match these glosses with the text, starting with 1, though this selection actually begins at the top of the second column of the inscription.

1   **subsidium**, -i n. *support, supplies* needed by him during his flight. **fugae**: dat. of purpose. **fuga**, -ae f. *flight, escape*. **divendo**, -ere, ——, divenditum *sell in separate lots* (rather than piece by piece). **margaritum**, -i n. *pearl*. **detracta**: neuter accusative plural since it takes its case from the nearer of the two paired nouns (**aurum** and **margarita**). **subinde** (adv.) *afterwards; from time to time*. **familia nummis fructibus**: ablatives of source; **familia**, -ae f. *household; slaves;* **nummus**, -i m. *coin; money*. **fructus**, -us m. *income; provisions*. **custos**, -odis m. *guards, armed men*; these were sent by their political enemies to hunt Turia's husband down. **locupleto** (1) *enrich, augment*. **quid**: this pronoun, best translated as *why*, introduces a series of rhetorical questions in the subjunctive (**eruam, conservatus sim**, etc.). **eruo**, -ere, -ui, -utum *bring up, bring to light; mention*.

5   **ut** *how*. **repentinus**, -a, -um *sudden, unexpected*. **vitanda** *dangers* (literally, *things to be avoided*). **audacia...temere**: "by foolhardy boldness" (on his part). **modestiora**: "plans more within the bounds of possibility." **receptaculum**, -i n. *place of refuge; place of safety*. **socios**: in apposition with **sororem tuam et virum eius C. Cluvium**. **ad me servandum**: "for saving me" (gerundive). **coniuncto omnium periculo**: by joining together to save Turia's husband, Turia, her sister, and Cluvius all put themselves in danger. **finiam...coner**: a future less vivid condition.

10   **salutariter** (adv.) *safely*. **lateo**, -ere, -ui, —— *go into hiding, disappear*. **acerbus**, -a, -um *bitter, harsh, grievous, painful*. **accido**, -ere, -cidi, —— *befall, come to pass, happen*: **tua vice** *in respect to you*. **fateor**, -eri, fassus, -a sum *confess, acknowledge*. **inutilis**, -is, -e *useless, ineffective*. **cive**: i.e., Turia's husband. **restitutio**, -onis f. *pardon* and *return*. **conlega**, -ae m. *colleague*; Lepidus and Augustus were members of the Second Triumvirate. **interpello** (1) *obstruct, interfere; object*. **prosterno**, -ere, -stravi, -stratum *throw* (oneself) *to the ground*. **humi**: locative, *on the ground*. **adlevo** (1) *lift up, raise*. **traho**, -ere, traxi, tractum *drag*.

15   **rapso** (1) *hurry away, carry away*. **livor**, -oris m. *black-and-blue mark; bruise*. **repletus**, -a, -um *filled with; covered with*. **gratulatione**: Augustus Caesar not only pardoned him, but wished him well in his return. **verbis**: i.e., Lepidus' words. **contumeliosus**, -a, -um *abusive, insulting*. **crudelis**, -is, -e *cruel, grievous*. **palam** (adv.) *openly, publicly*. **notesco**, -ere, -ui, —— *become known*. **pacatus**, -a, -um *pacified, made peaceful*; by this "politically correct" euphemism, Turia's husband means "when Octavian had successfully defeated his enemies in the Civil War that erupted after Caesar's death." **orbis**, -is m. *world*. **restitutus**, -a, -um *restored, re-established*. **felix**, -icis *happy; prosperous*.

ILS 8393, Funerary Inscription: the so-called *Laudatio Turiae* (excerpts), CIL 6.41062

Some scholars have identified the woman of this fragmentary epitaph of the late 1ˢᵗ century BCE with the *matrona* named Turia, whose brave protection of her husband is known from Valerius Maximus' *Memorable Deeds and Sayings* (6.7.2). After her husband Q. Lucretius Vespillo (consul in 19 BCE) had been proscribed by the First Triumvirate (43 BCE), Turia successfully hid him in her bedroom above the rafters, despite the fact that she would have been killed with him if he had been discovered.

In this fragmentary encomium, which reads like a spoken eulogy, the *matrona*'s husband praises her bravery, resolution, and devotion to her family, which she demonstrated several times: in avenging her parents' murders by political assassins; by assisting her husband to escape murder; by demanding at her own risk that his arch-enemy Lepidus allow him to return; by providing for her relations whose fortunes had been confiscated or lost during the Civil Wars; and by offering her husband a divorce when she did not produce children. He states that she failed him in only one way: by dying before him. (See the epitaph of Aurelia Philematium, whose husband makes a similar statement.)

1   Subsidia fugae meae praestitisti ornamentis divenditis cum omne aurum
       margaritaque corpori detracta tradidisti mihi et subinde familia nummis
       fructibus, deceptis adversariorum custodibus absentiam meam
              locupletasti...
       Quid ego nunc interiora nostra et recondita consilia secrete pectoris eruam?
5   Ut repentinis nuntiis ad praesentia et imminentia vitanda excitatus tuis
       consiliis conservatus sim? Ut neque audacia abripi me temere passa sis et
       modestiora cogitanti fida receptacula paraveris sociosque consiliorum
              tuorum
       ad me servandum dederis sororem tuam et virum eius C. Cluvium,
              coniuncto
       omnium periculo? Non finiam, si attingere coner. Sat est mihi tibique
10   salutariter me latuisse.
       Acerbissimum tamen in vita mihi accidisse tua vice fatebor, reddito iam
       non inutili cive patriae, beneficio et iudicio absentis Caesaris Augusti, cum
       per te de restitutione mea M. Lepidus conlega praesens interpellaretur et ad
       eius pedes prostrata humi, non modo non adlevata, sed tracta et servilem in
15   modum rapsata, livoribus corporis repleta, firmissimo animo eum
              admoneres
       edicti Caesari cum gratulatione restitutionis meae, auditisque verbis etiam
       contumeliosis et crudelibus exceptis vulneribus palam ea praeferres, ut
              auctor
       meorum periculorum notesceret....
       Pacato orbe terrarum, restituta re publica, quieta deinde nobis et felicia

Notes to Funerary Inscription, *ILS* 8393, *Laudatio Turiae* (excerpts):

20   **nobis**: dat. with **contigerunt**. **sors**, sortis f. *lot* (in life), *fortune*. **invideo**, -ere, invidi, invisum *begrudge*. **procedens aetas** *advancing age*. **diffido**, -ere, diffisus sum + dat. *despair* (*of*), *lose confidence in*. **orbitas**, -atis f. *lack of children*. **tenendo**: gerundive in abl. of means. **depono**, -ponere, -posui, -positum *lay aside, give up; abandon*. **causa**: ablative followed by the genitive (**eius**): *for the sake of*. **divertium**, -i n. *divorce*. **elocuta es**: this verb introduces a series of indirect statements, e.g., **tradituram** [esse], **futuros** [esse], etc. **alterius** (understand **feminae**). **non alia mente nisi**: "not out of any intention/thought except."

25   **condicio**, -onis f. *situation*. **quaereres pararesque**: subjunctive in a purpose clause (introduced by **ut**) in indirect statement. **habituram** [esse] *would consider*. **adfirmares**: also part of the **ut** purpose clause. **ministerium**, -i n. *assistance*. **seiungo**, -ere, seiunxi, seiunctum *separate, detach*. **socrus**, -us f. *mother-in-law*.

30   **deinceps** (adv.) *in turn*. **fateor**, fateri, fassus sum *confess, admit*; **fatear**: clause of purpose (with **ut** omitted) after **necesse est**. **exardesco**, -ere, exarsi, exarsus *become angry, be inflamed with anger*. **arbitrium**, -i n. *control*. **actus**, -us m. *action; offer*. **ut vix redderer mihi**: "that I could scarcely regain my self-control." **agito** (1) *consider, discuss, suggest*. **lex**, legis f. *law*; here, *decision*. **quare** (adv.) *on which account*. **desino**, -ere, desii, desitum *cease, stop, end*.

35   **quae tanta** *how great, what great*. **exuo**, -ere, -ui, -utum *pull or strip off; cast or put aside*. **muto** (1) *change*. **exuerem, mutarem**: subjunctives in result clauses. **mutarem certa dubiis**: "that I should exchange certainty for doubt"; Turia's husband means that he would be exchanging the marital happiness he enjoys for the mere possibility of having children. **dedecus**, -oris n. *disgrace, shame*. **communi infelicitate**: divorce would make both him and Turia unhappy. **utinam** (conj.) *would that*; introduces an optative subjunctive (subjunctive of wishing) clause. **patior**, pati, passus/a sum *allow, permit*. **donec** (conj.) *until*. **elato me maiore**: "after I, the elder (**maiore**), had been carried off (by death)." **iustus**, -a, -um *just, proper*. **supremus**, -a, -um *surviving, still living*.

40   **extorqueo**, -ere, extorsi, extortum *twist away, wrench out*. **vires**, -ium f. pl. *strength*. **maeror**, -oris m. *grief, mourning*. **mergo**, -ere, mersi, mersum *drown, sink*. **luctus**, -us m. *grief, sadness*. **mereo**, -ere, -ui, -itum *deserve*. **contingo**, -tingere, -tigi, -tactum + dat. *happen to, befall*; the subject of **contigisse** is **omnia**. **praesto**, -are, praestiti, praestitum *offer, present*; the direct object is **omnia**. Turia's husband means that though Turia deserved everything good, life did not allow him to present all these good things to her. **lex**, legis f. *law*. **mandatum**, -i n. *command*. **Lex** is predicative with **mandatum**: *as a law*; the thought, somewhat similar to our "your wish is my command," is that Turia's commands are his law. **extra** (adv.) *beyond*. **fuerit liberum mihi**: the subject is **quod** – "what will be free for me (to do), I will guarantee to do." **praesto**, -are, praestiti, praestitum *guarantee, be responsible for*. **tueor**, tueri, tutus/a sum *guard, protect*.

ILS 8393, Funerary Inscription: *Laudatio Turiae* (continued)

20   tempora contigerunt. Fuerunt optati liberi, quos aliqua mala sors
      inviderat.... procedens aetas spem finiebat.... [Tu] diffidens fecunditati
          tuae et
      dolens orbitate mea, ne tenendo in matrimonio te spem habendi liberos
      deponerem atque eius causa essem infelix, de divertio elocuta es:
          vacuamque
      domum alterius fecunditati te traditaram, non alia mente nisi ut nota
25   concordia nostra tu ipsa mihi dignam condicionem quaereres
          pararesque; ac
      futuros liberos te communes proque tuis habituram adfirmares; neque
      patrimoni nostri, quod adhuc fuerat commune, separationem facturam;
          sed in
      eodem arbitrio meo id et, si vellem, tuo ministerio futurum; nihil
          seiunctum,
      nihil separatum te habituram, sororis socrusve officia pietatemque mihi
30   deinceps praestituram.
      Fatear necesse est adeo me exarsisse, ut excesserim mente: adeo
      exhorruisse actus tuos, ut vix redderer mihi; agitari divertia inter nos,
      antequam fato dicta lex esset! posse te aliquid concipere mente, quare viva
      desineres esse mihi uxor, cum paene exule me vita fidissima permansisses!
35   Quae tanta mihi fuerit cupiditas aut necessitas habendi liberos, ut propterea
      fidem exuerem, mutarem certa dubiis? Sed quid plura? permansisti
          apud me;
      neque enim cedere tibi sive dedecore meo et communi infelicitate
          poteram…
      Utinam patiente utriusque aetate procedere coniugium potuisset, donec
      elato me maiore, quod iustius erat, suprema mihi praestares....
40   Naturalis dolor extorquet constantiae vires. Maerore mersor ad desiderium
          luctumque
      reservatus videor. Ultimum huius orationis erit omnia meruisse te neque
      omnia contigisse mihi ut praestarem tibi. Legem habui mandata tua: quod
      extra mihi liberum fuerit, praestabo.
      Te di manes tui et quietam patiantur atque ita tueantur opto.

Notes to *Funerary Inscription for Aurelia Philematium*:

1221a

1   **L.**: epigraphic abbreviation for Lucius. **l.**: epigraphic abbreviation for **libertus** *freedman*. **lanius**, -i m. butcher. **collis Viminalis** *the Viminal Hill*, one of Rome's seven hills.

2   **haec** f. nom. s. *this (woman), she*. **praecedo**, -ere, praecessi *precede in death* (**fato**). **corpore casto**: ablative of description. **castus**, -a, -um *chaste*.

3   **coniunx**, coniugis f. *wife*. **una**: *sole, one and only* (i.e., she was his one and only wife). **praeditus meo animo** *sharer of my mind*; with this phrase Hermia states that the two shared a single purpose or intention and that they lived in harmony always.

4   **fidus** + dat. *faithful, loyal*. **fido fida viro**: Hermia emphasizes their mutual fidelity through this iconic image, in which the adjective **fida**, referring to Philematium, is "embraced" by the two words referring to her husband. The theme of mutual fidelity is picked up again with the word **parili**. **studium**, -i n. *affection, love*. **parilis**, -is, -e *equal*. **cum** (conj.); **cum** used causally (*since, though*) usually takes the indicative in early Latin.

5   **avaritia**, -ae f. *avarice, greed*. **cum** + indicative *since* (causal); Hermia's thought is that the only way in which Philematium failed him was in dying before him. **cedo**, -ere, cessi *fail, give way*. **officium**, -i n. *duty* (as a wife). **l.**: epigraphic abbreviation for **liberta** *freedwoman*.

1221b

2   **Philematio**: The dative is written either in error, or the carver miscalculated the space for all the letters and found no room on the slab for an **m** (**Philematiom** is a first century BCE spelling for **Philematium**). **nominito** (1) *name*.

3   **pudens**, -entis *chaste, pure*. **vulgus**, -i n. *common crowd; the public in general*. **nescius**, -a, -um + gen. *being unknown to*. **vulgi nescia**: Philematium emphasizes that she was a wife who tended to her home and did not go gadding about in Rome.

4   **vir**, -i m. *husband*. **conlibertus**, -i m. *fellow-freedman*. **eidem**: dative *to this same one* (Lucius); Philematium explains that both she and Hermia had been slaves of the same man, Lucius Aurelius. **quo careo**: "whom I lack , of whom I am bereft (through my death)"; **careo** + ablatve. **eheu!** *alas!*

5   **re...et vero** *in fact and in truth*; the spelling **ree** on the epitaph has been regularized in our text. **plus superaque** *more than and above, more than and beyond*. **parens**: because, as she says in the next line, Hermia began to take care of her when she was seven years old.

6   **gremium**, -i n. *lap, bosom; heart*. **ipse**: i.e., Hermia.

7   **potior**, potiri, potitus/a sum *get, obtain, receive*. **necis potior**: "I reach death, I die."

8   **adsiduus**, -a, -um *diligent, unremitting*. **floreo**, -ere, florui *flourish, prosper*. **ad omnis** *in the eyes of all; before all*.

ILS 1221a, 1221b, Funerary Inscription for Aurelia Philematium

This stele of fine Tiburtine stone belonging to the 1st century BCE depicts Aurelia Philematium facing her husband, Lucius Aurelius Hermia; since she predeceased him she is shown bending her head to kiss his right hand farewell, a gesture of affection. Her head is covered by a *palla* in the traditional sign of wifely modesty. Aurelius' inscription (carved next to his image in somewhat awkwardly rendered lettering) and Philematium's inscription (carved next to her bust in lettering and spacing that is equally awkward) is painted with red pigment. Both Hermia and Philematium were freed by Lucius Aurelius and so took his *nomen* while retaining their slave names as *cognomina*, both Greek names. They were betrothed when she was seven years old but since slaves did not have the legal right to marry, they lived together as *contubernales* ("tent mates") until after their manumission. Hermia gives an encomium of his wife as though he were speaking her funeral eulogy. Philematium also speaks in the first person, as though she were alive. Both inscriptions are written in elegiac couplet.

1221a: L. Aurelius L. l. Hermia lanius de colle Viminale.

Haec quae me fato praecessit corpore casto
     coniunx una meo praedita amans animo,
fido fida viro vixit studio parili, cum
5   nulla in avaritia cessit ab officio.
Aurelia L. l.

1221b: Aurelia L. l. Philematio

Viva Philematium sum Aurelia nominitata,
     casta, pudens, vulgi nescia, fida viro.
Vir conlibertus fuit eidem, quo careo eheu!
5   re fuit et vero plus superaque parens.
Septem me natam annorum gremio ipse recepit;
     XXXX annos nata necis potior
Ille meo officio adsiduo florebat ad omnis.

Photo courtesy of *The VRoma Project*; permission ©Copyright The Trustees of the British Museum.

Notes to Funerary Inscription, *ILS* 8403, Claudia:

1   **hospes**, -itis m. *traveler*. **paulum**, -i n. *a little thing, a trifle*. **asto** (1) *stand near; stop and stand*. **perlego**, -ere, -exi, -ectum *read through; read thoroughly*.

2   Note the play on the syllables **pulchr**--- in this line. **haud** (adv.) *not*.

3   **Claudiam**: predicate accusative with a verb of naming.

4   **diligo**, -ere, -exi, -ectum *love, esteem, prize*.

6   **linquo**, -ere, liqui *leave behind*. **loco** (1) *bury, place*.

7   **sermo**, -onis m. *speech*. **Sermone** and **incessu**: ablatives of description. **lepidus**, -a, -um *charming, pleasant*; understand **erat**. **tum autem** (conj.) *but also, in addition*.**incessus**, -us m. *walk; poise, bearing*. **commodus**, -a, -um *proper; agreeable*.

8   **lana**, -ae f. *wool*; **lanam facere** *to spin and weave* (i.e., make clothing for her family).

Notes to Tacitus, *Agricola* 6:

6.1   **hinc** (adv.) *from here*. Having completed his service as military tribune in Britain with distinction, Agricola returned to Rome to enter the *cursus honorum*. **ad** + gerundive = purpose construction. **capesso**, -ere, -ivi, -itum *seize, try to reach, engage in*. **magistratus**, -us m. *office, magistracy*. **degredior**, degredi, degressus/a sum *descend, march down*. **Domitia Decidiana**: daughter of Decidius Domitius. Her father is identified in an inscription as having been a quaestor (a treasury official) and a praetor (a chief magistrate), making her a most suitable match for her ambitious husband. Also, her marriage to Agricola associated her family with the Julian *gens*. **natales**, -ium m. pl. *birth, origin*. **orior**, -iri, ortus/a sum *rise, spring, descend*. **iungo**, -ere, iunxi, iunctum *unite, join*; the marriage probably took place in 62 CE, when Agricola was 22 years old. It is possible that his decision to marry at this time was based on the preferment for office that married candidates enjoyed over unmarried ones and those with three children over those with fewer or none (see *Lex Papia Poppaea de maritandis ordinibus*, 9 CE). **nitor**, niti, nisus/a sum *climb, strive, press forward*. **decus**, -oris n. *honor, glory*. **robur**, -oris n. *strength*. **mira concordia**: ablative case. **mutuus**, -a, -um *mutual, reciprocal*. **caritas**, -atis f. *esteem, affection*. **in vicem** (<**vicis**) *by turns, alternately, reciprocally*. **antepono**, -ere, -posui, -positum *set before, prefer* + **se** (reciprocal use of the reflexive) = *each other*. **nisi quod**: *except that*. **tanto...quanto**: adverbs, correlative; *so much... as*. **mala**: supply **uxore**. **culpa**, -ae f. *blame, fault*; partitive genitive (**culpae**) with **plus**.

3   **augeo**, -ere, auxi, auctum *increase, enrich, bless with*. **subsidium**, -i n. *aid, assistance*. **tollo**, -ere, sustuli, sublatum *raise, lift*; in reference to a child, it means *acknowledge* or *bring up*. **brevi** (adv.) *soon, shortly*. **amitto**, -ere, -misi, -missum *lose, let go*.

ILS 8403, Funerary Inscription for Claudia, CIL 6.15346

The stele bearing this inscription was found at Rome but is now lost. Dated to circa 135-120 BCE, it bears testimony to the realities of a woman's life and the cultural expectations that framed a Roman woman's excellence – loyalty to husband, production of children, management of the house, weaving of wool. Rather uniquely, however, Claudia's husband distinguishes her for her personal graces – her beauty, her graceful speech, and her bearing. The meter is Senarii.

> Hospes, quod dico, paulum est: asta ac perlege.
> Hic est sepulchrum haud pulchrum pulchrae feminae.
> Nomen parentes nominarunt Claudiam.
> Suum maritum corde dilexit suo.
> 5   Natos duos creavit, horum alterum
> in terra linquit, alium sub terra locat.
> Sermone lepido, tum autem incessu commodo.
> Domum servavit, lanam fecit. Dixi. Abi.

Cornelius Tacitus, *Agricola* 6: Domitia Decidiana

In admiration of his father-in-law, Gnaeus Iulius Agricola (40-93 CE), Tacitus wrote *Agricola*, a monograph that has been called a eulogy in the guise of biography. He published it some five years after the death of his wife's father, who was rumored to have been poisoned by the Emperor Domitian out of envy for his reputation. Tacitus' mother-in-law, Domitia Decidiana, who is said to have avoided public notice successfully all of her life despite her husband's public roles, is mentioned only briefly, perhaps out of respect for her wish to avoid public attention. She is praised for being a worthy wife and partner to her husband's advancement. In Tacitus' statement that the family found some consolation from the birth of a daughter soon after the death of a son, her role as mother goes unnoticed.

> **6**   (1) Hinc ad capessendos magistratus in urbem degressus Domitiam Decidianam, splendidis natalibus ortam, sibi iunxit; idque matrimonium ad maiora nitenti decus ac robur fuit. vixeruntque mira concordia, per mutuam caritatem et in vicem se anteponendo, nisi quod in bona uxore tanto maior laus, quanto in mala plus culpae est.
>
> (3) Auctus est ibi filia, in subsidium simul ac solacium; nam filium ante sublatum brevi amisit.

Notes to Valerius Maximus, *Facta et Dicta Memorabilia* 6.7:

1   **ut** + subjunctive = purpose clause. **uxorius**, -a, -um *of a wife*. **attingo**, -ere, -tigi, -tactum *touch, mention*. **Tertia Aemilia**: she takes her name from her father's *nomen* or gens, the Aemiliani; when there are more daughters than one, they are named in birth order **maior**, **minor**, **tertia**, etc. Wife of Scipio Africanus Maior, she was sister of Paullus Aemilianus and the mother of two daughters named Cornelia and two sons. No other information about this exemplary woman is available. **Publius Cornelius Africanus Maior,** here named **Prior** (236-183 BCE) was a brilliant military strategist who defeated the Carthaginian armies during the Second Punic War in Spain, Sicily, and decisively at Zama near Carthage. **Cornelia Gracchorum**: Cornelia Minor (d. 100 BCE), wife of Tiberius Sempronius Gracchus; she bore twelve children, of whom only three survived. She was praised for being an *univira* (one-husband woman) and devoted mother of the Gracchi brothers, both reformers who were assassinated in the 2nd century BCE (see her letters in World of Learning). **comitas**, -atis f. *kindness, affability*. **ut** + subjunctive (**dissimulaverit**): result clause (introduced by **tantae**). **cum** + subjunctive (**sciret**): adversative, *although*. **ancillula**, -ae f. *young servant girl*. **ex suis**: understand **ancillis**. **gratus**, -a, -um + dative *pleasing, dear*. **dissimulo** (1) *conceal, ignore*. **ne** + subjunctive (**ageret**): negative purpose clause. **domitor**, -oris m. *lord*. **femina** is the subject of **ageret**; note how the word is surrounded and dwarfed by the status words used in reference to her husband. **reus**, -i m. **rea**, -ae f. *party to a lawsuit, defendant*; **reum agere** (idiom) *conduct legal proceedings against* + gen. of the charge. **vindicta**, -ae f. *punishment*. **ut** + subjunctive (**daret**): result clause (introduced by tantum). **manumitto**, -ere, -misi, -missum *emancipate, free from slavery*. **libertus**, -i m. *freedman*.

2   **Quintus Lucretius**: unknown. **proscribo**, -ere, -scripsi, -scriptum *proscribe, outlaw*. Proscription under Sulla included the death penalty for those proscribed; bounties for killing the proscribed; rewards for information leading to their capture; penalties for their concealment. **triumviri**, -orum m. an extra-constitutional commission of three men, formed by Octavian, Antony, and Lepidus in 43 BCE to punish Caesar's killers and govern Rome. **Turia**: some identify this woman as the subject of *Laudatio Turiae*. **camera**, -ae f. *vault*. **tectum**, -i n. *house roof*. **cubiculum**, -i n. *bedroom*. **abdo**, -ere, abdidi, abditum *hide, remove*; **abditum** modifies **Lucretium**. **conscius**, -a, -um *sharing the knowledge*; *confiding* (abl. absolute with **una ancillula**). **immineo**, -ere, -ui *threaten, impend*. **exitium**, -i n. *destruction*. **praesto**, -are, -stiti, -stitum *render; keep* (especially *safe*). **ut** + subjunctive (**retineret**): result clause. **cum** + subjunctive (**evaderent**): temporal clause, *when*. **cruciatus**, -us m. *torture, misfortune*. **evado**, -ere, evasi, evasum *escape from, pass*. **coniunx**, -iugis m/f. *husband, wife*. **sinus**, -us m. *bosom, protection, heart*. **salus**, salutis f. *life, health*. **retineo**, -ere, -tinui, -tentum *keep, preserve*.

3   **Sulpicia**: neither the love poet nor the wife of Calenus mentioned by Martial. **custodio**, -ire, -divi, -ditum *guard, keep watch over*. **ne** + subjunctive: negative purpose clause. **(Lucius Cornelius) Lentulus Cruscellio**: perhaps the admiral of Pompey mentioned by Appian in the *Bellum Civile*. **persequor**, -sequi, -secutus/a sum *follow, pursue*. **nihilo minus** *none the less*. **famularis** (adj.) *of servants*. **vestis**, -is f. *clothes, dress*. **sumo**, -ere, sumpsi, sumptum *put on, assume*. **duabus**: feminine ablative plural of **duo**. **totidem**: indecl. adj. *just as many*. **clandestinus**, -a, -um *secret*. **pervenio**, -ire, -veni, -ventum *come to, reach*. **recuso** (1) *be reluctant, refuse*. **ut** + subjunctive (**constaret**): purpose clause. **ei**: dat. of reference. **consto** (1) *stand firm, remain constant*.

Valerius Maximus, *Facta et Dicta Memorabilia* 6.7

The historian Valerius Maximus provides *exempla* in his handbook for orators, published after 31 CE. Under the heading *De Fide Uxorum Erga Viros*, "The Loyalty of Wives Toward their Husbands," he offers three examples of women who ought to be remembered for their virtuous behavior: Tertia Aemilia, the wife of Scipio Africanus Maior, who chose to ignore his liaison with a slave girl; Turia, who endangered her person by hiding her proscribed husband (now thought not to be the woman celebrated in *ILS* 8393, the so-called *Laudatio Turiae*); and Sulpicia, who followed her husband into exile, disregarding the consequences to herself.

(1)   Atque ut uxoriam quoque fidem attingamus, Tertia Aemilia, Africani prioris uxor, mater Corneliae Gracchorum, tantae fuit comitatis et patientiae, ut, cum sciret viro suo ancillulam ex suis gratam esse, dissimulaverit ne domitorem orbis Africanum femina magnum virum inpatientiae reum ageret, tantumque a vindicta mens eius afuit, ut post mortem Africani manu missam ancillam in matrimonium liberto suo daret.

(2)   Q. Lucretium proscriptum a triumviris uxor Turia inter cameram et tectum cubiculi abditum una conscia ancillula ab inminente exitio non sine magno periculo suo tutum praestitit singularique fide id egit, ut cum ceteri proscripti in alienis et hostilibus regionibus per summos corporis et animi cruciatus vix evaderent, ille in cubiculo et in coniugis sinu salutem retineret.

(3)   Sulpicia autem, cum a matre Iulia diligentissime custodiretur, ne Lentulum Cruscellionem, virum suum proscriptum a triumviris in Siciliam persequeretur, nihilo minus famulari veste sumpta cum duabus ancillis totidemque servis ad eum clandestina fuga pervenit nec recusavit se ipsam proscribere, ut ei fides sua in coniuge proscripto constaret.

Notes to Funerary Inscription, *CIL* 6.6593, *Carissima Coniunx*:

1   **placeo**, -ere, placui (+ abl.) *be pleasing to, please.*

2   **anima,**-ae f. *soul, spirit.* **in ore animam...deposui**: the Roman custom was for the nearest male relative to bend over the dying person to catch his/her last breath, which was thought to contain the **anima**. **frigida**: a euphemism for *deceased.*

3   **morior**, mori, mortuus/a sum *die.* **lumina**: metonymy for **oculos**. **premo**, -ere, pressi, pressus *press* (i.e., to close for the dead).

4   **obitus,** -us m. *death, decease.* **niteo**, nitere, nitui *shine, gleam.*

Notes to Valerius Maximus, *Facta et Dicta Memorabilia* 4.3.3 (Paragraph 1):

1   **laudibus**: abl. of respect. **virilis**, -e *manly, brave, bold.* **claritas**, -atis f. *celebrity, fame.* **supergredior**, -gredi, -gressus/a sum *surpass.* **maritus**, -i m. *husband.* **egregius**, -a, -um *outstanding, distinguished.* **penso** (1) *repay, compensate.* **excessus**, -us m. *death, departure.* **floreo**, -ere, florui *be in one's prime, flower.* **convictus**, -us m. *community life, living together.* **socrus**, -us f. *mother-in-law*, i.e., Livia (58 BCE-29CE), wife of Augustus. **pro** + abl.: *instead of, in place of.* **coniugium**, -i n. *marriage, husband, wife.* **torus**, -i m. *couch, bed.* **alterius...alterius**: *of the one...of the other.* **vigor**, -oris m. *energy.* **extinguo**, -ere, extinxi, extinctum *extinguish, destroy.* **viduitas**, -atis f. *widowhood, bereavement.* **consenesco**, -ere, -ui *grow old, fade.* **cubiculum**, -I n. *bedroom.* **experimentum**, -i n. *proof, experience* (here, of dedicated married love). **summa**, -ae f. *total, sum, culmination.* **impono**, -ere, imposui, impositum *place on, assign*; jussive subjunctive; Maximus marks this as the highest model of wifely decorum.

Notes to Valerius Maximus, *Facta et Dicta Memorabilia* 4.6.5 (Paragraph 1):

1   **ignes**: a common metaphor for passion, especially that of love. **Porcia**: (d. 43/42 BCE) daughter of the fierce Republican and Stoic Marcus Porcius Cato Uticensis (95-46 BCE) and the second wife of the tyrannicide Marcus Junius Brutus (85-42 BCE), she shared their political ideals and participated in the plot to kill Caesar. **debeo**, -ere, debui, debitum: perfect passive participle modifying **admiratione** *owed, destined, due.* **prosequor**, -sequi, -secutus/a sum + ablative *honor with.* **quae**: refers to Porcia. **cum** + subjunctive (**cognosses**): a temporal clause; translate *when.* **Philippi**, -orum m. pl. a city in Macedonia, site of the battle at which Octavian and Antony defeated Brutus and Cassius. **vinco**, -ere, vici, victum *conquer, defeat.* **interimo**, -imere, -emi, -emptum *kill, destroy.* **cognosses**: contracted form of **cognovisses**; < **cognosco**, -ere, -novi, -notum *learn.* **ferrum**, -i n. *sword, iron.* **ardeo, -**ere, arsi, arsum *be on fire, burn.* **carbo**, -inis m. *charcoal, embers.* **haurio**, -ire, hausi, haustum *take in, swallow.* **dubito** (1) *hesitate*; contracted form of **dubitavisti**. **muliebris...virilis** (adj.) *feminine... masculine.* **exitus**, -us m. *end, death.* **nescio an** *I rather think; I do not know whether.* **hoc**: neuter s. demonstrative pronoun, referring to **exitium**; supply **erat**. **usitatus**, -a, -um *familiar, usual*; supply **genere mortis absumptus est**. **absumo**, -ere, -sumpsi, -sumptum *kill.*

CIL 6.6593, Funerary Inscription: *Carissima Coniunx*

This epitaph names neither the deceased wife nor her husband, who erected her monument. The brief four-line poem, narrated by the dead woman, goes beyond conventional phrasing to include her husband's expression of grief (it is impossible to know whether she composed it herself or her husband commissioned it). The meter is elegiac couplet.

> Viva viro placui, prima et carissima coniunx
>> cuius in ore animam frigida deposui.
> Ille mihi lacrimans morientia lumina pressit.
>> Post obitum, satis hac femina laude nitet.

Valerius Maximus, *Facta et Dicta Memorabilia* 4.3.3

In his handbook for orators (1ˢᵗ century CE), Valerius considers the quality of marital fidelity. He presents Antonia Minor (36 BCE-37 CE), daughter of Mark Antony and Octavia, mother of three children including the Emperor Claudius, and grandmother of the Emperor Caligula, as a model of courage, devotion and female virtue, who refused to remarry after the death of her husband, the equally faithful Drusus Germanicus (9 CE), younger son of Livia.

> (1) Antonia quoque, femina laudibus virilem familiae suae claritatem supergressa, amorem mariti egregia fide pensavit, quae post eius excessum forma et aetate florens convictum socrus (pro coniugio) habuit, in eodemque toro alterius adulescentiae vigor extinctus est, alterius viduitatis experientia consenuit. hoc cubiculum talibus experimentis summam inponat.

Valerius Maximus, *Facta et Dicta Memorabilia* 4.6.5

Valerius considers marital love, declaring that *honestissimus amor* is "morte iungi quam distrahi vita" ("to be joined by death rather than to be torn apart by life"). Many women at the end of the Republic faced a threat as great as childbirth, but one in which they had a choice: they could join their husbands in death or exile or suffer the torments of living on alone in Rome, often shunned and in poverty. Unlike the wives of Cicero and Ovid, who remained behind with their children to work for their husband's return, Porcia, the wife of Caesar's assassin Brutus, joined her husband in death by committing suicide.

> (1) Tuos quoque castissimos ignes, Porcia M. Catonis filia, cuncta saecula debita admiratione prosequentur. quae, cum apud Philippos victum et interemptum virum tuum Brutum cognosses (quia ferrum non dabatur, ardentes ore carbones haurire non dubitasti, muliebri spiritu virilem patris exitum imitata. sed nescio an hoc fortius, quod ille usitato, tu novo genere mortis absumpta es.

Notes to Pliny, *Ep.* 7.5:

C. Plinius Calpurniae Suae S. This is a formula for the salutation of a letter: the name of the sender in the nominative, the addressee in the dative (often with **suae** or **suo** to show affection or close relationship), and the abbreviation **S.** (or **S. D.**), *salutem* (or *salutem dicit*), "says hello."

1   **desiderium**, -i n. *desire, longing.* **tui**: objective genitive.

2   **in causa [est]**: "is the cause," "is responsible." **deinde** (adv.) *next, then.* **quod** *the fact that.* **consuesco**, -ere, -suevi, -suetum *become accustomed*; in perfect, *be accustomed.* **absum**, abesse, afui *be away, be apart.*

3   **inde** *for this reason.* **noctium**: gen. pl of **nox**, noctis f. *night.* **in imagine tua**: i.e., "picturing you with my mind's eye," "dreaming of you." **vigil**, vigilis (adj.) *awake, sleepless.* **exigo**, -ere, -egi, -actum *drive out, pass* (of time). **interdiu** (adv.) *during the day.* **viso**, -ere, -i, -um *go to see, visit.* **diaeta**, -ae f. (from Greek) *a room, apartment.* Calpurnia had a room or suite of her own in Pliny's spacious villa. **ipsi**: with **pedes** (< **pes**, pedis). **ut…dicitur**: this phrase shows that **pedes ducunt** is a proverbial expression. **aeger**, -gra, -grum *sick, weak.* **maestus**, -a, -um *sorrowful, gloomy.* **similis excluso**: "like a lover shut out"; the **exclusus amator** is a favorite figure in Latin love poetry, as well as in modern romantic comedies. **limen**, -inis n. *threshold, doorway.* **careo**, -ere, carui *be free of* + abl.

4   **careo**, -ere, -ui + abl. *lack, be free of.* **quo**: "that in which" (refers to **tempus**). **in foro** *in public, in the courts.* Pliny was a well-respected pleader. **lis**, litis f. *lawsuit.* **contero**, -ere, -trivi, -tritum *crush, wear out.*

5   **aestima**: imperative of **aestimo** (1) *imagine.* **tu**: though unnecessary with the imperative, it adds to the pathos. **requies**, -etis f. *rest, peace.* **solacium**, -i n. *comfort, consolation, relief.* **requies in labore/ in miseria curisque solacium**: Pliny is very fond of crossed (chiastic) contrasts, especially at the ends of his letters. **vale**: the typical formula for closing a letter. There is no need for the writer to add his/her name because it is already at the top. **valeo**, -ere, valui, valitum *be well*, as a greeting, *farewell.*

Notes to Martial, *Epigrammata* 11.53:

1   **caeruleus**, -a, -um *blue, dark blue, dyed blue.* **cum** + subjunctive: concessive clause, *although.* **Britanni**, orum m. pl. *Britons.* **edo**, -ere, edidi, editum *produce, give birth to.* **quam**: here the exclamation *how!* **Latius**, -a, -um *Latin.* **pectus**, -oris n. *heart, mind.* **decus**, -oris n. *beauty, honor, virtue.* **Romanam**: translate with **esse; eam** understood. **Italides** (< Italis, -idis) *Italian*, modifies **matres. Atthides** (< Atthis, -idis) *Attic*; **matres** understood.

5   **di bene [faciant]**: "May the gods bless." **quod…quod…quod**: *because*; the anaphora gives force to the three-fold wishes. **sanctus**, -a, -um *pious, virtuous, sacred.* **pario**, parere, peperi, partum + dative *bear children to, give birth to*; the subject is Claudia. **fecundus**, -a, -um *fertile.* **sperat**: the subject is **puella** (i.e., Claudia). **gener**, -i m. *son-in-law.* **nurus**, -us f. *daughter-in-law.* **superi**, -orum m. pl. *the gods above.* **gaudeo**, -ere, gavisus + ablative *take joy in, rejoice in.* **natus**, -a, -um *offspring.* **tres**, trium *three.*

C. Plinius Caecilius Secundus (minor), *Epistulae* 7.5

Calpurnia is away and Pliny misses her terribly. Calpurnia, his second or third wife, was much younger than he, but they obviously enjoyed each other's company and a mutually satisfying relationship (see also *Ep.* 4.19, in the World of Learning). Here he reveals a physical pain over her unaccustomed absence, which seems to indicate that they traveled together on most occasions. Two other short letters to her survive (*Ep.* 6.4 and 6.7), in which he praises her writing style. He wrote them to her when she was away in Campania for her health and he had to stay behind on business.

C. PLINIUS CALPURNIAE SUAE S.
(1) Incredibile est quanto desiderio tui tenear. (2) In causa amor primum, deinde quod non consuevimus abesse. (3) Inde est quod magnam noctium partem in imagine tua vigil exigo, inde quod interdiu quibus horis te visere solebam ad diaetam tuam ipsi me, ut verissime dicitur, pedes ducunt, quod denique aeger et maestus ac similis excluso a vacuo limine recedo. (4) Unum tempus his tormentis caret, quo in foro amicorum litibus conteror. (5) Aestima tu quae vita mea sit, cui requies in labore, in miseria curisque solacium. Vale.

Marcus Valerius Martialis, *Epigrammata* 11.53

In this graceful octet of elegiac couplets, Martial celebrates, apparently sincerely, the Roman virtues displayed by a young woman from the northern provinces. Not only is Claudia Rufina beautiful, but she brings her husband the gifts of the traditional *matrona* in that she is fertile, willing to produce children, and anticipates her children's spouses. Martial's blessing on her marriage is that she be *univira* and that she enjoy three living children, a gift of the gods, since the mortality rate of infants and children was so high at this time.

Claudia caeruleis cum sit Rufina Britannis
    edita, quam Latiae pectora gentis habet!
Quale decus formae! Romanam credere matres
    Italides possunt, Atthides esse suam.
5   Di bene quod sancto peperit fecunda marito,
    quod sperat generos quodque puella nurus.
Sic placeat superis, ut conjuge gaudeat uno
    et semper natis gaudeat illa tribus.

Notes to Plautus, *Menaechmi* (Lines 602-615):

602   **ais**: defective verb, **aio, ais, ait, aiunt** *say*. The question is not meant to be taken literally, but in the spirit of comedy Matrona does so. **me...nuptam**: understand **esse** in indirect statement, continuing **ais**; understand **aio**. **nubo**, -ere, nupsi, nuptum *get married* (referring to a woman); **nuptus**, -a, um: perfect participle, *married to*. **satin = satis + -ne**. **illic = ille + -ce**; -ce is an enclitic particle, often reduced to -c, which is added to demonstratives for a deictic (or pointing) effect. **si sapiam...abeam**: future less vivid condition, "should...would" (Remember that Menaechmus is unaware that his wife and Peniculus are there and that his every word is being overheard). **sapio**, -ere, -ivi *have sense, be wise*. **abeo**, -ire, -ii/ivi, -itum *go away*. **hinc** (adv.) *from here*. **intro** *inside*. The scene has two doors, one representing Menaechmus' house, the other, conveniently, Erotium's. Here he points to his mistress's door. **ubi mi** (= **mihi**) **bene sit**: an idiom meaning, "where I can have a good time." The subjunctive is either potential or by attraction because of the condition. **mane**: imperative of **maneo**. **potius** (adv.) *rather, more*. **ne** (adv.) *truly*. **illam**: refers to the *palla* (a woman's outdoor garment) which Menaechmus stole earlier in the day and gave to Erotium. We might call it a *stole* for the obvious play on words. This *palla* is a major prop in the play. **ecastor**: expletive used by women, *by Castor!* **faenerato** (adv.) *at interest*; he'll pay for his indiscretion. **apstulisti** = **abstulisti**: < **aufero**, [ab- + fero] -ferre, abstuli, ablatum *carry away, steal*. **sic datur**: Peniculus praises Matrona for "giving it to him."

605   **clanculum** (adv.) diminutive of **clam**, *in secret*. **te**: subject of **facere** in the indirect statement. **flagitium**, -i n. *disgrace, crime*. **censeo**, -ere, -ui, -sum *think, imagine*. With **potis** understand **esse = posse**. **negoti**: partitive gen. with **quid**. **negotium**, -i n. *business*. **illuc = illud**. **men = mene** (me + question particle, -ne). **vin = visne** (vis < volo + -ne). **rogem**: subjunctive with **vis**, in a jussive noun clause. **aufer**: imperative of **aufero**. **palpatio**, -onis f. *caress*. Roman plays do not have stage directions, but we can often fill them in from what characters say about their actions. **pergo**, -ere, perrexi, perrectum *proceed, get on with it*. **mihi**: dat. with **tristis**. **quid** *why, for what, at what?* **tristis**, -e *sad, upset* (with + dat.). **te**: subject of **scire**. **oportet** *it behooves*, i.e., "you ought." **dissimulo** (1) *disguise, hide, pretend* (that something is not so). **pallam**: see note on **illam**, at line 604. **quidam**: subject of incomplete sentence "a certain party"; understand **abstulit pallam**. **paveo**, -ere, pavi *be frightened, be alarmed*.

610   **nil = nihil**, answers **quid**. **equidem** (adv.) *truly*. **unum**: picks up Menaechmus' **nil**. **pallor**, -oris m. *paleness; alarm*. **incutio**, -ere, -cussi, -cussum *cause, strike*. **at** (conj.) *but*. **ne comesses**: "you shouldn't have eaten up..." < **comedo**, -ere/-esse, -edi, -esum/-estum *eat up, devour*; the form is imperfect subjunctive in a jussive clause. **clam** (adv.) *in secret*; prep. + acc. or abl. *without the knowledge of*. **prandium**, -i n. *a midday meal*; this one was quite elaborate (see lines 208-213). **in** (prep.) + acc. *into, against*. **taceo**, -ere, -ui, -itum *be silent, shut up*. **hercle**: expletive, *by Hercules!* **nuto** (1) *nod, gesture*. **usquam** (adv.) *anywhere, in any way*. **quicquam**: internal accusative with **nuto** and **nicto**, *in any way, at all*. **nicto** (1) *wink* (at + dat.). **ne**: as in line 603. **mecastor**: like **ecastor** (expletive used by women) *by Castor!* **ego**: understand **sum**. **qui**: old abl. form, *why?* **expedi**: imperative of **expedio**, -ire, -ivi, -itum *extricate, explain*.

615   **confidentius**: comparative of **confidens**, -entis (adj.) *bold, shameless*. **hoc**: abl. of comparison. **pernego** (1) *deny flatly*.

Titus Maccius Plautus, *Menaechmi*: Act 4, Scene 2, Lines 602-652

Is Menaechmus' wife, Matrona, a shrew or a long-suffering wife? Since the *Menaechmi* is a comedy, she is both at once. The play takes place in Epidamnus, a Greek port city on the Adriatic coast, later called Dyrrhachium (modern Durazzo). Its far-fetched plot concerns twin brothers, long separated but sharing the same name, and depends on both of them being neither quick-witted nor overly scrupulous. The local Menaechmus steals a *palla* (mantle) from his wife to keep his mistress Erotium (from Greek *eros*, "love") happy. The comic crisis comes about when the other Menaechmus arrives from Syracuse in a long search for his twin. The Menaechmus from Syracuse has actually eaten the meal prepared for his brother, enjoyed his brother's mistress's favors, taken the *palla* to be refashioned as well as a gold bracelet to be repaired, or so Erotium believes; he actually has no intention of returning them. He can hardly believe his good luck. In this scene Peniculus (a professional parasite), under the mistaken impression that his patron, the local Menaechmus, has eaten dinner without him, tells Menaechmus' wife, Matrona. Peniculus and Matrona, in hiding, have just overheard the local Menaechmus confess to the crime of stealing his wife's *palla* to give to his mistress. The hen-pecked husband faces his indignant wife, who stands up for herself and her valuables. Wordplay such as assonance ("pallorem...palla," 610; 635), alliteration ("nuto neque nicto," 613; 614), and repetition (621-5) add to the delight of reading Plautus in Latin. Lines 603-4 are anapestic tetrameter catalectic; the rest are trochaic septenarius (meter used in lively dialogue,)

> PEN: Quid ais? MAT: Viro me malo male nuptam. PEN: Satin audis
>   quae illic loquitur?
> MAT: Satis. MEN: Si sapiam, hinc intro abeam, ubi mi bene sit. PEN:
>   Mane; male erit potius.
> MAT: Ne illam ecastor faenerato apstulisti. PEN: Sic datur.
> 605   MAT: Clanculum te istaec flagitia facere censebas potis?
> MEN: Quid illuc est, uxor, negoti? MAT: Men rogas? MEN: Vin hunc
>   rogem?
> MAT: Aufer hinc palpationes. PEN: Perge tu. MEN: Quid tu mihi
>   tristis es? MAT: Te scire oportet. PEN: Scit, sed dissimulat malus.
> MEN: Quid negotist? MAT: Pallam— MEN: Pallam? MAT: Quidam
>   pallam— PEN: Quid paves?
> 610   MEN: Nil equidem paveo. PEN: Nisi unum: palla pallorem incutit.
>   at tu ne clam me comesses prandium. perge in virum.
> MEN: Non taces? PEN: Non hercle vero taceo. nutat, ne loquar.
> MEN: Non hercle ego quidem usquam quicquam nuto neque nicto tibi.
> MAT: Ne ego mecastor mulier misera. MEN: Qui tu misera es? mi
>   expedi.
> 615   PEN: Nihil hoc confidentius, qui quae vides ea pernegat.

Notes to Plautus, *Menaechmi* (Lines 616-639a):

616   **per**: used in oaths with the accusative, *by*. **Iovem**: accusative of **Iuppiter**, Iovis m. Jupiter, Jove. **omnis**: accusative plural. **adiuro** (1) *swear*. **iste**, ista, istud "that of yours." **nutasse** = **nutavisse. de "isti,"**: about the word "isti." **illuc** (adv.) *to that place*. **redi**: imperative of **redeo**, -ire, -ii/-ivi, itum *return*. **quo** (adv.) *where*. **redeam**: deliberative subjunctive, with which one asks oneself a question. **ad phrygionem**: *to the gold embroiderer's*. **refer**: imperative of **refero. istaec** = **ista. quando** *since*. **haec** refers to Matrona. **res**, rei f. *affair, property*. **memini**, meminisse (defective verb in the perfect with a present meaning) *remember*.

620   **numquis** = **num + quis**; **num** is an interrogative particle that expects a negative answer. **quis**, qua, quid *anyone, someone*. **servorum**: partitive genitive with **numquis. delinquo**, -ere, -liqui, -lictum *do wrong, offend*. **ancilla**, -ae f. *slave woman*. **responso** (1) *answer, talk back, sass*. **eloquere**: imperative of **eloquor**, -loqui, -locutus/a sum *speak up*. **impune** (adv.) *without punishment*. **nugas agis**: "you are talking nonsense," "you've got to be kidding." **admodum** (adv.) *very*. **istuc** = istud. **familiares**, -ium m/f. pl. *household slaves* **aliquoi** = **alicui. iratus**, -a, -um *angry*. **num**: an interrogative particle that expects a negative answer, "Are you angry with me?! " (that is, "surely you are not angry with me, are you?") **saltem** (adv.) *at least*.

625   **edepol**: expletive used by men, *by Pollux!* **em** (interj.) *there!* **rursum** (adv.) *again*.

        dic: imperative of **dico**; **dic, duc, fac**, and **fer** lack the regular -e. **aegre est** (aegrest) *it is annoying*. **bellus**, -a, um *fine, handsome, pretty*; used sarcastically. **blandior**, -iri, -itus/a sum + dat. *fawn, flatter*. **potin** = **potis** + question particle -**ne. potis** *able*; understand **es. ut... ne**: with subjunctive in an exclamatory question. **molestus**, -a, -um *annoying*. **appello** (1) *address, talk to*. **aufer**: see 607. **properato**: imperative of **propero** (1) *hurry*. **apsente** (= **absente**) **me**: abl. absolute. **post** (adv.) *afterwards, next*. **ante** (prep. + acc.) *before, in front of*. **aedis/aedes**, -is f. *house, temple*. **corona**, -ae f. *crown, wreath, garland* (of flowers, worn as part of the festivities at dinner parties). **derideto**: future imperative of **derideo**, -ere, -risi, -risum *laugh at, mock*. **ebrius**, -a, -um *drunk*.

630   **prandeo**, -ere, prandi, pransum *eat one's midday meal*. **huc** (adv.) *here, to this place*. **tetuli** = **tuli**: reduplicated perfect of **fero**, a more ancient form, found in early Latin. **tun** = **tune** (**tu** + question particle -**ne**). **audacius**: comparative of **audax**, -acis (adj.) *bold, brazen*. **hoc homine**: ablative of comparison, "than." **non** for **nonne**: question particle that expects the answer "yes." **modo** (adv.) *just now*. **hic** (adv.) *here, in this place*. **floreus**, -a, -um *of flowers*. **asto**, -are, -stiti *stand at/near*. **quom** = **cum**. **nego** (1) *say (that something is) not*. **mi** = **mihi**: dative of reference (ethical dative); translate "my," "for me," "on me." **sinciput**, -pitis n. (< semi + caput, *half-head*) a comic word for *head, noggin*. **novisse**: perfect infinitive of **nosco**, -ere, novi, notum *come to know*; in perfect, *know*. The subject [**te**] is omitted as the same as the subject of the main verb (**aibas**). **peregrinus**, -a, -um *foreign*. **aibas** = **aiebas** < **aio**.

635   **quin** *why not?, truly*. **ut** (temporal) *when*. **dudum** (adv.) *long since*. **divorto** = **diverto**, -ere, -vorti/verti *turn/go away*. **aps** = **abs. demum** (adv.) *at last*. **domum**: acc. of place to which. **mihi**: dat. of possession. **qui** = **quo** *how, the wherewithal* + relative clause of purpose. **ulciscerer**: 1 s. imperfect subjunctive in indirect question. **nescio**, -ire, -scivi, -scitum *not know*. **ipsus** = **ipse. quidnam** *what in the world?* **quid taces?** – **quid** here means *why*. **quin**: see line

639   **quasi** *as if*. **mi** = **mihi**: dat. of separation, a variety of dat. of reference, *from me*.

Titus Maccius Plautus, *Menaechmi* (continued)

      MEN: Per Iovem deosque omnis adiuro, uxor, (satin hoc est tibi?)
          me isti non nutasse. PEN: Credit iam tibi de "isti": illuc redi.

      MEN: Quo ego redeam? PEN: Equidem ad phrygionem censeo. et
          pallam refer.

      MEN: Quae istaec palla est? PEN: Taceo iam, quando haec rem non
          meminit suam.

620   MEN: Numquis servorum deliquit? num ancillae aut servi tibi
      responsant? eloquere. impune non erit. MAT: Nugas agis.

      MEN: Tristis admodum es. non mi istuc satis placet. MAT: Nugas agis.

      MEN: Certe familiarium aliquoi irata es. MAT: Nugas agis.

      MEN: Num mihi es irata saltem? MAT: Nunc tu non nugas agis.

625   MEN: Non edepol deliqui quicquam. MAT: Em rursum nunc nugas
          agis.

      MEN: Dic, mea uxor, quid tibi aegre est? PEN: Bellus blanditur tibi.

      MEN: Potin ut mihi molestus ne sis? num te appello? MAT: Aufer
          manum.

      PEN: Sic datur. properato apsente me comesse prandium,
      post ante aedis cum corona me derideto ebrius.

630   MEN: Neque edepol ego prandi neque hodie huc intro tetuli pedem.
      PEN: Tun negas? MEN: Nego hercle vero. PEN: Nihil hoc homine
      audacius.

      non ego te modo hic ante aedis cum corona florea
      vidi astare? quom negabas mi esse sanum sinciput,
      et negabas me novisse, peregrinum aibas esse te?

635   MEN: Quin ut dudum divorti aps te, redeo nunc demum domum.
      PEN: Novi ego te. non mihi censebas esse, qui te ulciscerer.
      omnia hercle uxori dixi. MEN: Quid dixisti? PEN: Nescio,
      eam ipsus roga. MEN: Quid hoc est, uxor? quidnam hic narravit tibi?
      quid id est? quid taces? quin dicis quid sit? MAT: Quasi tu nescias.

639a [palla mi est domo surrepta. MEN: Palla surrepta est tibi?]

Titus Maccius Plautus, *Menaechmi* (continued)

640   MAT: Me rogas? MEN: Pol haud rogem te, si sciam. PEN: O hominem
         malum,
       ut dissimulat. non potes celare: rem novit probe.
       omnia hercle ego edictavi. MEN: Quid id est? MAT: Quando nil pudet
       neque vis tua voluntate ipse profiteri, audi atque ades.
       et quid tristis \<sim\> et quid hic mihi dixerit, faxo scias.
645   palla mi est domo surrupta. MEN: Palla surruptast mihi?
       PEN: Viden ut \<te\> scelestus captat? huic surruptast, non tibi.
       nam profecto tibi surrupta si esset—salva non foret.
       MEN: Nil mihi tecum est. sed tu quid ais? MAT: Palla, inquam, periit
       domo.
       MEN: Quis eam surrupuit? MAT: Pol istuc ille scit qui illam abstulit.
650   MEN: Quis is homo est? MAT: Menaechmus quidam. MEN: Edepol
         factum nequiter.
       quis is Menaechmust? MAT: Tu istic, inquam. MEN: Egone? MAT: Tu.
         MEN: Quis arguit?
       MAT: Egomet. PEN: Et ego. atque huic amicae detulisti Erotio.

Notes to Plautus, *Menaechmi* (Lines 640-652):

640   **pol** = **edepol** *by Pollux*. **rogem...sciam**: in old Latin, the present subjunctive is used in
       contrary-to-fact conditions in present time. **hominem malum**: accusative of exclamation. **ut**
       how. **dissimulo** (1) *pretend*. **celo** (1) *hide* (from). **probe** (adv.) *nicely*. **edicto** (1) *proclaim,
       tell*. **quando** *since*. **pudet**, -ere, -uit (impersonal verb) *put to shame*; **pudet me** *I am ashamed*.
       Here understand **te**. **vis** < **volo**. **voluntas**, -tatis f. *will*. **profiteor**, -eri, -fessus/a sum *admit,
       own up*. **ades**: imperative of **adsum**. **quid**: as in line 639; introduces an indirect question.
       \<sim\>: the angled brackets indicate a word that is not in the manuscripts, but has been added
       by an editor and accepted by future editors as belonging in the text. **faxo**: future perfect of
       facio; understand **ut** + subjunctive: "I'll see to it that." **scias**: subjunctive after **faxo** in a
       substantive clause of result.

645   **surrupta** = **surrepta** < **subripio**, -ere, -ui, -reptum *snatch, steal*. **scelestus**, -a, -um *wicked*.
       capto (1) *try to catch*. **profecto** (adv.) *actually, certainly*. **si esset...foret**: contrary-to-fact
       condition in mixed time: "had been...would be." **foret**: imperfect subjunctive of **sum**. **nil mihi
       tecum est** (idiom): "I have nothing to do with you." **tecum** is addressed to Peniculus; **te** to
       Matrona. **inquam** (defective verb) *I say* (often used parenthetically). **pereo**, -ire, -ivi/-ii, -itum
       perish, be lost, go missing. **istuc** = **istud**: object of **scit**.

650   **nequiter** (adv.) *badly, wickedly*. **Menaechmust** = **Menaechmus est**. **istic** = **iste**. **arguo**,
       -ere, -ui, -utum *make known, accuse*. **egomet**: the enclitic particle -**met** is attached to some
       pronouns for emphasis. **huic**: Peniculus points to the door of Erotium's house. **detulisti** <
       defero.

PART FOUR

THE WORLD OF THE FAMILY

The readings in this unit reflect the spectrum of female roles in the family (mother, wife, daughter, sister) and Roman social classes (senatorial, equestrian, plebeian, freed, foreign). They depict women as the mainstays of their families or criticize them for not exercising proper family virtues. Written between the second century BCE and the second century CE, the texts attest to the constancy of Roman ideals of womanhood. It is not surprising that the world of the family is the most Roman of all the worlds, the one in which even liberal men were strict traditionalists. The family was constituted in law as the primary source of Roman citizens; it was the first site of moral education and emotional bonding. Through the family cultural values were imparted: *pietas*, the honoring of familial, religious, and political obligations; *obsequium*, obedience to superiors, compliance, allegiance; and *affectio*, good will and affection. It is noteworthy that affection was a significant value but subsequent to notions of respect, obedience, loyalty and honor in the formation of Roman character.

Although our word *family* derives from the Latin *familia*, the Roman family was both larger than and different in composition from the contemporary nuclear family of mother, father, and children in that it was not solely a kin grouping. In ever-widening circles of association, it consisted of the *pater, mater, filii* (daughters and sons, including stepchildren and adopted children); the *domus* or household, with its *servi, liberti* (freed slaves, who carried the master's *nomen* in token of their relationship), properties, finances, and resident dependents. Also included were extended kin networks, both maternal and paternal, living elsewhere. The contractual nature of Roman marriage and the requirement of close alliances to obtain political advancement gave rise to a wide assortment of relationships which produced family solidarity.

Configurations of family were also affected by the high infant and child mortality rate, deaths of women in childbirth, and early deaths of men in war. Women married young to older men, so that some women lived long enough to bury two or three husbands, having had children by each. Stepmothers joined families damaged by death or divorce and produced half-siblings. Children of divorced couples remained with their father's family while the mother returned alone to her birth family. Childless couples or families without a male heir frequently adopted adult males from within and outside kin groups to safeguard the family wealth and name.

From earliest times, Roman law placed the family in the care of the oldest living male of the family, the *paterfamilias*, who held absolute power, *patria potestas*, over all its members as well as its finances and estates. Since he was the living representative of the family to the state, his household owed him respect and total obedience. As head of the household, he was responsible for the family's social, political, and financial success and in theory had the last word on the behavior of its members and the maintenance of family honor and reputation. With the goal of protecting family honor, the law permitted the *paterfamilias* to discipline its members even to death. However, there was an expectation that the father would place the interests and well-being of the state before his own will, seek advice from a family council, and act humanely. In the late first century BCE when Augustus passed legislation on adultery and marriage, the state took on duties of the *paterfamilias*. Thus, when Augustus exiled his daughter Julia it is unclear whether he acted as *paterfamilias* or *pater patriae*.

The goal of family life was not love or happiness, but rather domestic *concordia*, which was considered the duty of the *matrona*. The title *materfamilias*, mother of the family, was an honorific one, with no legal foundation. It designated a woman who in actual practice wielded considerable power, though she was legally under the authority of a father, husband, or state-approved guardian. From them she received both her socio-political identity and her status. Marriage and motherhood were the defining roles for Roman women. Latin had no word for a respectable adult woman who never married. Although the traditional ideal was for a woman to be faithful beyond the death of her husband (i.e., a *univira*), under Augustan law widows, especially noble wealthy ones, were expected to remarry and were penalized if they did not.

The first priority of a married woman, whose designation *matrona* is derived from *mater*, was to bear and rear legitimate citizens. Her proper domain was the *domus*, a locus for both public and private family activity, where she set an example of stern *pietas* for her children and household (a first-century BCE eulogy of a son to his mother Murdia provides a long list of expected matronly virtues: *modestia, probitas, pudicitia, obsequium, lanificium, diligentia, fides*). There she occupied herself with various duties, depending on her class and location. She had charge of the rearing and early education in morals and values of the sons who remained under the *patria potestas* until their father's death, and the daughters who remained under their father's power until their *manus* marriage or his death. As *domina*, she supervised slaves in work directed toward the maintenance of the household, with particular emphasis on the traditional wifely duty of weaving, which in late republican elite homes had become symbolic rather than actual. She presided over social and religious functions proper to her class and gender. She contributed to the family's status with her dowry and support of her husband's enterprises, which in the lower classes meant working in the family business. For the upper-class *matrona*, it meant keeping her honor untarnished and raising children who would bring glory to the family.

In *Dialogus* 28, Tacitus speaks of the ancestral family as the nursery of the best citizens and orators. Under the control of a traditional *matrona* whose virtue set the standard for behavior, sons could be trained and educated to greatness. In *Agricola* 4.2 he describes the influence that one such mother, Julia Procilla, exerted on the development of her son. In the *Consolatio ad Helviam* Seneca appeals to his mother's strength of character in an effort to comfort her during his exile and public disgrace. Cicero's letters to his wife reveal the changing fortunes of his family over years of political and domestic turmoil (58-47 BCE). His family does not speak for itself because their letters have not been preserved, but the outlines of their relationships can be reconstructed through Cicero's letters – his early dependence on his wife, his love for his daughter who divorces twice and dies in childbirth, his pride in his son's status, his fears for self and *familia*.

Evidence of close sibling affection is illustrated by an epitaph inscribed on a pyramid in Egypt by a sister for her brother in the second century CE. In letters preserved by the historian Nepos, Cornelia reproaches her son, Gaius Gracchus, for his disruptive politics. Cornelia invokes her position as *materfamilias* to exhort her last living son to respect the state by renouncing his plans to avenge the murder of his brother Tiberius in 133 BCE. However, sibling kinship was no guarantee of affection, especially in view of equal inheritance rights. Livy (*AUC* 1) records three notable tales of early sibling violence: Romulus' against Remus, Tullia Minor's against her sister, and Horatius' murder of his sister for mourning her betrothed, an enemy of the state.

In *Elegiae* 4.11, Propertius gives voice to another Cornelia, the wife of Paullus Aemilius Lepidus. Speaking in the first person from the grave, she extolls her life lived in compliance with tradition. Her language of duty and acceptance is reminiscent of Euripides' Alcestis, the selfless wife and mother of Greek myth, whose deathbed scene is frequently pictured on Roman sarcophagi as she bids farewell to her husband, whose death she traded for her own, and to her children. Propertius' Cornelia claims for herself pride of family lineage, faithfulness of the *univira* (the "one-man woman"), and the virtues associated with the *stola*, the concealing over-garment of the *matrona*. More generous than Alcestis, she invites Paullus to take another wife to help him bear his grief and loneliness.

We know little of lower-class families whose lives poverty often made brutal. There was no state assistance for the poor for much of Roman history, with the exception of the grain dole, the pittance given to clients by patrons at the morning *salutatio*, and sporadic benefactions of the emperors or of wealthy philanthropists. With respect to food, clothing, and shelter, slaves often fared better than the free poor, but they lacked the ability to form the bond that is the cornerstone of the family. Slaves were not permitted to marry, since the *iustum conubium* was a jealously protected right of Roman citizenship. Children born of slaves were the property of their masters; thus they were often separated from their birth parents and could be sold out of the master's *familia*.

Petronius' *Satyricon* gives us some idea of what kind of life house slaves and freedmen might have. Fortunata, Trimalchio's *contubernalis*, or bed-mate, was bought out of slavery by him after he was freed and they married. While his wife was instrumental to his success during a crisis in his finances, nevertheless Fortunata is made to understand her dependent position when Trimalchio publicly asserts his authority, threatening to divorce her and throw her out of the house penniless. Although exaggerated for satirical purposes, the *familia* of Trimalchio provides a valuable window on the life and manners of freedmen in the first century CE, those whose new-found wealth encouraged them to imitate the *mores* and ideals of the elite.

Notes to Tacitus, *De Vita Iulii Agricolae* 4 (Sections 1-4):

4.1   **Gnaeus Iulius Agricola** (40-93 CE), soldier and statesman, who rose to fame in Britain, where he proved an effective administrator and talented military commander; he was consul in 77 CE. **Foroiulienses**, -ium m. pl. *inhabitants of Forum Julii*, a colony in Gallia Narbonensis, founded by Julius Caesar for the 8th Legion; an important Roman naval station, it is modern Frejus, east of Nice in France. **ortus**, -a, -um *born* (perfect passive participle of **orior**, -iri, ortus/a sum *be born, arise*). **uterque**, utraque, utrumque *each of two, either, both*. **avus**, -i m. *grandfather, ancestor*. **procurator Caesarum** *imperial procurator*, also known as **Procurator Augustorum**, denoting a financial officer in the service of the emperor. These procurators could serve in Rome or abroad, sometimes as governors in the minor imperial provinces. **quae = haec**; predicate adjective with **nobilitas. equester**, -tris (adj.) *equestrian*. In the Empire, the Procurator Augustorum was created as the highest equestrian office; **Equites** who held this position became known as **illustres** or **splendidi. illi**: dative of possession; understand **erat. Iulius Graecinus**: Agricola's father, who was made a senator by Tiberius. He advanced as far as the praetorship. Seneca testifies (*De Beneficiis* 2.21) that he was an honorable and distinguished man, who died under Caligula (around 39-40 CE, just before Agricola's birth) for just that reason. **Gaius Caesar**: emperor of Rome from 37 to 41 CE, better known as Caligula. **mereor**, -eri, meritus/a sum *earn, win, acquire*; supply **est. Marcus Silanus**, governor of Africa, was the unfortunate father-in-law of Caligula, forced by him to commit suicide (38 CE). **iubeo**, -ere, iussi, iussum *order, command*. **abnuo**, -nuere, -nui, -nutum *refuse, deny*. **interficio**, -ere, -feci, -fectum *kill*.

2   **castitas**, -atis f. *chastity*; genitive of description. **sinus**, -us m. *bosom; love, heart*. It is possible that this is both literal (i.e., Agricola did not have a wet nurse) and figurative (his mother's loving attention). **indulgentia**, -ae f. *gentleness, indulgence*. **honestarum artium**: i.e. the **artes liberales**, consisting of grammar, logic, rhetoric, music, arithmetic, geometry, and astronomy – the education that produced a citizen leader. **cultus**, -us m. *training, culture, cultivation*. **pueritia**, -ae f. *childhood, youth*. **transago**, -ere, -egi, -actum *pass time, complete, spend*.

3   **arceo**, -ere, arcui, arctum *prevent, keep off*; the **quod** clause is the subject of this verb. **illecebra**, -ae f. *lure, attraction*. **pecco** (1) *go wrong, make a mistake, offend*. **praeter** + accusative *beyond, more than, in addition to*. **integer**, -gra, -grum *sound, upright, virtuous*. **quod** (conj.) *because, the fact that*. **statim** (adv.) *at once, immediately*. **magistra**, -ae f. *teacher* (note that the town is personified as a female). **Massilia**, -ae f. present-day *Marseilles* was founded by the Greeks in 600 BCE. In Tacitus' time it was preferred by the Romans to Athens as a scholarly and wholesome place to complete one's education. **comitas**, -atis f. *kindness, refinement, affability*. **parsimonia**, -ae f. *thrift*. **misceo**, -ere, miscui, mixtum *combine, mix, join*.

4   **soleo**, -ere, solitus/a sum *be accustomed, be in the habit*; **solitum**: modifies **ipsum** in the indirect statement introduced by **memoria teneo**. **iuventa**, -ae f. *youth*. **acrius** (comparative adv.) *more keenly, more eagerly*; translate with **hausisse. ultra [quam]**: preposition + accusative, *beyond, more than*. **concedo**, -ere, -cessi, -cessum *grant, allow, overlook*. **haurio**, -ire, hausi, haustum *draw in, drink up, devour*; **hausisse**: translate as if written **hausturum fuisse. ni = nisi. incendo**, -ere, incendi, incensum *inflame, rouse, set fire to*. **flagrans**, -antis *passionate, blazing, brilliant*. **coerceo**, -ere, coercui, coercitum *control, repress, check*.

Cornelius Tacitus, *De Vita Iulii Agricolae* 4.1-4: Julia Procilla

Tacitus wrote *Agricola* in 98 CE., a eulogy for his distinguished father-in-law in the guise of a biography. As is customary, he begins his record of Agricola's life by rehearsing his recent forebears. While it is no surprise that Agricola's male heritage receives primary attention, Tacitus gives due credit to Agricola's mother, Julia Procilla who, after the early death of her husband, presided over her son's development into a distinguished citizen. In this he provides some insight into the impact of the Roman *mater* at the critical early stages of her children's lives, even those of her children who were male. In Agricola's case, with his father dead, his mother's strength and virtue were dominant features of his early life. The passage below describes Julia Procilla's nurturance, paralleling its salutary effect to the healthful atmosphere of his "motherland."

4 (1) Gnaeus Iulius Agricola, vetere et inlustri Foroiuliensium colonia ortus, utrumque avum procuratorem Caesarum habuit, quae equestris nobilitas est. pater illi Iulius Graecinus senatorii ordinis, studio eloquentiae sapientiaeque notus, iisque ipsis virtutibus iram Gai Caesaris meritus: namque Marcum Silanum accusare iussus et, quia abnuerat, interfectus est. (2) mater Iulia Procilla fuit, rarae castitatis. in huius sinu indulgentiaque educatus per omnem honestarum artium cultum pueritiam adulescentiamque transegit. (3) arcebat eum ab inlecebris peccantium praeter ipsius bonam integramque naturam, quod statim parvulus sedem ac magistram studiorum Massiliam habuit, locum Graeca comitate et provinciali parsimonia mixtum ac bene compositum. (4) memoria teneo solitum ipsum narrare se prima in iuventa studium philosophiae acrius, ultra quam concessum Romano ac senatori, hausisse, ni prudentia matris incensum ac flagrantem animum coercuisset.

Tacitus describes Julia Procilla's fate (7.1) as one illustration of the devastating personal dangers and tragedies (even for women in private life) caused by the imperial succession after Nero, the last of the Julio-Claudian emperors. Tacitus records that in 69 CE, the "Year of the Four Emperors" (Galba, Otho, Vitellius, Vespasian), Otho landed a fleet on the coast of Liguria and ravaged the lands of Intemelius (modern-day Ventimiglia), which had opted for Vitellius, slaughtering its wealthy inhabitants, among them Julia Procilla, and seizing their possessions. Called to Vespasian's camp on his way to bury his mother, Agricola could not conduct her funeral rites or even mourn her loss.

Notes to Tacitus, *Dialogus* 28-29 (Sections 1-3):

28.1   **(1) descisco**, -ere, -ivi, -itum *fall off from, decline from.* **inopia**, -ae f. *need, lack.* **desidia**, -ae f. *laziness, idleness.* **inscientia**, -ae f. *neglect, ignorance.* **praecipio**, -cipere, -cepi, -ceptum *teach.* **oblivio**, -onis f. *forgetfulness.* **(2) mala**, -orum n. pl. *evils.* **fundo**, -ere, fudi, fusum *spread, pour.* **mano** (1) *flow, drip.* **(3) vestra** [**mala**]: i.e. in the provinces where Aper and Maternus find themselves. **proprius**, -a, -um *characteristic, one's own.* **vernaculus**, -a, -um *native; of a slave born in the master's house.* Tacitus labels these vices as inappropriate even to freeborn Romans. **excipio**, -cipere, -cepi, -ceptum *seize, grab.* **gradus**, -us m. *stage.* **cumulo** (1) *multiply, pile up.* **si prius** (adv.) *when...first.* **praedico**, -ere, -dixi, -dictum *mention beforehand.*

28.2   **(1) pridem** (adv.) *long ago.* **suus cuique** *each one's own.* **cellula**, -ae f. *little room.* While slaves' rooms were indeed very small, the diminutive also reflects the smallness of the slave nurse's mind and character. **emo**, -ere, emi, emptum *buy.* **nutrix**, -icis f. *nurse, nursemaid.* **gremium**, -i n. *lap.* **sinus**, -us m. *bosom; embrace.* **educo** (1) *rear, raise; educate.* **praecipuus**, -a, -um *special; particular.* **tueor**, tueri, tutus/a sum *protect, guard, take care of.* **inservio**, -ire, -ivi, -itum *serve; be devoted to.* **liberi**, -orum m.pl. *children.* **(2) eligo**, -ligere, -legi, -lectum *choose, select.* **natu**: ablative of respect after **maior**; **probo** (1) *approve, esteem*; dative with the compound verb **committeretur** (subjunctive in a relative clause of purpose). **suboles**, -is f. *offspring, children.* **coram**: prep. + abl., *in the presence of.* **fas** *right*; translate with **videretur** as well. **turpis**, -is, -e *base, dishonorable, ugly.* **dictum...factu:** ablative of the supine depending on **turpe...inhonestum**; translate as infinitives with the two adjectives. **inhonestus**, -a, -um *disgraceful, shameful; degrading.* **(3) non**...**modo**...**sed**...**etiam** *not only...but also.* **cura**, -ae f. *occupation, care.* **remissio**, -onis f. *free time, leisure.* **lusus**, -us m. *sport, game, play-time.* **sanctitas**, -atis f. *piety, purity.* **verecundia**, -ae f. *modesty, reverence.* **tempero** (1) *regulate, moderate.* **(4) Corneliam...Atiam**: mothers of the men named (understand **educationibus** with each). **praesum**, praeesse, praefui *be in charge of, direct.* **princeps**, principis *foremost, chief*. **accipio**, -ere, -cepi, -ceptum *hear; receive* (in a metaphorical sense of information transmitted). **(5) eo...ut** + subjunctive *to the extent...that.* **pertineo**, -ere, -ui *reach, concern.* **sincerus**, -a, -um *whole, sound, honest* (with **natura**). **integer**, -gra, -grum *whole, untouched, upright.* **pravitas**, -atis f. *depravity, vice.* **detortus**, -a, -um *twisted, distorted.* **pectus**, -oris n. *breast, chest*; here, *heart.* **adripio**, -ere, -ripui, -reptum *seize, learn quickly, appropriate.* **honestus**, -a, -um *admirable, worthy.* **sive...sive... sive** *whether...or...or.* **inclinasset**: syncopated form of **inclinavisset**; the subject is **natura**, subject also of **ageret, hauriret** (**haurio**, -ire, hausi, haustum *take in, drain*).

29.1   **delego** (1) *transfer, make over.* **graeculus**, -a, -um *Greek* (the diminutive is used scornfully). **ancilla, -**ae f. *maid.* **plerumque** (adv.) *generally, frequently.* **adiungo**, -ere, -iunxi, -iunctum *attach, add.* **vilis**, -e *cheap, common.* **serius**, -a, -um *important, critical.* **ministerium**, -i n. *duty, office, task.* **accommodatus**, -a, -um *fit for* (+ dat.). **(2) viridis**, -e (adj.) *green; young.* **rudis**, -e (adj.) *unformed, impressionable.* **imbuo**, -ere, -ui, -utus *infect, fill up.* **pensi habet** *considers of worth, thinks important.* **domo**: household slaves. **dominus**, -i m. *master.* **(3) quin etiam** *why even; but even.* **probitas**, -atis f. *virtue, honesty.* **adsuefacio**, -facere, -feci, -factum + dat. *accustom to.* **lascivia**, -ae f. *insolence, brashness.* **dicacitas**, -atis f. *slick or superficial talk.* **inrepo**, -ere, -repsi, -reptum *sneak in, creep in.* **contemptus**, -us m. *scorn, contempt.* **alienus**, -i m. *another, stranger.*

Cornelius Tacitus, *Dialogus de Oratoribus* 28-29.1-3

The *Dialogus*, closely modeled on Cicero's philosophical dialogues, is an imaginary conversation among three experts about the death of eloquence in Rome. In it Marcus Aper champions contemporary oratory; Curiatus Maternus considers oratory unnecessary in the peaceful climate of the benevolent Emperor Trajan; Vipstanus Messalla blames the decline of oratory on Roman mothers who have neglected their primary role as their children's first teacher of character and civic virtue. The selection opens with Messalla making his case to the others.

28.1 (1) Quis enim ignorat et eloquentiam et ceteras artis descivisse ab illa vetere gloria non inopia hominum, sed desidia iuventutis et neglegentia parentum et inscientia praecipientium et oblivione moris antiqui? (2) Quae mala primum in urbe nata, mox per Italiam fusa, iam in provincias manant. (3) Quamquam vestra vobis notiora sunt: ego de urbe et his propriis ac vernaculis vitiis loquar, quae natos statim excipiunt et per singulos aetatis gradus cumulantur, si prius de severitate ac disciplina maiorum circa educandos formandosque liberos pauca praedixero.

28.2 (1) Nam pridem suus cuique filius, ex casta parente natus, non in cellula emptae nutricis, sed gremio ac sinu matris educabatur, cuius praecipua laus erat tueri domum et inservire liberis. (2) Eligebatur autem maior aliqua natu propinqua, cuius probatis spectatisque moribus omnis eiusdem familiae suboles committeretur; coram qua neque dicere fas erat quod turpe dictu, neque facere quod inhonestum factu videretur. (3) Ac non studia modo curasque, sed remissiones etiam lususque puerorum sanctitate quadam ac verecundia temperabat. (4) Sic Corneliam Gracchorum, sic Aureliam Caesaris, sic Atiam Augusti praefuisse educationibus ac produxisse principes liberos accepimus. (5) Quae disciplina ac severitas eo pertinebat, ut sincera et integra et nullis pravitatibus detorta unius cuiusque natura toto statim pectore arriperet artes honestas, et sive ad rem militarem sive ad iuris scientiam sive ad eloquentiae studium inclinasset, id solum ageret, id universum hauriret.

29(1) At nunc natus infans delegatur Graculae alicui ancillae, cui adiungitur unus aut alter ex omnibus servis, plerumque vilissimus nec cuiquam serio ministerio accommodatus. (2) Horum fabulis et erroribus et virides teneri statim et rudes animi imbuuntur; nec quisquam in tota domo pensi habet, quid coram infante domino aut dicat aut faciat. (3) Quin etiam ipsi parentes non probitati neque modestiae parvulos adsuefaciunt, sed lasciviae et dicacitati, per quae paulatim impudentia inrepit et sui alienique contemptus.

Notes to Seneca, *Ad Helviam Matrem de Consolatione* 14.2-3; 16.1:

This work belongs to the genre of *consolatio*, a literary form datable to fifth-century BCE Greece.

14.2   **pars,** partis f. *point, item of consideration.* Seneca argues there are only two reasons for his mother to be so grieved: she lost the protective presence of her son, and she cannot bear the thought of being without him. **perstringo,** -ere, -strinxi, -strictum *touch upon, mention.* **in suis praeter ipsos:** "in your dear ones except themselves." **viderint:** hortatory subjunctive, the subject (**illae matres**) defined by the following three **quae** clauses; **video** here is *consider that, look out for that.* **exerceo,** -ere, -ui *exercise, make use of, employ.* **honores,** -um f. pl. *state offices,* including military. **illos:** i.e. *their sons.* **patrimonium,** -i n. *inheritance; wealth.* **exhaurio,** -ire, -hausi, -haustum *exhaust, use up.* **capto** (1) *seek to obtain, grasp at.* **commodo** (1) *lend, lend out;* understand **eloquentiam** as the object. **fatigo** (1) *wear out, exhaust;* the object is "their sons."

3   **gaudeo,** -ere, gavisus/a sum *rejoice, be joyful about/over; take pleasure in.* **bona,** -orum n. pl. *fortune, possessions, achievements.* **minimum usa:** understand **sed** or **autem. utor,** uti, usus/a sum + abl. *use, employ.* **modus,** -i m. *boundary, limit.* **cum** + subjunctive (**imponeres**): *although.* **tuae:** understand **liberalitati. filia familiae:** "a daughter living in her father's household." As such, Helvia did not have to contribute to her sons' patrimony since their father's inheritance might be thought sufficient. **locuples,** -etis *rich, wealthy.* **ultro** (adv.) *further, in addition.* **sic...ut** + subjunctive (**laborares, abstineres**): result clause. **administrasti:** a syncopated form of **administravisti. tamquam** (conj.) *as if.* **tuis...alienis:** understand **patrimoniis. abstineo,** -ere, -tinui, -tentum *refrain from.* **gratia,** -ae f. *favor, influence.* **parco,** -ere, peperci, parsus + dat. *spare, refrain from (using).* **impensa,** -ae f. *expense, outlay of money.* **pertineo,** -ere, -ui *apply, belong, concern.* **indulgentia:** understand **tua. utilitas,** -atis f. *self-interest;* understand **tuam. itaque** (conj.) *therefore, accordingly.* **ea:** defined by the following **quae** clause. **ereptus,** -a, -um *snatched away; taken (from one).* **incolumis,** -is, -e *unharmed, safe;* understand **filio.**

16.1   **est quod** + subjunctive (**utaris**): translate "you should not employ..." **excusatio,** -onis f. *defense, argument.* **muliebris nominis:** "of/belonging to the feminine sex." **immoderatus,** -a, -um *excessive, without measure, unbridled.* **ius,** iuris n. *right, appropriate custom.* **immensus,** -a, -um *unending, vast, unbounded.* **ideo** (adv.) *therefore, for that reason.* **maiores,** -um m. pl. *ancestors* (understand **nostri**). **lugeo,** -ere, luxi, luctum *mourn, weep for* (understand **uxoribus** with **lugentibus**); the direct object is **viros. vir,** viri m. *husband.* **pertinacia,** -ae f. *persistence; stubbornness, unyieldingness;* **cum pertinacia** should be translated after **deciderent. maeror,** -oris m. *grief; lamentation; mourning.* **constitutio,** -onis f. *ordinance, decree.* **decido,** -ere, decidi, decisum *come to terms with* (with **cum**). **finio,** -ire, -ivi, -itum *restrain, define, limit.* **et...et** *both...and;* this correlative sets up a parallel statement of opposite extremes. **carissimi,** -orum m. pl. "your nearest and dearest." **adficio,** -ficere, -feci, -fectum *influence, move, affect;* **adfici infinito dolore** is the subject of **est. duritia,** -ae f. *hardness, insensibility, austerity:* [adfici] nullo [dolore est] inhumana duritia. **temperamentum,** -i n. *compromise, moderation* (defined by the following two infinitives). **desiderium,** -i n. *sense of loss, longing.* **opprimo,** -ere, oppressi, oppressum *suppress, quell, put down.*

L. Annaeus Seneca (minor), *Ad Helviam Matrem de Consolatione* (excerpts)

This moving testimony to Helvia's character and learning by her son, Seneca the Younger, was written in 42/3 CE from exile in Corsica, where he had been sent on the charge of adultery with Caligula's sister, Julia Livilla. It offers a portrait of affectionate family bonding, especially with regard to the mother-son and sister relationships. Even before Seneca's exile Helvia had a hard life: her mother had died giving birth to her and she was raised by a stepmother; she suffered the loss of her own husband, her sister's husband, and three of her five grandchildren; and she found it necessary to migrate from her home in Corduba, Spain to Rome, preceded by her sister and her sons. Helvia was educated, but not to the level that Seneca could see her intellect and curiosity had inclined her, for her husband's old-fashioned values did not permit her to pursue her studies. Seneca appreciated the fact that philosophy was valuable as a guide to negotiate the hazards of life which his family, leaders by birth and achievement, often faced. Therefore, in the expectation that his mother could follow his reasoning, Seneca offers her logical argument and examples from Greek and Roman history to moderate her grief.

14   (2) Prior pars mihi leviter perstringenda est; novi enim animum tuum nihil in suis praeter ipsos amantem. Viderint illae matres quae potentiam liberorum muliebri inpotentia exercent, quae, quia feminis honores non licet gerere, per illos ambitiosae sunt, quae patrimonia filiorum et exhauriunt et captant, quae eloquentiam commodando aliis fatigant. (3) tu liberorum tuorum bonis plurimum gavisa es, minimum usa; tu liberalitati nostrae semper inposuisti modum, cum tuae non inponeres; tu, filia familiae, locupletibus filiis ultro contulisti; tu patrimonia nostra sic administrasti ut tamquam in tuis laborares, tamquam alienis abstineres; tu gratiae nostrae, tamquam alienis rebus utereris, pepercisti, et ex honoribus nostris nihil ad te nisi voluptas et inpensa pertinuit. Numquam indulgentia ad utilitatem respexit; non potes itaque ea in erepto filio desiderare quae in incolumi numquam ad te pertinere duxisti.

Seneca argues that his mother is unlike some women who use the excuse of their "natural" weakness to justify inordinate grief or who seek to make themselves beautiful or appear younger; rather, like Cornelia, mother of the Gracchi, her "jewels" were her children.

16   (1) Non est quod utaris excusatione muliebris nominis, cui paene concessum est inmoderatum in lacrimis ius, non inmensum tamen; et ideo maiores decem mensum spatium lugentibus viros dederunt ut cum pertinacia muliebris maeroris publica constitutione deciderent. Non prohibuerunt luctus sed finierunt; nam et infinito dolore, cum aliquem ex carissimis amiseris, adfici stulta indulgentia est, et nullo inhumana duritia: optimum inter pietatem et rationem temperamentum est: et sentire desiderium et opprimere.

Notes to Seneca, *Ad Helviam Matrem de Consolatione* 16.2-3; 19.1-2):

16.2   **semel** (adv.) *once* (modifies **sumptam**). **sumptus**, -a, -um *taken on, taken up*. **nosti** = **novisti**: "you know." **impositus**, -a, -um *put on*. **lugubria**, -orum n. pl. *mourning garments*. **exuo**, -ere, exui, exutum *put off, take off*. **plus** n. acc. s. *more*. **exigo**, -ere, exegi, exactum *demand, require*. **ab initio fortior**: modifies **vita**, "harsher from its beginning." **muliebris excusatio**: "the defense of being a woman." **contingo**, -ere, -tigi, -tactus + dat. *touch; pertain to*. **ei**: supply **feminae**. **vitium**, -i n. *flaw, weakness, vice*. **absum**, abesse, afui *be absent, be missing* (take with **a qua**).

3   **non te**: the first two sections of 16 open with the phrase **non est quod,** describing women in general; thus the reader expects a third general female situation here. Instead, Seneca contrasts his mother (**te** = Helvia) with the majority of women. **impudicitia**, -ae f. *immodesty*. **in numerum plurium**: "into the number of the majority of women." **adduco**, -ere, -duxi, -ductum *lead into, bring into*. **margarita**, -ae f. *pearl*. **flecto**, -ere, flexi, flexum *influence, persuade, bend*. **velut** (adv.) *as, just as*. **refulgeo**, -ere, -fulsi, -fulsum *gleam, shine*. **antiquus**, -a, -um *holding to the old ways, old-fashioned*. **institutus**, -a, -um *brought up, raised*. **periculosus** -a, -um + dat. *dangerous for*. **probus**, -a, -um *excellent, honest*; translate with **etiam** (understand **mulieribus**). **detorqueo**, -ere, -torsi, -tortum *pervert, divert*. **imitatio**, -onis f. *imitation*; translate with **peiorum** (understand **mulierum**). **fecunditas**, -atis f. *fertility*. **pudet**, -ere, puduit (impersonal verb) *shame, make someone* (acc.) *feel ashamed of* (genitive). **quasi exprobraret aetatem**: "as if it would reproach your mature age" (referring to women who do not acknowledge their grown children so as to seem young). **commendatio**, -onis f. *praise, recommendation*. **forma**, -ae f. *beauty, shape*. **tumesco**, -ere, -mui *begin to swell* (with pregnancy). **uterus**, -i m. *uterus* (here, *belly*). **abscondo**, -ere, -condi, -conditum *hide, conceal*. **indecens**, -entis *shameful*. **viscus**, -eris n. *inner organ*. **conceptus**, -a, -um *conceived*. **elido**, -ere, elisi, elisum *crush, strangle*.

19.1   **adhuc** (adv.) *up to this point*. **taceo**, -ere, -ui, -itum *pass over, leave unmentioned, be silent*. **pectus**, -oris n. *heart*; "soul." **pro indiviso** (adv.) *undividedly; without reserve; without holding back*. **maternus**, -a, -um *of a mother, maternal*. **misceo**, -ere, miscui, mixtum *mix, mingle; blend*. **respiro** (1) *breathe once more*, i.e., when Helvia felt faint with grief, her sister helped her go on. **sinus**, -us m. *bosom, embrace*.

2   **illa**: Helvia's sister, subject of **sequitur** and **dolet**. **adfectus**, -us m. *feeling, emotion*. **sequor**, sequi, secutus sum *share* (in), *partake, follow*. **persona**, -ae f. *character, part; case; person*. **non tantum** (adv.) *not only, not so much*. **perfero**, -ferre, -tuli, -latum *convey, bring, carry through*; i.e., when Seneca was a small child. **pius**, -a, -um *conscientious, attentive*. **nutricium**, -i n. *nursing; tending*. **aeger**, -gra, -grum *ill, sick*. **convalesco**, -ere, -valui *grow well; grow strong*. **pro**: prep. + abl. *on behalf of, for*. **quaestura**, -ae f. *quaestorship* (i.e., when Seneca was campaigning to be elected quaestor). **gratia**, -ae f. *support, influence*. **ne...quidem** *not even*. **sermo**, -onis m. *conversation, speech*. **salutatio**, -onis f. *greeting*. **audacia**, -ae f. *courage, daring*; i.e., his aunt suffered excessive shyness even in private life. **indulgentia**, -ae f. *love; devotion*. **verecundia**, -ae f. *shyness*. **nihil** (adv.) *not at all, in no way*. **seductus**, -a, -um *secluded, remote*. **petulantia**, -ae f. *boldness, impudence*. **rusticus**, -a, -um *old-fashioned*; translate with **in. . .petulantia** to describe **modestia**. **secretus**, -a, -um *sheltered, secluded*. **repositus**, -a, -um + **ad** *directed toward*. **obsto**, -are, -stiti + dat. *hinder, oppose*. **quominus**: conj. + subjunctive (**fieret**); translate "from becoming."

Seneca, *Ad Helviam Matrem de Consolatione* (continued)

16 (2) Non est quod ad quasdam feminas respicias quarum tristitiam semel sumptam mors finivit (nosti quasdam quae amissis filiis inposita lugubria numquam exuerunt): a te plus exigit vita ab initio fortior; non potest muliebris excusatio contingere ei a qua omnia muliebria vitia afuerunt. (3) Non te maximum saeculi malum, impudicitia, in numerum plurium adduxit; non gemmae te non margaritae flexerunt; non tibi divitiae velut maximum generis humani bonum refulserunt; non te, bene in antiqua et severa institutam domo, periculosa etiam probis peiorum detorsit imitatio; numquam te fecunditatis tuae, quasi exprobraret aetatem, puduit, numquam more aliarum, quibus omnis commendatio ex forma petitur, tumescentem uterum abscondisti quasi indecens onus, nec intra viscera tua conceptas spes liberorum elisisti.

Toward the end of his essay, Seneca encourages his mother to turn to her family for support, in particular to her sister, a woman of great courage and goodness who had already shown her deep regard for Helvia and for Seneca by bringing him to Rome, caring for him and promoting his career.

19 (1) Maximum adhuc solacium tuum tacueram, sororem tuam, illud fidelissimum tibi pectus, in quod omnes curae tuae pro indiviso transferuntur, illum animum omnibus nobis maternum. Cum hac tu lacrimas tuas miscuisti, in huius primum respirasti sinu. (2) Illa quidem adfectus tuos semper sequitur; in mea tamen persona non tantum pro te dolet. Illius manibus in urbem perlatus sum, illius pio maternoque nutricio per longum tempus aeger convalui; illa pro quaestura mea gratiam suam extendit et, quae ne sermonis quidem aut clarae salutationis sustinuit audaciam, pro me vicit indulgentia verecundiam.Nihil illi seductum vitae genus, nihil modestia in tanta feminarum petulantia rustica, nihil quies, nihil secreti et ad otium repositi mores obstiterunt quominus pro me etiam ambitiosa fieret.

Notes to Petronius, *Satyricon* 37.1; 67.1-2:

37.1   **nummus**, -i m. *coin.* **modius**, -i m. a measure of grain approximately equal to a bushel; hence, *a bushel basket.* **metior**, -iri, mensus/a sum *measure.* **modo** (adv.) *just now, just recently*; the repetition makes the statement more emphatic. **ignosco**, -ere, -novi, -notum + dat. *pardon*; *forgive.* **genius**, -i m. a *genius* was a kind of guardian spirit that was innate in people. One could make offerings to one's *genius*, particularly on a birthday. The guest politely begs pardon of Encolpius' *genius*, which might be offended at his words. **panis**, -is m. *bread.* **noluisses**: subjunctive in a contrary to fact condition (past time); understand as the protasis *If you had met her* (vel sim). **nec quid nec quare** *neither why nor wherefore*, or as we might say colloquially, "without rhyme or reason." **caelum**, -i n. *heaven*, i.e., she has risen in status. **topanta** n. pl. (Greek *to panta*) *everything, the whole world*; foreign expressions, sometimes misapplied, are sprinkled liberally throughout. **ad summam** *in short, in sum.* **merus**, -a, -um *pure, mere.* The word contributes more to sound (assonance) than to meaning. **meridies**, -ei f. *midday, noon.* **tenebrae**, -arum f. pl. *night, darkness.*

67.1   **quomodo** (adv.) *just as.* **nosti**: contraction of **novisti** < **nosco**, -ere, novi, notum *get to know*; perfect, *know.* **nisi** (conj.) *unless, until.* **argentum**, -i n. *set of silver serving dishes.* **compono**, -ponere, -posui, -positum *put away.* **reliquiae**, -arum f. pl. *remains of the food or meal, leftovers.* **puer**, -i m. *slave.* The slave's low station was indicated by this term. **divido**, -videre, -visi, visum *divide up, apportion.* **coniicio**, -icere, -ieci, -iectum *put, place.* **discumbo**, -cumbere, -cubui, -cubitum *recline, lie down.* **me apoculo**: "I'll take myself away," "I'll make myself scarce." **quater amplius** (adv.) *more than four times.* **familia**, -ae f. *company of slaves.* **galbinus**, -a, -um *greenish-yellow.* **succinctus**, -a, -um *belted, tied up with a belt.* **cingillum**, -i n. *a woman's belt* (especially one worn by a bride). **ita ut** (adv.) *in such a way that.* **cerasinus**, -a, -um *cherry red.* **periscelis**, -celidis f. *leg-band, anklet*; Fortunata has belted her tunic so that her ankles immodestly show. **tortus**, -a, -um *twisted*; these anklets are made of twisted metal, probably gold. **phaecasia**, -ae f. *white shoe*, a kind originally worn by Athenian priests. **inauratus**, -a, -um *gilded; decorated with gold.* **sudarium**, -i n. literally a *cloth used to wipe sweat* (**sudor**) off. **tergo**, -ere, tersi, tersum *wipe, wipe off, wipe down.* **collum**, -i n. *neck.* **applico** (1) *drape*; given Fortunata's vulgarity and lack of elegance, perhaps here it means to "plop down." **torus**, -i m. *couch.* **osculor** (1) *kiss, make a fuss over.* **plaudeo**, -ere, plausi, plausum *clap one's hands, applaud.* **est te...videre**: "Is it really you I see?"

2   **eo** (adv.) *to such a point.* **pervenio**, -ire, -veni, -ventum *reach, come to.* **armilla**, -ae f. *arm bracelets.* **crassus**, -a, -um *thick; fat, pudgy.* **lacertus**, -i m. *upper arm.* **ultimo** (adv.) *finally, lastly.* **resolvo**, -ere, -solvi, -solutum *loosen; take off, untie.* **reticulum**, -i n. *hairnet*; such golden hairnets have been found by archaeologists. **obrussa**, -ae f. *test, touchstone*, with **ex**, *of pure gold.* **noto** (1) *notice; be on the watch.* **omnia**: i.e., all Fortunata's jewelry. **afferri**: understand **ei**. **compes**, -pedis f. *shackles* or *fetters*; the anklets are worn as prisoners would wear shackles, but Trimalchio undoubtedly also means that women "bind" men to spend money on buying jewelry. **barcala**, -ae, m. *simpleton.* **sic nos barcalae despoliamur**: "thus we men get fleeced." **pondo** (adv.) *in weight, pounds.* **selibra**, -ae f. *one-half pound.* **nihilominus** (adv.) *nonetheless.* **mentior**, -iri, mentitus/a sum *lie; tell a lie.* **statera**, -ae f. *scales.* **approbari**: the scales were carried around so that the guests could verify that they weighed true. **pondus**, -eris n. *weight.*

C. Petronius, *Satyricon* 37.1; 67.1-2: Fortunata

In this excerpt from the mid-first-century CE *Cena Trimalchionis* (*Satyricon* 26-78), Fortunata is introduced as the wife of the crass and boorish freedman, Gaius Trimalchio; she was a former "dancer" in a house of prostitution whom he bought at auction, freed, and married. Now, as *domina*, she manages her husband's properties and knows his finances to the penny. Trimalchio's interactions with his wife, his freedpeople friends (Habinnas and Scintilla), his guests, and his slaves are a crude effort, anchored in wealth, to emulate elite attitudes and conduct. It is clear that Fortunata has not quite captured the role of lady: acting more like a slave overseer than a *materfamilias*, she presides over a dinner that is outrageous for the quantity, quality, and garishness of its offerings, language, and guest-host behaviors. Watching her scurry around the dining room, the novel's hero Encolpius asks one of the guests who she is.

37   (1) "Uxor" inquit "Trimalchionis. Fortunata appellatur. Quae nummos modio metitur. Et modo, modo quid fuit? Ignoscet mihi genius tuus. Noluisses de manu illius panem accipere. Nunc, nec quid nec quare, in caelum abiit et Trimalchionis topanta est. Ad summam, mero meridie si dixerit illi tenebras esse, credet."

At last Fortunata reclines for dessert, having in person attended to the disposition of the food and expensive utensils. She is outlandishly and tastelessly dressed, with manners to match, showing off her wealth. In this scene with their best friends Habinnas, a stone mason and tomb maker, and his wife Scintilla ("Sparkle"), both probably freedpeople, the husbands complain about their wives' taste for jewelry and spending.

67   (1) "Quomodo nosti," inquit, "illam" Trimalchio. "Nisi argentum composuerit, nisi reliquias pueris diviserit, aquam in os suum non coniciet."

"Atqui," respondit Habinnas, "nisi illa discumbit, ego me apoculo." Et coeperat surgere, nisi signo dato, "Fortunata" quater amplius a tota familia esset vocata. Venit ergo, galbino succincta cingillo, ita ut infra cerasina appareret tunica et periscelides tortae phaecasiaeque inauratae. Tunc sudario manus tergens, quod in collo habebat, applicat se illi toro in quo Scintilla Habinnae discumbebat uxor, osculataque plaudentem. "Est te," inquit, "videre?"

(2) Eo deinde perventum est, ut Fortunata armillas suas crassissimis detraheret lacertis Scintillaeque miranti ostenderet. Ultimo etiam periscelides resolvit et reticulum aureum, quem ex obrussa esse dicebat.

Notavit haec Trimalchio iussitque afferri omnia et, "Videtis," inquit, "mulieris compedes. Sic nos barcalae despoliamur. Sex pondo et selibram debet habere. Et ipse nihilominus habeo decem pondo armillam..." Ultimo etiam, ne mentiri videretur, stateram iussit afferri et circulatum approbari pondus.

C. Petronius, *Satyricon* 67.3-4; 76

67   (3) Nec melior fuit Scintilla, quae de cervice sua capsellam detraxit aureolam, quam Felicionem appellabat. Inde duo crotalia protulit, et Fortunatae in vicem consideranda dedit et, "Domini," inquit, "mei beneficio nemo habet meliora."

"Quid," inquit Habinnas, "excatarissasti me, ut tibi emerem fabam vitream. Plane si filiam haberem, auriculas illi praeciderem. Mulieres si non essent, omnia pro luto haberemus…"

(4) Interim mulieres sauciae inter se riserunt ebriaeque iunxerunt oscula, dum altera diligentiam matris familiae iactat, altera delicias et indiligentiam viri. Dumque sic cohaerent, Habinnas furtim consurrexit, pedesque Fortunatae correptos super lectum immisit. "Au, Au!" illa proclamavit, aberrante tunica super genua. Composita ergo in gremio Scintillae incensissimam rubore faciem sudario abdidit.

Toward the end of the dinner, Trimalchio praises Fortunata's loyalty in giving him all her belongings to start over again after he had lost his inheritance in trade.

76   (1) "Hoc loco Fortunata rem piam fecit. Omne enim aurum suum, omnia vestimenta vendidit et me centum aureos in manu posuit. Hoc fuit peculii mei fermentum."

Notes to Petronius, *Satyricon* 67 (Sections 3-4); 76:

67.3   **cervix**, -vicis f. *neck*. **capsella**, -ae f. *little box* (presumably worn on a chain). **aureolus**, -a, -um *little golden*. **Felicionem**: acc. "Lucky Boy." **crotalia**, -iorum n. pl. *drop pearl earrings*; Scintilla's earrings would jangle as she moved her head. **in vicem** (adv.) *in turn*. **consideranda** *to be inspected*. **dominus**, -i m. *husband*. **beneficium**, -i n. *generosity* (abl. of cause). **meliora**: understand **crotalia**. **quid** (interjection) *What!* **excatarissasti**: "you cleaned me out." **emo**, emere, emi, emptum *buy*. **faba**, -ae f. *bean*; Habinnas uses this word to disparage the earrings. **vitreus**, -a, -um *made of glass*. **plane** (adv.) *certainly*. **auricula**, -ae f. *little ear*. **praecido**, -ere, -cisi, -cisum *cut off*. **pro luto** *dirt cheap*.

67.4   **saucius**, -a, -um *wounded*; here, *tipsy*. **ebrius**, -a, -um *drunk*. **osculum**, -i n. *little mouth*; *kiss*. **diligentia**, -ae f. *attentiveness*, *thrift*. **iacto** (1) *keep talking about*. **deliciae**, -arum f. pl. *delights*. **indiligentia**, -ae f. *carelessness*. **vir**, viri m. *husband*. **cohaereo**, -ere, -haesi, -haesum *be occupied*. **furtim** (adv.) *stealthily*. **correptus**, -a, -um *grabbed*. **immitto**, -ere, -misi, -missum *fling*. **aberro** (1) *stray*. **genu**, -us n. *knee*. **compositus**, -a, -um *composed*, *ordered*. **gremium**, -i n. *lap*. **incensus**, -a, -um *inflamed* (blushing). **rubor**, -oris m. *red*. **abdo**, -dere, -didi, -ditum *hide*.

76   **hoc loco** *at this point*. **pius**, -a, -um *loyal and loving*. **aureus**, -i n. *gold coin*. **peculium**, -i n. *savings* (especially of a slave or minor). **fermentum**, -i n. *yeast* (metaphor for *start*, *beginning*).

ILS 1046a: Funerary Inscription, Terentia

This inscription, written and dedicated by Terentia to her brother, was carved on the pyramid of Cheops in Egypt in the 2nd century CE. Roman visitors often left their mark, anything from graffiti to poetry, on ancient Egyptian monuments. These lines were recorded by a fourteenth-century traveler, but the epigraph has since been lost through the removal of the facing of the pyramid. Apparently Terentia lost her brother while abroad and had to continue her travels without him. The poem, in dactylic hexameter, is incomplete (as the last line shows) but touching, especially in the affection expressed in the first three verses. Beginning in line 4 she lists the accomplishments of her brother, Decimus Terentius Gentianus, who was an up-and-coming young man during the reigns of Trajan and Hadrian. The inscription testifies to the learning achieved by some women of the upper classes, to the presence of women traveling outside of Rome in the Empire, and to a close brother-sister relationship.

> vidi Pyramidas sine te, dulcissime frater,
> et tibi, quod potui, lacrimas hic moesta profudi,
> et nostri memorem luctus hanc sculpo querulam.
> Sit nomen Decimi [G]entia[n]i pyramide alta,
> 5   pontificis comitisque tuis, Traiane, triumphis,
> lustra sex intra censoris, consulis esse . . .

Notes to Funerary Inscription, *ILS* 1046a:

1   **quod potui** *to the best of my ability, as well as I could.* **moestus** (= **maestus**), -a -um *unhappy, sad, grieving.* **profundo**, -ere, -fudi, -fusum *pour forth, shed.* Is there anything in this line that indicates that it was written by a woman? **memor**, -oris (adj.) *in memory, commemorative* (+ objective genitive). **luctus**, -us m. *sorrow, mourning.* **sculpo**, -ere, sculpsi, sculptum *carve.* **querulus**, -a, -um *mournful, plaintive*; translate as a noun, modified by **memorem**. **sit**: jussive subjunctive ("let..."). Here at last is the name of the of the honoree, **Decimus Gentianus**. The rest of his name, **Terentius**, is supplied from another inscription, *ILS* 1046 (also now lost) in which his rise through the *cursus honorum* is outlined. From **Terentius**, his *nomen*, we deduce that his sister had the name **Terentia**. She may have been the wife of the senator Lollianus Avitus, who was proconsul of Asia. **pyramide alta**: abl. of place where; **in** is often omitted in poetry.

5   **pontifex**, -icis m. *priest.* **comes**, -itis m. *companion.* **Traiane**: vocative of **Traianus**, *the emperor Trajan.* **lustrum**, -i n. originally a sacrifice for *purification*, it came to mean a *five-year period.* **censor**, -oris m. *censor*; in apposition with **pontificis** and **comitis**. Under the Empire this position was taken over by the Emperor. Terentius was **consul suffectus** under Trajan in 116 CE and **censitor** (*provincial tax officer*) under Hadrian in 120 (his sister in affectionate regard may have elevated him to **censor**). Some words are clearly missing; without them it is impossible to say whether it means he was only thirty when he died. **esse**: the transcription is unclear at this point. The letters **ese** could be read. The rest of the poem is missing. Another emendation, **exstet** (*be conspicuous, live on*), has been suggested, which would require the substitution in line 4 of **sic** for **sit**.

Notes to Nepos, *Fragmenta ex libris De Viris Illustribus* (Fragments 1-2):

1.1   **libro**: the book on Roman historians, extant only in small part, is one of about sixteen books of the *De Viris Illustribus* published around 34 BCE.

2   **ulciscor**, -i, ultus/a sum *take vengeance on*. **quispiam** *anyone, someone/something*. **atque** (conj. in a comparison) *than, to, as*. **licet**, -ere, -uit, -itum (impersonal verb) *it is permitted*. **re publica salva**: ablative absolute of circumstance, "on condition that." **persequor**, -i, -secutus/a sum *follow through, take vengeance*. **quatenus** *insofar as*. **multo tempore multisque partibus** "a lot of the time and in a lot of places." **pereo**, -ire, -ivi/ii, -itum *perish, be destroyed*. **potius quam** *rather than* (that). **profligo** (1) *destroy, overthrow, dash to the ground*.

2.1   **eadem** *the same woman* (i.e., Cornelia). **verbis conceptis**: ablative absolute, "if the words could be imagined." **deiero** (1) *swear, take a solemn oath*. **ausim**: perfect subjunctive of **audeo**, *I would venture, I would make bold*. **praeterquam** (adv.) *except, besides*. **neco** (1) *murder, kill*. **molestia**, -ae f. *annoyance*. **trado**, -ere, -didi, -ditum + dative *pass on, give*. **oportet**, -ere, -uit (impersonal) *it is fitting*. **antehac** *before this, previously*. **liberi**, -orum m. pl. *children*. **pars**, partis f. *role, part*; **partis**: acc. pl. **tolero** (1) *bear, support*; Cornelia expects Gaius, the last of her sons, to take up the duties of his deceased siblings in regard to her. **ut, uti** clauses depend on **curare**; substantive clauses of result. **quam minimum** *as little as possible* + genitive. **sollicitudo**, -inis f. *anxiety, trouble*. **senecta**, -ae f. (also **senectus**, -tutis f.) *old age*. **quaecumque**: n. pl. of **quicumque**, *whoever, whatever*. **velles**: imperfect subjunctive of **volo**. **placeo**, -ere, -ui, -itum + dat *please, satisfy*. **nefas** (indecl. n. noun) *contrary to divine law, deeply wicked*. **res maiores** *important matters*. **praesertim** (adv.) *especially*. **resto** (1) *remain, be left*.

2   **ne quidem** *not even*. **opitulor** (1) *help*. **quin** *but that; (preventing) from* + subjunctive. **adversor** (1, depon.) + dative *oppose, set oneself against*; **adversere**: an alternate form of **adverseris**. **pausa**, -ae f. *end, stop, respite*. **ecquando** *ever? when...ever?* **modus**, -i m. *limit, end*. **desino**, -ere, -i *cease, leave off*. **et habentes et praebentes molestiis desistere?** Two translations have been suggested for this difficult passage: "both having vexations and offering to desist from them" (Snyder) or "stop taking and giving offense" (Skinner). **perpudesco**, -ere *begin to feel very ashamed at* (impersonal + ablative). **omnino** (adv.) *entirely, at all*.

3   **petito, facito**: future imperatives. **tribunatus**, -us m. *tribunate, office of the tribune*. **per me** *for my sake, as far as I am concerned*. **lubet = libet**: *it pleases*. **parento** (1) *sacrifice in honor of one's dead parents*. **deus parens** *departed spirit of a parent*. **deum = deorum**. **expeto**, -ere, -ivi, -itum *desire, demand, aim at*. **prex**, precis f. *good wishes, prayers*.

4   **ne** + perfect subjunctive in a jussive construction; **sirit** (<**sino**, -ere, sivi/sii, situm *allow, permit*) is an archaic form; **sirit** is an archaic perfect subjunctive form and therefore appropriate to the speech of Cornelia. **ea**: internal object of **perseverare**. **persevero** (1) *persist*. **vereor**, -eri, veritus/a sum *fear, be afraid*. **tibi**: dative of reference. **laboris**: partitive genitive. **culpa tua**: ablative of cause. **tute** = emphatic form of **tu**.

Cornelius Nepos, *Fragmenta, De Viris Illustribus*: Cornelia

Excerpts from letters, perhaps by Cornelia, mother of the Gracchi, to her son Gaius (written before 123 BCE), survive today as part of a huge work by the first-century BCE biographer Cornelius Nepos. Although Atticus and Quintilian read Cornelia's letters with admiration for their style, scholars dispute whether these passages are direct quotations from her letters. If indeed they are hers, they are a testament to the fine education that some elite women received, a unique female voice from the 2nd century BCE probably preserved because of its stern support of Roman patriarchal values. The letters show a mother's continued influence on her grown son, her expectation that her instructions would be heeded, and her passionate insistence that personal considerations must take second place to respect for the state and its gods.

Fragment 1: *Verba ex epistula Corneliae Gracchorum matris ex libro Cornelii Nepotis de Latinis historicis excerpta*

(2) Dices pulchrum esse inimicos ulcisci. id neque maius neque pulchrius cuiquam atque mihi esse videtur, sed si liceat re publica salva ea persequi. sed quatenus id fieri non potest, multo tempore multisque partibus inimici nostri non peribunt atque, uti nunc sunt, erunt potius quam res publica profligetur atque pereat.

Fragment 2: *Eadem alio loco*

Verbis conceptis deierare ausim, praeterquam qui Tiberium Gracchum necarunt, neminem inimicum tantum molestiae tantumque laboris, quantum te ob has res, mihi tradidisse; quem oportebat omnium eorum, quos antehac habui liberos, partis eorum tolerare atque curare ut quam minimum sollicitudinis in senecta haberem, utique quaecumque ageres, ea velles maxime mihi placere, atque uti nefas haberes rerum maiorum adversum meam sententiam quicquam facere, praesertim mihi, cui parva pars vitae restat.

(2) ne id quidem tam breve spatium potest opitulari, quin et mihi adversere et rem publicam profliges? denique quae pausa erit? ecquando desinet familia nostra insanire? ecquando modus ei rei haberi poterit? ecquando desinemus et habentes et praebentes molestiis desistere? ecquando perpudescet miscenda atque perturbanda re publica?

(3) sed si omnino id fieri non potest, ubi ego mortua ero, petito tribunatum; per me facito quod lubebit, cum ego non sentiam. ubi mortua ero, parentabis mihi et invocabis deum parentem. in eo tempore non pudebit te eorum deum preces expetere, quos vivos atque praesentes relictos atque desertos habueris?

(4) ne ille sirit Iuppiter te ea perseverare, nec tibi tantam dementiam venire in animum. et si perseveras, vereor ne in omnem vitam tantum laboris culpa tua recipias, uti in nullo tempore tute tibi placere possis.

Notes to Propertius, *Elegiae* (Lines 1-4, 33-36, 43-56):

1   **desino**, -sinere, -sii, -situm *leave off from, cease*. **urgeo**, -ere, ursi *weigh down; oppress*. **pando**, -ere, pandi, passus *open*. **ianua**, -ae f. *door (of her tomb)*. **prex**, precis f. *prayer, entreaty*. **cum semel** *when once*. **infernus**, -a, -um *of death, of the underworld*. **intro** (1) *enter; reach*. **funus**, -eris n. *corpse; funeral*. **exoro** (1) *persuade, win by entreaty*. **sto**, stare, steti *stand (open)*. **adamas**, -antis m. *hard stone*; hence, something that is unyielding. **viae**: the roads back to the land of the living.

33   **praetexta**, -ae f. The **toga praetexta** was worn by boys before the coming-of-age ceremony and unmarried girls. **maritus**, -a, -um *of marriage, of a wedding*. **vincio**, -ire, vinxi, vinctum *encircle, fasten*. **et**: postpositive; translate before **vinxit**. **acceptus**, -a, -um *received, taken up*. **vitta**, -ae f. *headband*; traditionally, married women wore a distinctive hair style fashioned with fillets or ribbons. **coma**, -ae f. *hair; lock of hair*. **iungo**, -ere, iunxi, iunctus *unite, yoke to* (+ dative). **discessura**: "fated to leave it too soon." **cubile**, -is n. *bed, marriage bed*; **cubili**: dat. with **iungor**. **lapis**, -idis f. *stone*, i.e., *tombstone*. **uni nupta**: *spouse to one man*; until the late Republican period, this was seen to be a virtue of the *matrona*, who, if widowed, was not expected to remarry. Many tombstones memorialize the "one-man woman" who came to be termed *univira*. **lego**, -ere, lexi, lectus *read; describe*.

43   **exuviae**, -arum f. pl. *spoils of war*; i.e., glory gained by victory. **damnum**, -i n. *(cause of) harm*. **quin** (adv.) *nay rather*. **aetas**, -atis f. *life, age*. **crimen**, -inis n. *slander, cause of reproach*. **insignis**, -is, -e *famed*. **utramque facem**: i.e., the torch of marriage and the torch of the pyre. **mi = mihi**. **a sanguine** "from my blood-line." **iudicis metu**: ablative of cause, "from fear of the judge." **quilibet**, quaelibet, quodlibet (pronoun) *any, anyone at all*. **tabella**, -ae f. *voting tablet*. **austerus**, -a, -um *stern, severe*.

50   **turpis**, -e *morally foul; guilty*. **assessus**, -us m. *the position of being seated side by side*; translate with **meo**. **ulla**: understand **femina**. **vel tu...vel (tu) cui**: dative of possession, *whether (that woman be) you...or you for whom*. **tardus**, -a, -um *hesitant; unmoving*. **Cybeben**: accusative singular of **Cybele**, an eastern Mother Goddess brought to Rome in 204 BCE by the Romans in response to a prophecy that she would help them win the Second Punic War (see the World of the State). Cornelia's ancestor Claudia's chastity was established when she led the goddess' mired boat from Ostia to Rome. **funis**, -is m. *rope*. **turritus**, -a, -um *turreted*; Cybele wore a crown that resembled a city wall with turrets. **rarus**, -a, -um *unequalled, unrivalled*. **ministra**, -ae f. *servant; priestess*. **iuratus**, -a, -um *sworn* (to keep). **reposco**, -poscere, -poposci *demand again*. **exhibeo**, -ere, -ui *show; produce*. **vivus**, -a, -um *alive, (still) aflame*. **carbasus**, -i f. *canvas, linen clothing*. **albus**, -a, -um *white*, of the garment worn by the Vestals. The Vestal Aemilia, accused of letting Vesta's sacred fire die out, was vindicated when the fire automatically rekindled after she put a piece of her robe on the hearth.

55   **caput**, -itis n. *head*; by metonymy, *source, origin*. **Scribonia**: Scribonia, sister of L. Scribonius Libo, had three husbands, one a member of the *gens* Scipio and father of her daughter Cornelia; the third was Octavian, whom she married in 40 BCE and to whom she bore Julia, ironically Cornelia's step-sister. **laedo**, -ere, laesi, laesum *harm, hurt; wrong*. **in me** *in my case*. **nisi fata** *except my fate* (of dying so young). **velis**: potential subjunctive.

Sextus Propertius, *Elegiae* 4.11: Cornelia (excerpts)

This long lovely poem, a testament to the ideal of the *materfamilias* and to the values of the *familia*, was written on the occasion of the death of the young aristocrat Cornelia (16 BCE). Propertius imagines Cornelia delivering her own eulogy over her tomb, in defense of her brief but virtuous life: *ipsa loquor pro me* (27). In the selections below she addresses her grieving husband, Paullus Aemilius Lepidus, and their now motherless children with loving concern and instruction; she proudly greets her parents and forbears; she fearlessly seeks from the spirits of the underworld justification and favor. Cornelia claims a place of honor among her famous ancestors, both male and female Cornelii Scipiones, having earned, as a loyal wife and caring mother, the fame appropriate to women, that of a virtuous *matrona*. The meter is elegiac couplet, typical of funerary inscriptions.

1   desine, Paulle, meum lacrimis urgere sepulcrum:
        panditur ad nullas ianua nigra preces;
    cum semel infernas intrarunt funera leges,
        non exorato stant adamante viae.

    mox, ubi iam facibus cessit praetexta maritis,
        vinxit et acceptas altera vitta comas,
35   iungor, Paulle, tuo sic discessura cubili:
        in lapide hoc uni nupta fuisse legar.

    non fuit exuviis tantis Cornelia damnum:
        quin et erat magnae pars imitanda domus.
45   nec mea mutata est aetas, sine crimine tota est:
        viximus insignes inter utramque facem.
    mi natura dedit leges a sanguine ductas,
        ne possem melior iudicis esse metu.
    quaelibet austeras de me ferat urna tabellas:
50   turpior assessu non erit ulla meo,
    vel tu, quae tardam movisti fune Cybeben,
        Claudia, turritae rara ministra deae,
    vel cui, iuratos cum Vesta reposceret ignes,
        exhibuit vivos carbasus alba focos.
55   nec te, dulce caput, mater Scribonia, laesi:
        in me mutatum quid nisi fata velis?

Notes to Propertius, *Elegiae* (Lines 61-64, 67-74, 95-98):

61   **generosus**, -a, -um *ennobling, noble, eminent.* **vestis [materna]** = *the stola,* the concealing over-garment worn by the Roman matron of the upper classes, indicating her married status. **sterilis**, -is, -e *childless.* **rapina**, -ae f. *a stealing, rape* (in the sense of Pluto's rape of Persephone). Cornelia has been taken from her family and home by an early death. **Lepide**: Cornelia's son, Marcus Aemilius Lepidus. **Paulle**: Cornelia's other son, L. Aemilius Paullus. **levamen**, -inis n. *solace, comfort*; understand **estis**. **condo**, -ere, condidi, conditum *close, shut.* **lumina**, -um n. pl. *lights*; by metonymy, *eyes.* **sinus**, -us m. *embrace.*

67   **specimen**, -inis n. *sign, mark; pattern, example*; predicate nominative with **nata** (perfect passive participle of **nascor**). **fac [ut]** + subjunctive (**teneas**) *be sure to, take care to.* **unum... virum**: i.e., to be a *univira* like Cornelia. **serie** (adv.) *in turn.* **fulcio**, -ire, fulsi, fultum *be a prop, support* (i.e., by begetting children and continuing the line). **mihi...volenti** *for me going willingly.* **cumba**, -ae f. the *boat* of Charon. **solvo**, -ere, solvi, solutum *untie, loose* (i.e., set sail). **aucturis...meis** "since my descendants will enrich the number of my deeds." **merces**, -edis f. *reward, recompense.* **triumphus**, -i m. *triumphal procession*; Cornelia equates women's good reputation and contribution of children to the family line with the triumph, the highest male honor. **emeritus**, -a, -um *fully deserved, discharged from service* (term used for military veterans); modifying **rogum** (*funeral pyre*), it may refer to the function of freeing her body from its reputation or from the opulence of the rites. **libera**: translate as an adverb, "freely." **tibi**: i.e., her husband Paullus. **commendo** (1) *commend, entrust.* **cura**, -ae f. *care, concern; worry*; Cornelia means that a mother's concern for her children survives even after death. **et** (adv.) *even, still, yet.* **inustus**, -a, -um *branded, unburned.*

95   **accedat**: optative subjunctive. **proles**, -is f. *offspring, children*; ablative of accompaniment. **iuvo**, -are, iuvi, iutum *help, comfort*; hortatory subjunctive. **bene habet** *it is good, it is well.* **lugubrium**, -i n. *mourning dress.* **sumo**, -ere, sumpsi, sumptum *dress oneself in/with, don, put on*; Cornelia is happy that none of her children died before her, since child mortality was high in antiquity. **exsequiae**, -arum f. pl. *funeral.* **caterva**, -ae f. *flock, group, crowd.* **causa**, -ae f. *case, pleading.* **peroro** (1) *argue(a case) to the end, wind up a speech.* **surgo**, -ere, surrexi, surrectum *rise, stand up* (as in a court). **gratus**, -a, -um *grateful, pleasing.* **rependo**, -ere, -pendi, -pensum *pay back, reward.* **humus**, -i f. *earth, ground.* **mos**, moris m. *good morals, virtue.* **pateo**, -ere, patui + dat. *open up, unbar.* **mereo**, -ere, merui, meritum *receive a reward, merit, gain.* **vehor**, -i, vectus/a sum *sail, be borne.*

Sextus Propertius, *Elegiae* 4.11 (continued)

61   et tamen emerui generosos vestis honores
       nec mea de sterili facta rapina domo.
    tu, Lepide, et tu, Paulle, meum post fata levamen:
       condita sunt vestro lumina nostra sinu.

    filia, tu specimen censurae nata paternae,
       fac teneas unum nos imitata virum.
    et serie fulcite genus: mihi cumba volenti
70   solvitur aucturis tot mea facta meis.
    haec est feminei merces extrema triumphi,
       laudat ubi emeritum libera fama rogum.
    nunc tibi commendo communia pignora natos:
       haec cura et cineri spirat inusta meo.

95   quod mihi detractum est, vestros accedat ad annos:
       prole mea Paullum sic iuvet esse senem.
    et bene habet: numquam mater lugubria sumpsi;
       venit in exsequias tota caterva meas.
    causa perorata est. flentes me surgite, testes,
100   dum pretium vitae grata rependit humus.
    moribus et caelum patuit: sim digna merendo,
       cuius honoratis ossa vehantur avis.

Notes to Cicero, *Ad Familiares* 14.4 (Paragraphs 1-4):

Paragraph numbers have been inserted throughout for convenience in locating the notes.

Salutation: abbreviations expressing greetings at the opening of Latin letters are common. **Scr. = scripta [epistula]** or **scripsi**: *written/ I wrote*. **Brundisii**: *at Brundisium* (modern-day Brindisi); the locative is used for cities. **prid. = pridie Kalendas Maias**: *the day before the Kalends of May:* April 30th. On Roman dates, see Allen and Greenough §§ 630-631. **A.U.C. 696 = ab urbe condita (anno urbis conditae)**: *the 696th year from the founding of the city* (58 BCE). **S. D. = salutem dicit**: *says hello, gives greeting*. **suis**: *his own, his dear ones; his family*.

1   **do**, dare, dedi, datum (in the context of letter-writing) *write, send.* **propterea quod** *because.* **conficio**, -ere, -feci, -fectum *consume, subdue, sweep away; accomplish, complete, settle.* **quod**: in transitions, *and in fact, and yet.* **vitae**: objective genitive depending on **cupidi**. **utinam** + subjunctive of wish: *if only, would that!* **fuissemus**: Cicero is speaking of himself in the plural. The optative subjunctive or subjunctive of wish; the pluperfect indicates a wish unfulfilled in past time. **vidissemus**: unfulfilled potential, equivalent to the conclusion clause of a contrary-to-fact condition in past time. **quod si** *and if, but if.* **commodum**, -i n. *advantage, benefit.* **aliquando** (adv.) *at some time, ever.* **quam primum** *as soon as possible.* **complexus**, -us m. *embrace.* **emorior**, emori, emortuus/-a sum = **morior** *die.* **colo**, -ere, colui, cultum *worship, cherish, honor.* **refero**, -ferre,- tuli, -latum + **gratiam** *be grateful.*

2   **caput**, -itis n. *life, person, civil rights.* **prae** + abl.: *before, compared with.* **improbus**, -a, -um *wicked.* **deduco**, -ere, -duxi, -ductum *deflect, divert.* **quo minus = ut eo minus** *so that...not, from* + subjunctive after **deductus est**, a verb of hindering. **praesto** (1) *surpass, exhibit, show.* **officium, -**i n. *service, duty, sense of duty.* **aliquando** (adv.) *some time, ever.* **habebimus gratiam** = "I will be grateful."

3   **proficiscor**, -i, profectus/a sum + abl. *set out.* **a.d. II K. Mai. = ante diem II Kalendas Maias**: *the second day before the Kalends of May* (April 29). **peto** *head for*; the direct object is Cyzicum, a town on the Propontus sea in Asia. **perdo**, -ere, perdidi, perditum *ruin, destroy*; **me perditum, afflictum**: accusatives of exclamation. **rogem**: deliberative subjunctive, for asking oneself a question – *should I...?* **reditus**, -us m. *return.* **adiuvo** (1) *assist, help.* Both **confirmes** and **adiuves** are subjunctives in a jussive noun clause with **ut** omitted. **sin** (conj.) *but if.* **transigo**, -ere, -egi, -actum *finish, settle.* **fac [ut]** + subjunctive: *bring it about that.*

4   **scito**: second person singular imperative from **scio**. **plane** (adv.) *plainly, certainly, quite.* **Tulliola**: an affectionate diminutive of **Tullia**, Cicero's much-loved daughter. **se res habebit** *the case will stand.* **servio**, -ire, -ivi-, -itum *be a slave*; + dat. *serve, be of use to, be devoted to, accommodate oneself to.* **sinus**, -us m. *bosom, heart.*

M. Tullius Cicero, *Ad Familiares* 14 (selections): Terentia

Cicero's letters to Terentia demonstrate aspects of Roman life that are rarely seen. First, they reveal a respectable *matrona* acting with courage and loyalty in the public sphere to support her endangered family and protect their assets during Cicero's long absences from Rome. Then, they show Cicero's deep affection for and dependence on his family and *domus*. Finally they chart the dissolution of an elite marriage which crumbles under the weight of separation, financial setbacks, politics, family tragedy, and the maturation of the *matrona*. This first letter, written at the start of Cicero's exile from Rome (58 BCE), is addressed to Terentia and their children, Tullia and the younger Cicero. When Cicero fled from Rome in fear of prosecution for his handling of the Catilinarian conspiracy, he became a public enemy: his family was treated dishonorably, his money was seized, and his house on the Palatine was looted and destroyed.

14.4. Scr. Brundisii prid. Kalendas Maias A.U.C. 696

TULLIUS S. D. TERENTIAE ET TULLIAE ET CICERONI SUIS.

(1) Ego minus saepe do ad vos litteras, quam possum, propterea quod cum omnia mihi tempora sunt misera, tum vero, cum aut scribo ad vos aut vestras lego, conficior lacrimis sic ut ferre non possim. Quod utinam minus vitae cupidi fuissemus! certe nihil aut non multum in vita mali vidissemus. Quod si nos ad aliquam alicuius commodi aliquando recuperandi spem fortuna reservavit, minus est erratum a nobis; si haec mala fixa sunt, ego vero te quam primum, mea vita, cupio videre et in tuo complexu emori, quoniam neque di, quos tu castissime coluisti, neque homines, quibus ego semper servivi, nobis gratiam rettulerunt.

(2) Nos Brundisii apud M. Laenium Flaccum dies XIII fuimus, virum optimum, qui periculum fortunarum et capitis sui prae mea salute neglexit neque legis improbissimae poena deductus est, quo minus hospitii et amicitiae ius officiumque praestaret: huic utinam aliquando gratiam referre possimus! habebimus quidem semper.

(3) Brundisio profecti sumus a. d. II K. Mai.: per Macedoniam Cyzicum petebamus. O me perditum! O afflictum! Quid enim? Rogem te, ut venias? Mulierem aegram, et corpore et animo confectam. Non rogem? Sine te igitur sim? Opinor, sic agam: si est spes nostri reditus, eam confirmes et rem adiuves; sin, ut ego metuo, transactum est, quoquo modo potes ad me fac venias.

(4) Unum hoc scito: si te habebo, non mihi videbor plane perisse. Sed quid Tulliola mea fiet? iam id vos videte: mihi deest consilium. Sed certe, quoquo modo se res habebit, illius misellae et matrimonio et famae serviendum est. Quid? Cicero meus quid aget? iste vero sit in sinu semper et complexu meo.

Notes to Cicero, *Ad Familiares* 14.4 (Paragraphs 5-9):

5   **queo** (defective verb) *be able to.* **maeror** -oris m. *sorrow, grief.* **egeris**: perfect subjunctive of **ago**; Cicero refers to Terentia's financial status. **utrum...an** + subjunctive in indirect question *whether...or.* **spolio** (1) *strip, plunder, despoil.* **Pisonem**: Cicero's son-in-law, Gaius Calpurnius Piso Frugi, Tullia's first husband, who died before Cicero's return from exile. **fore = futurum esse. de familia liberanda**: gerundive, "concerning the freeing of the household slaves." **promitto**, -ere, -missi, -missum *give a promise to* (+ dat. **tuis [servis]**). **mereo**, -ere, merui, meritum *deserve, earn.* **in officio esse** *be true to one's duty.* **adhuc** (adv.) *until now, so far.* **praeterea** (adv.) *besides.* **magno opera = magnopere** (adv. of **magnus**) *greatly, particularly.* **causa, -** ae f. *position, case.* **abeo**, -ire, -ivi, -itum *pass away, become lost,* i.e., if his estates have been confiscated. **libertus**, -i m. *freedman.* **obtineo**, -ere, -tinui, -tentum *prevail, maintain,* i.e., their claim of freedom against those making claims on Cicero's property, who might accuse him of evading confiscation by freeing his slaves. **pertineo**, -ere, -tinui, -tentum *belong, pertain*; the subject is **res. praeterquam** *except, beyond, besides.* **oppido** (adv.) *very.*

6   **ut sim...habeam**: jussive noun clause depending on **hortaris. salus**, -utis f. *welfare, life, health.* **eiusmodi...ut** *such...that.* **quas = tuas litteras** *your letter.* **exspecto** (1) *wait for, hope for*; **exspectassem** is a contracted form of **exspectavissem. licet**, -ere, licuit, licitum est (impersonal verb) *it is permitted*; **si esset licitum**: contrary-to-fact condition. **per nautas = a nautis. tempestas**, -tatis f. *weather* (good or bad); here, *good weather.* **praetermitto**, -ere, -misi, -missum *let pass.*

7   **quod reliquum** *what remains.* **sustento** (1) *hold up, keep up, support* (frequentative of **sustineo**). **floreo**, -ere, florui *prosper, flourish*; Cicero is referring here to himself, not to them both. **adfligo**, -ere, -flixi, -flictum *crush, throw down.* **una...cum**: *together...with.* **ornamentum**, -i n. *distinction, decoration.* **quamquam** (conj.) *although.* **ferenda non sunt** *they are things that should not be borne.* **confirmo** (1) *encourage, strengthen.*

8   **Clodius, Sallustius**, and **Pescennius** are probably Cicero's freedmen. **impedio**, -ire, -ivi, -itum *hinder, hamper.* **valetudo**, -tudinis f. *health* (good or bad). **perbenevolus**, -a, -um *very friendly* **observo** (1) + dat. *guard, watch over.* **Sicca**: a friend of Cicero who owned a property at Vibo, a town in the toe of Italy. **discedo, -**ere, -cessi, -cessum + abl. *depart from, go away.*

9   **quoad** (adv.) *as far as.* **existimo** (1) *think, suppose, consider.*

Notes to Cicero, *Ad Familiares* 14.20:

       Salutation: de Venusino: *from his villa near Venusia* (in Apulia). **Kalendis Octobribus A.U.C. 707**: October 1, 47 BCE.

1   **Tusculanus**, -a, -um *of Tusculum* (a town in Latium); **Tusculanum**, -i n. *an estate at Tusculum.* **postridie** (adv.) *the day after.* **ut sint** and later **ut sit**: understand **cura** or **fac. diutius**: comparative adv. of **diu**, *for a long time.* **labrum**, -i n. *basin, bathtub.* **balineum = balneum**, -i n. *bath.* **item** (adv.) *likewise.* **victus**, -us m. *sustenance.*

M. Tullius Cicero, *Ad Familiares* 14 (continued)

(5) Non queo plura iam scribere: impedit maeror. Tu quid egeris, nescio: utrum aliquid teneas an, quod metuo, plane sis spoliata. Pisonem, ut scribis, spero fore semper nostrum. De familia liberanda nihil est quod te moveat: primum tuis ita promissum est, te facturam esse, ut quisque esset meritus; est autem in officio adhuc Orpheus, praeterea magno opere nemo; ceterorum servorum ea causa est, ut, si res a nobis abisset, liberti nostri essent, si obtinere potuissent, sin ad nos pertineret, servirent praeterquam oppido pauci.

(6) Sed haec minora sunt. Tu quod me hortaris, ut animo sim magno et spem habeam recuperandae salutis, id velim sit eiusmodi, ut recte sperare possimus. Nunc miser quando tuas iam litteras accipiam? quis ad me perferet? quas ego exspectassem Brundisii, si esset licitum per nautas, qui tempestatem praetermittere noluerunt.

(7) Quod reliquum est, sustenta te, mea Terentia, ut potes. Honestissime viximus, floruimus: non vitium nostrum, sed virtus nostra nos afflixit; peccatum est nullum, nisi quod non una animam cum ornamentis amisimus; sed, si hoc fuit liberis nostris gratius, nos vivere, cetera, quamquam ferenda non sunt, feramus. Atqui ego, qui te confirmo, ipse me non possum.

(8) Clodium Philetaerum, quod valetudine oculorum impediebatur, hominem fidelem, remisi. Sallustius officio vincit omnes. Pescennius est perbenevolus nobis, quem semper spero tui fore observantem. Sicca dixerat se mecum fore, sed Brundisio discessit.

(9) Cura, quoad potes, ut valeas et sic existimes, me vehementius tua miseria quam mea commoveri. Mea Terentia, fidissima atque optima uxor, et mea carissima filiola et spes reliqua nostra, Cicero, valete. Pr. K. Mai. Brundisio.

Cicero's last letter to Terentia directs her to prepare his home in Tusculum for his return. The tone is curt, unlike his affectionate letter of a decade earlier. In 47/6 BCE, their estrangement, apparently over money matters, ended in divorce, which required Cicero to return Terentia's dowry. Shortly thereafter Cicero married his wealthy ward Publilia, whom he divorced after Tullia's death in childbirth (Feb. 45 BCE). Terentia remarried well and lived to 103, if Pliny the Elder is to be believed; he writes: *Terentia Ciceronis ciii* (*NH* 7.48.158).

14.20. Scr. de Venusino Kal. Octobribus A.U.C. 707.

TULLIUS S. D. TERENTIAE SUAE.

(1) In Tusculanum nos venturos putamus aut Nonis aut postridie: ibi ut sint omnia parata – plures enim fortasse nobiscum erunt et, ut arbitror, diutius ibi commorabimur. Labrum si in balineo non est, ut sit, item cetera, quae sunt ad victum et ad valetudinem necessaria. Vale. K. Oct. de Venusino.

ILS 8394: *Laudatio Funebris Murdiae,* CIL 6.10230

A marble tablet of the 1ˢᵗ century BCE preserves part of an encomium by a son for his mother, Murdia. In the portion below, he describes her as excelling in the virtues of a *matrona* and honoring the members of both her marriages in her will.

(5) Quibus de causis cum omnium bonarum feminarum simplex similisque esse laudatio soleat, quod naturalia bona propria custodia servata varietates verborum non desiderent, satisque sit eadem omnes bona fama digna fecisse, et quia adquirere novas laudes mulieri sit arduum, cum minoribus varietatibus vita iactetur, necessario communia esse colenda ne quod amissum ex iustis praeceptis cetera turpet.

(6) Eo maiorem laudem omnium carissima mihi mater meruit, quod modestia, probitate, pudicitia, obsequio, lanificio, diligentia, fide par similisque ceteris probis feminis fuit, neque ulli cessit virtutis laboris sapientiae periculorum...

Notes to *ILS* 8394: *Laudatio Funebris Murdiae* (Paragraphs 5-6):

5   Since women do not act in public, their lives are similar and they are similarly praised. **cum**: introduces two subjunctives in a causal clause. **simplex**, -plicis (adj.) *simple, uncomplicated.* **naturalis**, -e (adj.) *natural, by nature.* **bona,** -orum n. pl. *good qualities.* **proprius,** -a, -um *one's own, personal, characteristic*; translate as an ablative of means, modifying **custodia**. **custodia**, -ae f. *oversight, care, restraint, protection.* **servo** (1) *preserve, guard, keep*; agrees with **bona**. **varietas**, -atis f. (in the plural, with **verborum**) *varied expressions.* **desidero** (1) *feel the want of, miss.* **satis sit**: belongs to the **cum** concessive clause and introduces **omnes fecisse**. **dignus**, -a, -um *worthy* + abl. (**bona fama**). **quia** (conj.) *since*; continues the causal construction with **sit arduum. arduus**, -a, -um *difficult, hard.* **minoribus varietatibus** *less significant changes, lesser variations of fortune.* **cum** + subjunctive of **iacto** (1) *shake, disturb, disquiet*; the subject is **vita [feminarum]. necessario** (adv.) *of necessity, unavoidably.* **communia** *common virtues* (that all women share). **colo,** -ere, -ui, cultum *cherish, protect, cultivate*; understand **nobis** with **colenda esse. ne [ali]quod amissum** + subjunctive: *so that anything lost...may not...* **praeceptum**, -i n. *precept, maxim, order.* **cetera** *the other virtues* (refers to **communia**). **turpo** (1) *soil, dishonor, disgrace.*

6   **eo** (adv.) *for that reason.* **modestia**: this quality, and those following, are ablatives of respect. **lanificium**, -i n. *wool-working*; spinning and weaving were the traditional duties of wives, which demonstrated their domestic piety. **cedo,** -ere, cessi, cessum + dat. (**ulli [feminae]**) *yield, be inferior to.* The remainder of the text is lost.

UNIT FIVE
THE WORLD OF THE BODY

In this unit we turn from the moral, social, and educational worlds to the physical. This world embraces both health issues and adornment, the internal and external body. Women's bodies were the site of tensions about respectability and proper behavior in ways that men's bodies were not, for women's honor was dependent on preserving the chastity of their bodies. Thus even bathing, which Roman men considered essential for health and an important social activity, was somewhat problematic for women. For the Romans, bathing was a daily social and communal event frequently conducted in public facilities similar to modern spas or health clubs, though the wealthy sometimes had several rooms for bathing built into their grand houses. Women used the public baths, but the sexes did not bathe together: some bathhouses had separate, usually smaller sections for women, and other baths set aside earlier, less desirable hours for women, who usually had to pay higher fees as well, though all fees for the baths were relatively low. The bathhouses contained a series of rooms most of which had pools or large tubs heated to different temperatures, matching the temperature of the room (cold, warm, hot); the bather moved through the rooms in an order determined by beliefs about health. The bathhouses also included facilities for exercising (probably used mostly by men), massage, and other bodily services like hair-plucking; large imperial baths also had gardens and even libraries. Although Roman citizens were proud of their baths and considered them a mark of the superiority of Roman culture, their ambivalence about women's use of the baths testifies to the strength of taboos about the female body. Hence elite women concerned about their reputations may have used the public baths less than women of the lower classes.

The readings in this unit, dating from the third century BCE to the second century CE, begin with views of women's biology and end with observations on women's self-presentation and adornment. Since all the passages were written by men, they reflect men's thoughts and visions of women's physical attributes rather than women's views of themselves; they also reveal some of the cultural tensions about women's bodies.

The first two passages, from Celsus and the elder Pliny, are "scientific." They concern the remarkable effects of women's bodily fluids (with special attention paid to menstrual blood) which are viewed as problematic deviations from the male "norm" but ultimately are accepted because they relate to the production of children. As Amy Richlin writes, "Evidently the female body itself is intrinsically powerful — both harmful and helpful; almost uncanny, evidently due to its special processes, not only menstruation but also childbirth and lactation" (1997: 201). Women's bodies are places of concealment; their dampness is a sign of both pollution and lack of control (Gold, 1998: 375). This "knowledge" seems fantastical to us, but it reflects lore and prejudices that have had a long history and carry over to our day. Often the science of the ancient world, even medical science, owed more to philosophy than to observation, experimentation, and common sense; more often science was concerned with how things "should be" according to the logic of the male intellect. To men of the ancient world, the male was the ideal; women were both strange and familiar beings, more closely tied to the world of nature than men and more interested in creature comforts, possessions, and sex. The Romans seem more comfortable with the physical differences of women than the Greeks, to whom women were alien and chaotic beings. Judith Hallett suggests that the Roman elite seems to have had a double view of women, one of polarity and the other of unity or sameness, which enabled them to ascribe to exceptional women the qualities they valued in men. This second view she attributes to a recognition of the "similarities between elite Roman women and their male blood kin" (1989: 59)

The next two readings take us to the mortal enemies of female life: miscarriage and death in childbirth. Girls could be married as young as twelve, an age when their bodies were not sufficiently developed to carry a pregnancy to term. In addition, Roman women often endured more pregnancies than their bodies could support. Since such a small percentage of children survived to adulthood, it is common to hear of women giving birth to twelve or more children (Agrippina Maior, for example, had nine children; twelve children were born to Cornelia, mother of the Gracchi, but only three reached adulthood and only one survived her). The Greek medical writer Soranus, who practiced in Rome in the first century CE, has many sensible things to say about women's bodies, including an accurate description of Premenstrual Syndrome. He considered fit for child-bearing women who were between the ages of 15 and 40. The younger Pliny's wife, almost certainly in her teens, suffered a miscarriage which Pliny attributes to her youth and inexperience with pregnancy. Evidently Calpurnia had no slave woman who could recognize or was privy to the cessation of her menses, nor do we know what sexual and reproductive knowledge young women received before they entered marriage. Julia, daughter of Caesar and wife of Pompey, lost her baby and her life in childbirth, an event all too common in antiquity. This particular loss was both a personal tragedy for her father and her husband and a disaster for the state, since it contributed to the end of the alliance between Caesar and Pompey that had been cemented by Julia's marriage. It is a sober reminder that even a Roman woman's body was not her own, but could be used by her father, husband, or guardian to advance his political career or social and financial aspirations. Whatever her rank, a woman's duty to her family was to marry and bear children – and risk her life in the process.

The remaining passages address women's concern for their appearance, which has as much to do with the Roman male's reliance on appearance to indicate worth as with the supposed vanity of the women themselves. Lucretius writes of a woman who makes herself attractive through her kind-heartedness, her obliging ways, and her physical closeness to the man with whom she shares her life. In the other passages, more elaborate and expensive ways of pleasing a man come into play, all potentially comic or tragic, depending on what happens to the girl or woman involved. Like other poets of love, Ovid has more interest in male than in female desire, but he does take some notice of the plight of women who have to fend for themselves in a man's world. His mistress has lost her hair in her attempt to make it more beautiful. What chance will she have to advance herself and her prospects with her clientele? It is interesting that male poets pay so little attention to the physical characteristics and social standing of the *puellae* they celebrate that these women seem almost disembodied and without identity (Fantham et al., 1994). This certainly cannot be said of the one Roman female love poet whose works are extant, Sulpicia (see the World of Flirtation). The poem from "Sulpicia's Garland" extols the striking beauty of this young woman poet – her shining eyes, her hair which becomes her whether loose or styled, her natural grace, and her elegant dress – arrayed for the festival of Mars. This literary piece parallels typical artistic representations of women in that it is both idealized and personal, combining the physical with the moral.

Finally, in the two passages about dress, we see two quite different women plying their antithetical professions. A Vestal Virgin has been observed too saucily attired and is admonished to be more discreet. In the Plautus piece, the *meretrix* (courtesan) has a wardrobe of the most exotic and alluring style, each item named with an exuberance equal to its fabric and manufacture.

Wall painting from the Roman villa at Stabiae of a female in transparent clothing reclining on a couch and holding a drinking horn (30-50 CE). Photo courtesy of *The VRoma Project*; permission ©Copyright The Trustees of the British Museum.

Notes to Celsus, *De Medicina* 2.8 (Section 16); 4.27 (Sections 1-4) :

2.8   (16) **vomo**, -ere, -ui, -itum *vomit*. **profusus**, -a, -um *excessive*. **menstruum**, -i n. *menstrual period, the menses*. **libero** (1) *relieve, ease*. **purgo** (1) *cleanse, clear (up)*. **naris**, -is f. *nostril*. **fundo**, -ere, fudi, fusum *pour, pour forth*. **vaco** (1) + abl. *be freed from, cleared of* . **loca**, -arum n. pl. *female genitals; womb*. **partus**, -us m. *childbirth, labor*. **sternumentum**, -i n. *sneeze, sneezing*. **levo** (1) *alleviate, ease*.

4.27.1   **vulva**, -ae f. *the womb, uterus*. **vehemens**, -entis (adj.) *violent, strong*. **malum**, -i n. *illness, ailment*. **proxime** *next* (in frequency). **haec** refers to **vulva**. **adficio**, -ere, -feci, -fectum *affect, influence*. **interdum** (adv.) *at times*. **exanimo** (1) *weaken, tire out*; the direct object is an understood **feminam**. **morbus**, -i m. *sickness*. **comitialis morbus** *epilepsy*. **prosterno** (1) *afflict, prostrate, lay a person low*. **disto** (1) *differ*. **casus**, -us m. *event, disorder*. **eo** = *epilepsy* (abl. of comparison). **spuma**, -ae f. *foam, spittle*. **profluo**, -fluere, -fluxi, -fluxum *flow forth*. **nervus**, -i m. *sinew, tendon*. **distendo**, -ere, -tendi, -tentum *stretch tight, spasm*. **sopor**, -poris m. *deep sleep, coma, stupor*. **tantum** (adv.) *only*. **crebro** (adv.) *frequently*. **perpetuus**, -a, -um *everlasting*, i.e. lasting throughout the rest of her life.

2   **vis**, viris f. *strength, vitality* (**virium**, gen. pl.: gen. of the whole = partitive genitive). **adiuvo** (1) *help*. **parum** (adv.) *too little* (strength or vitality). **cucurbitula**, -ae f. *little cup*. Blood-letting was sometimes facilitated by applying heated, small cups upside down on the skin. As the cups cooled, a vacuum was created inside them, which caused the blood to be drawn into the capillaries near the surface of the skin, so that a puncture (**cute incisa**) would bleed more freely. **defigo**, -figere, -figi, -fixum *apply, attach to*. **inguen**, inguinis n. *groin*. **iaceo**, -ere, -ui *lie prostrate, lie exhausted*. **alioqui** (adv.) *in general*. **nares**, -ium f. pl. *nose*. **extinctus**, -a, -um *extinguished, put out* (i.e., of something burned). **lucerna**, -ae f. *lamp*. **linamentum**, -i n. *linen lamp wick*. **foedus**, -a, -um *foul-smelling, smelling bad*. **rettuli** (< **refero**): refers to 3.20.1 where Celsus lists such strong-smelling stimulants as pitch, onion, garlic, greasy wool. **excito** (1) *rouse, stimulate*. **perfusio**, -onis f. *affusion, a pouring*. **efficio**, -ficere, -feci, -fectum *bring about, be effective, have an effect*. **ad se redire** (idiom): "to regain one's senses, become conscious again." **circumcido**, -ere, -cidi, -cisum *cut off entirely, deprive of*. **casus**, -us m. *attack* (of an illness), *recurrence* (of an illness).

3   **purgatio**, -onis f. *menstruation*. **mulieri**: dat. with **noceo**. **remedio**: dative of purpose. **cutis**, -is f. *skin*. **mamma**, -ae f. *breast*. **malignus**, -a, -um *malign*. **subicienda sunt medicamenta**: Celsus recommends the application of an herbal mixture to bring about the flow of the menses from the uterus. **costum**, -i n. *an aromatic plant, perfume*. **puleium**, -i n. *pennyroyal (an herb)*. **viola**, -ae f. *violet* (the flower). **apium**, -i n. *parsley*. **nepita**, -ae f. *catmint*. **stureia**, -ae f. *savory*. **hysopum**, -i n. *hyssop*. **aptus**, -a, -um *suitable*. **porrum**, -i n. *leek*. **ruta**, -ae f. *rue*. **cyminum**, -i n. *cumin*. **caepa**, -ae f. *onion*. **sinapi**, -is n. *mustard*. **olus**, -eris n. *vegetable*.

4   **ex inferiore parte**: "the genital area." **tricesimus**, -a, -um *thirtieth*. **vitium**, -i n. *illness, affliction*. **sano** (1) *cure, heal*; **sanasse** = **sanavisse**. **dolor capitis** *headache*. **brachium**, -i n. *upper arm*. **curasti**: contracted form for **curavisti**.

Aulus Cornelius Celsus, *De Medicina* 2, 4 (selections)

Although ancient medical authors rarely profiled individual women, women's biology featured prominently in their writings. While Celsus and other known authors on medical theory were male, there were women doctors and, of course, midwives, whose knowledge and experience were doubtless incorporated in the treatises. Another important source of information on the subject was the women patients themselves and their "folk remedies," which were as effective as the doctors' remedies. The passages below indicate that ancient medicine had a concept of feminine biology quite different from that of modern times. Good health for both men and women depended upon having the proper amounts of four bodily humors (blood, phlegm, black bile, and yellow bile). Illness was due to a deficiency, or more commonly an excess, of one of these humors (usually blood). Women's bodies were considered more porous and softer than men's and thus more absorbent of moisture. Therefore women had more difficulty maintaining the right balance of humors and thus periodically shed excess blood through menstruation to compensate. Roman doctors believed that sometimes the menstrual blood was not shed through the vagina, but was either retained in the body or was released through another orifice.

2.8 (16) Mulier sanguinem vomens profusis menstruis liberatur. Quae menstruis non purgatur, si sanguinem ex naribus fudit, omni periculo vacat. Quae locis laborat aut difficulter partum edit, sternumento levatur.

4.27 (1) Ex vulva quoque feminis vehemens malum nascitur proximeque ab stomacho vel adficitur haec vel corpus adficit. Interdum etiam sic exanimat, ut tamquam comitiali morbo prosternat. Distat tamen hic casus eo, quod neque oculi vertuntur nec spumae profluunt nec nervi distenduntur: sopor tantum est. Idque quibusdam feminis crebro revertens perpetuum est.

(2) Ubi incidit, si satis virium est, sanguis missus adiuvat; si parum est, cucurbitulae tamen defigendae sunt in inguinibus. Si diutius aut iacet aut alioqui iacere consuevit, admovere oportet naribus extinctum ex lucerna linamentum, vel aliud ex iis, quae foedioris odoris esse rettuli quod mulierem excitet. Idemque aquae quoque frigidae perfusio efficit. ... Deinde ubi ad se redit, circumcidendum vinum est in totum annum, etiamsi casus idem non revertitur...

(3) At si purgatio nimia mulieri nocet, remedio sunt cucurbitulae cute incisa inguinibus vel etiam sub mammis admotae. Si maligna purgatio est, subicienda sunt medicamenta quae evocent sanguinem: costum, puleium, violae albae, apium, nepita et stureia et hysopum. In cibum quoque accipiat quae apta sunt: porrum, rutam, cyminum, caepas, sinapi, vel omne acre olus.

(4) Si vero sanguis, qui ex inferiore parte erumpere solet, is ex naribus eruperit, incisis inguinibus adponenda est cucurbita idque per tres vel quattuor menses tricesimo quoque die repetieris: tunc scias hoc vitium sanasse. Si vero non se sanguis ostenderit, scias ei dolores capitis surgere. Tunc ex brachio ei sanguis emittendus est et statim curasti eam.

Notes to Plinius (maior), *Naturalis Historia* 28 (Sections 20.70-21.72):

20.70   **quae**: "those things which." **trado**, -ere, tradidi, -ditum *pass down, report*; Pliny is using oral tradition. **portentum**, -i n. *phenomenon*. **miraculum**, -i n. *marvel, wonder*. **accedo**, -ere, -cessi, -cessum *come to, be added to*. **ut sileamus** *not to speak of, to say nothing of*. **membratim** (adv.) *limb from limb*. **in scelera** *for criminal purposes*. **abortus**, -us m. *miscarriage, dead foetus*. **mensis**, -is m. *month, menstrual flow*. **piaculum**, -i n. *offering for expiation*; perhaps the undoing of spells cast with menstrual discharge. **obstetrix**, -icis f. *midwife*. **meretrix**, -icis f. *courtesan*. Tradition has it that various prose and verse works on sexual topics were written by courtesans. According to Suetonius, the emperor Tiberius kept the sex manuals of a Greek courtesan (*hetaira*) named Elephantis as a reference for his orgies. **prodo**, -ere, prodidi, proditum *thrust out, hand down*; **prodidere = prodiderunt**. Pliny offers examples of lore passed down by courtesans and midwives. **capillus**, -i m. *hair*. **cremo** (1) *burn, cremate*. **fugo** (1) *put to flight*. **fugari**, **respirare**, **emendari**, and **sisti** are infinitives in an indirect statement. **nidor**, -oris m. *strong smell, fumes*. **vulva**, -ae f. *womb*. **vulvae morbus** = *hysteria*. **strangulo** (1) *suffocate, choke*. **respiro** (1) *breathe*.

71   **cinis**, -eris m. *ashes*. **testa**, -ae f. *piece of burned clay, pot*. **spuma argenti** *foam of silver, lead monoxide*, formed when air is blown over molten lead. **scabritia**, -ae f. *inflamed condition* (especially of the eyes or eyelids), *scab*. **prurigo**, -inis f. *itching, irritation*. **emendo** (1) *free from faults, correct*. **emendari**: the same verb applies to the other conditions down to **sacrum ignem**. **item** (adv.) *likewise*. **verruca**, -ae f. *wart*. **ulcus**, -eris n. *sore, ulcer*. **mel**, mellis n. *honey*. **sinus**, -us m. *curve, fold, cavity*. **addito melle ac ture**: abl. absolute. **tus**, turis n. *frankincense*. **panus**, -i m. *an abscess* (named from its shape). **podagra**, -ae f. *gout*. **adeps**, -ipis m/f. *soft animal fat*. **suillus**, -a, -um *of pigs*; **adeps suillus** *lard*. **ignis sacer**: "holy fire"; used of various skin diseases including *erysipelas* (Greek for "red skin" = Saint Anthony's fire), *herpes*, and *anthrax*. **sanguis**, -inis m. *blood*; i.e., *hemorrhage*. **sisto**, -ere, stiti, statum *stop, check*. **inlino**, -ere, -levi, -litum *smear on*. **inlito**: understand **cinere**; ablative absolute. **formicatio**, -onis f. *the sensation that ants are crawling over one's skin*.

21.72   **lac**, lactis n. *milk*. **usus**, -us m. *use*. **convenit**: *it is generally agreed*. **dulcis**, -e *sweet*. **mollis**, -e *gentle, mild*. **febris**, -is f. *fever*. **coeliacus**, -a, -um (< Greek) *affecting the bowels*. **utilis**, -e *useful*. **maxime** (adv.) *especially*. **eius**: "of that woman"; antecedent of **quae**. **removeo**, -ere, -movi, -motum *remove, wean*. **malacia**, -ae f. (< Greek) *nausea, sickness*. **stomachus**, -i m. *alimentary canal, stomach*. **rosio**, -onis f. *eating away, smarting*. **efficax**, -acis *effective*. **experior**, -i, -pertus/a sum *try, experience*; **experiuntur**: the subject is a general "they" (understand **lac esse** in indirect statement with the predicate adj. **efficacissimum**). **mamma**, -ae f. *breast*. **collectio**, -onis f. *abscess*; **collectionibus**, **oculo** are dat. of advantage ("for"). **ictus**, -us m. *blow*. **cruor**, -oris m. *blood*. **suffundo**, -ere, -fudi, -fusum *pour into, blur*. **epiphora**, -ae f. *inflammation* (esp. of the eyes). **inmulgeo**, -ere *milk into*; the milk is squeezed into the eye. **prosum**, prodesse, -fui *be useful, do good*. **magis**: comp. adv. *more*. **sucus**, -i m. *juice, sap*. **pollen**, -inis n. *fine flour*. **super** (adv.) *besides*. With **eius quae** understand **lac est**. **mas**, maris *male, masculine*. **enitor**, -i, -xus/a sum *give birth to*. **geminus**, -i m. *twin*. **vinum**, -i n. *wine*. **cibus**, -i m. *food*. **acer**, -cris, -cre *sharp, pungent*. **abstineo**, -ere, -ui, -tentum + abl. *keep away from*; **abstineat**: subjunctive in a general condition.

C. Plinius Secundus (maior), *Naturalis Historia* 28.20-23

Women's bodies could be harvested as a natural source of medicines, and women themselves must sometimes have actively cooperated in the cures and procedures (Richlin 1997: 205). In these selections from his *Natural History*, Pliny (23/24-79 CE) describes the mysterious powers derived from women's bodies, especially from their bodily fluids, and credits women with extraordinary physical potency. Pliny begins his treatment of remedies derived from women's bodies with a reference to forbidden magical practices involving a miscarried fetus. He goes on to give recipes for cures prepared from a woman's burnt hair (70-1), from breast milk, from saliva, and from menstrual discharge. Among Pliny's sources for this book (see *NH*. I) are midwives and prostitutes, two groups of professional women with great practical knowledge of women's health. He names several: Sotira, a midwife (83); Salpe of Lemnos, who wrote on women's diseases; Olympias of Thebes, who was concerned with women's reproductive health; Elephantis, who wrote on erotic matters. These passages give some idea of the type of lore about women that has had a long and lurid life.

20   (70) Quae ex mulierum corporibus traduntur, ad portentorum miracula accedunt, ut sileamus divisos membratim in scelera abortus, mensum piacula quaeque alia non obstetrices modo, verum etiam ipsae meretrices prodidere: capilli si crementur, odore serpentes fugari; eodem nidore vulvae morbo strangulatas respirare;
(71) cinere eo quidem, si in testa sint cremati vel cum spuma argenti, scabritias oculorum ac prurigines emendari, item verrucas et infantium ulcera, cum melle capitis quoque vulnera et omnium ulcerum sinus, addito melle ac ture panos, podagras, cum adipe suillo sacrum ignem, sanguinem sisti, inlito item formicationes corporum.

21   (72) De lactis usu convenit dulcissimum esse mollissimumque et in longa febri coeliacisque utilissimum, maxime eius, quae iam infantem removerit. et in malacia stomachi, in febribus, rosionibus efficacissimum experiuntur; item mammarum collectionibus cum ture, oculo ab ictu cruore suffuso et in dolore aut epiphora, si inmulgeatur, plurimum prodest, magisque cum melle et narcissi suco aut turis polline, superque in omni usu efficacius eius, quae marem enixa sit, multoque efficacissimum eius, quae geminos mares, et si vino ipsa cibisque acrioribus abstineat.

Notes to Plinius (maior), *Naturalis Historia* 28 (Sections 22-23.77):

22.75   **eius**: antecedent of **quae**, referring to the mother of a girl; understand **lac** as the subject of **praevalet**. **ad vitia sananda**: gerundive of purpose; **sano** (1) *cure, restore to health*. **facies**, -ei f. *face*. **praevaleo**, -ere, -ui *be very powerful*. **pulmo**, -onis m. *lung*. **incommodum**, -i n. *trouble*. **cui**: dative with compound verb; the antecedent is **lac**. **admisceo**, -ere, -ui, -tum *mix in with, add to*. **inpubes**, -is (adj.) *youthful, prepubescent*. **urina**, -ae f. *urine*. **Atticus**, -a, -um *Athenian*. **omnia**: refers to the three ingredients; we would say "each." **cochleare**, -is n. *spoon* (< **cochlea**, *snail*; the **cochleare** was used to extract a snail from its shell); as now, a "spoon" is a standard measurement. **singuli**, -ae, -a *one each, single*. **mensura**, -ae f. *measure, measurement* (abl. of means). **vermis**, -is m. *worm*. **auris**, -is f. *ear*. **eicio**, -ere, eici, -iectum *cast out*. **pario**, -ere, peperi, partum *give birth to*. **gusto** (1) *taste*. **canis**, -is m/f. *dog*. **rabiosus**, -a, -um *rabid*. **nego** (1) *say (that) not*.

76   **saliva**, -ae f. *spit*. **ieiunus**, -a, -um *fasting*. **diiudico** (1) *determine*; the subject is a generalized "they." **cruentus**, -a, -um *bloody, bloodshot*. **epiphora**: see 72. **ferveo**, -ere, -bui *be inflamed*. **angulus**, -i m. *corner*. **subinde** (adv.) *repeatedly*. **madefio**, -eri, -factum *be wet, be soaked*. **pridie** (adv.) *the day before*. **fascia**, -ae f. *band for a woman's breasts, brassiere*. **alligo** (1) *bind*. **minuo**, -ere, -ui, -utum *lessen*.

23.77   **nullus est modus**: i.e., "of a woman's power." **modus**, -i m. *measure, limit*. **abigo**, -ere, -egi, -actum *drive away*; infinitive in indirect statement (understand **dicunt**). **grando**, -inis f. *hail*. **turbo**, -inis m. *whirlwind*. **fulgur**, -is n. *lightning flash*. **mensis**: see 70. **nudo** (1) *expose*; **mense nudato**: abl. absolute (a difficult passage: the woman is exposed, not just the discharge). **averto**, -ere, -verti, -versum *turn aside*. **violentia caeli** *stormy weather*. **tempestas**, -atis f. *storm*. **menstruum**, -i n. *menstrual discharge*; at sea she can prevent a storm even if she is not menstruating.

Notes to Valerius Maximus, *Facta et Dicta Memorabilia* 4 (Section 6.4):

4   **consimilis**, -e *very similar*. **adfectus**, -us m. *disposition, fondness* (the **honestissimus amor** of which Valerius Maximus spoke in 4.6.3). **Iuliae filiae**: subjective genitive. She is the object of **adfectus**; her father **C. Caesaris** (100-44 BCE) is subjective gen. **quae = illa** (Julia). **adnoto** (1) *comment on*. **cum** + subjunctive: *when*. **aedilicius**, -a, -um *of the aedile* (a municipal officer). **comitia**, -orum n. pl. *assembly for election*; *elections*. **Pompeius Magnus**: awarded this title in 81 BCE at his triumph for victory in Africa, Gnaeus Pompeius (106-48 BCE) was killed by Caesar's followers. **coniunx**, -iugis m/f. *husband, wife*. **vestis**, -is f. *clothing*. **cruor**, -oris m. *blood*. **respergo**, -ere, respersi, respersum *splash*. **campus**, -i m. *plain*; here, the *Campus Martius*, where the assemblies met to vote. **refero**, -ferre, -tuli, -latum *bring back*. **terreo**, -ere, terrui, territum *frighten*. **ne**: introduces a clause of fearing in the subjunctive mood; *lest, that*. **qua = aliqua** (after **ne**), adjectival pronoun modifying **vis**. **adfero**, -ferre, attuli, adlatum/ allatum *use against, bring to*. **exanimis**, -e *lifeless*. **concido**, -ere, -cidi *fall*. **partus**, -us m. *birth*. **subitus**, -a, -um *sudden*; **subita consternatione**: abl. of cause. **consternatio**, -onis f. *dismay, tumult*. **eicio**, -ere, eieci, eiectum *expel*. **cogo**, -ere, -egi, -actum *compel*. **magno... cum...detrimento**: translate as **cum magno detrimento**. **cuius**: refers to **totus terrarum orbis**. **civilis**, -e *civil, political*. **truculentus**, -a, -um *wild*. **perturbo** (1) *upset*; **perturbata esset**: conclusion of the past contrary-to-fact condition ("had...would have"). **communis**: genitive singular modifying **sanguinis**. **vinculum**, -i n. *bond, tie*. **constringo**, -ere, -strinxi, -strictum *bind, restrain*.

C. Plinius Secundus (maior), *Naturalis Historia* 28 (continued)

22 (75) eius vero, quae feminam enixa sit, ad vitia tantum in facie sananda praevalet. pulmonum quoque incommoda lacte mulieris sanantur; cui si admisceatur inpubis pueri urina et mel Atticum, omnia coclearium singulorum mensura, vermes quoque aurium eici invenio. eius, quae marem pepererit, lacte gustato canes rabiosos negant fieri.

(76) Mulieris quoque salivam ieiunam potentem diiudicant cruentatis oculis et contra epiphoras, si ferventes anguli oculorum subinde madefiant, efficacius, si cibo vinoque se pridie ea abstinuerit. invenio et fascia mulieris alligato capite dolores minui.

23 (77) post haec nullus est modus. iam primum abigi grandines turbinesque contra fulgura ipsa mense nudato; sic averti violentiam caeli, in navigando quidem tempestates etiam sine menstruis.

Valerius Maximus, *Facta et Dicta Memorabilia* 4.6.4

Valerius Maximus, in describing admirable love between wife and husband, gives the *exemplum* of Julia (83-54 BCE), who was the daughter of Julius Caesar and Cornelia and the wife of Pompey the Great. While marriage was a means for the Roman *paterfamilias* to forge politically or financially advantageous connections, in some cases these arrangements fostered real affection between the two parties. The marriage of Julia and Pompey was the bond that cemented the grudging coalition of the rival generals Caesar and Pompey in 60 BCE, each seeking supreme power in Rome. Julia struggled to keep her husband and father, both of whom she loved, on speaking terms, like her kinswoman Octavia, who was later to broker peace between her husband Antony and her brother Octavian. Julia's death in childbirth without an heir contributed to the dissolution of the accord between Caesar and Pompey and the resumption of civil war.

6.4 Consimilis adfectus Iuliae C. Caesaris filiae adnotatus est. quae, cum aediliciis comitiis Pompei Magni coniugis sui vestem cruore respersam e campo domum relatam vidisset, territa metu ne qua ei vis esset adlata, exanimis concidit partumque, quem utero conceptum habebat, subita animi consternatione et gravi dolore corporis eicere coacta est magno quidem cum totius terrarum orbis detrimento, cuius tranquillitas tot civilium bellorum truculentissimo furore perturbata non esset, si Caesaris et Pompei concordia communis sanguinis vinculo constricta mansisset.

Notes to Pliny Minor, *Epistulae* 8.10:

C. Plinius Fabato Prosocero: a formula for the salutation of a letter: the name of the sender in the nom., the addressee in the dat. (often with **suo** or **suae**), and the abbreviation **S**. (or **S. D.**), **salutem** (or **salutem dicit**), "says hello." Calpurnius Fabatus was a censorious old man (see *Ep.* 8.11, 6.12; 7.11). He died when Pliny and Calpurnia were in Bithynia. **prosocer**, -eri m. *wife's grandfather*.

1   **quo magis...hoc tristior** *the more...the more sad(ly)*. **pronepos**, -otis m. *great-grandson*. **tristis**, -e *sad*. **neptis**, -is f. *granddaughter*. **abortum facere** *to suffer a miscarriage*. **praegnans**, -antis (adj.) *pregnant*. **puellariter** (adv.) *in a girlish manner, in youthful inexperience*. This adverb implies that she was under seventeen, even though she had probably been married to Pliny for three or four years. Women were sometimes married even under age twelve, though the marriage was not legally recognized until they reached twelve. Contemporary medical writers oppose child marriage for girls: Soranus sets the age of conception between 15 and 40; to Rufus 18 was the youngest a woman could safely carry a child. **per hoc** *as a result of this*. **custodio**, -ire, -ivi/-ii, -itum *guard, watch out for*. **facit omittenda**: that is, she engaged in activities she should not have, had she known she was pregnant. Pliny the Elder included amulets to be worn and activities to be avoided by pregnant women (see, for example *NH* 28.23.81; 28.27.98; 28.77.246-7). **documentum**, -i n. *lesson*. **expio** (1) *atone for*.

2   This sentence is very carefully constructed, perhaps to indicate the complexity of the feelings expressed and the difficulty Pliny feels in expressing them. **ut** *as* (followed by **sic** *so*). **graviter accipere** (~ **graviter ferre**) *to be grieved (at); to take* [something] *hard*. **accipias**: subjunctive in a result clause after **necesse est**; **ut** is often omitted. **senectus**, -utis f. *old age*; **senectutem** is subject of **destitutam** [**esse**] in indirect statement. **paratis posteris**: abl. of separation with **destitutam**; **posteri**, -orum m. *descendants*. **destituo**, -ere, -ui, -utum *forsake, leave without*. **dis**: dat. pl. of **deus**. **negaverunt, servarent, reddituri**: the subject of these verbs is **di**, understood from **dis**. **illos** and **quorum** refer to the hoped-for children. **reddituri** < **reddo**. **quamquam** *although*. **parum** (adv.) *too little, not enough, not* (related to **parvus**). **prospere** (adv.) *successfully, favorably* (< **prosperus**). **exploro** (1) *put to the test, try out*. **fecunditas**, -atis f. *fertility*.

3   **isdem**: antecedent of **quibus**; supply **verbis** or **sententiis** or similar. **hortor moneo confirmo**: notice the use of asyndeton to express the emotional urgency of the advice to both his grandfather-in-law (**te**) and himself (**me**). **confirmo** (1) *strengthen, reassure*. **ardentius**: comparative of **ardens** *eager*. **tu**: understand **cupis**. **liberi**, -orum m. pl. *children*. **latus**, -eris n. *side*. **pronus**, -a, -um *leaning towards, headed for, proceeding without difficulty*. **pronum**: translate with **iter**. **subitus**, -a, -um *sudden, sudenly arising, made in a hurry*. **imago**, -inis f. *representation, likeness, death-mask* of an ancestor who had held office. These were displayed in the houses of elite families and were carried or worn by actors in funeral processions, which were awesome ceremonies. Pliny believes that any progeny he and his wife produce will be able to display the **imagines** of many generations of illustrious ancestors on both sides. **relicturus**: translate with **videor**. **nascantur, mutent**: jussive subjunctives. **gaudium**, -i n. *joy*. **vale**: the typical formula for closing a letter. There is no need for the writer to add his/her name because it is already at the top. **valeo**, -ere, valui, valitum *be well*; as a greeting, *farewell*.

C. Plinius Caecilius Secundus (minor), *Epistulae* 8.10

Calpurnia, Pliny's wife, has suffered a miscarriage. Pliny writes to Fabatus, his wife's grandfather, to break the sad news. Calpurnia's extreme youth and lack of education in practical matters of feminine health are tragically brought to the fore. Always the optimist, Pliny is still hopeful and takes consolation in the fact that the miscarriage is proof of his wife's fertility. Pliny wrote another letter on this subject, the next in the collection, to Calpurnia Hispulla, his wife's kindly aunt, in which he asks her to explain the accident to her father ("excusa patri tuo casum") because it is the sort of thing that women are more ready to make allowances for, and thus she could better comfort him ("cui paratior apud feminas venia," *Ep.* 8.11.3). His anxiety over his grandfather-in-law's reaction may account for the paternalistic tone some readers find in this letter. In fact, Pliny never did father any children. Though childless, Calpurnia and he were awarded the *ius trium liberorum* for their service to the state.

C. PLINIUS FABATO PROSOCERO

(1) Quo magis cupis ex nobis pronepotes videre, hoc tristior audies neptem tuam abortum fecisse, dum se praegnantem esse puellariter nescit, ac per hoc quaedam custodienda praegnantibus omittit, facit omittenda. Quem errorem magnis documentis expiavit, in summum periculum adducta.

(2) Igitur, ut necesse est graviter accipias senectutem tuam quasi paratis posteris destitutam, sic debes agere dis gratias, quod ita tibi in praesentia pronepotes negaverunt, ut servarent neptem, illos reddituri, quorum nobis spem certiorem haec ipsa quamquam parum prospere explorata fecunditas facit.

(3) Isdem nunc ego te quibus ipsum me hortor moneo confirmo. Neque enim ardentius tu pronepotes quam ego liberos cupio, quibus videor a meo tuoque latere pronum ad honores iter et audita latius nomina et non subitas imagines relicturus. Nascantur modo et hunc nostrum dolorem gaudio mutent. Vale.

Notes to Incertus Auctor, *De Sulpicia Elegiae* 1:

1   **colo**, -ere, -ui, cultum *till, tend, attend, worship, dress, adorn*. **tuis kalendis**: abl. of time when, *the first of March*. This refers to the feast of the Matronalia, a woman's version of the Saturnalia, when women dressed to the nines and sacrificed to Juno. The kalends of every month were sacred to Juno; the kalends of March were also sacred to Mars. During this festival women waited on their servants and received gifts from the men in their lives. **spectatum**: supine (translate with "to" as a purpose construction) with **veni**, imperative of **venio**. **ipse**: gods are traditionally invited to ceremonies in their honor. **sapio** *have sense, be wise*. **ignosco**, -ere, -novi, -notum *forgive, pardon*. Venus and Mars were an item. **violentus**, -a, -um *aggressive, impetuous*; an epithet appropriate to the god of war. **caveto**: future imperative of **caveo**, -ere *beware, take care, watch out* + substantive clause with **ne** *lest, that...not*. **tibi miranti**: dat. of advantage/disadvantage. **turpiter** (adv.) *disgracefully*. **cado**, -ere, cecidi, casum *fall*.

5   **exuro**, -ere, -ussi, -ustum *burn up, consume*. **divus**, -i m. *god*. **accendo**, -ere, -cendi, -censum *kindle, set on fire*. **geminus**, -a, -um *twin*. **lampas**, -adis f. *torch*. **quoquo** (adv.) *whenever*. **vestigium**, -i n. *footstep*. **compono**, -ere, -posui, -positum *arrange, set in order*. **furtim** (adv.) *stealthily*. **subsequor**, -i, -secutus/a sum *attend* (as her footman or maid). **Decor**, -oris m. *Beauty, Charm* (personified). **seu** (**sive**)...**seu** (**sive**) *whether...or*. **solvo**, -ere, -vi, -utum *unbind, loosen*. **crinis**, -is m. *hair*. **fundo**, -ere, fudi, fusum *pour, spread*. **decet** *it becomes* (impersonal verb). **capillus**, -i m. *hair*; **fusis capillis**: abl. of description.

10   **como**, -ere, compsi, comptum *arrange, dress*. **venerandus**, -a, -um *to be admired*. **coma**, -ae f. *hair*; **comptis comis**: abl. of cause. **uro**, -ere, ussi, ustum *burn, set on fire*. **Tyrius**, -a, -um *Tyrian* (designating luxury). **palla**, -ae f. *mantle*; *stole*; a Roman woman's regular cloak, typically worn over her tunic and *stola*. **niveus**, -a, -um *snowy*. **candidus**, -a, -um *shining white*. **vestis**, -is f. *clothes*. **talis**, -e *such as, of such a kind* (used to introduce a simile). **felix**, -icis (adj.) *fruitful, prosperous*. **Vertumnus**, -i m. an Etruscan god, associated by the Romans with the changes of the seasons (because of the resemblance of the name to the Latin verb *vertere*). He was the god of exchange and trade and had a statue near the booksellers' stalls. **ornatus**, -us m. *fine array*. **habeo**, -ere, -ui, -itum *have, wear*. **decenter** (adv.) *becomingly*.

15   **puellarum**: partitive gen. with **sola**. **mollis**, -e *soft*. **carus**, -a, -um *dear*. **vellus**, -eris n. *fleece*. **det**: subjunctive in a relative clause of characteristic; the subject is **Tyros**. **sucus**, -i m. *sap, moisture*. **bis madefacta**: the Greeks had a word for this – *dibapha* (*twice-dipped*) a treatment that resulted in a luxurious deep purple wool. **Tyros**, -i m. *Tyre*, a Phoenician city, famous for its dye; "Tyrian purple" was a color between red and purple. **meto**, -ere, messui, messum *reap, gather*. **oleo**, -ere, olui *smell*. **arvum**, -i n. *farmland*. **cultor**, -oris m. *farmer*. **odoratus** *fragrant*. **dives**, -itis (adj.) *rich*. **Arabs**, -is (adj.) *Arabian*. **seges**, -etis f. *field*. **niger**, -gra, -grum *black*. **ruber**, -bra, -brum *red*. **litus**, -oris n. *coastline*. **gemma**, -ae f. *jewel*.

20   **proximus**, -a, -um *nearest*. **Eous**, -a, -um *of dawn, eastern* (from Eos, *Dawn, goddess of dawn*); **Eois** modifies **aquis** (dat. with **proximus**). **Indus**, -i m. *an Indian*. **hanc**: refers to Sulpicia. **Pieris**, -idis, f. *daughter of Pierus, a Muse*; pl., *the Muses*. **festus**, -a, -um *of holidays, festive*. **canto** (1) *sing of, celebrate in song*. **testudineus**, -a, -um *made of tortoise shell*. **superbus**, -a, -um *proud*. **lyra**, -ae f. *lyre*. **sollemnis**, -e *annual, established, festive, religious*. **sumo**, -ere, sumpsi, sumptum *take up, receive*. **vestro choro**: abl. with **dignior** (comparative of **dignus**).

Incertus Auctor, *De Sulpicia Elegiae* 1

Sulpicia's Garland 1 (found as Tibullus, Book 3.8), of uncertain authorship, is a tribute to Sulpicia the poet, a sort of greeting card to accompany a gift to her on the occasion of the festival of Mars on the Kalends (1st) of March. It is the introduction to a group of six poems called "Sulpicia's Garland." The poem is rich in vocabulary (three words for hair, several for apparel and for fields and farmlands) and in the sensual delights, colors juxtaposed, scents, textures, and finally music. It ranges from the Roman festival to the distant luxurious east (Tyre, Arabia, India) and adds quite a few gods along the way, all of them paying court to Sulpicia. The meter is elegiac couplet.

> Sulpicia est tibi culta tuis, Mars magne, kalendis;
> > spectatum e caelo, si sapis, ipse veni;
> hoc Venus ignoscet; at tu, violente, caveto
> > ne tibi miranti turpiter arma cadant:
> 5 illius ex oculis, cum vult exurere divos,
> > accendit geminas lampadas acer Amor.
> Illam, quidquid agit, quoquo vestigia movit,
> > componit furtim subsequiturque Decor;
> seu soluit crines, fusis decet esse capillis:
> 10 seu compsit, comptis est veneranda comis.
> Urit, seu Tyria voluit procedere palla:
> > urit, seu nivea candida veste venit.
> Talis in aeterno felix Vertumnus Olympo
> > mille habet ornatus, mille decenter habet.
> 15 Sola puellarum digna est cui mollia caris
> > vellera det sucis bis madefacta Tyros,
> possideatque, metit quidquid bene olentibus arvis
> > cultor odoratae dives Arabs segetis,
> et quascumque niger rubro de litore gemmas
> 20 proximus Eois colligit Indus aquis.
> Hanc vos, Pierides, festis cantate kalendis,
> > et testudinea Phoebe superbe lyra.
> Hoc sollemne sacrum multos haec sumet in annos:
> > dignior est vestro nulla puella choro.

Notes to Plautus, *Epidicus* 221-234:

221   **viden**: contracted form of **videsne**. **venefica**, -ae f. *she who poisons*; Periphanes means his son's mistress. We might call her a "witch" who "bewitches" young men.

222   **sed** "but yes." Understand **erat**, *she was*. **vestitus**, -a, -um *clothed*. **auratus**, -a, -um *gilded, bedecked in gold*. **ornatus**, -a, -um *arrayed, adorned*. **ut** (adv.) *how*. **lepide** (adv.) *splendidly*. **concinne** (adv.) *elegantly*. **nove** (adv.) *in the latest style*.

223   **quid** (interrog.) *how?* **indutus**, -a, -um *dressed, garbed*. **regilla inducula**: "royal robe." **mendicula (inducula)** *plain robe*; a **mendicula** was a beggar-woman.

224   **impluviata** "skylight" (robe); the **impluvium** was the skylight in the ceiling of the atrium. The term here may mean the garment had four sides like an impluvium, or perhaps was light or gauzy like the sky (or even "see-through" as one could see through the **impluvium** to the sky). **istaec**: emphatic form of **istae [feminae]**. **faciunt nomina**: "make up names for."

225   **utin fuerit**: "Was she really….?" Periphanes thinks that Epidicus means the prostitute literally was wearing an impluvium. **quid** *why?* **istuc**: emphatic of **istud**.

226   **quasi…multae incedant** + subjunctive, in a present contrary-to-fact condition; in Plautus' time the present subjunctive was used in such conditions. **fundus**, -i m. *estate, piece of property*. Epidicus picks up on Periphanes' misunderstanding and makes a joke: women can dress so expensively that they practically wear their estates or property "on their backs." **exornatus**, -a, -um *adorned, decked out*.

227   **tributus**, -i m. *payment of a tax*. **impero** (1) *demand, require*. **pendi potis** (understand **esse**): "it can be paid."

228   **illis**: abl. of agent, *the prostitutes*. **quibus**: dative; Epidicus uses the metaphor of taxation to refer to the fee that clients pay prostitutes for their services (which is certainly larger than the tax the prostitutes are charged by the state for giving such service).

229   **vestis**, -is f. *clothing, garment*. **quotannis** (adv.) *every year*.

230   **rallus**, -a, -um *thin*. **spissus**, -a, -um *thick*. **linteolum caesicium** *little linen dress, blue in color*.

231   **indusiatam** *a dress with an under-tunic*. **patagiatam** *a dress that has a border*. **caltulus**, -a, -um *golden; marigold*. **crocotulus**, -a, -um *saffron, orange-yellow*.

232   **subparum**, -i n. *an all-linen under-dress*. **subnimium**, -i n. *a gauzy dress*. **rica**, -ae f. *a veil*. **basilicus**, -a, -um *royal*. **exoticus**, -a, -um *foreign*.

233   **cumatilis**, -is, -e *having a "wave" pattern*; *colored like the waves*. The meaning of this term is not clear. Perhaps this term refers to cloth resist-dyed to make such a pattern, or it may refer to a weaving pattern that creates undulations of color. If the term denotes color, then perhaps it indicates a sea-green or deep blue. **plumatilis**, -is, -e *having the appearance of feathers*. This term is also unclear, but it may refer to a weaving pattern that produces a feather-pattern, or to color(s) that perhaps shimmer like feathers or are varicolored like some birds' feathers are. **carinus**, -a, -um *walnut brown*, i.e., a kind of deep reddish brown. **cerinus**, -a, -um *of the color of wax*, i.e., brownish yellow. **gerrae**, -arum f. pl. *trifles*.

234   **adimo**, -ere, -emi, -emptum *take from*. **Laconicus**, -a, -um *Laconian, Spartan*. Epidicus' meaning is unclear. Perhaps the dress was the color of the famed dog breed from Laconia.

T. Maccius Plautus, *Epidicus* 221-234

      Clothes may not make the woman, but in the oldest profession, the flashier the outfits, the better. Plautus' *Epidicus* is named after its main character, the crafty slave who assists his young master in a forbidden love-affair, a typical New Comedy plot. In this selection Epidicus describes to Periphanes, the young man's father, the various types of clothing that prostitutes invest in to attract young men. While scholars disagree on the meanings of some of the terms Epidicus uses (he may be inventing them for fun), it is clear that the Roman fabric industry produced even as early as the 2nd century BCE a variety of weaves and dyes with fashionable names to induce them (or have them persuade their patrons) to buy the very latest and the best. The meter is trochaic octonarii.

<blockquote>

PE: viden veneficam?
EP: sed vestita, aurata, ornata ut lepide, ut concinne, ut nove!
PE: quid erat induta? an regillam induculam an mendiculam?
EP: impluviatam, ut istaec faciunt vestimentis nomina.
225   PE: utin impluvium induta fuerit? EP: quid istuc tam mirabile est?
quasi non fundis exornatae multae incedant per vias.
at tributus cum imperatus est, negant pendi potis:
illis quibus tributus maior penditur, pendi potest.
quid istae quae vesti quotannis nomina inveniunt nova?
230   tunicam rallam, tunicam spissam, linteolum caesicium,
indusiatam, patagiatam, caltulam aut crocotulam,
subparum aut—subnimium, ricam, basilicum aut exoticum,
cumatile aut plumatile, carinum aut cerinum—gerrae maximae!
cani quoque etiam ademptumst nomen. PE: qui? EP: vocant Laconicum.

</blockquote>

Notes to Lucretius, *De Rerum Natura* 4.1278-87:

1278   **divinitus** (adv.) *by divine inspiration*. **interdum** (adv.) *meanwhile, at times*. **Venus**, Veneris f. *Venus*. **sagitta**, -ae f. *arrow*.

1279   **deterior**, -oris (adj.) *less desirable*; **deteriore forma**: abl. of quality or description. **fio**, fieri, factus/a sum (passive of **facio**) *be done, happen* + substantive clause of result with **ut**. **muliercula**, -ae f.: diminutive of **mulier**, perhaps used to diminish her, though sometimes diminutives are affectionate (as if he were anticipating the friendship to come). **ametur**: subjunctive in a substantive clause of result after **fit**.

1280   **facit + ut** (1282): with substantive clause of result; notice the old-fashioned alliteration in this and the previous line. **morigerus**, -a, -um *obliging, winning* (to her husband or partner, something desirable in a woman). **munde**: adv. of **mundus**, -a, -um *clean, neat, dainty, elegant*. **culto** < **colo**, -ere, -ui, cultum *worship, dwell, adorn*.

1282   **facile**: adv. **insuesco**, -ere, -suevi, -suetum *accustom, inure*. **<te>**: the angle brackets mean that this word was added to the text. **dego**, -ere, -i *pass* (time), *live*.

1283   **quod superest** *as for what is next, for the rest, further*; not an expression one expects to find in poetry. **consuetudo**, -inis f. *custom, cohabitation*. **concinno** (1) *bring about*.

1284   **quamvis** *however*, with **leviter**. **leviter** (adv.) *lightly*. **quod** *that which* (subject of **tunditur**). **creber**, -bra, -brum (adj.) *dense, frequent*. **tundo**, -ere, tetudi, tunsum/tusum *beat, pound*. **ictus**, -us m. *blow, stroke*, (the) *beat*. **labasco**, -ere *begin to give way*. **gutta**, -ae f. *drop*. **saxum**, -i n. *rock*. **cadentis** accusative plural. **pertundo**, -ere, -udi, -usum *beat through, perforate*.

Notes to Livy, *Ab Urbe Condita* 4.44 (Paragraph 1):

King Numa is said to have created the Vestals, who were charged with keeping a fire on the state hearth burning, cleansing the shrine of Vesta daily with water from the Egerian spring, and participating in state religious rites. But before the founding of Rome, Rhea Silvia, the mother of Romulus and Remus, was forced by her uncle to become a Vestal so that she could not produce royal heirs. Six priestesses inhabited the Vestal residence, which was built into the side of the Palatine hill and entered from the Forum. They were chosen by the Pontifex Maximus from freeborn children between the ages of 6 and 10 years old for 30 years of service (see Aulus Gellius, World of Childhood.).

1   **virgo vestalis** f. *a virgin maid of Vesta*, the Roman goddess of the hearth. **causam dicere** *defend oneself*. **incestus**, -us m. *unchastity, sexual impurity*. **innoxius**, -a,- um *innocent, harmless* + abl. of separation. **suspicio**, -onis f. *mistrust, suspicion*. **propter** + acc. *on account of*. **cultus**, -us m. *attire, style*. **amoenus**, -a, -um (comparative form) *delightful, attractive*. **ingenium**, -i n. *nature, character*. **liber**, -era, -erum (comparative form) *free, bold*. **parum** (adv.) *too little, scarcely*. **abhorreo**, -ere, -ui *shrink from, be free from*. **amplio** (1) *adjourn for further investigation* (legal); *enlarge, extend*. **deinde** (adv.) *then, next*. **absolvo**, -ere, -ui, -utum *acquit, set free*. **pro** + abl. *on behalf of, for*. **collegium**, -i n. *college*, i.e,. **collegium pontificum** or college of priests. **pontifex maximus**: the pontifex maximus was the head of the College of Priests; as the highest priest in Rome, he was responsible for a number of cults, among them the Vestals, near whose residence he had his office, the Regia. **abstineo**, -ere, -ui, -entum *refrain from* (+ abl. of separation). **iocus**, -i m. *joke, jest*. **colo**, -ere, -ui, cultum *adorn* (translate as middle voice). **sancte** (adv.) *chastely, piously*. **scite** (adv.) *smartly, tastefully*.

T. Lucretius Carus, *De Rerum Natura* 4.1278-87

Even a woman who falls short of the ideal of physical beauty can win the love of her life partner with good grooming and considerate ways. Lucretius (ca. 94-55 BCE) wrote a didactic epic on *The Way Things Are* in six books, bringing atomic physics and Epicurean philosophy to Latin speakers. At the end of Book 4, he departs from a graphic discussion of sex and addresses the subject of love and of living together in harmony. His style is somewhat archaic, incorporating more alliteration and assonance than is usually found in the classical period. The meter is dactylic hexameter.

> Nec divinitus interdum Venerisque sagittis
> deteriore fit ut forma muliercula ametur;
> 1280   nam facit ipsa suis interdum femina factis
> morigerisque modis et munde corpore culto,
> ut facile insuescat secum <te> degere vitam.
> quod superest, consuetudo concinnat amorem;
> nam leviter quamvis quod crebro tunditur ictu,
> 1285   vincitur in longo spatio tamen atque labascit.
> nonne vides etiam guttas in saxa cadentis
> umoris longo in spatio pertundere saxa?

Titus Livius, *Ab Urbe Condita* 4.44

In the year 420 BCE, in the midst of difficult military campaigns and election tensions, Livy devoted two sentences of his history *Ab Urbe Condita* to a prosecution involving one of the Vestal Virgins. Since the purity of the Vestals was linked with the integrity of Rome, Vestals were punished severely for dereliction of duty and given distinctive honors for performing their office well. Vestals were expected to observe decorum and dress simply and modestly. In the following passage, Livy describes a public charge brought against the Vestal Postumia. Unlike other accusations recorded against Vestals (e.g., those against Sextilia, Caparronia, Tuccia, Marcia, Licinia, etc.), this one ends on a rather humorous note. While Postumia was found not guilty of the charge of sexual misconduct, she was told to be more seemly in her words and comportment.

> (1)   Eodem anno Postumia virgo vestalis de incestu causam dixit, crimine innoxia, ab suspicione propter cultum amoeniorem ingeniumque liberius quam virginem decet parum abhorrens. Eam ampliatam, deinde absolutam pro collegii sententia pontifex maximus abstinere iocis colique sancte potius quam scite iussit.

P. Ovidius Naso, *Amores* 1.14.1-5, 13-18

In this light first-century BCE poem, Ovid teases his girl over the loss of her once-beautiful tresses, sacrificed to her vanity or to her desire to please her lover. He chides her that now she will wear the hair of German captives with embarrassment, but closes with the sanguine advice that her hair will grow back, provided she leave it alone. The meter is elegiac couplet.

> Dicebam "medicare tuos desiste capillos!"
>> Tingere quam possis, iam tibi nulla coma est.
>
> At si passa fores, quid erat spatiosius illis?
>> Contigerant imum, qua patet usque, latus.
>
> 5   Quid, quod erant tenues, et quos ornare timeres?
>
> ------------
>
> Adde, quod et dociles et centum flexibus apti
>> Et tibi nullius causa doloris erant.
>
> 15   Non acus abrupit, non vallum pectinis illos.
>> Ornatrix tuto corpore semper erat;
>
> Ante meos saepe est oculos ornata nec umquam
>> Bracchia derepta saucia fecit acu.

Notes to Ovid, *Amores* 1.14 (Lines 1-5, 13-18):

1   **dicebam**: the imperfect for repeated action. **medico** (1) *doctor up, dye.* **desisto**, -ere, -stiti, -stitum *leave off, quit* (+ infinitive). **capillus**, -i m. *hair.* **tingo**, -ere, tinxi, tinctum *dip, color.* **quam**: the antecedent is **coma. tibi**: dat. of possession (**tibi est coma = habes comam**). **coma**, -ae f. *hair.* **passa**: perfect participle of **patior**, -i, passus/a sum *suffer, let alone.* **fores = esses.** **si passa fores, quid erat**: a mixed condition: contrary-to-fact and a question; the changes in moods convey emotion. **spatiosius**: comparative adj. (neuter) of **spatiosus**, -a, -um *ample, full.* **illis**: abl. of comparison ("than"), referring to **capillos. contingo**, -ere, -tigi, -tactum *touch.* **imus**, -a, -um *lowest, the base of* (with **latus**). **qua** with **usque** (adv.) *all the way, as far as.* **pateo**, -ere, -ui *lie open, stretch.* **latus**, -eris n. *side; the waist.* **quid** (transitional adv.) *what of?* **quod** *the fact that.* **tenuis**, -e *fine, thin.* **quos**: refers to **capilli** in a relative clause of characteristic ("of the sort which" + subjunctive **timeres**). **orno** (1) *adorn, embellish.*

13   **quod** *the fact that.* **docilis**, -e *manageable.* **flexus**, -us m. *bend, curling* (of the hair). **aptus**, -a, -um *fitted, suited, conformable.* **dolor**, -oris m. *pain.* **acus**, -us f. *needle, pin, hairpin.* **abrumpo**, -ere, -rupi, -ruptum *break off, tear.* **vallum**, -i n. *wall, rampart, palisade* (or item resembling spiked palisades). **pecten**, -inis m. *comb.* **ornatrix**, -icis f. *hairdresser.* **tuto corpore**: abl. of description; **tutus**, -a, -um *safe, secure.* That is, the hairdresser was safe from her mistress' anger, because the hair was so easy to manage that she never pulled it with the comb. One can only imagine what happened to the poor woman after all the hair fell into the lady's lap (line 54, **antiquos gremio...capillos**). **bracchium**, -i n. *arm.* **saucius**, -a, -um *wounded.*

PART SIX
THE WORLD OF THE STATE

The readings in this unit present six impressive women from different time periods and socio-political levels who variously challenged prevailing feminine stereotypes: Queen Tanaquil, by birth an Etruscan; her daughter-in-law, Queen Tullia Minor; the patrician *mater* Veturia; the noble *matrona* Claudia Quinta; the courtesan Hispala Faecenia; the wealthy plebeian Sempronia; and the imperial *matrona* Agrippina Maior. This world was challenging for all Romans, but particularly for women. Here tensions arising from gender expectations became explosive. While Roman law denied women both a political role in the state and public self-expression, history preserves instances of women violating or circumventing these restrictions and of men accommodating or even rewarding their behavior.

For men, the state was the field in which honor and reputation were earned. With the exception of the six state priestesses, the Vestal Virgins, women could properly earn honor only through the production of children and their assimilation into the state. A woman's honor was earned negatively; she remained outside the public eye, did not seek fame except through the males of her family, and conformed to the dependent role of the stereotypical *matrona*, the mature married woman with children. Elite women had some role in public life in that they shared the status of their fathers, husbands, and sons; they owned property; they held priestly office; they endowed public works; they were patrons of worthy causes; and they set an example to others by their conduct and character. Furthermore, inscriptions in Rome and the provinces testify that even working-class women helped increase the family holdings, held local religious offices, and arranged advantageous marriages for their children.

Roman history documents the cultural schizophrenia that resulted from denying citizen women equal access to the rights, duties, and privileges of their state and relegating them before the law to the category of children. While the initial impulse may have been to protect the more vulnerable sex in a chiefly agricultural and militaristic culture, early Roman law and custom were founded on clear gender bias. Roman law showed little confidence in women's ability to manage themselves or be a credit to their family and state. All free women were subordinate to one of three types of male legal authority: *patria potestas* (paternal), *manus* (marital), or *tutela* (guardianship, a surrogate for parents or husband), described by Gaius in the *Institutes*, a record of laws in force in the second century CE. *Tutela* required that, in the absence of *patria potestas* or *manus* marriage, all freeborn women (Vestals excepted) have a guardian for life to approve their legal transactions. Gaius speculates that the original law, largely irrelevant by the Augustan period, was framed to protect women *propter animi levitatem* ("on account of their lightness of mind"), an opinion he does not share.

Despite prejudicial law and customs, from earliest times Roman women ventured into the public arena alone and in groups when necessary, making contributions to the *res publica* that were considered valuable and even rewarded. Legend celebrates the Sabine Women, the founding mothers of the Roman nation, for intervening with their infants on the battlefield between their husbands and their fathers who sought revenge for their kidnapping. The legendary Cloelia was honored with a statue of herself in toga and on horseback, a tribute considered equal to her "male courage" in leading a hostage escape. Conversely, women found guilty of public criminal behavior were strictly punished by their families, condemned by name, and vilified as *exempla* of reprehensible female tendencies. Tarpeia became a byword for female greed and treason. She admitted an invading army in exchange for what the soldiers bore on their right arms; however, she was rewarded not with their gold bracelets, but by being crushed to death with their shields. This legend became a cautionary tale to men about the perfidy of women and their need of male supervision, and to women about the consequences of autonomy.

Five of the six women in this unit are described by Livy, who brings a first-century CE sensibility to bear on the narratives he reconstructs from documents, tradition, and earlier histories. Tanaquil, responsible for Servius' becoming the sixth king of Rome, and Tullia, responsible for ending his reign, are two faces of the ambitious woman who cannot hold political office herself but wields power through men. Tanaquil arranged the election of her son-in-law Servius as king after the murder of her husband Tarquinius Priscus, and so secured a good leader for Rome and a smooth transition of government. While Livy says nothing about Tanaquil's deception, he paints Tullia, whose lust for power brings about the deaths of her sister, her first husband, and her father, as an *exemplum* of the evil woman who arrogantly forces her will on her private and public worlds.

Veturia, mother of the exiled patrician Coriolanus, who commanded a foreign army against Rome in the fifth century BCE, is presented as the traditional stern *materfamilias*. When the Roman Senate was able neither to raise an army against him nor persuade Coriolanus to retreat, the matrons turned to Veturia. She led them, along with Coriolanus' wife Volumnia and their two sons, to his battle camp to beg him to halt his attack. Invoking her role as her son's first educator and moral instructor, Veturia shamed him into withdrawing. Livy approves the fact that the women were granted public honors, including a memorial temple, for saving the state.

Claudia Quinta's act of piety is briefly mentioned by Livy, who is more concerned with the role of Rome's leaders in introducing the cult of the Magna Mater, who was to bring success in the Second Punic War. Ovid, on the other hand, makes Claudia Quinta's miraculous conveyance of the statue of the Magna Mater from Ostia to Rome the central focus of his story in the *Fasti*, where it becomes the means by which Claudia's shady reputation is cleared by the goddess. The story dramatically illustrates the connection for Romans between female chastity and the good of the state and the importance of public honor for women.

Livy describes Hispala Faecenia as a courtesan who modestly plied her trade to support herself after manumission by her mistress. Fearing for her young patrician lover, at great risk to herself she revealed information that led to the suppression of the second-century BCE Bacchanalian cult widespread in Italy. Her act was publicly rewarded by the Senate with money, lifetime protection, and citizen privileges that wiped the slate clean of her background and occupation.

Beginning with the last century BCE, Rome saw a growth in tolerance for women's public action, perhaps as an outcome of the ongoing civil wars and political instability.

Although conservatives remained quick to condemn women they judged to be "out of control," public monuments and tombstones testify to wider recognition of individual women for their virtue, their accomplishments, and their patronage of worthy causes. A good example is the women's protest in 42 BCE against the passage of a war tax to be levied on those who had lost husbands, fathers, and sons to proscriptions. On their behalf Hortensia, daughter of the orator Hortensius, entered the Forum to argue their case before the Triumvirs. Her speech won the admiration and support of the gathered citizens, which forced the leaders to withdraw the proposal.

In Sempronia, Sallust offers a different, less flattering model of the "new" Roman woman who became visible in the late Republic and flourished during the Empire. Although Sempronia is not a key figure in the Catilinarian conspiracy, she uses her familial status to support those who were. Conceding her beauty and brilliance, Sallust contrasts her with her older kinswoman, Cornelia, a chaste, refined *matrona* who was also learned and talented. Sempronia's abilities and education are shown to have provided her a freedom from oversight that led only to immoral behavior and treason. The perceived inability of families to limit the excesses of their women gave a rationale for Augustus' program of social reform. Ironically, Augustan legislation was aimed at strengthening family values and private morality, but by giving public recognition to women's roles as *matrona* and *materfamilias*, it increased the independence from male oversight of all free women. Augustus' *ius trium liberorum* released women who had borne three children from the rule of *tutela* by making them *sui iuris*, responsible for themselves before the law. Under Augustus' direction the Senate extolled Octavia and Livia, his sister and wife, as ideals of traditional Roman womanhood and voted them honors which were normally reserved for male achievement. At the same time Augustus showed his intolerance for public immorality by exiling his daughter Julia and then his granddaughter for adultery.

Agrippina Maior follows the example of Cloelia and Tanaquil rather than that of her mother-in-law Livia, who boasted that she never entered the Senate or the camps. On campaign with her husband and children in Germany, Agrippina startled everyone with her involvement in military affairs and her courage. A fierce advocate for her husband, Germanicus, and after his death for her sons in imperial succession, she received cold treatment from Tacitus, who was as critical of the excesses spawned by imperial power as of women who ignored gender boundaries. He gave scant praise to Agrippina, despite her status as a model *matrona* and prolific *mater*, proof that the tensions of gender expectation remained strong into the empire. Fully subscribing to ancient Roman values, he exemplifies male hostility to women who display any sort of public presence.

Notes to Gaius, *Institutionum Commentarii Quattuor* (Sections 144-5; 148-150):

144   **parens,** -entis m. *parent, father, mother* (dat. with **permissum est**); here, Gaius is referring only to fathers. **liberi,** -**orum** m. pl. *children* (dat. with **dare**). **potestate**: i.e., **patria potestas,** the legal power of the father over his family. **testamentum,** -i n. *will*; abl. of place or means. **tutor,** -oris m. *legal guardian*; Gaius refers to two kinds of guardian for the two types of guardianship that existed: the **tutor impuberum** and the **tutor mulierum. masculinus,** -a, -um *masculine.* **sexus,** -us m. *sex, gender.* **femininus,** -a, -um *feminine* (supply **sexus**). **impubes,** -eris (adj.) *before puberty*; *youthful, chaste.* The **tutor impuberum** was the guardian of a minor without a father. He administered the minor's estate until the minor reached the age of puberty (twelve for girls, fourteen for boys). **pubes,** -eris (adj.) *post puberty*; *adult.* The **tutor mulierum** was the guardian of an adult woman who had neither a **paterfamilias** nor a **manus** marriage. The tutor's authorization was needed for particular legal and financial actions. **nubo,** -ere, nupsi, nuptum *be married* (used for women); the subjunctive is used here in a **cum** circumstantial clause, meaning *when.* **veteres,** veterum m. pl. *(our) forefathers.* **perfectae aetatis** *of mature age.* **levitas,** -atis f. *shallowness, frivolity.* **tutela,** -ae f. *legal guardianship* (**tutela mulierum**).

145   **quis = aliquis** after **si, nisi, num, ne. pubertas,** -atis f. *puberty*; *sexual maturity.* **pervenio,** -ire, -veni, -ventum *reach, come to.* **desino,** -ere, -sivi, -situm *stop.* **nihilominus** *none the less.* **tantum** (adv.) *only.* **lege Iulia et Papia Poppaea**: passed in 18 BCE, this law regulated Roman marriages, stating what marriages between classes and individuals were valid, and encouraging, through penalties, men and women (including widows) to marry and have children. **iure [trium] liberorum**: *the right of three children*; this right was granted by Augustus to women who had given birth to three children, releasing them from the **tutela mulierum. excipio,** -ere, -cepi, -ceptum *remove, exempt, make exception of*; ablative absolute construction. **vestalis,** -is (adj.) *Vestal,* the virgin priestesses of Vesta, who were exempt from **tutela. sacerdotium,** -i n. *priesthood.* **lege XII tabularum**: *the law of the Twelve Tables.* **caveo,** -ere, cavi, cautum *decree, stipulate, guarantee.*

148   **in manu**: Gaius explains that **manus** marriage, in which the bride passes from her father's **potestas** to her husband's authority, can take place in one of three ways: by **usus** (living continuously with him), by **confarreatio** (a special ceremony involving sacrifice of a meal cake to Jupiter Farreus) or by **coemptio** (by a fictional "sale"). By Augustan times **manus** marriage had become rare, since it placed women under complete legal control of husbands who might not have their best interests at heart (see World of Marriage). **proinde ac** *just as.* **nurus,** -us f. *daughter-in-law.* **neptis,** -is f. *grand-daughter.*

149   **Lucium Titium**: Lucius Titius is the Roman equivalent of "John Doe."

150   **persona,** -ae f. *person.* **recipio,** -ere, -cepi, -ceptum *admit, accept, guarantee*; **optio** is the subject. **optio,** -onis f. *choice.* **licet** *it is lawful.* **ei**: i.e., the wife. **Titiae**: Titia is the Roman equivalent of "Jane Doe." **casus,** -us m. *case, situation.* **vel...vel** *either...or.* **res,** rei f. *aspect* (of the woman's life).

Gaius, *Institutionum Commentarii Quattuor* 1.144-145, 148-150

While there are references to laws under the monarchy, the Twelve Tables are Rome's earliest extant law, published in 451 BCE by a special commission in response to plebeian demands. The original document, inscribed on bronze tablets and displayed in the Forum, was burned during the Gallic invasion of Rome, but a later partial text of short imperative statements in archaic and later Latin survives. In the following centuries the Senate passed new laws which superceded the Twelve Tables, but they were never abolished. Since Roman legal procedure depended upon precedents, juridical wisdom was acquired through study and consultation with legal scholars and ex-magistrates. By 160 CE, the laws and precedents had become so numerous and contradictory that a jurist, known only by the name Gaius, compiled and published in the *Institutes* those laws that were still in force. While our most important source on Roman law is the sixth-century CE *Digest* of Emperor Justinian in fifty volumes, the *Institutes* is the most complete legal work from the classical period and our only authority for *tutela mulierum*. This provision bound women (except Vestal Virgins) not under *patria potestas* or *manus* to the legal guardianship/control of a close male relative or a state-appointed guardian. Augustan legislation removed freeborn women who had borne three children from *tutela mulierum*, and by the time of Gaius this type of guardianship had clearly lost much of its force.

144 Permissum est itaque parentibus liberis, quos in potestate sua habent, testamento tutores dare, masculini quidem sexus impuberibus, feminini vero impuberibus puberibusque, vel cum nuptae sint. Veteres enim voluerunt feminas, etiamsi perfectae aetatis sint, propter animi levitatem in tutela esse.

145 Itaque si quis filio filiaeque testamento tutorem dederit et ambo ad pubertatem pervenerint, filius quidem desinit habere tutorem, filia vero nihilominus in tutela permanet: tantum enim ex lege Iulia et Papia Poppaea iure liberorum a tutela liberantur feminae. Loquimur autem exceptis virginibus Vestalibus, quas etiam veteres in honorem sacerdotii liberas esse voluerunt: itaque etiam lege XII tabularum cautum est.

148 Uxori, quae in manu est, proinde ac filiae, item nurui, quae in filii manu est, proinde ac nepti tutor dari potest.

149 Rectissime autem tutor sic dari potest: **Lucium Titium liberis meis tutorem do** vel **uxori meae tutorem do.**

150 In persona tamen uxoris, quae in manu est, recepta est etiam tutoris optio, id est ut liceat ei permittere, quem velit ipsa, tutorem sibi optare, hoc modo: **Titiae uxori meae tutoris optionem do.** Quo casu licet uxori tutorem optare vel in omnes res vel in unam forte aut duas.

Notes to Livy, *Ab Urbe Condita* 1 (Chapters 39.1-3, 41.1-5):

39.1   **regia**, -ae f. *palace*. **visus**, -us m. *sight*; abl. of respect with **mirabile**. **eventus**, -us m. *outcome*. **dormio**, -ire, dormivi, -itum *sleep*. **Servius Tullius**: sixth King of Rome. **ardeo**, -ere, arsi, arsum *be on fire, shine*. **ferunt** *they report*. **conspectus**, -us m. *sight*.

2   **plurimo...clamore...orto**: abl. of means after **excitos**. **ad** + accusative: *in regard to*; dependent on **orto**. **excio**, -ire, -ivi -itus *rouse, summon*; supply **esse** in indirect statement; the subject is **reges**. **cum** + subjunctive in a temporal construction: *when*. **familiaris**, -is m. *domestic servant; friend*. **restinguo**, -ere, restinxi, restinctum *extinguish*; **ad** + gerund = purpose construction. **retineo**, -ere, retinui, retentum *hold back, restrain*; supply **eum** and **esse** in indirect statement. **sedo** (1) *calm*; abl. absolute with **tumultu**. **veto**, -are, vetui, vetitum *forbid, prohibit*; **eam**: subject of the infinitive in indirect statement. **donec** + subjunctive: *until* **sua sponte** *of its own accord, unaided*. **expergiscor**, -gisci, experrectus/a sum *wake up*.

3   **abeo**, -ire, -ivi, -itum *go away*; **flammam**: subject of the infinitive in indirect statement. **abduco**, -ere, -duxi, -ductum *lead away*. **secretum**, -i n. *privacy, remote place*. **viden = vides + -ne**. **humilis**, -e *lowly, poor*. **cultus**, -us m. *care, training*. **educo** (1) *bring up, rear*. **licet** + infinitive: *one can, one may*. **hunc**: understand **puerum** (Servius), subject of **futurum [esse]** in indirect statement. **lumen**, -inis n. *light, glory*. **quidam**, quaedam, quoddam *a certain*. **dubius**, -a, -um *uncertain, precarious*. **praesidium**, -i n. *protection, support*. **adfligo**, -ere, -flixi, -flictum *crush, throw down*; **adflictae**: in apposition to **regiae**. **proinde** (adv.) *therefore, just as*. **materia**, -ae f. *matter, occasion*. **ingens**, -entis *huge*. **publice** (adv.) *for the State*. **privatim** (adv.) *at home*. **indulgentia**, -ae f. *indulgence, gentleness*. **nutrio**, -ire, -ivi, -itum *rear*; supply **eum**.

41.1   **claudo**, -ere, clausi, clausum *shut*. **arbiter**, arbitri m. *witness, judge*. **eicio**, -ere, eieci, eiectus *drive out, put out*. **simul...simul** *both...and*. **quae**: subject of **sunt**. **curando vulneri**: gerundive in the dative following **opus**, "for curing the wound." **opus** (indecl.) *needful, necessary*; predicate adjective with thing needed in the nominative. **tamquam**: conj. with the subjunctive, *as if*. **subsum**, -esse *be at hand*. **sedulo** (adv.) *busily, purposely*. **comparo** (1) *collect, gather*; supply **ea**, object and antecedant of **quae**. **destituo**, -ere, -stitui, -stitutum *forsake*. **molior**, moliri, molitus/a sum *build, work at*.

2   **propere** (adv.) *hastily*. **accio**, -ire, -ivi, -itum *summon*. **cum**: *when*, with temporal subjunctive. **exsanguis**, -e *lifeless*. **inultus**, -a, -um *unavenged*. **socer**, soceri m. *father-in-law*. **socrus**, -us f. *mother-in-law*. **ludibrium**, -i n. *mockery, joke*.

41.3   **facinus**, -oris n. *crime, deed*. **fecere = fecerunt**. **erigo**, -ere, erexi, erectum *raise up, encourage*. **duces**: in apposition to **deos**. **clarus**, -a, -um *famous*; predicate adjective with **caput**. **fore**: future infinitive. **quondam** (adv.) *formerly, at one time*. **circumfundo**, -ere, -fudi, -fusi *surround*; abl. of means with **portenderunt**. **portendo**, -ere, -tendi, -tentum *predict*. **excito** (1) *provoke*. **peregrinus**, -i m. *foreigner*; in apposition to **nos**. **reputo** (1) *reflect*. **subitus**, -a, -um *sudden*. **torpeo**, -ere *be numb, stupified*. **at** (conj.) *still, but*.

4   **impetus**, -us m. *press, attack, charge*. **sustineo**, -ere, -tinui, -tentum *control, check*. **aedes**, aedium f. pl. *house*. **fenestra**, -ae f. *window*. **Nova via**: this street began at the Porta Mugionia and circled the Palatine on the north. **ad Iovis**: understand **templum**.

5   **sopio**, -ire, -ivi, -itum *put to sleep, stun*. **ictus**, -us m. *blow*. **alte** (adv.) *deeply*. **se redeo**, -ire, -ivi, -itum *return to oneself*. **abstergeo**, -ere, abstersi, -sum *wipe away*. **salubris**, -e *healthy*. **propediem** (adv.) *soon*. **confido**, -ere, confisus/a sum *trust, be confident*. **iubere**: understand **Tanaquil dixit regem**. **dicto audiens** + dat. *obey*. **obeo**, -ire, -ivi, -itum *perform, meet, go to, die*. **munia**, -orum n. pl. *official duties*.

Titus Livius, *Ab Urbe Condita*, Book 1: 39.1-3, 41.1-5: Tanaquil

Livy describes Rome's first Etruscan queen, Tanaquil, as strong, resourceful, and proud. An aristocrat of Tarquinia, she married the half-Etruscan son of Damaratus, a refugee from Corinth, but realized that, despite her husband's talent for leadership, as the son of an immigrant he had little chance of attaining high position in Tarquinia. She urged him to emigrate to Rome, a city of growing power without a native aristocracy, where he became Lucius Tarquinius Priscus and, fulfilling an omen she interpreted on their arrival, the fifth King of Rome (616-579 BCE). Tanaquil influenced the course of Roman history two more times: responding to another omen, she arranged for the talented young Servius Tullius to be educated and married to her daughter, and, after the fatal attack on her husband, she addressed the anxious Romans on Servius' behalf.

39 (1) Eo tempore in regia prodigium visu eventuque mirabile fuit. Puero dormienti, cui Servio Tullio fuit nomen, caput arsisse ferunt multorum in conspectu; (2) plurimo igitur clamore inde ad tantae rei miraculum orto excitos reges, et cum quidam familiarium aquam ad restinguendum ferret, ab regina retentum, sedatoque eam tumultu moveri vetuisse puerum donec sua sponte experrectus esset; (3) mox cum somno et flammam abisse. Tum abducto in secretum viro Tanaquil "Viden tu puerum hunc" inquit, "quem tam humili cultu educamus? Scire licet hunc lumen quondam rebus nostris dubiis futurum praesidiumque regiae adflictae; proinde materiam ingentis publice priuatimque decoris omni indulgentia nostra nutriamus."

41 (1) Tarquinium moribundum cum qui circa erant excepissent, illos fugientes lictores comprehendunt. Clamor inde concursusque populi, mirantium quid rei esset. Tanaquil inter tumultum claudi regiam iubet, arbitros eiecit. Simul quae curando volneri opus sunt, tamquam spes subesset, sedulo comparat, simul si destituat spes, alia praesidia molitur. (2) Seruio propere accito cum paene exsanguem virum ostendisset, dextram tenens orat ne inultam mortem soceri, ne socrum inimicis ludibrio esse sinat.

41 (3) "Tuum est" inquit, "Serui, si vir es, regnum, non eorum qui alienis manibus pessimum facinus fecere. Erige te deosque duces sequere qui clarum hoc fore caput divino quondam circumfuso igni portenderunt. Nunc te illa caelestis excitet flamma; nunc expergiscere vere. Et nos peregrini regnauimus; qui sis, non unde natus sis reputa. Si tua re subita consilia torpent, at tu mea consilia sequere." (4) Cum clamor impetusque multitudinis vix sustineri posset, ex superiore parte aedium per fenestras in Nouam viam versas—habitabat enim rex ad Iovis Statoris—populum Tanaquil adloquitur. (5) Iubet bono animo esse; sopitum fuisse regem subito ictu; ferrum haud alte in corpus descendisse; iam ad se redisse; inspectum volnus absterso cruore; omnia salubria esse; confidere propediem ipsum eos visuros; interim Ser. Tullio iubere populum dicto audientem esse; eum iura redditurum obiturumque alia regis munia esse.

Notes to Livy, *Ab Urbe Condita* 1 (Chapters 47-48.3-7):

Servius' kingship was engineered by Tanaquil, wife of Rome's fifth king, Tarquinius Priscus, who was murdered by the sons of Rome's fourth king. To secure his throne, Servius married his two daughters to Tarquin's two sons. Tullia Minor, having killed her husband and sister to marry her brother-in-law, grows restless at her father's long life.

47.1   **in dies**: *daily*. **infestior**: comparative of **infestus** *unsafe, dangerous*. **spectare...pati**: historical infinitives. **interdiu** *by day*. **ne** + subjunctive: purpose clause. **gratuita** *gratuitous, for nothing*; a predicate adjective.

2   **defuisse...defuisse** + dat.; indirect statement with **dixit** understood. **serviret** < **servio**, -ire, -ivi, -itum *be a slave*.

3   **appello**: supply **te** as object. **sin minus** *if not*. **eo peius...quod** *for the worse...that*. **istic** (adv.) *in this, on this occasion*. **quin** *why not?* **accingeris**: translate as reflexive.

4   **necesse est** + dat. (**tibi...patri tuo**). **ab**: understand **veniente**. **te...regem**: the word order emphasizes Tullia's claim.

5   **parum...animi**: partitive genitive. **facesse**: present active imperative < **facesso, -ere, -ivi, -itum** *go away, retire*. **devolvere**: present imperative of **devolvo**, -ere, -volui, -volutum, passive acting as a middle voice – *fall headlong, tumble down*. **stirpem**: from **stirps**, -is f. *family, stock*. **similior**: comparative of **similis** + dat.

6   **increpando**: gerund, abl. of means, from **increpo** (1) *rebuke*. **instigat** < **instigo** (1) *goad*. **si**: see **ipsa** below (Tullia). **cum Tanaquil potuisset**: "while Tanaquil had been able." **moliri** < **molior**, -iri, -itus/a sum *strive for*. **tantum...ut**: introduces a result clause. **si...nullum momentum...faceret**: "if she were exerting no influence." **in dando...regno**: gerundive, "in giving and removing power."

48. 3   **iam et**: *now even*. **cogente...audere**: **cogo** is followed by the acc. (understand **eum**) and infinitive. **multo...validior**: adv. + comparative, "far more powerful." **medium**: agrees with the noun it modifies: "Servius by the waist." **adripio**, -ere, -ripui, -reptum *seize*. **effero**, -ferre, -tuli, -latum *carry out*. **in inferiorem partem per gradus**: "onto the lower level," "down the steps." **ad cogendum senatum**: purpose construction with the gerundive.

4   **apparitor**, -oris m. *attendant*; despite the word order, **fit fuga** refers to them, not to **regis**. **ipse...fugientem...interficitur**: all refer to Servius. **exsanguis**, -inis (adj.) *pale, feeble*. **comitatus**, -us m. *escort, retinue*. **se**: reflexive with **recipio** *return*.

5   **creditur**: *it is believed*; followed by indirect statement **factum [esse]**. **abhorreo**, -ere, -horrui *shrink from*; subject is Tullia. **carpentum**, -i n. *a two-wheeled coach*. **invehor**, -vehi, -vectus/a sum *ride, drive*; refers to Tullia. **revereor**, -eri, -itus/a sum *stand in awe of*. Tullia's entrance in the Forum is shocking, especially in a carriage, a Vestal privilege.

6   **facesso**, -ere, -ivi, -itum (intransitive) *retire, go away*. **summum...Esquiliarum**: on Cyprian street, former site of Diana's temple, to the Urbian incline, up the Esquiline hill. **flectenti** < **flecto, -ere**, flexi, flectum *bend, turn*, refers to Tullia; the dative follows **restitit** < **resisto**, -ere, -stiti *resist, stop short*. Her reaction is different from her driver's. **trucido** (1) *kill cruelly*.

7   **traditur**: impersonal use; **trado**, -ere, tradidi, traditum *is told*. **monumento**: dat. of purpose; **monumentum**, -i n. *reminder, memorial*. **sceleratus**, -a, -um *accursed, infamous*. **quo** (adv.) *where*. **Furia**, -ae f. *Fury* (avenging spirit, especially of spilled kin blood); *rage*. **Tullia... egisse...tulisse**: indirect statement after the impersonal **fertur**. **contamino** (1) *defile, pollute*. **quibus iratis**: abl. absolute, refering to the Penates. **exitus**: m. pl., subject of **sequerentur**. **similes**: modifies **exitus**, followed by **malo principio** in the dative. **propediem** (adv.) *soon*.

Titus Livius, *Ab Urbe Condita* 1.47-48: Tullia Minor

The story of Tullia, daughter-in-law of Tanaquil, younger daughter of Rome's sixth king, Servius Tullius (578-535 BCE), wife of Tarquinius Superbus, last king of Rome (534-510 BCE), is one of envy, greed and blood lust. Livy terms her *ferox* for her grisly deeds against husband, sister, and father, and censures her instigation to violence. Her familial and civic *impietas* joined to masculine traits of ambition, cruelty and arrogance create a chilling picture of viciousness.

47 (1) Tum vero in dies infestior Tulli senectus, infestius coepit regnum esse; iam enim ab scelere ad aliud spectare mulier scelus. Nec nocte nec interdiu virum conquiescere pati, ne gratuita praeterita parricidia essent: (2) non sibi defuisse cui nupta diceretur, nec cum quo tacita serviret; defuisse qui se regno dignum putaret, qui meminisset se esse Prisci Tarquini filium, qui habere quam sperare regnum mallet. (3) "Si tu is es cui nuptam esse me arbitror, et virum et regem appello; sin minus, eo nunc peius mutata res est quod istic cum ignauia est scelus. Quin accingeris? (4) Non tibi ab Corintho nec ab Tarquiniis, ut patri tuo, peregrina regna moliri necesse est: di te penates patriique et patris imago et domus regia et in domo regale solium et nomen Tarquinium creat vocatque regem. (5) Aut si ad haec parum est animi, quid frustraris civitatem? quid te ut regium iuvenem conspici sinis? Facesse hinc Tarquinios aut Corinthum; devolvere retro ad stirpem, fratri similior quam patri." (6) His aliisque increpando iuvenem instigat, nec conquiescere ipsa potest si, cum Tanaquil, peregrina mulier, tantum moliri potuisset animo ut duo continua regna viro ac deinceps genero dedisset, ipsa regio semine orta nullum momentum in dando adimendoque regno faceret.

48 (3) Tum Tarquinius necessitate iam et ipsa cogente ultima audere, multo et aetate et viribus validior, medium arripit Servium elatumque e curia in inferiorem partem per gradus deiecit; inde ad cogendum senatum in curiam rediit. (4) Fit fuga regis apparitorum atque comitum; ipse prope exsanguis cum sine regio comitatu domum se reciperet ab iis qui missi ab Tarquinio fugientem consecuti erant interficitur. (5) Creditur, quia non abhorret a cetero scelere, admonitu Tulliae id factum. Carpento certe, id quod satis constat, in forum inuecta nec reuerita coetum virorum evocavit virum e curia regemque prima appellavit. (6) A quo facessere iussa ex tanto tumultu cum se domum reciperet pervenissetque ad summum Cyprium vicum, ubi Dianium nuper fuit, flectenti carpentum dextra in Urbium clivum ut in collem Esquiliarum eveheretur, restitit pavidus atque inhibuit frenos is qui iumenta agebat iacentemque dominae Servium trucidatum ostendit. (7) Foedum inhumanumque inde traditur scelus monumentoque locus est—Sceleratum vicum vocant—quo amens, agitantibus furiis sororis ac viri, Tullia per patris corpus carpentum egisse fertur, partemque sanguinis ac caedis paternae cruento vehiculo, contaminata ipsa respersaque, tulisse ad penates suos virique sui, quibus iratis malo regni principio similes propediem exitus sequerentur.

Notes to Livy, *Ab Urbe Condita* 39.9 (Sections 5-7); 10 (Sections 5-9):

9.5   **scortum**, -i n. *prostitute* (literally, *a skin, hide*). **libertina**, -ae f. *freedwoman*. **dignus**, -a, -um + abl. *worthy of*. **quaestus**, -us m. *occupation*. **ancillula**, -ae f. *a little serving-maid* (diminutive). **adsuesco**, -ere, adsuevi, adsuetum *train, accustom*. **manumitto**, -mittere, -misi, -missum *emancipate, free*. **genus**, -eris n. *way, respect* (i.e., *kind of occupation*). **tueor**, tueri, tuitus or tutus/a sum + **se** *keep oneself*.

6   **huic** = Hispala Faecenia. **consuetudo**, -dinis f. *familiarity, love affair*. **iuxta** (prep. + acc.) *close to*. **vicinitas**, -atis f. *neighborhood*. **res**, rei f. *property, wealth*. **damnosus**, -a, -um (+ gen.) *harmful to*. **ultro** (adv.) *unasked, voluntarily* (i.e., she pursued Aebutius). **appeto**, -ere, -petivi, -petitum *desire, approach*. **maligne** (adv.) *grudgingly*. **praebeo**, -ere, -ui, -itum *supply, offer*; abl. absolute construction. **sui**, suorum m. pl. *one's own* (i.e., family, friends). **meretricula**, -ae f. *a public prostitute, courtesan* <**meretrix, -icis f.** "she who earns her money". **munificentia**, -ae f. *generosity*; ablative case. **sustineo**, -ere, -tinui, -tentum *support, maintain*. **quin** (adv.) *rather, indeed*. **eo**: adverb followed by **ut**, *to the point...that*.

7   **procedo**, -ere, -cessi, -cessum *go on, continue, advance*. **patronus**, -i m. *protector, patron*. **in...manu**: a legal term describing the power (**manus**) over a wife transferred from father to husband upon marriage. **tutor**, -oris m. *guardian*; one exercising a legal protectorate (see Gaius on **tutela**). Having no family, Hispala got a state-appointed **tutor** to assist her preparation of her will. **tribunus**, -i m. *tribune*; he defended plebeian rights against encroachment by patricians. **praetor**, -oris m. *praetor*; a magistrate charged with the administration of justice. **peto**, -ere, petivi, petitum *seek for, sue for*. **cum** + subjunctive *when*. **testamentum**, -i n. *will, testament*. **instituo**, -ere, -tui, -tutum *establish*. **heres**, -edis m/f. *heir*.

10.5   **ancilla**, -ae f. *handmaid or female slave*; in apposition to **se** (speaking of herself). **comes**, -ites m/f. *companion*. **sacrarium**, -i n. *shrine, chapel*. **intro** (1) *enter*; **intrasse** is a contracted form of **intravisse** (this and the following infinitives depend on **ait**). **accedo**, -ere, -cessi, -cessum *go to, approach*.

6   **scire**: dependent on **ait**; the subject is Hispala. **corruptela**, -ae f. *corruption, bribery*. **eam**: refers to **sacrarium** but is attracted to the gender and case of **officinam**. **officina**, -ae f. *factory; workshop*. **biennium**, -i n. *two-year period*. **consto** (1) impersonal use: *be well-known, established*. **nemo**, -inis m/f. *no one*. **initio** (1) *initiate*.

7   **ut**: *as soon as*; subjunctive because the clause is within a reported statement. **introduco**, -ducere, -duxi, -ductum *bring in, introduce*. **velut** (adv.) *just as if*. **trado**, -ere, tradidi, traditum *hand over, betray*. **sacerdos**, -dotis m/f. *priest, priestess*. **deduco**, -ducere, -duxi, -ductum *lead away*; the subject is **sacerdotes**. **circumsono** (1) *resound on all sides*. **ululatus**, -us m. *wailing, shrieking*. **cantus**, -us m. *singing, playing*. **symphonia**, -ae f. *orchestra*. **cymbalum**, -i n. *cymbal*. **tympanum**, -i n. *drum*. **pulsus**, -us m. *beat*. **ne** + subjunctive (**possit**) in a negative purpose construction. **quirito** (1) *cry out, wail*. **cum**: con. + causal subjunctive (**inferatur**) *seeing that, since*. **stuprum**, -i n. *lewdness, debauchery;* with **inferatur** = *rape*. **infero**, -ferre, -tuli, illatum *introduce, put on*. **exaudio**, -audire, -audivi, -auditum *listen to, hear clearly*.

8   **oro** (1) *pray, beg*; historical infinitive (Hispala is subject). **obsecro** (1) **ut** + subjunctive (**discuteret**) *implore*. **discutio**, -ere, -cussi, -cussum *smash, dispel, scatter*; the subject is Aebutius. **eo** (adv.) *there*. **praecipito** (1) + **se** *rush headlong, fall*. **infandus**, -a, -um *unspeakable*. **patior**, pati, passus/a sum *suffer* (with **essent**). **deinde** (adv.) *then*.

9   **dimitto**, -ere, -misi, -missum *send away, let go*. **sacrum**, -i n. *rite, worship*. **tempero** (1) *abstain, forbear*.

Titus Livius, *Ab Urbe Condita* 39 (excerpts): Hispala Faecenia

Women are critical to Livy's dramatic story of the suppression of the second-century BCE "Bacchanalian Conspiracies," but they remain in the background, supporting male actors. Whether history or legend, Livy's narrative illustrates the interplay of forces – public and private, privileged and voiceless, civic and social – which were often polarized and gendered in Roman life. The Bacchic cult (Livy calls it a "woman's religion" 13.8) came from the east and spread quickly through Italy. Its rites were secret (night-time celebrations involving both sexes and the use of wine), and its rumored practices were criminal (murders, forgeries, and stolen wills). Hispala Faecenia, whom Livy calls "scortum nobile libertina," is the reluctant hero who exposes this threat to the state out of concern for her lover, Publius Aebutius. Four other women are involved: Duronia, the vicious mother of Aebutius, who jeopardizes his life for the sake of her second husband; Aebutia, the paternal aunt of Aebutius, "proba et antiqui moris femina" (11.5); Sulpicia, the consul's mother-in-law, "nobilis et gravis femina" (12.2); Paculla Annia, the Campanian priestess who turned the Bacchic rites into orgiastic celebrations with young male initiates. The cult was ruthlessly suppressed through state and family punishments and decrees enacted in 186 BCE by a shocked Senate and Assembly (a bronze copy of the *Senatus Consultum de Bacchanalibus* is the oldest surviving decree). Aebutius and Hispala were voted generous public honors.

9   (5) Scortum nobile libertina Hispala Faecenia, non digna quaestu, cui ancillula adsuerat, etiam postquam manumissa erat, eodem se genere tuebatur. (6) huic consuetudo iuxta vicinitatem cum Aebutio fuit, minime adulescentis aut rei aut famae damnosa: ultro enim amatus appetitusque erat, et maligne omnia praebentibus suis meretriculae munificentia sustinebatur. (7) quin eo processerat consuetudine capta, ut post patroni mortem, quia in nullius manu erat, tutore ab tribunis et praetore petito, cum testamentum faceret, unum Aebutium institueret heredem.

10   (5) Ancillam se ait dominae comitem id sacrarium intrasse, liberam numquam eo accessisse. (6) scire corruptelarum omnis generis eam officinam esse; et iam biennio constare neminem initiatum ibi maiorem annis viginti. (7) ut quisque introductus sit, velut victimam tradi sacerdotibus. eos deducere in locum, qui circumsonet ululatibus cantuque symphoniae et cymbalorum et tympanorum pulsu, ne vox quiritantis, cum per uim stuprum inferatur, exaudiri possit. (8) orare inde atque obsecrare, ut eam rem quocumque modo discuteret nec se eo praecipitaret, ubi omnia infanda patienda primum, deinde facienda essent. (9) neque ante dimisit eum, quam fidem dedit adulescens ab his sacris se temperaturum.

Notes to Livy, *Ab Urbe Condita* 2.40:

40.1   **ad** + acc. *to, at.* **Gnaeus Marcius Coriolanus**: an aristocrat whose successful campaign against the Volscians earned him the name Coriolanus, after their chief town. Charged with tyrannical conduct and criticized for opposition to grain distribution to the starving plebs during a period of famine, he angrily withdrew from Rome and joined the Volscians in a seige of Rome. **frequens**, -entis *crowded, in large numbers.* **coeo**, -ire, -ivi, -itum *assemble, meet.* **consilium**, -i n. *consultation, counsel.* **an** (conj.) *or.* **parum** (adv.) *too little.* **invenio**, -ire, -veni, -ventum *find out, discover.*

2   **pervinco**, -vincere, -vici, -victum *prevail*; **pervicere = pervicerunt**. **ut** + subjunctive (**irent et...defenderent**): introduces a purpose construction following **pervinco**; *seeing that.* **Marcius**: Coriolanus. **quoniam**: conj. with subjunctives (**possent...**), *since.* **prex**, precis f. *entreaty, prayer.*

3   **ventum est...nuntiatum est**: impersonal usage. **adsum**, -esse, -fui *be present, come.* **agmen**, -minis n. *procession, battle line.* **ut qui** + subjunctive (**motus esset**): *seeing that he.* **maiestas**, -atis f. *dignity*; abl. of means. **legatus**, -i m. *an envoy, deputy, or army commander.* **sacerdos**, -dotis m. *priest.* **offundo**, -ere, -fudi, -fusum + dat. *pour out, fill.* **religio**, -onis f. *sanctity, reverence, awe*; with **tanta**, abl. of means. **obstinatus**, -a, -um *firm, resolute.* **adversus** (prep. + acc.) *towards, against.*

4   **dein = deinde** (adv.) *then, next.* **familiaris**, -is m. *friend, servant.* **insignis**, -e *distinguished.* **maestitia**, -ae f. *sadness*; abl. with **insignis**. **nurus**, -us f. *daughter-in-law.* **nepos**, -otis m. *grandson.* **frustror** (1, deponent) *deceive, trick.* **coniunx**, -iugis m/f. *husband, wife.*

5   **prope** (adv.) + **ut**: *almost as.* **amens**, -entis *mad, crazy*; used as a substantive, *madman.* **consterno** (1) *startle, confuse.* **sedes**, -is f. *seat, chair.* **cum** + subjunctive: a circumstantial clause, *when.* **obvius**, -a, -um *encountering, against.* **complexus**, -us m. *embrace.* **verto**, -ere, verti, versum *change, turn.* **sine** (+ subjunctive) **sciam**: "allow me to know"; supply **utrum** before **ad** and before **captiva**.

6   **in hoc**: translate *for this.* **senecta**, -ae f. *old age.* **traho**, -ere, traxi, tractum *draw, drag.* **materne = mater + -ne**. **exsul**, exsulis m. *exile.* **populor** (1, depon.) *lay waste, destroy.* **gigno**, -ere, genui, genitum *give birth to, bear.* **alo**, alere, alui, altum *nourish.*

7   **quamvis** (conj.) *although.* **infestus**, -a, -um *hostile, dangerous.* **minax**, minacis (adj.) *threatening.* **ingredior**, -i, -gressus/a sum *enter.* **cum** + indicative: temporal construction, *when.* **succurro**, -ere, -curri, -cursum *occur (to you), come into (your) mind.* **Penates**, -ium m. pl. *guardians of the family pantry*; with Vesta and the Lares, these early deities were the chief private cult of every Roman house and were worshiped at an altar in the atrium.

8   **pario**, -ere, peperi, partum *bear, produce*; contrary-to-fact condition. **oppugno** (1) *attack, assault.* **diu** (adv.) *a long time.* **turpis**, -e *disgraceful, ugly.* **usquam** (adv.) *in any way.* **nec ut**: translate "and although."

9   **videris**: perfect subjunctive as imperative: *See about these!* **pergo**, -ere, perrexi, rectum *proceed, continue, go on.* **immaturus**, -a, -um *untimely.* **servitus**, -tutis f. *slavery, service.* **amplector**, -cti, -plexus/a *embrace*; the subject is **uxor ac liberi**. **fletus**, -us m. *weeping.* **orior**, -iri, ortus/a sum *rise, spring up.* **comploratio**, -onis f. *loud lamentation.* **frango**, -ere, fregi, fractum *break down, shatter*; **fregere = fregerunt**, the subjects of which are **uxor, liberi, fletus, comploratio**.

10   **dimitto**, -ere, -misi, -missum *send away.*

11   **invideo**, -ere, -vidi, -visum + dat. *begrudge, envy.* **vivebatur**: impersonal. **adeo** (adv.) *for in fact, to such an extent.* **obtrectatio**, -onis f. *disparagement.* **monumentum**, -i n. *monument*; dat. of purpose. **quoque** *also, too.* Try the following word order: **quoque templum, quod monumento esset, Fortunae muliebri aedificatum [est]**. **aedifico** (1) *build, construct.*

Titus Livius, *Ab Urbe Condita* 2.40: Veturia

This story takes place at the intersection of public and private in the Roman aristocratic family, where the real power of women beneath their lack of public status becomes visible. When Rome was threatened in 491 BCE by a Volscian army and their leader Coriolanus refused all suits for peace, the matrons of Rome went to his camp with his mother, his wife, and his children to beg him not to attack his homeland. Like the Sabine women of early history, they employed feminine weapons: tears, entreaties, and their children. Coriolanus remained unmoved until his mother stepped forth to sternly remind him of his responsibilities to his state, the gods, the family honor, and to her, as the woman who bore, nurtured, and educated him.

40 (1) Tum matronae ad Veturiam matrem Coriolani Volumniamque uxorem frequentes coeunt. Id publicum consilium an muliebris timor fuerit, parum invenio: (2) pervicere certe, ut et Veturia, magno natu mulier, et Volumnia duos parvos ex Marcio ferens filios secum in castra hostium irent et, quoniam armis viri defendere urbem non possent, mulieres precibus lacrimisque defenderent. (3) Vbi ad castra ventum est nuntiatumque Coriolano est adesse ingens mulierum agmen, ut qui nec publica maiestate in legatis nec in sacerdotibus tanta offusa oculis animoque religione motus esset, multo obstinatior adversus lacrimas muliebres erat; (4) dein familiarium quidam qui insignem maestitia inter ceteras cognoverat Veturiam, inter nurum nepotesque stantem, "nisi me frustrantur" inquit, "oculi, mater tibi coniunxque et liberi adsunt." (5) Coriolanus prope ut amens consternatus ab sede sua cum ferret matri obviae complexum, mulier in iram ex precibus versa "sine, priusquam complexum accipio, sciam" inquit, "ad hostem an ad filium venerim, captiva materne in castris tuis sim. (6) In hoc me longa vita et infelix senecta traxit ut exsulem te deinde hostem viderem? Potuisti populari hanc terram quae te genuit atque aluit? (7) Non tibi, quamvis infesto animo et minaci perveneras, ingredienti fines ira cecidit? Non, cum in conspectu Roma fuit, succurrit: intra illa moenia domus ac penates mei sunt, mater coniunx liberique? (8) Ergo ego nisi peperissem, Roma non oppugnaretur; nisi filium haberem, libera in libera patria mortua essem. Sed ego mihi miserius nihil iam pati nec tibi turpius usquam possum, nec ut sum miserrima, diu futura sum: (9) de his videris, quos, si pergis, aut immatura mors aut longa servitus manet." Vxor deinde ac liberi amplexi, fletusque ob omni turba mulierum ortus et comploratio sui patriaeque fregere tandem virum. (10) Complexus inde suos dimittit: ipse retro ab urbe castra movit.

After speculating about Coriolanus' end, Livy approves the public honors by which the early Roman state recognized the bravery of its citizen women.

(11) Non inviderunt laude sua mulieribus viri Romani—adeo sine obtrectatione gloriae alienae vivebatur—; monumento quoque quod esset, templum Fortunae muliebri aedificatum dedicatumque est.

Notes to Ovid, *Fasti* 4 (Lines 293-314):

293   **eques**, equitis m. *knight*. **misceo**, -ere, miscui, mixtum *mingle, join*. **gravis**, -e *serious, stern*. **plebs**, plebis f. *lower orders, plebeians*. **obvius**, -a, -um *to meet*; *at hand*. **Tuscus**, -a, -um *Etruscan*; i.e., the Tiber River, which goes north into Etruscan territory. **flumen**, -inis n. *stream, river*. **os**, oris n. *mouth, entrance*, i.e., Ostia, the seaport of Rome, situated at the place where the Tiber River joins the Tyrrhenian Sea (the Mare Nostrum, or western Mediterranean).

295   **procedo**, -ere, -cessi, -cessum *advance, progress*. **pariter** (adv.) *equally, at the same time, together*. **nata**, -ae f. *daughter*. **nurus**, -us f. *daughter-in-law*. **colo**, -ere, colui, cultum *cherish, honor*. **virginitas**, -tatis f. *maidenhood*. **focus**, -i m. *hearth; altar*. **sedulus**, -a, -um *busy, diligent*. **funis**, -is m. *rope, ship's cable*. **contentus**, -a, -um *strained, tense*. **bracchium**, -i n. *arm*. **lasso** (1) *tire, weary*. **vix** (adv.) *with difficulty, hardly*. **subeo**, -ire, -ivi, -itum *advance*. **adversus**, -a, -um *against, opposite*. **hospitus**, -a, -um *foreign, strange, guest*. **siccus**, -a, -um *dry, thirsty*. **diu** (adv.) *a long time*. **tellus**, -uris f. *earth, land, ground*. **sitis**, -is f. *drought, thirst*. **uro**, -ere, ussi, ustum *scorch, parch, burn*.

300   **sedeo**, -ere, sedi, sessum *sit, settle, be idle*. **limosus**, -a, -um *muddy*. **pressus**, -a, -um *burdened*. **carina**, -ae f. *keel* (by metonymy, *ship*). **vadum**, -i n. *shallow, bottom*. **adest operi**: "is present for work." **pro parte** *to the best of one's ability*. **adiuvo** (1) *help*; translate **et** first. **sono** (1) *sounding*. **illa** = the ship. **velut** (adv.) *just as*. **stabilis**, -e *firm, steady*. **pontus**, -i m. *sea*. **attonitus**, -a, -um *astonished*. **monstrum**, -i n. *marvel, portent*. **paveo**, -ere, pavi *be terrified, dread*.

305   **Claudia Quinta**: named after her father, one of the Claudii; she is his fifth daughter. **genus**, -eris n. *birth, descent*. **Clausus**, -i m. a Sabine leader who is helpful to Aeneas (see *Aeneid* 7.706); the ancestor of the famous Claudian gens. **refero**, -ferre, -tuli, -latum *trace back to*. **altus**, -a, -um *noble, high*. **facies**, -ei f. *face*. **impar**, -paris (adj.) *unequal, inferior to*. **castus**, -a, -um *pure, chaste, innocent*. **credo**, -ere, -didi, -ditum *believe, suppose, trust*; supply **est**. **iniquus**, -a, -um *unfavorable, unfair, adverse*. **laedo**, -ere, laesi, laesum *hurt, wound*. **crimen**, -inis n. *charge, guilt, crime*. **rea**, -ae f. *defendant*; with **acta est** = *she is accused* (i.e., she is made a defendant). **cultus**, -us m. *attire, style*. **ornatus**, -a, -um *embellished, adorned*. **prodeo**, -ire, -ii, -itum *appear*. **varie** (adv.) *variously, changeably*. **capillus**, -i m. *hair*.

310   **obsum**, -esse, -fui *be against, harm*. **rigidus**, -a, -um *strict, inflexible*. **promptus**, -a, -um *ready, easy*. **lingua**, -ae f. *speech, tongue*. **senex**, -is m. *old man*. **conscius**, -a, -um *conscious of* (+ gen.). **rectum**, -i n. *virtue, right*. **mendacium**, -i n. *lie*. **rideo**, -ere, risi, risum *laugh at*. **vitium**, -i n. *fault, flaw, defect*. **credulus**, -a, -um *credulous of, trusting toward*. **turba**, -ae f. *crowd, mob*; in apposition with the subject in **sumus**. **agmen**, -inis n. *procession*. **haurio**, -ire, hausi, haustum *draw off, take, drink*.

Publius Ovidius Naso, *Fasti* 4.293-328, 343-344

The story of the importation from Phrygia to Rome in 204 BCE of the statue of the Mother Goddess Cybele is told by both Ovid and Livy (*AUC* 29.11-15), who tells us that the Senate consulted the Sibylline Books for a remedy against the disease raging in the army and Hannibal's invasion of Rome. Livy focuses on the diplomatic negotiations, envoys, and search, guided by the Delphic Oracle, for a "vir optimus in civitate" (best man in the state): Publius Cornelius Scipio (soon to be *Africanus* after his victory over Hannibal). Claudia Quinta is mentioned briefly by Livy among the "matronae primores civitatis" (leading matrons of the state) only because "her reputation, previously in doubt, made her modesty more distinguished for posterity by so devout a service" (29.14). Ovid, on the other hand, makes Claudia Quinta the hero of the legend in his *Fasti*, a religious, political, and historical calendar poem. The festival of the Magna Mater was celebrated annually on the day before the *Nones* of April (the 4th), when the statue of the goddess was first brought from the East to Rome. In his lengthy discussion of the Great Mother's festival, Ovid dramatizes the role of Claudia Quinta, whose reputation was tarnished by three *vitia* (faults): her style of dress, her elegant hairdos, her forward (*prompta*) speech to her elders (see also Postumia in the World of the Body). The meter is elegiac couplet.

<blockquote>

omnis eques mixtaque gravis cum plebe senatus
    obvius ad Tusci fluminis ora venit.

295   procedunt pariter matres nataeque nurusque
    quaeque colunt sanctos virginitate focos.

sedula fune viri contento bracchia lassant,
    vix subit adversas hospita navis aquas.

sicca diu fuerat tellus, sitis usserat herbas,

300   sedit limoso pressa carina vado.

quisquis adest operi, plus quam pro parte laborat,
    adiuvat et fortes voce sonante manus:

illa velut medio stabilis sedet insula ponto;
    attoniti monstro stantque paventque viri.

305   Claudia Quinta genus Clauso referebat ab alto
    (nec facies impar nobilitate fuit),

casta quidem, sed non et credita: rumor iniquus
    laeserat, et falsi criminis acta rea est.

cultus et ornatis varie prodisse capillis

310   obfuit ad rigidos promptaque lingua senes.

conscia mens recti famae mendacia risit,
    sed nos in vitium credula turba sumus.

haec ubi castarum processit ab agmine matrum
    et manibus puram fluminis hausit aquam,

</blockquote>

Notes to Ovid, *Fasti* 4 (Lines 315-328, 343-344):

315   **inroro** (1) *sprinkle on.* **aether**, -eris m. *sky, heaven.* **aspico**, -ere, aspexi, aspectum *look at.* **careo,** -ere, carui + abl *be without, not have, lack.* **mente carere**: *to be crazy.* **summitto,** -ere, -misi, -missum *lower, let down.* **genu**, -us n. *knee.* **voltus = vultus,** -us m. *face, eyes.* **figo**, -ere, fixi, fixtum *fix, fasten.* **edo**, -ere, -idi, -itum *declare, utter.* **crinis**, -is m. *hair.* **iaceo,** -ere, -ui *hang loose, be neglected, be in ruins.* **supplex**, -icis (adj.) *suppliant.* **almus**, -a, -um *nourishing, kindly.* **genetrix**, -icis f. *mother.* **fecundus**, -a, -um *fertile, fruitful.*

320   **condicio**, -onis f. *condition, terms.* **prex**, precis f. *prayer, entreaty, request.* **casta negor**: supply **esse**. **damno** (1) *condemn.* **mereo**, -ere, -ui, -itum *deserve, earn.* **fateor,** -eri, fassus/a sum *confess, reveal.* **luo**, -ere, lui *pay, atone for.* **poena**, -ae f. *penalty, punishment.* **iudex**, -icis m. *judge*; ablative absolute with **dea**. **pignus**, -oris n. *pledge, assurance.* **res**, rei f. *case, matter, affair*; **re**: translate *in fact, actually.*

325   **exiguus**, -a, -um *slight.* **conamen**, -inis n. *effort, attempt.* **mirus**, -a, -um *strange, wonderful.* **scaena**, -ae f. *stage*; scan to find the case. This is probably a reference to the sacred drama played out on the stage for the festival of the Magna Mater. **testificor** (1, depon.) *vouch for, give evidence.* **index**, -icis m. *witness, indication*; in apposition with **sonus**.

343   **celeber**, celebris: superlative adjective, *crowded, honored.* **vix** (adv.) *with difficulty.* **tandem** (adv.) *finally, at last.* **pudicus**, -a, -um *modest, chaste.* **testis**, -is m/f. *witness.*

Publius Ovidius Naso, *Fasti* 4 (continued)

315   ter caput inrorat, ter tollit in aethera palmas
             (quicumque aspiciunt, mente carere putant),
       summissoque genu voltus in imagine divae
             figit, et hos edit crine iacente sonos
       "supplicis, alma, tuae, genetrix fecunda deorum,
320   accipe sub certa condicione preces.
       casta negor; si tu damnas, meruisse fatebor;
             morte luam poenas iudice victa dea;
       sed si crimen abest, tu nostrae pignora vitae
             re dabis, et castas casta sequere manus."
325   dixit, et exiguo funem conamine traxit;
             mira, sed et scaena testificata loquar:
       mota dea est, sequiturque ducem laudatque sequendo;
             index laetitiae fertur ad astra sonus.
             ----
343   Claudia praecedit laeto celeberrima voltu,
             credita vix tandem teste pudica dea;

Notes to Sallust, *Bellum Catilinae* 24 (Sections 4-5); 25:

24.4   **tempestas**, -tatis f. *time, season, weather.* **plurumos = plurimos. genus**, -eris n. *class, birth, descent.* **ascisco**, -ere, -ivi, -itum *admit* (to his conspiracy), *receive, appropriate*; the subject of the main verb and this infinitive is **Catilina. aliquot** (indecl. adj.) *some.* **ingens**, -gentis (adj.) *huge, great*; **ingentis = ingentes. sumptus**, -us m. *expense, cost*; acc. pl. **stuprum**, -i n. *debauchery, prostitution.* **tolero** (1) *support, sustain.* **tantummodo** (adv.) *only.* **quaestus**, -us m. *profit, income.* **luxuria**, -ae f. *extravagance, excess*; Sallust attributes much of the decline in the morality of the late Republic to this vice. **aes alienum =** *borrowed money, debt.* **conflo** (1) *produce, cause* (literally *ignite, inflame, melt down metals*); here a metaphoric use signifying *run up debts.*

5   **servitium**, -i n. *slavery*; n. pl. *slaves.* **sollicito** (1) *incite, rouse, stir up.* **incendo,** -ere, -i, incensum *set on fire, inflame.* **adiungo**, -ere, -iunxi,-iunctum *attach, add, ally.* **interficio**, -ere, -feci, -fectum *kill, destroy.*

25.1   **eis**: dissolute older women attracted to Catiline because he encouraged their vices. **virilis**, -e (adj.) *masculine*; gen. of description. **facinus**, -oris n. *crime.* **committo**, -mittere, -misi, -missum *commit, perform.*

2   **genus**, -eris n. *birth, descent, class*; **genere** and the following ablatives of respect are dependent upon **fortunata. praeterea** (adv) *besides, moreover.* **viro**: supply **et** before **liberis** and again below, between **psallere** and **saltare**. The term for omission of connectives is asyndeton. **doctus**, -a, -um *learned, taught, educated*; the two following clauses are dependent upon **docta. psallo**, -ere *sing, play the lyre.* **salto** (1) *dance.* **elegantius** (comparative adv.) + **quam** *more elegantly.* **probus**, -a, -um *modest, proper* (in morals); dat. following **necesse est. multa alia**: acc. of respect after **docta.**

3   **carior**, -oris (comparative adj.) *dearer, more beloved* (< **carus**). **decus**, -oris n. *decendy, virtue; good reputation.* **pudicitia**, -ae f. *modesty; sexual purity.* [**utrum**]...**an** *whether...or*; introduces indirect question with a subjunctive verb. **parco,** -ere, peperci, parsum + dat. *spare; use carefully.* **discerno,** -ere, -crevi, -cretum *distinguish, decide*; potential subjunctive.

4   **creditum**, -i n. *loan.* **abiuro** (1) *forswear, deny on oath*; Sempronia swore that she had never received the money. **caedes**, -is f. *murder.* **conscius**, -a, -um *accomplice.* **inopia,** -ae f. *lack, need, want*; **luxuria** and **inopia** are abl. of cause. **praeceps** (adv.) *headlong* (into vice). **abeo**, -ire, -ivi, -itum *depart; be changed.*

5   **ingenium,** -i n. *intelligence, natural ability.* **absurdus**, -a, -um *senseless, illogical.* **posse = potis erat. versus**, -us m. *poetry, verse.* **iocum movere** *be witty.* **mollis**, -e (adj.) *sensitive, gentle.* **procax**, -acis (adj.) *bold, shameless, salacious.* **prorsus** (adv.) *in short, in sum.* **facetiae**, -arum f. pl. *clever talk, wittiness.* **lepos**, -oris m. *charm, attractiveness.* **insum**, -esse, -fui *be in, belong* (understand **Sempronia**).

Gaius Sallustius Crispus, *Bellum Catilinae* 24.4-5, 25

As part of his strategy to explain how serious was the aristocrat Catiline's attempt to overthrow the Republic in 63 BCE, Sallust emphasizes the utter depravity of Catiline's followers, both male and female. He chooses to create a vivid portrayal of Sempronia, one of the corrupted older wealthy women who surrounded the desperate and violent Catiline, despite the fact that she had apparently not played a major role in the conspiracy. Daughter of a distinguished plebeian family that included among its ancestors that most proper and esteemed woman, Cornelia, mother of the Gracchi, she is described as a talented, daring "new" woman whose charming manners, loose morals and untraditional behavior reflected badly on her family and on her husband, Decimus Brutus, an aristocrat and staunch Republican who was absent from Rome during the conspiracy.

24 (4) Ea tempestate plurumos cuiusque generis homines adscivisse sibi dicitur, mulieres etiam aliquot, quae primo ingentis sumptus stupro corporis toleraverant, post, ubi aetas tantummodo quaestui neque luxuriae modum fecerat, aes alienum grande conflaverant. (5) Per eas se Catilina credebat posse servitia urbana sollicitare, urbem incendere, viros earum vel adiungere sibi vel interficere.

25 (1) Sed in eis erat Sempronia, quae multa saepe virilis audaciae facinora commiserat. (2) haec mulier genere atque forma, praeterea viro, liberis satis fortunata fuit.Litteris Graecis et Latinis docta, psallere saltare elegantius quam necesse est probae, multa alia quae instrumenta luxuriae sunt. (3) Sed ei cariora semper omnia quam decus atque pudicitia fuit. Pecuniae an famae minus parceret, haud facile discerneres; lubido sic accensa, ut saepius peteret viros quam peteretur. (4) Sed ea saepe antehac fidem prodiderat, creditum abiuraverat, caedis conscia fuerat, luxuria atque inopia praeceps abierat. (5) Verum ingenium eius haud absurdum: posse versus facere, iocum movere, sermone uti vel modesto vel molli vel procaci; prorsus multae facetiae multusque lepos inerat.

Notes to Tacitus, *Annales* 1.33 (Section 6); 40 (Sections 1-4); 69 (Section 1):

33.6   **accedo**, -ere, -cessi, -cessum + dat. *be added, come in addition*; the subjects are **offensiones** and **Agrippina**. **muliebris**, -e *of women*. **offensio**, -onis f. *complaint*. **novercalis**, -e *of step-mothers*. **Livia**: wife of Augustus, mother of Tiberius and Drusus. **stimulus**, -i m. *provocation*. **paulo** (adv.) *a little*. **commotior,** -oris (comparative adj.) *rather excitable*, from **commoveo**, -ere, -movi, -motum *unsettle*. **nisi quod** *were it not for the fact that*. Tacitus elides his thought here: Agrippina was emotional and stubborn, but she had good qualities. **castitas**, -tatis f. *purity, virtue*. **maritus**, -i m. *husband*. **quamvis** (adv.) *however much*. **indomitus**, -a, -um *unbridled, intractable*.

40.1   **eo in metu**: i.e., the fear caused by the military uprising. **arguo**, -ere, -ui, -utum *denounce*; **arguere = arguerunt**. **omnes**: i.e., the staff officers. **superior exercitus** = the army of upper Germany (**Germania Superior**). **pergo**, -ere, -rexi, -rectum *proceed, go on*; subjunctive after **quod** (*because*) in a clause giving a reason that is not the writer's own (i.e., the reason given by the staff officers). **obsequium**, -i n. *obedience*; understand **essent**. **rebellis = rebelles**, -ium m.pl. *rebels*. **superque** *and more*. **missio**, -onis f. *discharge from service*. **mollis**, -e *lenient*. **consultum,** -i n. *decree*. **pecco** (1) *blunder, do wrong*; **peccatum [esse]**: used impersonally in indirect statement.

2   **vilis**, -e *cheap*. **ipsi**: dat. with **vilis**; refers to Germanicus. **salus**, -utis f. *safety*. **filium parvulum**: the *toddler* Gaius (Caligula), then two years old. Their other children were in Rome. **gravidus**, -a, -um *pregnant*. **coniunx**, -iugis f/m. *wife, husband*. **furens**, -entis (present participle of **furo**) *riotous*. **omnis**: genitive (agrees with **iuris**). **violator**, -oris m. *violator*. **haberet**: subjunctive in indirect question, introduced by **cur**. **avus**, -i m. *grandfather*: Tiberius, uncle and adoptive father of Germanicus. **reddo**, -ere, -didi, -ditum *return*; subjunctive in indirect command (the subject is Germanicus)**.**

3   **cunctor** (1, depon.) *delay, hesitate*. **aspernor** (1, depon.) *reject*; her rationale is presented in the causal **cum** clause that follows. **uxorem**: object of **complexus** and **perpulit**. **se**: subject of **ortam [esse]**, referring to Agrippina; in indirect statement following **testaretur**. **divus**, -a, -um *divine*; **divo Augusto**: abl. of source. **orior**, -iri, ortus/a sum *spring from, be born*. **degener**, -is (adj.) *inferior* (to one's ancestors). **testor** (1, depon.) *declare, call as witness*; subjunctive in **cum** causal clause (the subject is Agrippina). **postremo** (adv.) *finally*. **uterus**, -i m. *womb*, including her unborn child. **fletus**, -us m. *weeping*. **complector**, -i, -plexus/a sum *embrace*; the subject is Germanicus. **abeo**, -ire, -ivi, -itum *go away*; the subject is Agrippina. **abiret**: subjunctive in a jussive noun clause after **perpulit ut**. **perpello**, -ere, -puli, -pulsum *prevail upon*; the subject is Germanicus.

4   **incedo**, -ere, -cessi, -cessum *proceed on foot*. Tacitus dramatizes the sad and solemn march of the women. It is a delicate twist that the women go forward as in a battle line (**agmen**) while the men remain behind in their camp. **agmen**, -inis n. *line of march*. **profugus**, -a, -um *in flight*. **sinus**, -us m. *bosom*. **lamentor** (1, depon.) *wail*. **circum** (adv.) *around*. **simul** (adv.) *at the same time*. **traho**, -ere, traxi, tractum *drag* (translate as middle/reflexive). **tristis**, -e *sad*. **quae...qui**: the women left; the men stayed.

69.1   **pervado**, -ere, -vasi, -vasum *spread through*. **interim** (adv.) *meanwhile*. **circumvenio**, -ire, -veni, -ventum *surround*, i.e., the Roman army. **fama**, -ae f. *rumor*. **infestus**, -a, -um *hostile*. **Gallia**, -ae f. *Gaul* (**tres Galliae: Belgica, Lugdunensis, Aquitania**). **peto**, -ere, -ivi, -itum *attack*; infinitive in indirect statement, depending on **fama**. **ni = nisi**: *if not*. **inpono**, -ere, -posui, -positum *placed over*. **Rhenus**, -i m. *the Rhine*. **pons**, pontis m. *bridge*. **solvo**, -ere, solvi, solutum *break down*. **solvi**: infinitive with **prohibuisset** (translate "from"). **flagitium**, -i n. *disgraceful deed*. **formido**, -inis f. *fear*. **audeo**, -ere, ausus/a sum *dare*; subjunctive in relative clause of characteristic, introduced by **erant qui**.

Cornelius Tacitus, *Annales* 1.33, 40, 69: Agrippina Maior

Agrippina the Elder, daughter of Augustus' daughter Julia and Marcus Agrippa, was happily married to Germanicus, son of the Empress Livia's second son Drusus, until his early death. Agrippina and Germanicus had many children, among them Gaius (the Emperor Caligula) and Agrippina the Younger (the powerful mother of Nero). Livia and Tiberius were not fond of the couple, perhaps because of Augustus' favor and their own ambitions. Tacitus characterizes Agrippina the Elder as a loyal and virtuous wife, but he recognizes her aggressive advocacy for Germanicus, a favorite especially with the army, to succeed Augustus.

33 (6) Accedebant muliebres offensiones novercalibus Liviae in Agrippinam stimulis, atque ipsa Agrippina paulo commotior, nisi quod castitate et mariti amore quamvis indomitum animum in bonum vertebat.

This dramatic passage opens with the staff officers' critique of Germanicus' actions during the military uprising in 15 BCE.

40 (1) Eo in metu arguere Germanicum omnes quod non ad superiorem exercitum pergeret, ubi obsequia et contra rebellis auxilium: satis superque missione et pecunia et mollibus consultis peccatum, (2) vel si vilis ipsi salus, cur filium parvulum, cur gravidam coniugem inter furentis et omnis humani iuris violatores haberet? illos saltem avo et rei publicae redderet. (3) diu cunctatus, aspernantem uxorem, cum se divo Augusto ortam neque degenerem ad pericula testaretur, postremo uterum eius et communem filium multo cum fletu complexus, ut abiret perpulit. (4) incedebat muliebre et miserabile agmen, profuga ducis uxor, parvulum sinu filium gerens, lamentantes circum amicorum coniuges quae simul trahebantur nec minus tristes qui manebant.

Agrippina's heroic behavior while stationed in Germany with her husband does credit to her personal legacies from Augustus and Agrippa. In Germanicus' absence, Agrippina courageously saves the bridge and cares for the helpless, thus incurring further the enmity of Tiberius and his henchman Sejanus.

69 (1) Pervaserat interim circumventi exercitus fama et infesto Germanorum agmine Gallias peti, ac ni Agrippina inpositum Rheno pontem solvi prohibuisset, erant qui id flagitium formidine auderent.

Cornelius Tacitus, *Annales*: Agrippina Maior (continued)

69   (2) sed femina ingens animi munia ducis per eos dies induit, militibusque, ut quis inops aut saucius, vestem et fomenta dilargita est. (3) tradit C. Plinius Germanicorum bellorum scriptor, stetisse apud principium pontis laudes et grates reversis legionibus habentem. (4) id Tiberii animum altius penetravit: non enim simplicis eas curas, nec adversus externos militem quaeri. (5) nihil relictum imperatoribus, ubi femina manipulos intervisat, signa adeat, largitionem temptet, tamquam parum ambitiose filium ducis gregali habitu circumferat Caesaremque Caligulam appellari velit.

Notes to Tacitus, *Annales* 1.69 (Sections 2-5):

69. 2   **ingens**, -entis *huge*; with **animi**, gen. of description. **munia**, -orum n.pl. *duties, functions of office*. **induo**, -ere, -ui, -utum *put on, assume*. **miles**, -itis m. *soldier*; in singular as a collective. **ut** *as*. **quis = aliquis** *anyone*. **inops**, -is (adj.) *in need*. **saucius**, -a, -um *wounded*. **vestis**, -is f. *clothing*. **fomentum**, -i n. *soothing application, bandage*. **dilargior**, -iri, -itus/a sum *give generously*.

3   **trado**, -ere, -didi, -ditum *pass down*; **tradit** is regularly used in citing a source, rather like "op. cit." **C. Plinius**: Pliny the Elder wrote a now-lost history of the German Wars (Pliny, *Ep.* 3.5.4). **stetisse**: supply **Agrippinam**. **principium**, -i n. *head*. **grates** (no gen.) f. *thanks*. **reversis legionibus**: dat. after **grates**.

4   **altius**: comparative adv. < **altus**. **penetro** (1) *enter*; **in animum...penetravit**: introduces an indirect statement of Tiberius' thoughts. **simplex**, -icis (adj.) *simple*; **non simplex** *disingenuous*; **simplicis**: predicate gen. of characteristic, referring to Agrippina, understand **esse**. **adversus** (prep.+ acc.) *towards, against*. **externus**, -a, -um *foreign, of a foreign enemy*; here, used substantively. **militem**: used as a collective, *the army*; object of **quaeri** (understand **Agrippinam** as subject). **quaero**, -ere, -sivi, -situm *seek, try to obtain*. Tacitus suggests that Tiberius suspected that Agrippina wanted to win over the army in order to promote Germanicus' claims to succession.

5   **relictum [esse]** < **relinquo**, -ere, -liqui, -lictum leave behind (pass. *remain, be left*); indirect statement continuing the thought of Tiberius. The remaining verbs are subjunctives because dependent clauses in the indirect statement. **imperator**, -is m. *victorious general, commander*. **manipulus**, -i m. *maniple* (a military unit): "the troops." **interviso**, -ere, -i, -um *look over, review*. **signum**, -i, n. *military standard* (pl.) *ranks*. **adeo**, -ire, -ii, -itum *approach*; *address*. **largitio**, -onis f. *largesse, bribery*. **tamquam parum ambitiose**: "ás if with little ambition" (adverbial phrase). **dux**, ducis m. *general*. **gregalis**, -e (adj.) *of the herd, common*. **habitus**, -us m. *clothing*; translate **gregali habitu** as "ordinary soldier's uniform." **circumfero**, -ferre, -tuli, -latum *carry around, parade around*. **velit** < **volo**, velle, volui *wish, want*. **appello** (1) *name, call*. **Caligula** diminutive < **caliga**, -ae f. *hob-nailed boot worn by a soldier*; **Caesarem Caligulam** thus means "Caesar wearing little boots." Agrippina apparently had a miniature pair of soldier's boots made for her toddler, who continued to bear the nickname **Caligula** even in adulthood.

PART SEVEN
THE WORLD OF WORK

Even today it is difficult to get an accurate picture of women's work. Women are estimated to form about one-third of the world's "waged" labor force. Many women, however, are employed as domestic servants or market vendors and so often go uncounted. It is even more difficult to form a picture of women's work in antiquity. We have tried, instead, to select sources which give some idea of the kinds of work women undertook in addition to the never-ending task of home-making. Our readings include two selections from "books of advice" for those who owned large landed properties (*latifundia*). In the first selection, Cato addresses the duties and character of the female overseer (*vilica*), while in the second, Columella gives advice on providing incentives for slave women to breed slave children. Some women had public careers of a sort, as is shown by the inscriptions honoring Naevoleia Tyche, public benefactor. The epitaph of an *obstetrix* and the Elder Pliny's brief listing of women painters and actresses give some idea of the range of careers in which women engaged. The *meretrices* (courtesans) in Plautus' *Cistellaria* illustrate the hard choices faced by unmarried women who lacked the assistance of a patron or who had received no training for skilled occupations. Vergil's surprising comparison of the hard-working divine smith, Vulcan, to the hard-working woman who keeps house for her family is instructive and sensitive. Was Vergil recalling his mother's work in his vignette of the tireless and selfless housewife?

References by Roman authors to occupations are few (if we except Vitruvius and military writings), which makes Cato's short passage on the duties and knowledge of a *vilica* (female overseer of an estate) valuable indeed. Inscriptions, however, are a rich source of information about work. While a definitive study of inscriptions that relate to work remains to be undertaken, Natalie Kampen's *Image and Status: Roman Working Women in Ostia* makes a solid contribution in this direction. Sandra Joshel examined inscriptions found in Rome and its environs (*Work, Identity, and Legal Status at Rome: a study of the occupational inscriptions*) and found that inscriptions reveal a built-in bias towards those who had money to spend on commissioning an inscription or who were associated with the elite and therefore had a patron willing to erect a monument for them. Thus, what we can learn about work from inscriptions is connected with social status as well as gender. Women, we may surmise, were less likely to have money to spare and perhaps were less likely to be valued as workers and so commemorated by their owners or patrons. Joshel's study reveals how unevenly the two genders are represented in epigraphical evidence: out of 1,470 inscriptions at Rome that listed a job title, only 208 referred to women. These inscriptions list women engaged in a number of fields: manufacture (such as jewelers, makers of clothing, producers of cloth, dyers); sales (such as dealers in food products, cloth, and clothing); professional services (such as midwives); skilled services (such as hairdressers, masseuses, entertainers); domestic service (such as child attendants, nurses, personal servants); and administration (such as administrators of a household). The general occupations for most women recorded in inscriptions were connected, not surprisingly, with cloth and production of clothing: silk worker (*sericaria*); spinner (*quasillaria*); wool weigher or spinning supervisor (*lanipenda*); weaver (*staminaria*); dyer of purple (*purpuraria*); tailor (*vestiaria* or *vestifica*); seamstress of cloth of gold (*auri vestrix*); and mender or seamstress (*sarcinatrix*). Related occupations for women include jeweler (*gemmaria*); pearl setter (*margaritaria*); gilder (*brattiaria*); ironsmith (*ferraria*); and manager of a workshop (*officinatrix*). Many inscriptions commemorate men and women co-workers as *colliberti*, indicating that they maintained the work friendships or alliances they had developed during their slavery.

Another source of evidence for women's occupations is art. One terracotta plaque found in Ostia depicts a saleswoman selling chickens, rabbits, and snails; sitting on her counter are two monkeys, perhaps to attract customers as well as for sale. A second Ostian terracotta tomb relief shows a midwife delivering a baby. A wall painting from a Pompeian tavern shows a waitress serving wine to two men who are vying for her attention (and for the drink she is carrying).

We may imagine the hardships faced by poor working women, slave or free, by considering the lives of workers in certain modern societies that provide little in the way of social services, financial aid or legal protection. Roman workers would find even a short illness potentially catastrophic unless they belonged to a *collegium* (guild) that provided temporary assistance or unless they had close ties with a patron or former master. They doubtless hoped each day to earn enough to feed themselves and their families and pay the rent. While it is unclear to what extent elite households needed to buy items not furnished by their estates or by slave production, the numerous shops lining the streets of Pompeii, Herculaneum, and Ostia indicate that many workers were employed in retail.

Male and female workers may have had difficulty in coming up with the money needed to establish a business, but cooperative ventures could solve this problem: *colliberti* might pool their *peculia* (slave savings). Their patrons might also make loans to them as an investment in their enterprise. Certain occupations, such as dyeing, were closed to those who had not trained as young apprentices. Anyone wishing to enter an occupation which required literacy, such as medicine, was handicapped by the fact that free education was not provided by the state. For such careers parents either paid for the occupational training of their children or, if possible, apprenticed them out. The epitaph of Eucharis (see the World of Childhood) shows that work could begin very early for a child. Certain occupations (e.g., fighting or hunting in the arena, acting and miming, and prostitution) were considered *infamis*, that is, of such ill repute that citizens could not engage in them without losing many civic rights. Nonetheless, some *libertae* like Syra and Melaenis in Plautus' *Cistellaria* might have turned to prostitution to stay alive. What we must not forget in a culture of household machines and maid services is how hard poor women worked just to maintain a household: bearing and raising children, cooking and washing, perhaps without the assistance of a single slave.

Religion provided elite women with a culturally approved venue of work. In addition to the small number of Vestals and *flaminicae*, there were many local religious offices open to them. It is not known what sort of remuneration they received beyond food and housing, as in the case of the Vestals, but for them the status was more important than the money. Women also had important roles to play at funerals. While female kin washed and dressed the body and conducted laments within the house, professional mourners were hired to amplify the procession and sing dirges. Although some elite women engaged in leisure activities from dawn to dusk, there were others who "worked" in various ways, supervising large numbers of slaves personally or with the assistance of a housekeeper or steward, receiving clients, keeping records. Joshel's study of inscriptions of the household of the Statilii shows the scope of the *matrona's* responsibilities: there were bodyguards to oversee, personal and room servants, cooks, provisioners, caretakers, and at least one social organizer. Personal attendants included bedchamber servants, waiters, and carvers, while caretakers included doorkeepers, cleaners, gardeners, keepers of jewelry and garments, clothes pressers, and maids. The elite *matrona* was also expected to oversee the education of her children and supervise their nurses and tutors. A woman who was legally *sui iuris* (free from *patria potestas* and not under her husband's *manus*) might own and supervise several estates. Another task might be to serve as hostess for receptions and dinners whose purpose would be to display the *familia* and its resources, to form and maintain alliances, and to stay informed about the most recent political, cultural and social gossip.

Notes to Cato, *De Agricultura* 142-3 (excerpts):

142.1 **hoc amplius** (adv.) *furthermore, in addition.* **oportet:** supply **vilico**, "a farm manager ought to." **utor,** uti, usus sum + acc. *manage, supervise, direct;* in early Latin **utor** was sometimes transitive and so took the accusative case instead of the ablative. **eae:** dative of **ea;** used instead of **ei,** for which the gender would be ambiguous. **uti:** an alternative spelling of the conjunction **ut,** here introducing a purpose clause. **adventus,** -us m. *arrival, visit.* **quae opus sunt** *what things there is need of;* this phrase is the subject of **parentur curenturque.**

143.1 **vilicae:** take with **officia. curato faciat:** future imperative sing. + subjunctive, "take care that"; the subject of **faciat** is **vilica. tibi:** Cato speaks to the *vilicus* directly in this and the next sentence. **esto:** future imperative 2nd s. of **esse. ea:** abl. with **contentus. facito:** future imperative 2nd s. of **facere. metuo,** -ere, metui, metutum *fear, respect deeply.* **siet = sit** (archaic subjunctive). The subject of **metuo** and **siet** is **vilica. utor,** uti, usus sum + acc. *be acquainted with, associate with.* **neve...neve** *neither...nor.* **domum [eas] recipere** *receive them at home, welcome them into the house.* **ad sese** *into her part of the house.* **cenam:** "out to meals." **ne [ali]quo** = *not anywhere.* **ambulatrix,** -tricis f. *social butterfly, visitor.* **rem divinam** *religious rites.* **ni:** archaic form of **ne;** introduces two negative hortatory subjunctives, **faciat** and **mandet. mando** (1) *order, request* (understand: "others to perform"). Understand **alicui** as antecedent of **qui. pro ea** *for her, on her account.* **iniussu** (adv.) *without the order.* **scito:** future imperative 3rd s. of **scire;** the subject is **vilica. familia,** -ae f. *family.*

2 **mundus,** -a, -um *neat, tidy; clean.* **conversus,** -a, -um *well-turned out; neat, tidy.* **focus,** -i m. *hearth; hearth-fire.* **circumversus,** -a, -um *neat, tidy;* supply **et** between **purum** and **circumversum. priusquam** takes the subjunctive to show purpose. **cubitum eat** *go to bed;* a preposition is not used in this supine phrase. **Kalendis, Idibus, Nonis:** The first day of any month was called the **Kalendae** (*Calends*). The **Idus** (*Ides*) occurred on the fifteenth day of March, May, July and October, but on the thirteenth day of the other months. The **Nonae** (*Nones*) occurred on the seventh day of March, May, July and October, but on the fifth day of the other months. **corona,** -ae f. *garland, wreath.* **indo,** -ere, -idi, -itum *place, hang.* **per** + acc. *through, during.* **lar, laris** m. The *Lar familiaris* was the deity that protected the house and its family. **supplico** (1) + dat. *pray to, worship, make offering to.* **supplicet:** hortatory subjunctive. **copia,** -ae f. *resources, means.* **pro copia** (adv.): "to the extent she has the resources to do so." **uti:** an alternative spelling of the conjunction **ut,** here introducing a purpose clause. **coctus,** -a, -um *cooked; hot; prepared.*

3 **gallina,** -ae f. *hen.* **ovum,** -i n. *egg.* **uti:** infinitive of **utor,** *use* (in cooking). **pirum,** -i n. *pear.* **aridus,** -a, -um *dried; preserved by drying.* **sorbum,** -i n. *fruit of the sorb tree;* the sorb, or service tree, is an ash that produces a small, brown, edible fruit. **ficus,** -i m. *fig.* **uva,** -ae f. *grape.* **passus,** -a, -um *dried.* **sapa,** -ae f. *new wine boiled down; the must of wine.* **dolium,** -i n. *jar.* **mala** n. (acc. pl.) *apples.* **strutea** (or **struthea**) *of sparrows;* it is unknown what kind of apples these were. **vinacium,** -i n. *grape pulp, mashed grapes.* **urceus,** -i m. *jug, amphora.* **obrutus,** -a, -um *buried, covered over.* **nux,** nucis f. *nut.* **Praenestinus,** -a, -um *of Praeneste,* a city near Rome. **recens,** -entis *new, newly picked.* **Scantiana:** *Scantianian, of Scantianum;* the location of Scantianum is unclear, but one possibility is in the Maremna area of Tuscany. **condo,** -dere, -didi, -ditum *preserve.* **silvaticus,** -a, -um *wild, of the forest.* **quotannis** (adv.) *every year, yearly.* **farina,** -ae f. *flour.* **far,** farris n. *spelt* (a kind of grain). **subtilis,** -is, -e *finely ground down, ground into very small pieces.*

Marcus Porcius Cato, *De Agricultura* 142-3 (excerpts)

Cato (234-149 BCE) is best known for his advocacy of the traditional Roman values associated with male virtue: *gravitas*, *pietas*, and *simplicitas*. These were intimately connected with Rome's origin as an agricultural community. Farming was the traditional occupation of Rome's elite and Cato gained first-hand experience in farming growing up on his father's Sabine farm near Reate; nevertheless, like many wealthy aristocrats, he devoted himself to a career in politics while his large estates were run by slave labor. His writing, our earliest surviving Latin prose narrative, resembles a farmer's notes, jotted down at the end of the day's activities. In these selections he discusses the duties and character of the *vilica*, the wife of the slave overseer. Her husband, the *vilicus*, is expected to direct and manage her, as though she would otherwise perform her duties inadequately.

142 (1) ...Hoc amplius, quo modo vilicam uti oportet et quo modo eae imperari oportet, uti adventu domini quae opus sunt parentur curenturque diligenter.

143 (1) Vilicae quae sunt officia, curato faciat. Si eam tibi dederit dominus uxorem, ea esto contentus. Ea te metuat facito. Ne nimium luxuriosa siet. Vicinas aliasque mulieres quam minimum utatur neve domum neve ad sese recipiat. Ad cenam ne quo eat neve ambulatrix siet. Rem divinam ni faciat neve mandet, qui pro ea faciat, iniussu domini aut dominae. Scito dominum pro tota familia rem divinam facere. (2) Munda siet; villam conversam mundeque habeat; focum purum circumversum cotidie, priusquam cubitum eat, habeat. Kalendis, Idibus, Nonis, festus dies cum erit, coronam in focum indat, per eosdemque dies lari familiari pro copia supplicet. Cibum tibi et familiae curet uti coctum habeat. (3) Gallinas multas et ova uti habeat. Pira arida, sorba, ficos, uvas passas, sorba in sapa et pira et uvas in doliis et mala strutea, uvas in vinaciis et in urceis in terra obrutas et nuces Praenestinas recentes in urceo in terra obrutas habeat. Mala Scantiana in doliis et alia quae condi solent et silvatica, haec omnia quotannis diligenter uti condita habeat. Farinam bonam et far subtile sciat facere.

Notes to Columella, *De Re Rustica*:

1   **feminis**: indirect object of **dedimus**. **fecundus**, -a, -um *fertile*. **suboles**, -is f. *offspring, children*. **honoro** (1) *honor, respect*. **otium**, -i n. *leisure time; release from work*. **nonumquam** (adv.) *sometimes, a few times*. **natus**, -i m. *son*. It is unclear, however, whether Columella is using the plural as a collective noun referring to children of both sexes. **educo** (1) *rear, raise*. **educassent = educavissent**; the subject is **feminae**.

2   **vacatio**, -onis f. *exemption from work due to service*. **contingo**, -ere, -tigi, -tactum + dat. *befall, fall to* (someone). The subject is **vacatio** and **libertas**.

3   **et...et** (conj.) *both...and*. **cura**, -ae f. *care, attention; trouble; exertion, industry*. **patris familias** (objective gen.): i.e., the master; **familia** can also denote the slaves of a particular master. **confert**: "confers much (benefit)," *contributes to*. **augendo patrimonio**: gerundive; dative after **confert**, "by increasing his wealth." The slave's children were also slaves and so essentially increased the master's total wealth.

Notes to Funerary Inscription, *CIL* 6.6647:

1   **Hygiae**: dative case: understand "This monument is for Hygia." This midwife was named after or in honor of Hygia, the goddess of health.

2   **Flaviae Sabinae**: the owner of Hygia.

3   **opstetrix = obstetrix**, -icis f. *midwife*. The alternation of "b" and "p" is common in the Latin vulgate. **vixit**: the subject is Hygia.

5   **contubernalis**, -is m/f. "tent-mate," a term also used for the informal unions slaves were allowed instead of marriage.

6   **carissimae**: understand **posuerunt**.

L. Iunius Columella, *De Re Rustica* 1.8.19

Columella wrote the *De Re Rustica* in the mid 1st century CE. It consists of twelve books of advice on running an agricultural estate. Chapter 8 is devoted to the assignment of work to slaves and how to best care for them in order to maintain and increase their productivity. In this selection he argues that since a slave woman's "work" in bearing children profits her master, she should be rewarded for her fecundity. Varro, a contemporary who also wrote a treatise on the running of an estate, had a different opinion. He recommended that only *vilici* be rewarded with privileges, with *peculium* (a slave's savings with which he might buy his freedom) and with female slave companions; Varro was apparently unconcerned with how a slave woman might perceive this use of her body.

19   (1) Feminis quoque fecundioribus, quarum in subole certus numerus honorari debet, otium nonnumquam et libertatem dedimus, cum plures natos educassent. (2) Nam cui tres erant filii, vacatio, cui plures libertas quoque contingebat. (3) Haec et iustitia et cura patris familias multum confert augendo patrimonio.

CIL 6.6647: Funerary Inscription for Hygia

On this epitaph, found in Rome, two men commemorate their fellow slave, an *obstetrix* (midwife) aptly name Hygia ("Health"). The two slaves called themselves Hygia's *contubernales* ("tent-mates"), a term which may also indicate that they had a recognized "living-together" relationship with her.

Hygiae

Flaviae Sabinae

opstetr(ici) vixit ann(is)

XXX

Marius Orthrus et

Apollonius contubernali

carissimae

Notes to Funerary Inscription, *ILS* 6373:

1   **Augustalis**, -e *of the emperor Augustus*; as a noun, *priest of the deified Augustus*. The emperor Tiberius established a "college" (**collegium**) of priests to offer sacrifices to the deified Augustus in every **municipium**. Each collegium had six priests, who were formally titled **sevir Augustalis** (se- < **sex**).

2   **paganus**, -i m. *man of the countryside.*

3   **decurio**, -onis m. *senator of a municipium* such as Pompeii.

4   **bisellium**, -i n. *honorific stone seat.* **meritum**, -i n. *service* (to the city of Pompeii).

6   **libertabus**: archaic ablative plural, first declension. **Caii Munati Fausti**: a genitive parallel to **suis**.

Tomb of Naevoleia Tyche, on the street of tombs outside the Herculaneum Gate in Pompeii. Photo courtesy of *The VRoma Project*.

ILS 6373: Funerary Inscription for Naevoleia Tyche

This inscription is found on the first-century CE tomb that was built outside the Herculaneum Gate of Pompeii by Naevoleia Tyche for herself, for her husband, C. Munatius Faustus, and for their freed slaves. The stone tomb is shaped like an altar (a not uncommon form for a tomb) and decorated with reliefs. The relief below the inscription may depict some part of the funerary ceremony; the one to the right of the inscription contains a boat, referring to Faustus' and Naevoleia's shipping business. Towards the top of the monument is a relief of a bust of a woman, presumably Naevoleia. The social and commercial importance of Faustus and Naevoleia is shown by the fact that the *decuriones* of Pompeii voted them a *bisellium*, an honorific seat to be used on public occasions. Naevoleia and Faustus were proud of this honor and had a bas-relief of their *bisellium* with a footstool carved to the left of the inscription.

> Naevoleia L(ucii) lib(erta) Tyche sibi et
> C(aio) Munatio Fausto Aug(ustali) et pagano
> cui decuriones consensu populi
> bisellium ob merita eius decreverunt.
> 5   Hoc monumentum Naevoleia Tyche libertis suis
> libertabusq(ue) et C(ai) Munati Fausti viva fecit.

Street of tombs: rear of Naevoleia Tyche tomb. Photo courtesy of *The VRoma Project*.

Notes to Pliny maior, *Naturalis Historia* 35.40 147-8:

147   **Iaia Cyzicena** *Iaia of Cyzicus*. **perpetua virgo** *never married*. **iuventa**, -ae f. *youth*; abl. of time within which. **M. Varro**: Marcus Terentius Varro, philologist and scholar, 1st century BCE. **penicillum**, -i n. or **penicillus**, -i m. *a paint-brush*. **cestros**, -i m. (from Greek) a pointed tool (used in encaustic painting). She worked in both genres, tempera and encaustic (paint made of pigment mixed with beeswax and fixed with heat after its application). **ebur**, -oris n. *ivory*. **imago**, -inis f. *likeness*, *image*, *portrait*. **maxime** (adv.) *especially*. **Neapoli** (locative) *in Naples*. **anus**, -us f. *old woman*. **speculum**, -i n. *mirror*.

148   **ullus**, -a, um; (gen.) ullius, (dat.) ulli *any*. **velox**, -ocis (adj.) *swift*. **artis**: partitive genitive with **tantum**. **tantum...ut** + result clause. **multum** (adv.) *much, by far*. **manipretium**, -i n. *payment for workmanship*. **antecedo**, -ere, -cessi, -cessum *go before, surpass, be larger than*. **celeber**, -bris, -bre *busy, distinguished*. **Sopolis**: a Greek painter, otherwise unknown. **Dionysius** (*NH* 35.40.113), an artist who painted only figures and was called **anthropographos** ("painter of people"). **pinacotheca**, -ae f. *picture-gallery*. **inpleo**, -ere, -evi, -etum *fill in, fill up*. **Olympias**: a painter and teacher; both she and her pupil **Autobulus** are otherwise unknown. **memoro** (1) *speak, mention*.

Notes to Pliny maior, *Naturalis Historia* 7.48.158:

158   **mima**, -ae f. *actress in mime*. **scaena**, -ae f. (< Greek **skene**) *stage*. **pronuntio** (1) *proclaim*; of an actor, *speak one's lines*. This may mean that she played a role at the age of 100 or that she had a stage career lasting 100 years, in which case she would have started very young; there is a precedent for this in an epitaph of a child acrobat who died at 18 months. **emboliaria**, -ae f. (< Greek **embolion**: *entr'acte, interlude*) *a performer of interludes*. **Caio Poppaeo Quinto Sulpicio coss.**: abl. absolute of time, indicating the date by naming the two consuls for the year; **coss.**: abbreviation of **consulibus**. The year was 8 CE. **ludus**, -i m. *game*; in pl., *festival games* or *theatrical shows*. **divus**, -a, -um *divine, deified*; Pliny wrote *NH* after Augustus' death when it was customary to call him **Divus Augustus**. **votivus**, -a, -um (with **ludis**) *performed in fulfillment of a vow*. **agens**: participle of **ago** in the sense of *leading, living*. **produco**, -ere, -duxi, ductum *bring forth, bring on to the stage*. **tirocinium**, -i n. *newness to a profession*; **tirocinio**: "for her debut." **Marcus Pomponius**: plebeian aedile in 82 BCE; he seems to be otherwise unknown. **aedilis plebis**: *aedile of the plebs*, one of the officials charged with care of the streets of Rome, distribution of grain, and supervision of the public games. **Caius Marius** and **Gnaeus Carbo** were the consuls in 82 BCE. **ante** (adv.) *before this/ that, ago*. **annos XCI**: accusative of time, *how long*. **Magnus Pompeius**: Pompey the Great commissioned Rome's first stone theater, which was dedicated in 55 BCE. **dedicatione**: abl. of time when. **anus**, -us f. *old woman*. **pro** (prep. + abl. or acc.) *by way of, as*. **miraculum**, -i n. *marvel, amazing event, freak*. **vivo**, -ere, vixi, victum *live*; **vixisse**: infinitive in indirect statement depending on **auctor est** as if a verb of writing/speaking. **auctor**, -oris m. *author, source*. **Pedianus Asconius**: Quintus Asconius Pedianus, a scholar of the 1st century CE who wrote a commentary on Cicero of which only fragments are extant.

C. Plinius Secundus (maior), *Naturalis Historia* 35.40 (selections)

Women painters are listed in chapter 40 of book 35, in which Pliny presents a history of painting, a description of the making of natural pigments, and an overview of the lives and works of painters, including some women. Most of the female painters mentioned by Pliny were Greek, but the last one, Iaia, worked in Italy in the 1st century BCE. Pliny notes that women artists were known for their preference for certain subjects: for example, Iaia of Cyzicus made her mark as a portrait painter of women, including herself. Iaia was one of the most successful and well-compensated painters of her day. Unfortunately, these female artists are all but unknown outside of Pliny's account, and even here, except for Iaia, they are little more than names.

147 Iaia Cyzicena, perpetua virgo, M. Varronis iuventa Romae et penicillo pinxit et cestro in ebore imagines mulierum maxime et Neapoli anum in grandi tabula, suam quoque imaginem ad speculum.

148 nec ullius velocior in pictura manus fuit, artis vero tantum,/ut multum manipretiis antecederet celeberrimos eadem aetate imaginum pictores Sopolim et Dionysium, ⌐quorum tabulae pinacothecas inplent. pinxit et quaedam Olympias, de qua hoc solum memoratur, discipulum eius fuisse Autobulum.

C. Plinius Secundus (maior), *Naturalis Historia* 7.48.158

Pliny lists a number of women known for their longevity, including Terentia, wife of Cicero, who lived to 103, and one Clodia, Ofilius' wife, who not only lived to 115, but bore fifteen children. He also names actresses who were very long-lived. Such age statistics cannot always be trusted, since no legal birth records were kept. In the case of Galeria Copiola, Pliny goes out of his way to establish the time frame of her stage career with definite external dates.

158 (1) Lucceia mima C annis in scaena pronuntiavit. Galeria Copiola emboliaria reducta est in scaenam C. Poppaeo Q. Sulpicio coss. ludis pro salute Divi Augusti votivis annum CIIII agens; producta fuerat tirocinio a M. Pomponio aedile plebis C. Mario Cn. Carbone coss. ante annos XCI; a Magno Pompeio magni theatri dedicatione anus pro miraculo reducta. Sammulam quoque cx annis vixisse auctor est Pedianus Asconius.

Notes to Plautus, *Cistellaria* (Lines 38-41):

38   **libertina**, -ae f. *freedwoman.* **ambo**, -ae, -a *both.* **meretrix**, -icis f. *prostitute.* **te**: Selenium, her friend Melaenis' daughter, actually an abandoned child that Melaenis brought up. **hanc**: Gymnasium, Syra's daughter. **educo** (1) *raise, rear, bring up.*

40   **ex** + abl. *out of;* here, *begotten of.* **conventicius**, -a, um *coming together;* here, *customer.* **superbia**, -ae f. *haughtiness.* **causa** + gen. *because of, account of;* this preposition generally comes after its object (**superbiae**). **pello**, -ere, pepuli, pulsum *compel, force.* **meretricius**, -a, -um *pertaining to prostitutes.* **quaestus**, -us m. *occupation; source of income.* **nisi** (conj.) *save only, but only.* **esurio**, -ire, —, -itum *go hungry; starve.*

Notes to Plautus, *Cistellaria* (Lines 123-124, 133-144):

123   **illanc**: Selenium; the -c(e) is an indeclinable intensifying suffix which also appears in certain case forms of hic, haec, hoc. **hinc** (adv.) *from here.* **fleo**, -ere, flevi *weep, cry.* **parvolus**, -a, -um *very small* or *little.* **proicio**, -icere, -ieci, -iectum *throw forth* or *out; abandon, throw away.* **angiportum**, -i n. *narrow street, alley.* **tollo**, -ere, sustuli, sublatum *lift up; rescue.*

133   **eam**: Selenium. **amica**: Melaenis. **dono**: dat. of purpose, "as a gift" **mecum**: literally *with me,* but here translate as "to me, in my presence."

135   **puerum aut puellam**: Melaenis wanted a child; a boy is mentioned first because her client would be more willing to support an illegitimate son. **alicunde** (adv.) *from some place or another.* **reperio**, -perire, -pperi, -pertum *find, discover.* **recens** (adv.) *recently.* **natus**, -a, -um *born.* **eapse**: nominative of **ea** + **-pse,** an indeclinable, intensifying suffix. **quod** + subjunctive: a relative clause of purpose, in which the antecedent of **quod** is **natum. suppono**, -ponere, -posui, -positum *put in the place of, substitute for.* **potestas**, -atis f. *power; chance* (to do something). **primum** (adv.) *first.* **evenit**, -venire, -ventum est (impersonal) *happen, come about.* **ilico** (adv.) *immediately, instantly.* **copia**, -ae f. *resources; means, opportunity.* **facere copiam** + dat. *take the opportunity for.* **eius**: "of Melaenis' request." **ei** *for her* (Melaenis). **oro** (1) *beg, ask.*

140   **pario**, -ere, peperi, partum. *bring forth, give birth to;* Melaenis, however, only pretended to give birth to the baby girl. **obstetrix**, -icis f. *midwife.* **opera**, -ae f. *work.* **dolor**, -oris m. *pain; labor pain.* **item ut** *such as.* **malum**, -i n. *evil; trouble.* **quaero**, -ere, quaesivi, quaesitum *seek out, look for.* **amator**, -oris m. *lover.* **aio**: (defective verb) *say.* **peregrinus**, -a, -um *from foreign parts, from abroad.* **sibi**: dative of possession with **esse**; take with **amatorem. suppositio**, -onis f. *substitution.* **gratia** + gen. *for the sake* (of someone), *on* (someone's) *account;* this preposition generally comes after its object (**eius,** her lover).

Titus Maccius Plautus, *Cistellaria* (excerpts)

This play is a serious comedy with a potentially tragic love story, which through chance ends happily. It was written in the 2nd century, near the end of the Second Punic War. In it, a young man, Alcesimarchus, is in love with a young woman, Selenium, who is a *meretrix* (prostitute) like her mother, Melaenis. Alcesimarchus wants to marry Selenium, but his father wishes him to marry a respectable young woman. The title comes from the jewelry casket containing items that prove Selenium's identity as the daughter of a citizen, thus enabling her to marry the man she loves. Though the *Cistellaria* is an adaptation of a play by Menander, the foremost Greek writer of New Comedy, Plautus' Roman audience was familiar with the harsh aspects of the life of a *meretrix*. The plot focuses on the female characters in the play, such as the young but generous Selenium; Syra, an old *meretrix* who softens the hardships of her life with drink; and the resourceful Melaenis, who tries to ensure some security for herself by tricking her erstwhile lover, a man who turns out to be Alcesimarchus' father.

38-41 Syra explains how she and Melaenis came to be *meretrices*:

> SYRA: quia nos libertinae sumus, et ego et tua mater, ambae
> meretrices fuimus: illa te, ego hanc mihi educavi
> 40   ex patribus conventiciis. neque ego hanc superbiai
> causa pepuli ad meretricium quaestum, nisi ut ne esurirem.

123-24, 133-44 Syra explains how Selenium, abandoned by her family shortly after her birth, came to be Melaenis' adopted daughter:

> SYRA: nam ego illanc olim, quae hinc flens abiit, parvolam
> puellam proiectam ex angiportu sustuli.
>
> -------------
>
> eam meae ego amicae dono huic meretrici dedi,
> quae saepe mecum mentionem fecerat
> 135   puerum aut puellam alicunde ut reperirem sibi,
> recens natum, eapse quod sibi supponeret.
> ubi mihi potestas primum evenit, ilico
> feci eius ei quod me oravit copiam.
> postquam eam puellam a me accepit, ilico
> 140   eandem puellam peperit quam a me acceperat,
> sine obstetricis opera et sine doloribus,
> item ut aliae pariunt, quae malum quaerunt sibi.
> nam amatorem aibat esse peregrinum sibi
> suppositionemque eius facere gratia.

Publius Vergilius Maro, *Aeneis* 8.407-415

Vergil's famous epic on the founding of Rome gives us compelling portraits of goddesses and legendary women, but none capture the feeling of lived existence like the nameless housewife in this simile. This glimpse into the world of women's work serves as a discreet bridge between Venus' seduction of her husband Vulcan and his fulfillment of his promise to forge weapons for her son, Aeneas. Not until *haud secus* on line 414 do we realize the force of this imagery: the two subjects and their tasks could not be more different, but Vergil uses this image of the hard-working, nurturing *materfamilias* as an illustration of the divine metalsmith's selfless and tireless dedication to his trade. Long before modern society was ready to accept the idea, this simile validates woman's work as real work.

> Inde ubi prima quies medio iam noctis abactae
> curriculo expulerat somnum, cum femina primum,
> cui tolerare colo vitam tenuique Minerva
> 410   impositum, cinerem et sopitos suscitat ignis
> noctem addens operi, famulasque ad lumina longo
> exercet penso, castum ut servare cubile
> coniugis et possit parvos educere natos:
> haud secus ignipotens nec tempore segnior illo
> 415   mollibus e stratis opera ad fabrilia surgit.

Notes to Vergil, *Aeneis* 8.407-415:

Aeneis, -idos f. *The Aeneid.*

407   **inde** (adv.) *then, from that.* **abactus,** -a, -um *finished, passed*; describes **noctis. curriculum,** -i n. *course, career.* **expello,** -ere, -puli, -pulsum *drive away, expel, remove.* **primum** (adv.) *first.* **tolero** (1) *support, sustain, bear.* **colus,** -i f. *distaff* (the staff from which wool is pulled for spinning). **tenuis,** -e *slight, poor, thin.* **Minerva,** -ae f. patron goddess of wisdom, war, and the arts; here, the word means *weaving, working in wool.*

410   **impono,** -ere, -posui, -positum + dative *impose on, assign to, lay upon*; impersonal, supply **est. cinis,** -eris m. *ashes, embers.* **sopio,** -ire, -ivi, -itum *put to sleep*; **sopitos** modifies **ignis** (i.e., **ignes**). **suscito** (1) *stir, rouse, awaken.* **addo,** -ere, addidi, additum *add* (**noctem**) *to* (**operi**). **famula,** -ae f. *handmaid; house servant.* **lumen,** -inis n. *lamp, torch, light.* **longus,** -a, -um *tedious, long, vast.* **exerceo,** -ere, -ui, -itum *keep busy, supervise, train.* **pensum,** -i n. *allotment of wool to be spun; task.* **castus,** -a, -um *clean, pure* (moral and physical). **ut** + subjunctive (**possit**): purpose construction. **cubile,** -is n. *bed, couch.* **coniunx,** -iugis m/f. *husband, wife.* **educo,** -ere, -duxi, -ductum *raise up, rear, train.* **natus, nata** m/f. *male offspring, female offspring.* **haud secus** *not at all otherwise* (i.e., "just the same as"). **ignipotens,** -entis (adj.) *fire-working.* **segnis,** -e *slow, sluggish, lazy* (comparative form).

415   **mollis,** -e *soft.* **stratum,** -i n. *coverlets, bed, couch.* **fabrilis,** -e *of the craftsman, of the smith.* **surgo,** -ere, -rexi, -rectum *arise, get up.*

PART EIGHT
THE WORLD OF FLIRTATION

Although the intense elegies of Catullus, Propertius, and Tibullus typify the genre of passionate love poetry, the lighter tone of the World of Flirtation is best captured in the work of Horace, Ovid, and Sulpicia. The selections in this unit open with a brief but multi-layered passage in which Propertius pretends to prefer a *meretrix* to his beloved who professes a respectability which her behavior belies. Horace delicately captures the light and playful spirit of attraction in the banter between a lover and his estranged beloved in *Carmina* 3.9, where Lydia gives as good as she gets and has the final word. Ovid, in the guise of a "professor of love" in his scandalous *Ars Amatoria*, instructs unmarried women – not respectable *matronae*, he insists (*AA* 1.31 ff.) – about where to find potential lovers, how to dress seductively, and how to win over men and gain power. Sulpicia uniquely addresses the genre in a female voice, an elite one at that. Known as the Roman Sappho, she inverts the dominant male-submissive female roles of Latin love elegy, adapting its conventions to her elegant *persona*.

This is the most un-Roman of the Worlds, the one furthest removed in spirit and content from the *mos maiorum* ("customs of the ancestors"). With its focus on art and artifice and the expression of emotion, it celebrates what Romans typically condemned in Greek culture as alien to *Romanitas*. In this "modern" world of male-female intimacy outside of marriage lived the "new" liberated woman as *dominatrix* and her willing male "slave," a prisoner of love and madly addicted to his "disease." During the Republic, the state rarely involved itself in adult sexual activities, with the notable exception of the Senate's interdiction in 186 BCE on Bacchanalian practices in Italy (Livy, *AUC* 39.8-20, the World of the State). For the most part the family, highly sensitive to any blemishes on its reputation, monitored the behavior of its members, until Augustus took steps to punish even prominent individuals for counter-cultural behavior which he saw as a threat to public and family well-being.

The literature of dalliance was in fact a borrowing from Greek drinking songs, lyric poetry, new comedy, and Hellenistic poetry. It exalted youth, infatuation, and sex. It was a world of no consequences, despite the tragedies its poets invoked to throw its focus into high relief. It was a fluid world of shifting feelings, few constraints, and a single goal – the acquisition of the beloved. It was a feminine world, seen almost exclusively through the eyes of a male author. At the center of this world was a daring new character, the literary creation of a sophisticated citizen woman from a good family who turned her back on the stuffy *matrona* in her concealing *stola* and emulated instead the *meretrix*, from whom traditionally she had always been separated. This literary figure set the fashion. Married to an older man by parental arrangement, she could attend late-night parties in the most revealing attire, choose her lovers, and accept expensive gifts; in the absence of domestic responsibilities in the form of weaving or children, she spent her day preparing her toilette and planning trysts, drunk on her power and her notoriety.

Even in Rome this construct was not a totally new creation of the love poets. It was reminiscent of the rebellious world of young men, whose behaviors are indulged in Roman Comedy because, despite their flaunting of the *patria potestas*, the plot always ended in an acceptable marriage. It evoked the world of prostitution and the underground behavior of married men, long sanctioned by tradition, who quite commonly had extra-marital relations with foreign women, slaves, and prostitutes. Caesar and Antony stand out as notable examples of leaders who faced public criticism of their private sexual indulgences, but only when these had political ramifications (with Cleopatra).

What was new was the genre of late Republican love poetry, which literarily emancipated the high-class Roman *matrona* from her father and husband and permitted her autonomy over her body, independence of spirit, and disdain for her reputation. It is difficult to know to what extent this construct reflects the attitudes of real women of the time and to what extent it is male fantasy. The generation that was born and flourished in this short-lived climate of sexual freedom was attracted to it for many reasons, but chief among them was its opposition to the paternal world of stern *Romanitas* that had so failed in its promises. Careers in the military and politics, which now brought status without power, had become less attractive to men. Civil wars, political chaos, contact with other cultures, the availability of luxury items, leisure, and wealth were all factors which added to the appeal of this lifestyle. Talented and intelligent women of the higher social classes found themselves unfulfilled by the life open to respectable women, not merely because they themselves were so little appreciated by men but also because the covenants of their marriage had been violated by the turmoil of the century. Elite marriage was a contract of convenience, frequently arranged and broken by the *paterfamilias* for reasons of political alliance and family finances. Citizenship seemed of so little value in comparison to their sexual freedom that some women were willing to have themselves classified as prostitutes before the law in order to avoid prosecution for adultery. The woman who had a single husband in her lifetime (termed *univira* in post-classical Latin) continued to be praised in public and privately ignored by the upper classes.

The World of Flirtation was also a dangerous one for real women. Elite married women who attempted to participate in practices forbidden to them soon faced serious consequences, as evidenced by the suffering of those who had flouted tradition and failed, such as Sempronia, Augustus' daughter and granddaughter Julia, as well as the love instructor himself, Ovid. While Augustus' legislation did not eradicate wanton behavior, as Seneca, Petronius, and Juvenal would later testify, it put an end to public expression of its values and, with the exile and death of Ovid, it smothered the flame of elegiac love poetry.

Sextus Propertius, *Elegiae* 2.23. 12-20

The woman Propertius celebrates in the lines below is a streetwalker, one who is "free" of the constraints of respectable clothing and chaperones and thus is more accessible. He claims to prefer her kind to the beloved of love elegy who closes her door – not out of modest virtue, like the traditional *matrona*, but rather because she claims the prerogative of conducting affairs behind her husband's back while maintaining appearances (look for her voice in lines 17-20). The meter is elegiac couplet.

<blockquote>

a pereant, si quos ianua clausa iuvat!

contra, reiecto quae libera vadit amictu,

    custodum et nullo saepta timore, placet?

15   cui saepe immundo Sacra conteritur Via socco,

    nec sinit esse moram, si quis adire velit;

differet haec numquam, nec poscet garrula quod te

    astrictus ploret saepe dedisse pater,

nec dicet "Timeo, propera iam surgere, quaeso

20   infelix, hodie vir mihi rure venit."

</blockquote>

Notes to Propertius, *Elegiae* 2.23

12   **a** (interj.) *Ah!* **pereo**, -ire, -ii, -itum *perish, die.* **quos = aliquos** after **si. iuvo**, -are, iuvi, iutum *please; give pleasure to*; the subject is **ianua clausa. ianua**, ae f. *house-door; entrance.* **claudo**, -ere, -si, -sum *block, close, shut.* **contra** (adv.) *on the contrary.* **reicio**, -ere, –ieci, -iectum *throw back, throw over the shoulder.* **quae**: supply as the antecedent **illa femina. vado**, -ere *stride, go quickly, make one's way.* **amictus**, us m. *mantle, cloak, wrap*; the effect is to display her figure, since she is certainly not wearing the *stola* of the married woman. **custos**, -odis m.f. *guard*; translate with **timore. saepio**, -ire, -si, -tum *fence in, protect*; **saepta** and **libera** modify **quae. placeo**, -ere, -ui, -itum + dat. (**mihi** understood) *please, satisfy*; the subject is **illa femina** (understood).

15   **immundus**, -a, -um *unclean, dirty.* **Sacra...Via**: the word order emphasizes the contrast between the prostitute's pursuits and the sacred and political traditions of this ancient pathway into the Roman Forum. **contero**, -ere-, -trivi, -tritum *grind, wear out.* **soccus**,-i, m. *low-heeled slipper*; since this footwear was associated with the Greek comic stage, the following lines suggest comic stereotypes and themes, such as the "stingy father" who complains about giving his son money to spend on lovers. **sino**, -ere, sivi, situm *allow.* **mora**, ae f. *delay, pause.* **adeo**, -ire, -ii, -itum *approach; address; apply to.* **differo**, -ferre, distuli, dilatum *put off*; the object is **te** (note how the verb and its object frame the line). **posco**, -ere, poposci *demand, require*; the object is **id** understood, antecedent of **quod. garrulus**, -a, -um *babbling, talkative.* **astrictus**, -a, -um *stingy; tight.* **ploro** (1) *bewail, whine*; subjunctive in a relative clause of characteristic. **[se]...dedisse**: indirect statement after **ploret. propero** (1) *hurry, do with haste.* **surgo**, -ere, surrexi, surrectum *arise; get up.* **quaeso**, -ere *beg, ask.*

20   **infelix**, -icis (adj.) *unhappy, unlucky* (may modify the girl speaking or be a direct address to the lover: "unhappy man"). **vir**, viri m. *man; husband.* **rure**: *from the country.*

Notes to Ovid, *Ars Amatoria* 1 (Lines 135-162):

135   **fugio**, -ere, fugi *escape one's notice*; jussive subjunctive. **certamen**, -inis n. *contest, competition*. **capax**, -acis (adj. + gen.) *capable of holding; spacious*. **commoda**, -orum n. pl. *favorable circumstances*. **nil** (= **nihil**) **opus est** + abl. *there is no need of*. **digitus**, -i m. *finger* (i.e., making signs with your hands). **arcanum**, -i n. *secret*. **tibi accipienda est**: passive periphrastic with the dative of agent. **nutus**, -us m. *nod of the head, motion of the head*. **proximus a(b)** + abl. *nearest to, next to* (superlative of **propior**). **sedeto**: future active imperative, 2nd and 3rd person singular.

140   **latus**, -eris n. *side* (of the body). **qua potes usque** *as near as you can*. **bene**: supply **est**. **linea**: subject of **cogit**; the Circus had markings on the benches that indicated seat limits. **si nolis…iungi**: as an unlikely supposition, the verb is in the subjunctive, followed by a complementary infinitive. **lege…loci**: "by the circumstance of her position." **quaero**, -ere, quaesivi, quaesitum *seek, look for*; jussive subjunctive. **socius**, -a, -um *shared, common, mutual*. **sonus**, -i m. *utterances, sounds;* understand **tuos**.

145   **facito…requiras**: future imperative with subjunctive in indirect command: "be sure to ask". **studiose** m. *eager one; my student* (vocative). **mora**, -ae f. *delay, pause*. **faveo**, -ere, favi, fautum + dat. *favor, support, befriend*. **pompa**, -ae f. *procession*; the games were opened by a parade around the Circus of images of the gods, white as ivory (**caelestibus eburnis**). **frequens**, -entis (adj.) *crowded, populous*. **plaudeo**, -ere, plausi, plausum + dat. *applaud; give applause to*. **utque** (adv.) *as frequently*. **gremium**, -i n. *bosom, lap*. **pulvis**, -eris m. *dust, powder*.

150   **decido**, -ere, -cidi *fall down, come down*. **excutio**, -ere, -cussi, -cussum *flick something out; remove*. **etsi** (conj.) *even if*. **quilibet**, quaelibet, quodlibet *anything at all you please*. **officium**, -i n. *service, favor* (i.e., his touching her garment). **aptus**, -a, -um + abl. *fitted to, suitable to*. **pallium**, -i n. (pl. used for s.) *cloak* or *mantle*, in the Greek style (dress of Greek and Roman prostitutes). **demissus**, -a, -um *trailing, dragging*. **colligo**, -ligere, -legi, -lectum *gather up; pick up*. **inmundus**, -a, -um *clean; unspotted, undirtied*; scan to determine the case. **sedulus**, -a, -um *attentive, careful*. **effero**, -ferre, -tuli, -latum *lift up, carry away from*. **humus**, -i f. *ground; dirt*.

155   **protinus** (adv.) *immediately, without pause*. **pretium**, -i n. *reward; prize*. **crus**, cruris n. *lower leg*. **contingo**, -ere, -tigi, -tactum *be near; happen*. **respice**: supply **ei**, the antecedent of **quicumque praeterea** (adv.) *furthermore, moreover*. **ne**: introduces a negative result clause. **premo**, -ere, pressi, pressum *press; thrust*. **mollis**, -is, -e *soft; tender; delicate*. **tergum**, -i n. (plural frequently used for singular) *back* (i.e., of the *puella*). **genu**, -us n. (abl. here) *knee* (of the person sitting behind her). **levis**, -is, -e *capricious, fickle*.

160   **pulvinus**, -i m. *cushion*; since the Circus seats were made of stone, many people found it necessary to bring cushions. **facilis**, -is, -e *courteous, well-mannered*. **compono**, -ponere, -posui, -positus *smooth, plump up, arrange*. **prosum**, prodesse, profui *be of use, be helpful*; impersonal use. **ventos movisse**: "to fan." **tenuis**, -is, -e *light, trifling*. **tabella**, -ae f. *writing tablet*. **cavus**, -a, -um *hollow*. **tener**, tenera, tenerum *soft, delicate*. **scamnum**, -i n. *bench, stool*.

Publius Ovidius Naso, *Ars Amatoria* 1.135-162

One of Ovid's most sophisticated works is his *Ars Amatoria*, a didactic poem published in 1 BCE. It is a mock handbook on flirtation that teaches the tricky game of conducting a love affair. In Books 1-2 he teaches men how to pick up women, win their hearts, keep their interest, and finally break off the relationship. He suggests the Circus, where the horse races take place, as the perfect pick-up spot, since it is the traditional haunt of girls of easy virtue and men and women were permitted to sit together. The perspective is entirely male, with the woman as a passive target. This passage follows a tongue-in-cheek retelling of the Rape of the Sabine Women (111-134), in which Romulus, Rome's first king, establishes the practice of finding a mate at the public festivals. The meter is elegiac couplet.

135	Nec te nobilium fugiat certamen equorum;
	Multa capax populi commoda Circus habet.
	Nil opus est digitis, per quos arcana loquaris,
	Nec tibi per nutus accipienda nota est:
	Proximus a domina, nullo prohibente, sedeto,
140	Iunge tuum lateri qua potes usque latus;
	Et bene, quod cogit, si nolis, linea iungi,
	Quod tibi tangenda est lege puella loci.
	Hic tibi quaeratur socii sermonis origo,
	Et moveant primos publica verba sonos.
145	Cuius equi veniant, facito, studiose, requiras:
	Nec mora, quisquis erit, cui favet illa, fave.
	At cum pompa frequens caelestibus ibit eburnis,
	Tu Veneri dominae plaude favente manu;
	Utque fit, in gremium pulvis si forte puellae
150	Deciderit, digitis excutiendus erit:
	Etsi nullus erit pulvis, tamen excute nullum:
	Quaelibet officio causa sit apta tuo.
	Pallia si terra nimium demissa iacebunt,
	Collige, et inmunda sedulus effer humo;
155	Protinus, officii pretium, patiente puella
	Contingent oculis crura videnda tuis.
	Respice praeterea, post vos quicumque sedebit,
	Ne premat opposito mollia terga genu.
	Parva leves capiunt animos: fuit utile multis
160	Pulvinum facili composuisse manu.
	Profuit et tenui ventos movisse tabella,
	Et cava sub tenerum scamna dedisse pedem.

Notes to Ovid, *Ars Amatoria* 3 (Lines 129-136, 239-42, 298-304):

129   **carus**, -a, um *dear; expensive, costly*. **onero** (1) *burden, laden*. Ovid uses the second person plural form to address his female readers. **lapillus**, -i m. *little* (precious) *stone*. The **lapillus viridis** was the emerald that the Romans imported from India. **lego**, -ere, lexi, lectus *select, choose*; here, *lift out*. **viridis**, -is, -e *green*. **decolor**, -oris *dusky, dark-skinned*. **Indus**, -i m. *inhabitant of India*. **prodeo**, -ire, -ii, -itum *go out, appear in public*. **gravis**, -is, -e *heavy; laden down*; modifies the reflexive pronoun [**vos**], which is understood. **insutus**, -a, -um *sewn onto, attached*; a common fashion in feminine dress was to have a woman's garment bordered with a golden band. **peto**, -ere, -ivi, -itum *seek; hunt out*. **fugo** (1) *put to flight; chase off*. **opes**, -is f. *wealth; luxury; display of wealth*.

133   **munditiae**, -arum f. pl. *elegance*. **sine lege**: "unarranged," "blown by the wind." **admotus**, -a, -um *applied, made use of*. **manus admotae**: "hands used to arrange the hair." **unus**, -a, -um *sole; one and only*. **ornatus**, -us m. *embellishment, dress*. **quamque**: "each woman." **decet** (impersonal) *befit; make* (someone) *beautiful*. **eligo**, -ere, -elegi, -electum *select, choose*. **ante** (adv.) *first of all*. **speculum**, -i n. *mirror*.

239   **tutus**, -a, -um *safe; unharmed; unbeaten, unpunished*. **ornatrix**, -tricis f. *hairdresser*. Many hairstyles were elaborate, involving curling and dyeing hair, or using hair pieces. An **ornatrix** was a specially trained slave who would be expensive to purchase. **odi quae**: understand **dominam** as direct object of **odi** and antecedent of **quae**. **saucio** (1) *wound, hurt*. **ora**, -um n. pl. *face* (of the **ornatrix**). **unguis**, -is m. *finger-nail*. **raptus**, -a, -um *snatched*. **bracchium**, -i n. *arm*. **fingo**, -ere, fixi, fixum *stab, jab, gash*. **acus**, -us f. *pin; hairpin*. **devoveo**, -ere, -vovi, -votum *curse*; **illa** [**ornatrix**] is the subject. **et tangit**: "even while she touches." **simulque** *and at the same time*. **ploro** (1) *weep, cry*. **invisus**, -a, -um *hated*. **sanguinolentus**, -a, -um *dripping blood, bleeding*.

298   **disco**, -ere, didici *learn, learn how to*. **gradus**, -us m. *step, pace; walk, way of walking*. **incessus**, -us m. *walking, gait; step; a way of walking*. **pars**, partis f. (with **decoris**): "a share of beauty," "an amount of beauty." **allicio**, -licere, -lexi, -lectus *allure, entice; draw to* (oneself). **ignotus**, -a, -um *unknown* (to one). **ille**: understand **incessus**. **haec**: understand **femina**. **latus**, -eris n. *side; flank* (of the body). **fluens**, -entis *fluttering, blowing about*. **aura**, -ae f. *breeze*. **extensus**, -a, -um (modifies **pedes**) *long, lengthy; high*. Ovid means that one (**superba**) woman walks about in an exaggerated manner.

303   **velut** *as if she were*. **Umber**, Umbra, Umbrum *Umbrian*; Umbria was an area of Italy known for its rusticity and boorishness. **rubicundus**, -a, -um *sun-burned*. **ingens**, -entis (adj.) *large, huge*. **varicus**, -a, -um *with feet spread wide apart, straddling, waddling*.

Publius Ovidius Naso, *Ars Amatoria* 3.129-36, 239-42, 298-304

Speaking as a man who admires and pursues women, Ovid gives advice to women who wish to attract men in Book 3 of his poetic handbook *Ars Amatoria* (1 BCE). In the following passages, he urges women to pay attention to their looks and be responsive to male needs, focusing on the less assertive arts of attraction through dress, cosmetics, and receptive flirting. They should enhance their best features while concealing their defects. They should speak, laugh, walk, sit, sing, and dance in ways that men find charming. He recommends that they learn how to play games with their boyfriends, such as dice or *latrunculi* (like chess), and make sure that they sometimes lose. Ovid's purpose is ambiguous: does he expect women to read his poem or is he divulging female secrets to his male audience? The meter is elegiac couplet.

129-136: Ovid suggests elegance, not opulence, and a personal style.

> vos quoque non caris aures onerate lapillis,
> 130   quos legit in viridi decolor Indus aqua
> nec prodite graves insuto vestibus auro:
>   per quas nos petitis, saepe fugatis, opes.
> munditiis capimur: non sint sine lege capilli;
>   admotae formam dantque negantque manus.
> 135   nec genus ornatus unum est: quod quamque decebit,
>   eligat et speculum consulat ante suum.

239-242: Ovid advises sparing application of cosmetics and perfume, in private. Although boyfriends like to watch hair being fixed, women should not show anger at the slave who tugs at a snarl (a common reaction, to judge from the love poets).

> tuta sit ornatrix: odi, quae sauciat ora
> 240   unguibus et rapta brachia figit acu;
> devovet, et tangit dominae caput illa simulque
>   plorat in invisas sanguinolenta comas.

298-304: Ovid observes that graceful movement is as important as appearance.

> discite femineo corpora ferre gradu:
> est et in incessu pars non contempta decoris;
> 300   allicit ignotos ille fugatque viros.
> haec movet arte latus tunicisque fluentibus auras
>   accipit, extensos fertque superba pedes;
> illa, velut coniunx Umbri rubicunda mariti,
>   ambulat, ingentis varica fertque gradus.

Notes to Horace, *Carmina* 3.9 (Lines 1-24):

1   **donec** *while, as long as.* **gratus,** -a, -um + dat. *dear to, pleasing to.* **quisquam,** quaequam, quicquam/quidquam *any, anyone*; with **nec**: *and no one,* modifying **iuvenis** (line 3). **potior,** -oris (comparative adj.) *better, preferable.* **bracchium,** -i n. *arm*; accusative of respect. **candidus,** -a, -um *white, beautiful.* **cervix,** -icis f. *neck.* **vigeo,** -ere, vigui *thrive, flourish.*

6   **ardeo,** -ere, arsi + abl. *burn, be passionate for.* **Chloe,** Chloes f. Chloe, a Greek name in the Greek accusative (**Chloen**). **nomen,** -inis n. *fame, reputation*; *name, title*; genitive of description. **Ilia,** -ae f. another name for Rhea Silvia, who bore Romulus and Remus to the god Mars; use of this name emphasizes the connection of Rome with Ilium (Troy).

9   **Thressa,** -ae f. *Thracian woman*; inhabitant of Thrace, a land of unstable fierce tribes north of Greece, which finally became a Roman province in 46 CE. **doctus, -**a, -um *learned, skilled, clever.* **modus,** -i m. *meter, music, measure*; *way.* **cithara,** -ae f. *lute*; genitive after **sciens**. **metuam...si parcent**: present subjunctives in a future less vivid condition ("should...would"). **morior,** mori, mortuus/a sum *die.* **parco,** -ere, peperci, parsum + dat. s*pare.* **anima,** -ae f. *life, soul* (a reference to his girlfriend). **superstes,** -stitis (adj.) *surviving.*

13   **torreo,** -ere, torrui, tostum *scorch, roast.* **fax,** facis f. *torch, wedding torch, flame.* **Thurinus,** -a, -um *of Thurii,* a town in the south colonized by the Greeks in pre-Roman times and noted for its wealth. **bis** *two times, twice.* **patior,** pati, passus/a sum *suffer, experience, endure.*

17   **priscus,** -a, -um *old, ancient.* **diduco,** -ere, -duxi, -ductum *part, divide, separate.* **iugum,** -i n. *yoke.* **aeneus,** -a, -um *of bronze.* **flavus,** -a, -um *yellow, golden*; *golden-haired.* **excutio,** -ere, -cussi, -cussum *cast off, discard.* **reicio,** -ere, -ieci, -iectum *cast off, reject.* **pateo,** -ere, patui *be open, accessible*; the convention is that the woman opens or closes her door to her unhappy lover, the **exclusus amator,** who is often the subject of Latin love poetry. **ianua,** -ae f. *door, entrance.*

21   **quamquam** (conj.) *although, and yet.* **sidus,** -eris n. *star, planet.* **levis,** -e (adj.) *light, easy.* **cortex,** -icis m. *cork, bark.* **improbus,** -a, -um *cruel, perverse, rebellious.* **iracundus,** -a, -um *angry* (probably in jealousy). **Hadria,** -ae m. *Adriatic Sea.* **obeo,** -ire, obivi, obitum *die*; potential subjunctive. **lubens,** -entis (adj.) *be willing*; *gladly.* The anaphora of **tecum** and the placement of **amem** and **lubens** each at the end of their clauses emphasize her eagerness to resume their relationship.

Quintus Horatius Flaccus, *Carmina* 3.9

In this playful poem the voices of a lover and his ex-girl are structured in three pairs of four-line stanzas. The female exhibits the personal freedom of a courtesan. The names and places are from outside of Rome. The poem's playfulness flaunts Roman *gravitas* (this Venus is a far cry from the mother-goddess of Rome). In this poem published in 23 BCE, Horace captures the flavor of lovers' recriminations, the singing contests of Greek pastoral poetry, and the *suasoriae* (persuasive speeches) of Roman rhetorical education. The meter is Second Asclepiadean.

The unnamed **lover** speaks first, describing his past happiness with his girl:
> Donec gratus eram tibi
> nec quisquam potior bracchia candidae
> cervici iuvenis dabat,
> Persarum vigui rege beatior.

Lydia admits she was happy with her lover before he strayed:
> 5   Donec non alia magis
> arsisti neque erat Lydia post Chloen,
> multi Lydia nominis,
> Romana vigui clarior Ilia.

He brags of the musical talents of his current girl, Chloe from Thrace:
> Me nunc Thressa Chloe regit,
> 10   dulcis docta modos et citharae sciens,
> pro qua non metuam mori,
> si parcent animae fata superstiti.

She counters with the status of her new boyfriend, Calais from South Italy:
> Me torret face mutua
> Thurini Calais filius Ornyti,
> 15   pro quo bis patiar mori,
> si parcent puero fata superstiti.

He wonders if they could resume their relationship:
> Quid si prisca redit Venus
> diductosque iugo cogit aeneo,
> si flava excutitur Chloe
> 20   reiectaeque patet ianua Lydiae?

She answers unambiguously:
> Quamquam sidere pulchrior
> ille est, tu levior cortice et inprobo
> iracundior Hadria,
> tecum vivere amem, tecum obeam lubens.

Notes to Sulpicia, *Elegidia* 1-3:

1.1   **pudori, mihi**: double dative (of purpose and reference): "At last love has come, such that (**qualem**) it would be more shameful for me to have hidden it than to have uncovered it to anyone." **pudor**, -oris m. *shame*. **tego**, -ere, texi, tectum *cover, clothe*. **nudo** (1) *strip, bare, unclothe, expose*; **nudasse** is the contracted form of **nudavisse**. **Texisse** and **nudasse** form a playful opposition and paradox, literal and figurative, of clothing or words. **Sit** (subjunctive in characteristic clause) makes the time of the event more general. **exoro** (1) *win by entreaty, persuade*. **Cytherea** = *Aphrodite*; note the use of the Greek **Cytherea** and the Latin **Venus**. Both have answered Sulpicia's prayers. Perhaps she thinks of Sappho's poem to Aphrodite (Sappho, Fragment 1) as well as her own verses. **Camenae**: originally water goddesses, they are the Roman version of the *Muses*, i.e., *poetry*. **illum** = Cerinthus, named in poems 2 and 4. **depono**, -ere, -posui, -positum *put down, plant, entrust for safekeeping*. **sinus**, -us m *lap, bosom*.

5   **exsolvo**, -ere, -ui, -utum *fulfill, pay off*. **promissum**, -i n. *promise*. **narret**: jussive subjunctive. **gaudium**, -i n. *joy, delight*. **si quis** *if anyone*; Sulpicia offers her story to any unrequited lover. The condition is future less vivid ("should...would"). **non**: if taken with **mandare**, rather than **velim,** she wishes she did not have to seal her letters. **signatis tabellis**: dative; "sealed tablets" refer to letters or drafts of poems. **ne...nemo**: the double negative causes an ambiguity in a poem which is full of paradoxes; **nemo**, neminis m/f. *nobody*; *some nobody* (anyone who is not her beloved, **meus**). The text is in doubt here: another reading which solves this problem is **me legat ut nemo**. The double negative can be explained by its being used for emphasis and by the fact that a verb of fearing is implied. **quam...ante = antequam. meus** *my own true love*. **pecco** (1) *err, do wrong, make a blunder*. Note the tenses of the infinitives and their introductory verbs: the present indicative (**iuvat**) with the perfect (**peccasse** is a contracted form of **peccavisse**) indicates that the action has already taken place. **iuvo** (1) *help, cause to be glad*. **vultus**, -us m. *expression, face, one's view*. **conpono**, -ere, -posui, -positum *arrange, compose, write*. **famae**: see line 2.

10   **taedet**, -ere, -uit (impersonal verb) *it wearies, it annoys* (understand **me**). **cum...fuisse**: a euphemism for sexual intercourse. **ferar** "may I be said/reported to..."

2.1   **invisus**, -a, -um *hateful, horrid*. **natalis**, -e *of birth* (understand **dies**). **rus**, ruris n. *the country*; **rure** *in the country*. **molestus**, -a, -um *annoying, nasty*. **qui**: the subject is [**dies**] **natalis**. **dulcius**: comparative of **dulcis**, -e *sweet, pleasant*. **urbe**: ablative of comparison. **an**: a question-particle sometimes used for indignation or surprise (*surely not*; *what!*). **villa**, -ae f. *farmhouse, country-house*. **sit**: potential subjunctive. **aptus**, -a, -um *suitable*. **Arretinus**, -a, -um *of Arretium*, a town in Etruria. **amnis**, -is m. *river*.

5   **nimium** (adv.) *too much* (with **studiose**). **Messalla** is her guardian. **mei**: objective genitive with **studiose**, voc. of **studiosus**, -a, -um *solicitous*. **heu** *alas* (for + gen. or dat.); other texts read **neu** or **non. tempestivus** *early, in season*. **propinquus**, -a, -um *near*; as a noun, *relative*. A suggested reading is **neu tempestivae saepe**, taking **propinque** in the adjectival sense of "near to, on the point of" with the genitive (i.e., "often on the point of an unseasonable journey"), as if Messalla always planned inconvenient outings for her. In the text printed here **tempestivae viae** depends on **heu. abducta < abduco**: she pretends she has been kidnapped. **hic** (adv.) *here*. **arbitrium**, -i n. *judgment, control*. **arbitrio...meo**: abl. of description, "at my own discretion," "to be the boss of me." **quamvis** (rel. adv.) *no matter how, however*. **sino**, -ere, sivi, situm *permit*.

Sulpicia, *Elegidia* 1-6

Standing alone in extant Latin poetry, Sulpicia, a young poet of the late 1st century BCE, gives voice to a woman's love in six poems (Tibullus, Book 3.13-18). The aristocratic daughter of Servius Sulpicius Rufus (poem 4), she was the ward of Valerius Messalla Corvinus (poem 2), a gifted patron of the arts whose circle also included Tibullus. In the tradition of Latin love poetry, she chronicles her love for Cerinthus and her budding fame as a poet. Long overlooked as the work of a naive teenage girl, Sulpicia's poetry finally became the object of scholarly attention in the late 1970s. The meter is elegiac couplet.

1. Sulpicia sings of her love for Cerinthus and her discovery of her talent as a poet:

> Tandem venit amor, qualem texisse pudori
> > quam nudasse alicui sit mihi fama magis.
> Exorata meis illum Cytherea Camenis
> > adtulit in nostrum deposuitque sinum.
> 5 Exsolvit promissa Venus: mea gaudia narret,
> > dicetur si quis non habuisse sua.
> Non ego signatis quicquam mandare tabellis,
> > ne legat id nemo quam meus ante, velim,
> sed peccasse iuvat, vultus conponere famae
> 10 > taedet: cum digno digna fuisse ferar.

2. Sulpicia resents celebrating her birthday in the country with her guardian Messala, without Cerinthus:

> Invisus natalis adest, qui rure molesto
> > et sine Cerintho tristis agendus erit.
> Dulcius urbe quid est? an villa sit apta puellae
> > atque Arretino frigidus amnis agro?
> 5 Iam nimium Messalla mei studiose, quiescas,
> > heu tempestivae saepe, propinque, viae!
> Hic animum sensusque meos abducta relinquo,
> > arbitrio quamvis non sinis esse meo.

Notes to Sulpicia, *Elegidia* 3-6:

3.1 **triste**: translate with *iter*. **sublatum** < **suffero**, -ferre, sustuli, sublatum *lift*. **Romae**: locative, *in Rome*. **omnibus...nobis**: dative of agent. **agatur**: jussive (hortatory) subjunctive, "let...," "may ..." **ago**: here, *spend* (time). **qui** refers to **dies**. **opinor** (1, depon.) *suppose, imagine* **nec opinanti/necopinanti**: *unaware, unsuspecting*. **forte** (adv.) *by chance*.

4.1 **gratum est** (= **gratias ago**), "thanks a lot" (sarcastic). **securus**, -a, -um *carefree, unconcerned*. **quod** *the fact that*. **multum tibi permittis**: " you allow yourself plenty of freedom." **subito** (adv.) *suddenly*. **male** (adv.) *badly, awfully* (intensifies the negative **inepta**). **ne cadam**: negative purpose clause; **cado**, -ere, cecidi, casum *fall*. **ineptus**, -a, um *silly, absurd* (**inepta** refers to Sulpicia; translate as an adverb). **toga**, -ae f. *a lower-class woman* of "loose character" (used generally); the only women who wore togas in Rome were prostitutes. **togae**: objective genitive (translate "for") with **cura**. **potior** (adj.) *preferable, more desirable*; followed by **quam**. **premo**, -ere, pressi, pressum *squeeze, weigh down*. **quasillum/quasillus** *wool basket*. Sulpicia shows the scorn of an upper-crust lady for the woman who has to work for her living. If Cerinthus really is carrying on with a **quasillaria**, it is hard to see how she would have any time or energy for him after working on wool-making from dawn to dark, let alone for writing him verses. **scortum**, -i n. *a prostitute* (the one Cerinthus is hanging out with). **Servi filia Sulpicia**: her official name with patronymic, as it would appear on her epitaph. Is this a veiled taunt, that he does not know what he is missing?

5 **sollicitus**, -a, -um *troubled, anxious, uneasy*. The subject is [**ei**] antecedent to **quibus**. **illa**: translate with **maxima causa**. **dolori**: dative of purpose ("for"), with **causa**. **cedam** < **cedo**, -ere, cessi, cessum *yield to, give up my place to*. **ignotus**, -a, -um *unknown, obscure, low*. **torus**, -i m. *couch, bed, liaison*.

5.1 **tuae puellae**: objective genitive, translate "for." **pius**, -a, -um *devoted, loving*. **vexo** (1) *trouble, afflict*. **fessus**, -a, -um *tired, weary*. **calor**, -oris m. *fever* (of passion or illness). **a** (interj.) *Ah!* **aliter** (adv.) *otherwise*. **evinco**, -ere, -vici, -victum *overcome, prevail over*. **optarim** (= **optaverim**) and **putem**: subjunctives in future less vivid condition ("would...should").

5 **prosum**, prodesse, profui + dat. *be of use, do good, be helpful*; **prosit**: potential subjunctive in a mixed condition. **lentus** *slow, easy, indifferent*. Notice the interlocked word order: **nostra mala** (*ills*) surrounds **potes ferre** which in turn embraces **lento pectore**. She plies her syntax to overwhelm her lover's imagined lack of feeling.

6.1 **sim**: optative subjunctive ("may"). **mea lux**: she means that he is the light of her life. **aeque** (adv.) *equally*. **fervidus**, -a, -um *burning, intense, hot*. **ac** (conj.) *as*. **ante** (adv.) *ago, before*. **tota iuventa**: ablative (of time within which); **iuventa**, -ae f. *youth*. **conmitto**, -ere, -misi, -missum *bring together, bring about*. **stulta**: nominative; **stultus**, -a, -um *stupid, foolish*. **cuius**: objective genitive with **paenituisse** (translate as subject of the impersonal). **fateor**, -eri, fassus/a sum *confess*; potential subjunctive. **paenitet**, -ere, -uit *it causes regret*; **me paenitet** *I regret* (+ genitive of the thing that causes regret). **magis...quam** *more...than*.

5 **hesternus**, -a, -um *of yesterday, yesterday's*. **quod** *the fact that*. **relinquo**, -ere, reliqui, relictum *leave, abandon*. Notice the word order: he is left in the night, while she stands outside. **ardor**, -is m. *heat, passion*. **dissimulo** (1) *pretend* that something is not, *hide, conceal*. The word order reveals her failure to disguise the heat of her passion.

Sulpicia, *Elegidia* 1-6 (continued)

3. Her guardian relents. leaving Sulpicia free to spend the day with Cerinthus:

> Scis iter ex animo sublatum triste puellae?
>> natali Romae iam licet esse suo.
> Omnibus ille dies nobis natalis agatur,
>> qui nec opinanti nunc tibi forte venit.

4. Sulpicia angrily suspects that Cerinthus has another girlfriend:

> Gratum est, securus multum quod iam tibi de me
>> permittis, subito ne male inepta cadam.
> Sit tibi cura togae potior pressumque quasillo
>> scortum quam Servi filia Sulpicia:
> 5   Solliciti sunt pro nobis, quibus illa dolori est,
>> ne cedam ignoto, maxima causa, toro.

5. Sulpicia, ill with a fever, hopes Cerinthus is thinking of her and wishes her well:

> Estne tibi, Cerinthe, tuae pia cura puellae,
>> quod mea nunc vexat corpora fessa calor?
> A ego non aliter tristes evincere morbos
>> optarim, quam te si quoque velle putem.
> 5   At mihi quid prosit morbos evincere, si tu
>> nostra potes lento pectore ferre mala?

6. In this small gem, Sulpicia regrets her abrupt departure from Cerinthus, leaving him to spend the previous night alone:

> Ne tibi sim, mea lux, aeque iam fervida cura
>> ac videor paucos ante fuisse dies,
> si quicquam tota conmisi stulta iuventa,
>> cuius me fatear paenituisse magis,
> 5   hesterna quam te solum quod nocte reliqui,
>> ardorem cupiens dissimulare meum.

LIST OF WOMEN NAMED IN THE READINGS
The names of fictitious women are in italics

Agrippina Maior, the daughter of Marcus Agrippa and Julia; wife of Germanicus (ca. 14 BCE-33 CE).
  C. Tacitus, *Annales* 1.33, 40, 69 (excerpts). (State)

Antonia Minor, the daughter of Marcus Antonius and Octavia; wife of Drusus (36 BCE-37 CE).
  Valerius Maximus, *Facta et Dicta Memorabilia* 4.3.3. (Marriage)

Atia, the daughter of Marcus Atius Balbus; mother of Octavius (Augustus) and Octavia (d. 43/42 BCE.).
  C. Tacitus, *Dialogus de Oratoribus* 28-29 (excerpts). (Family)

Aurelia, the mother of Caesar; reported Clodius' violation of the women's festival (d. 54 BCE).
  C. Tacitus, *Dialogus de Oratoribus* 28-29 (excerpts). (Family)

Aurelia Philematium, a freedwoman, wife of the butcher Hermia (1st century BCE).
  ILS 1221, Funerary Inscription. (Marriage)

Calpurnia, the young second or third wife of Pliny (fl. late 1st century CE.).
  C. Plinius Caecilius Secundus (minor), *Epistulae* 4.19, 7.5, 8.10. (Learning, Marriage, Body).

Calpurnia Hispulla, the sister of Calpurnia's dead father (fl. mid-late 1st century CE).
  C. Plinius Caecilius Secundus (minor), *Epistulae* 4.19. (Learning)

Chloe, a music girl from Thrace (late 1st century BCE).
  Q. Horatius Flaccus, *Carmina* 3.9. (Flirtation)

Claudia, a *matrona* (ca. 135-120 BCE).
  ILS 8403, Funerary Inscription. (Marriage)

Claudia Quinta, *matrona* who led the ship of the *Magna Mater* to Rome (fl. 204 BCE).
  P. Ovidius Naso, *Fasti* 4.293-328, 343-344. (State)

Claudia Rufina, wife of Martial's friend Pudens (fl. mid-late 1st century CE).
  M. Valerius Martialis, *Epigrammata* 11.53. (Marriage)

Cornelia 1, the daughter of P. Cornelius Scipio Africanus maior; wife of Tiberius Sempronius Gracchus; mother of Sempronia, Tiberius and Gaius Gracchus (fl. 2nd century BCE).
  M. Fabius Quintilianus, *Institutio Oratoria* 1.1.6 (Learning); C. Tacitus, *Dialogus de Oratoribus* 28-29 (excerpts), C. Nepos, *De Viris Illustribus*, frag. 1-2. (Family)

Cornelia 2, the daughter of Cornelius Scipio and Scribonia; wife of Paullus Aemilius Lepidus (d. 16 BCE).
  Sextus Propertius, *Elegiae* 4.11 (excerpts). (Family)

Domitia Decidiana, the wife of Iulius Agricola; Tacitus' mother-in-law (fl. 1st century CE).
  C. Cornelius Tacitus, *Agricola* 6.1, 3. (Marriage)

Eucharis, a singer and actress (2nd -1st century BCE).
  ILS 5213, Funerary Inscription. (Childhood)

Fortunata, the wife of Trimalchio (mid 1st century CE).
  C. Petronius Arbiter, *Satyricon* 37, 67, 76 (excerpts). (Family)

Galeria Copiola, an actress (1st century BCE).
>C. Plinius Secundus (maior), *Naturalis Historia* 7.48.158. (Work)

Gymnasium, the daughter of *Syra*; a *meretrix* (early 2nd century BCE).
>T. Maccius Plautus, *Cistellaria* 38-41, 123-4, 133-44. (Work)

Helvia, the mother of Seneca (fl. 1st century CE).
>L. Annaeus Seneca, *Ad Helviam Matrem de Consolatione* 14, 16, 19 (excerpts). (Family)

Hispala Faecenia, a freedwoman and courtesan (fl. 186 BCE).
>T. Livius, *Ab Urbe Condita* 39.9-10 (excerpts). (State)

Hortensia, the eloquent daughter of the orator Q. Hortensius Hortalus (1st century BCE).
>M. Fabius Quintilianus, *Institutio Oratoria* 1.1.6. (Learning)

Hygia, a midwife (1st century CE).
>*CIL* 6.6647: Funerary Inscription. (Work)

Iaia Cyzicena, a painter (1st century BCE).
>C. Plinius Secundus (maior), *Naturalis Historia* 35.40.147-8. (Work)

Julia, the daughter of Julius Caesar and Cornelia; wife of Pompey (ca. 83-54 BCE).
>Valerius Maximus, *Facta et Dicta Memorabilia* 4.6.4. (Body)

Julia, the daughter of Octavian (Augustus) and Scribonia (39 BCE-CE 14).
>C. Suetonius Tranquillus, *Vita Divi Augusti* 64.2-3. (Learning)

Julia, the daughter of Julia and Agrippa; granddaughter of Augustus (ca.19 BCE-29 CE).
>C. Suetonius Tranquillus, *Vita Divi Augusti* 64.2-3. (Learning)

Julia Procilla, the mother of Gnaeus Julius Agricola (1st century CE).
>C. Tacitus, *Agricola* 4.1-4. (Family)

Laelia, the wife of Q. Mucius Scaevola (fl. 2nd -1st century BCE).
>M. Fabius Quintilianus, *Institutio Oratoria* 1.1.6. (Learning)

Livia Drusilla, Livia, the wife of Augustus (58 BCE-29 CE).
>Cornelius Tacitus, *Annales* 1.33, 40, 69 (excerpts). (State)

Lucceia, an actress (ca. late 1st century BCE).
>C. Plinius Secundus (maior), *Naturalis Historia* 7.48.158. (Work)

Lydia, one of Horace's literary girlfriends (late 1st century BCE).
>Q. Horatius Flaccus, *Carmina* 3.9. (Flirtation)

Matrona, wife of Menaechmus (early 2nd century BCE).
>T. Maccius Plautus, *Menaechmi* 602-652. (Marriage)

Melaenis, the mother of *Selenium*; a *meretrix* (early 2nd century BCE).
>T. Maccius Plautus, *Cistellaria* 38-41, 123-4, 133-44. (Work)

Minicia Marcella, the 13-year-old daughter of Fundanus (ca. 100-110 CE).
>C. Plinius Caecilius Secundus (minor), *Epistulae* 5.16. (Childhood)

Murdia, honored daughter, wife, and mother (1st century BCE).
>*ILS* 8394: *Laudatio Funebris Murdiae*: (excerpts). (Family)

Naevoleia Tyche, a wealthy Pompeiian businesswoman and benefactor (1st century CE).
>*ILS* 6373: Funerary Inscription. (Work)

Olympias, a painter (n.d.).
>C. Plinius Secundus (maior), *Naturalis Historia* 35.40.147-8. (Work)

Perilla, poet, stepdaughter, and literary protégé of Ovid (fl. early 1st century CE).
>P. Ovidius Naso, *Tristia* 3.7. (Learning)

Porcia, the wife of M. Junius Brutus (d. 43 BCE).
>Valerius Maximus, *Facta et Dicta Memorabilia* 4.6.5. (Marriage)

Postumia, a Vestal Virgin (420 BCE).

 T. Livius, *Ab Urbe Condita* 4.44. (Body)

Sammula, an actress (n.d).

 C. Plinius Secundus (maior), *Naturalis Historia* 7.48.158. (Work)

Sappho, Greek lyric poet of Lesbos (fl. 6th century BCE).

 P. Ovidius Naso, *Tristia* 3.7 (Learning); M. Valerius Martialis, *Epigrammata* 10.35 (Marriage)

Scintilla, the wife of Habbinas; best friend of *Fortunata* (mid-1st century CE).

 C. Petronius Arbiter, *Satyricon* 37, 67, 76 (excerpts). (Family)

Selenium, the daughter of *Melaenis*; a *meretrix* (early 2nd century BCE).

 T. Maccius Plautus, *Cistellaria* 38-41, 123-4, 133-44. (Work)

Sempronia, the wife of D. Brutus; member of the Catilinarian Conspiracy (fl. 63 BCE).

 C. Sallustius Crispus, *Bellum Catilinae* 24-25 (excerpts). (State)

Sulpicia 1, poet, the daughter of Servius Sulpicius Rufus; ward of M. Valerius Messalla Corvinus (fl. late 1st century BCE)

 Incertus Auctor, *De Sulpicia* 1. (Body); Sulpicia, *Elegidia* 1-6. (Flirtation)

Sulpicia 2, poet, wife of Calenus (fl. late 1st century CE).

 Sulpiciae Conquestio lines 7-11 (Learning); M. Valerius Martialis, *Epigrammata* 10.35. (Marriage)

Sulpicia 3, the wife of Cornelius Lentullus Cruscellio (fl. mid 1st century BCE).

 Valerius Maximus, *Facta et Dicta Memorabilia* 6.7. (Marriage)

Syra, the mother of *Gymnasium*; a *meretrix* (early 2nd century BCE).

 T. Maccius Plautus, *Cistellaria* 38-41, 123-4, 133-44. (Work)

Tanaquil, the Etruscan-born queen; wife of Tarquinius Priscus (6th century BCE).

 T. Livius, *Ab Urbe Condita* 1.39, 41 (excerpts). (State)

Terentia, the sister of D. Terentius Gentianus (fl. 130 CE).

 ILS 1046a: Funerary Inscription for her brother. (Family)

Terentia, the wife of Cicero (1st century BCE).

 M. Tullius Cicero, *Epistulae ad Familiares* 14.4, 20. (Family)

Tertia Aemilia, the wife of P. Cornelius Scipio Africanus maior (3rd century-2nd century BCE).

 Valerius Maximus, *Facta et Dicta Memorabilia* 6.7. (Marriage)

Titia, the name signifies "Jane Doe."

 Gaius, *Institutiones* 1.144-145, 148-150. (State)

Tullia, the daughter of Cicero and Terentia (79-45 BCE).

 M. Tullius Cicero, *Epistulae ad Familiares* 14.4, 20. (Family)

Tullia Minor, the younger daughter of Servius Tullius; queen; wife of Tarquinius Superbus (fl. 6th century BCE).

 T. Livius, *Ab Urbe Condita* 1.47-48 (excerpts). (State)

Turia, a *matrona*; perhaps also wife of Q. Lucretius Vespillo (1st century BCE).

 ILS 8393 "*Laudatio Turiae*" (excerpts); Valerius Maximus, *Facta et Dicta Memorabilia* 6.7. (Marriage)

Veturia, the mother of Coriolanus (fl. 493 BCE).

 T. Livius, *Ab Urbe Condita* 2.40. (State)

Volumnia, the wife of Coriolanus (fl. 493 BCE).

 T. Livius, *Ab Urbe Condita* 2.40. (State)

LIST OF AUTHORS OF TEXT SELECTIONS

Anonymous: *De Sulpicia* 1, from Tibullus, Book 3 (Body); Funerary and Honorary Inscriptions from *CLE*, *CIL*, *ILS* (Childhood, Marriage, Family, Work).

Cato the Elder: Marcus Porcius Cato, statesman, senator, censor, and farmer (234-149 BCE); work: *De Re Rustica* (*On Agriculture*); selection: from *De Re Rustica* 142, on the farmer's wife. (Work)

Celsus: Aulus Cornelius Celsus, polymath, (fl. 14-37 CE); work: encyclopedia on agriculture, rhetoric, military science, and philosophy, of which only *De Medicina* (*On Medicine*) survives; selection: from *De Medicina* 2, 4, on women's health. (Body)

Cicero: Marcus Tullius Cicero, orator, consul, man of letters (106-43 BCE); work: orations, rhetorical treatises, philosophical works, letters; selection: from *Epistulae ad Familiares* 14. (Family)

Columella: L. Iunius Moderatus Columella, (mid-1st century CE); work: *De Re Rustica* (*On Agriculture*); selection: from *De Re Rustica* 1, on slave mothers. (Work)

Cornelia: Cornelia, daughter of Scipio Africanus, wife of Tiberius Sempronius Gracchus, mother of Sempronia, Tiberius and Gaius Gracchus (2nd century BCE); selection: from her letters in Nepos, *De Viris Illustribus*. (Family)

Gaius: Gaius, jurist (2nd century CE); work: *Institutiones* (*Institutes*) and other legal compilations; selection: from *Institutiones* I, on *tutela* (guardianship). (State)

Gellius: Aulus Gellius, scholar (2nd century CE); work: *Noctes Atticae* (*Attic Nights*); selection: *Noctes Atticae* 1, on choosing Vestals. (Childhood)

Horace: Quintus Horatius Flaccus, poet (65-8 BCE); work: *Carmina* (*Odes*), epistles, satires; selection: *Carmina* 3.9, on Lydia. (Flirtation)

Juvenal: Marcus Junius Juvenalis, satiric poet (ca. 65-127 CE); work: *Saturae* (*Satires*); selection: from *Satura* 6, on the intellectual woman. (Learning)

Livy: Titus Livius, historian (59 BCE to 17 CE); work: *Ab Urbe Condita* (*From the Founding of the City*), originally 142 books, of which 35 are extant; selection: from *Ab Urbe Condita* 1, 3, 4, 29, 39. (Body, Family, State)

Lucretius: Titus Lucretius Carus, poet, philosopher (ca. 94-55 BCE); work: *De Rerum Natura* (*On the Nature of Things*); selection: from *De Rerum Natura* 4, on true loveliness. (Body)

Martial: Marcus Valerius Martialis, poet (ca. 40-104 CE); work: *Epigrammata* (*Epigrams*); selection: from *Epigrammata* 3, 10, 11. (Learning, Marriage)

Naevius: Gnaeus Naevius, poet (3rd century BCE); work: comedies, tragedies, epic poem *Bellum Poenicum*, from which fragments survive; selection: from a lost comedy. (Childhood)

Nepos: Cornelius Nepos, historian, biographer (ca. 99-24 BCE); work: *De Viris Illustribus* (*On Famous Men*), and others surviving only in fragments; selection: *De Viris Illustribus*, from the letters of Cornelia. (Family)

Ovid: Publius Ovidius Naso, poet (43 BCE to 17 CE); work: *Amores, Heroides, Ars Amatoria, Metamorphoses, Fasti, Tristia.*; selection: from *Amores* 1, *Ars Amatoria* 1, 3, *Fasti* 4, *Tristia* 3. (Learning, State, Flirtation)

Petronius: Petronius Arbiter, satirical novelist (1st century CE); work: *Satyricon*; selection: from *Satyricon* 37, 67, 76, on Fortunata. (Family)

Plautus: Titus Maccius Plautus, comic playwright (fl. 205-184 BCE); work: 21 surviving comedies; selection: from *Menaechmi, Epidicus, Cistellaria*. (Marriage, Body, Work)

Pliny the Elder: Gaius Plinius Secundus (maior), scholar (23-79 CE); work: *Naturalis Historia* (*Natural History*), and other lost technical treatises; selection: from *Naturalis Historia* 7, 28, 35. (Body, Work)

Pliny the Younger: Gaius Plinius Caecilius Secundus (minor), lawyer, statesman, man of letters (ca. 61-112 CE) work: *Epistulae* (*Letters*), *Panegyricus*; selection: from *Epistulae* 4, 5, 7, 8 (Childhood, Learning, Marriage, Body)

Propertius: Sextus Propertius, poet (ca. 54-2 BCE); work: *Elegiae* (*Elegies*); selections: from *Elegiae* 2.23 on the *meretrix* and 4.11, on Cornelia. (Family, Flirtation)

Quintilian: Marcus Fabius Quintilianus, teacher of rhetoric (ca. 30/5-100 CE); work *Institutio Oratoria* in ten books; selection: from *Institutio* 1, on women's elegant speech. (Learning)

Sallust: Gaius Sallustius Crispus, historian (86-35 BCE); work: *Bellum Catilinae, Bellum Iugurthinum, Historiae*; selection from *Bellum Catilinae* 24-25, on Sempronia. (State)

Seneca: Lucius Annaeus Seneca, man of letters, philosopher, tutor of Nero (ca.4 BCE-65 CE); work: *Dialogi* (ethical treatises), tragedies; selection: from *Ad Helviam de Consolatione* 14, 16, 19, on grieving women. (Family)

Suetonius: Gaius Suetonius Tranquillus, historian, biographer (70-ca. 130 CE); works: *De Viris Illustribus* (*About Famous Men*), *De Vita Caesarum* (*On the Lives of the Caesars*), others now lost; selection: from *De Vita Augusti* 64, on the education of his daughters. (Learning)

Sulpicia 1: Sulpicia, daughter of Servius Sulpicius Rufus, love poet (fl. late 1st century BCE); work: *Elegidia* (*Short Elegies*); selection: *Elegidia* 1-6, from Tibullus, *Carmina* 3. (Flirtation)

Sulpicia 2: Sulpicia, wife of Calenus, poet (1st century CE); work: poetry, now lost; selection: fragment, *Conquestio* 7-11, on a woman writing epic; tribute by Martial, *Epigrammata* 10.35. (Learning, Marriage)

Tacitus: Cornelius Tacitus, historian (ca. 56-115 CE); work: *Agricola, Annales* (*Annals*), *Dialogus* (*Dialogue*), *Germania, Historiae* (*Histories*); selection: from *Agricola, Annales, Dialogus*, on mothers and wives. (Marriage, Family, State)

Terentia: Terentia, upper-class Roman woman (2nd century CE); work: unknown; selection: fragment of an epigraphical poem to her brother. (Family)

Valerius Maximus: Valerius Maximus, historian (fl. 14-37 CE); work: *Factorum ac Dictorum Memorabilium libri ix* (*Memorable Deeds and Words*); selection: from *Memorabilia* 4, 6, on exemplary women. (Marriage, Body)

Vergil: Publius Vergilius Maro, poet (70-19 BCE); work: *Aeneis* (*Aeneid*), *Georgica* (*Georgics*), *Ecloga* (*Eclogues*); selection: from *Aeneis* 8, on the housewife. (Work)

BIBLIOGRAPHY

Books

Arietti, James A. 1997. "Rape and Livy's View of Roman History." In *Rape in Antiquity*. Edited by Susan Deacy and Karen F. Pierce, 209-229. London and Swansea: Duckworth and The Classical Press of Wales.

Beard, Mary, John North, and Simon Price. 1998. *Religions of Rome. Volume 1: A history, Volume 2: A sourcebook*. Cambridge: Cambridge University Press.

Bonner, Stanley F. 1977. *Education in Ancient Rome: From the Elder Cato to the Younger Pliny*. Berkeley and Los Angeles: University of California Press.

Bradley, Keith R. 1991. *Discovering the Roman Family: studies in Roman social history*. Oxford and New York: Oxford University Press.

Braund, Susanna Morton. 2002. *Latin Literature*. London and New York: Routledge.

Copley, Frank O. 1981. *Exclusus Amator: a study in Latin love poetry*. Chico, CA: Scholars Press.

D'Ambra, Eve. 1993. *Private Lives, Imperial Virtues: the frieze of the Forum Transitorium in Rome*. Princeton: Princeton University Press.

------. 2000. "Nudity and Adornment in Female Portrait Sculpture of the Second Century AD." In *I, Claudia*. Edited by Diana E. E. Kleiner and Susan B. Matheson, 101-114. Austin: University of Texas Press.

Dixon, Suzanne. 1992. *The Roman Family*. Baltimore and London: Johns Hopkins University Press.

------. 2001. *Reading Roman Women: sources, genres and real life*. London: Duckworth.

Fantham, Elaine, Helene Peet Foley, Natalie Boymel Kampen, Sarah B. Pomeroy, and H. A. Shapiro. 1994. *Women in the Classical World: image and text*. Oxford and New York: Oxford University Press.

Fraschetti, Augusto, ed.. 2001. *Roman Women*. Translated by Linda Lappin. Chicago: University of Chicago Press.

Gardner, Jane F. 1986. *Women in Roman Law & Society*. London: Croom Helm.

------ and Thomas Wiedemann. 1991. *The Roman Household: a sourcebook*. London and New York: Routledge.

Grubbs , Judith. 2002. *Women and the Law in the Roman Empire: a sourcebook on marriage, divorce, and widowhood*. London and New York: Routledge.

Habinek, Thomas. 1998. *The Politics of Latin Literature: writing, identity, and empire in ancient Rome*. Princeton: Princeton University Press.

Hallett, Judith P. 1984. *Fathers and Daughters in Roman Society: women and the elite family*. Princeton: Princeton University Press.

-----. 1999. "Women in the Ancient Roman World." In *Women's Roles in Ancient Civilizations*. Edited by Bella Vivante, 259-289. Westport, CT and London: Greenwood Press.

Hallett, Judith P. and Marilyn B. Skinner. 1997. *Roman Sexualities*. Princeton: Princeton University Press.

Harvey, Brian K. 2004. *Roman Lives: ancient Roman life as illustrated by Latin inscriptions*. Newburyport MA: Focus.

Hemelrijk, Emily A. 1999. *Matrona Docta: educated women in the Roman elite from Cornelia to Julia Domna*. London and New York: Routledge.

Hoffer, Stanley E. 1999. *The Anxieties of Pliny the Younger*. Atlanta: Scholars Press.

Joshel, Sandra R. 1992a. "The Body Female and the Body Politic: Livy's Lucretia and Verginia." In *Pornography and Representation in Greece and Rome*. Edited by Amy Richlin, 112-30. Oxford and New York: Oxford University Press. Reprinted in *Sexuality and Gender in the Classical World*. Edited by Laura K. McClure, 163-187. Oxford: Blackwell.

-----. 1992b. *Work, Identity, and Legal Status at Rome: a study of the occupational inscriptions*. Norman: University of Oklahoma Press.

Kampen, Natalie Boymel. 1981. *Image and Status: Roman working women in Ostia*. Berlin: Mann.

Kleiner, Diana E. E. 1996. "Imperial Women as Patrons of the Arts in the Early Empire." In *I, Claudia*. Edited by Diana E. E. Kleiner and Susan B. Matheson, 28-41. New Haven: Yale University Art Gallery. Distributed by the University of Texas Press, Austin.

Kleiner, Diana E. E. and Susan B. Matheson (eds.). 1996. *I, Claudia: women in ancient Rome*. New Haven: Yale University Art Gallery. Distributed by the University of Texas Press, Austin.

-----. 2000. *I, Claudia II: women in Roman art and society*. Austin: University of Texas Press.

Kraemer, Ross S. 1988. *Maenads, Martyrs, Matrons, Monastics: a sourcebook on women's religions in the Greco-Roman world*. Philadelphia: Fortress Press.

-----. 2004. *Women's Religions in the Greco-Roman World: a sourcebook*. Oxford and New York: Oxford University Press,

LaFollette, Laetitia. 1994. "The Costume of the Roman Bride." In *The World of Roman Costume*. Edited by Judith Lynn Sebesta and Larissa Bonfante, 54-64. Madison, WI: University of Wisconsin Press.

Lefkowitz, Mary and Maureen Fant. 1992. *Women's Life in Greece and Rome: a source book in translation*. 2d ed. Baltimore: Johns Hopkins University Press.

McClure, Laura K., ed. 2002. *Sexuality and Gender in the Classical World: readings and sources*. Oxford: Blackwell.

McManus, Barbara F. 1997. *Classics and Feminism: gendering the classics*. New York and London: Twayne Publishers and Prentice Hall International.

Plant, I. M. 2004. *Women Writers of Ancient Greece and Rome: an anthology*. Norman: University of Oklahoma Press.

Rawson, Beryl, ed. 1986. *The Family in Ancient Rome: new perspectives*. Ithaca: Cornell University Press.

-----. 2003. *Children and Childhood in Roman Italy*. Oxford: Oxford University Press.

Rawson, Beryl and Paul Weaver. 1997. *The Roman Family in Italy: status, sentiment, space*. Oxford: Clarendon Press.

Richlin, Amy. 1997. "Pliny's Brassiere." In *Roman Sexualities*. Edited by Judith P. Hallett and Marilyn B. Skinner, 197-220. Princeton: Princeton University Press.

Sebesta, Judith Lynn. 1994. "Symbolism in the Costume of the Roman Woman." In *The World of Roman Costume*. Edited by Judith Lynn Sebesta and Larissa Bonfante, 46-53. Madison, WI: University of Wisconsin Press.

-----. 1998. "Women's Costume and Feminine Civic Morality in Augustan Rome." In *Gender and the Body in the Ancient Mediterranean*. Edited by Maria Wyke, 529-

541. Oxford: Blackwell.

Shelton, Jo-Ann. 1998 2nd ed. *As The Romans Did: a sourcebook in Roman social history*. 2d ed. Oxford and New York: Oxford University Press.

Snyder, Jane M. 1989. *The Woman and the Lyre: women writers in classical Greece and Rome*. Carbondale and Edwardsville, IL: Southern Illinois University Press.

Treggiari, Susan. 1991. *Roman Marriage:* iusti coniuges *from the time of Cicero to the time of Ulpian*. Oxford and New York: Clarendon Press and Oxford University Press.

Turcan, Robert. 2000. *The Gods of Ancient Rome: religion in everyday life from archaic to imperial times*. Translated by Antonia Nevill. London and New York: Routledge.

Veyne, Paul, ed. 1987. *A History of Private Life. Volume I: From Pagan Rome to Byzantium*. Translated by Arthur Goldhammer. Cambridge, MA and London: Belknap Press of Harvard University Press.

Wallace-Hadrill, Andrew. 1994. *Houses and Society in Pompeii and Herculaneum*. Princeton: Princeton University Press.

Warrior, Valerie M. 2002. *Roman Religion: a sourcebook*. Newburyport MA: Focus.

Wiedemann, Thomas. 1989. *Adults and Children in the Roman Empire*. New Haven and London: Yale University Press.

-----. 1981. *Greek and Roman Slavery*. Baltimore: Johns Hopkins University Press.

Zanker, Paul. 1998. *Pompeii: public and private life*. Translated by Deborah L. Schneider. Cambridge, MA: Harvard University Press.

Periodicals

Finley, Moses I. 1965. "The Silent Women of Rome." *Horizon* 7.1: 57-64. Reprinted in *Sexuality and Gender in the Classical World*. Edited by Laura K. McClure, 147-160. Oxford: Blackwell, 2002.

Flory, Maureen. 1993. "Livia and the History of Public Honorific Statues for Women in Rome." *Transactions of the American Philological Association* 123: 287-308.

Gold, Barbara. 1998. "The House I Live In Is Not My Own: women's bodies in Juvenal's *Satires*." *Arethusa* 3: 369-86.

Grebe, Sabine. 2003. "Marriage and Exile: Cicero's letters to Terentia." *Helios* 30: 127-46.

Hallett, Judith P. 1989. "Women as 'Same' and 'Other' in Classical Roman Elite." *Helios* 16: 59-78.

Hemelrijk, Emily A. 2004. "Masculinity and Femininity in the *Laudatio Turiae*." *The Classical Quarterly* 54.1: 183-197.

Kleiner, Diana E. E. 1987. "Women and Family Life on Roman Imperial Funerary Altars." *Latomus* 46: 545-554.

Latin Text Commentaries and Epigraphical Sources

Balme, Maurice and James Morwood. 2003. *On the Margin: marginalized groups in ancient Rome*. Oxford and New York: Oxford University Press.

Birley, Anthony R. 2000. *Onomasticon to the Younger Pliny: letters and panegyric*. München and Leipzig: K. G. Saur.

Buecheler, Franz. and E. Lommatzsch, eds. 1972. *Carmina Latina Epigraphica (CLE)*, 3 vols. Leipzig: Teubner, 1895-; reprinted Amsterdam.

Corpus Inscriptionum Latinarum (CIL). 1869-. Berlin: G. Reimerum, de Gruyte.

Dessau, Herman, ed.. 1979. *Inscriptiones Latinarum Selectae (ILS)*. Chicago: Ares Publishers, reprint.

Goodyear, Francis Richard David. 1972-1981. *The Annals of Tacitus, books 1-6*. Cambridge: Cambridge University Press.

Ogilvie, Robert Maxwell. 1970. *A Commentary on Livy, books 1-5*. Oxford: Clarendon Press, 1965; reprinted with *addenda*.

Sherwin-White, A. N. 1966. *The letters of Pliny: a historical and social commentary*. Oxford, Clarendon Press.

Internet Sites

Forum Romanum: Corpus Scriptorum Latinorum
http://www.forumromanum.org/literature/authors_a.html
Diotima: Women and Gender in the Ancient World
http://www.stoa.org/diotima
Ad Fontes Academy: The Latin Library
http://www.thelatinlibrary.com
The Perseus Digital Library: Greek and Roman Materials
http://www.perseus.tufts.edu/cache/perscoll_Greco-Roman.html
The Stoa Consortium
http://www.stoa.org
VRoma: A Virtual Community for Teaching and Learning Classics
http://www.vroma.org
WORDS 1.97: *William Whitaker's Dictionary program*
http://users.erols.com/whitaker/words.htm

VOCABULARY

The Vocabulary contains all words from the texts that do not appear in the glosses. Excerpted with permission from William A. Whitaker's on-line Latin-English Dictionary Program WORDS 1.97

A

ab *prep.* w/ abl. by (agent), from; after

abduco, abducere, abduxi, abductus *v.* lead away; entice, seduce; withdraw

abhorreo, abhorrere, abhorrui, -- *v.* abhor; be averse to, shudder at; differ from

abigo, abigere, abegi, abactus *v.* drive off; steal; seduce; cure; force birth

abripio, abripere, abripui, abreptus *v.* snatch away; wash away; kidnap

absentia, absentiae *n.* f. absence; non-appearance; lack

absolutus -a -um, absolutior/-us, absolutissimus -a -um *adj.* complete; perfect, pure; unconditional

abstineo, abstinere, abstinui, abstentus *v.* withhold; abstain; refrain (from); avoid

ac *conj.* and, and also, and besides

accedo, accedere, accessi, accessus *v.* approach; agree; be added to (w/ ad or in + acc.); constitute

accendo, accendere, accendi, accensus *v.* kindle; illuminate; arouse; make bright

acceptus -a -um, acceptior/-us, acceptissimus -a -um *adj.* welcome, pleasing; popular; received

accuso, accusare, accusavi, accusatus *v.* accuse, blame, find fault; charge (w. offense)

acer, acris -e, acrior/-us, acerrimus -a -um *adj.* sharp, bitter, shrill; keen; severe, vigorous

actum, acti *n.* n. deed, transaction; acts (pl.); chronicles, record

ad *prep.* acc. to, up to, towards; at; according to

addo, addere, addidi, additus *v.* add, insert, say in addition; increase; associate

adeo, adire, adivi(ii), aditus *v.* approach; attack; visit; undertake; take possession

adfecto, adfectare, adfectavi, adfectatus *v.* desire, aspire, try, lay claim to; pretend

adfero, adferre, adtuli, adlatus *v.* convey; report, allege; produce, cause

adfirmo, adfirmare, adfirmavi, adfirmatus *v.* affirm; confirm, ratify; emphasize

adhuc *adv.* thus far, to this point; still; besides

adiuvo, adiuvare, adiuvi, adiutus *v.* aid, encourage, favor; sustain; be profitable

adloquor, adloqui, adlocutus sum *v.* speak to; address, harangue; call on

administro, administrare, administravi, administratus *v.* manage, direct; operate, conduct

admiratio, admirationis *n.* f. wonder, surprise; admiration, regard

admoneo, admonere, admonui, admonitus *v.* admonish; suggest, advise; urge; warn

admoveo, admovere, admovi, admotus *v.* move up; lean on, conduct; draw near; apply

adpono, adponere, adposui, adpositus *v.* place near, set before, serve up; appoint

adprobo/approbo, adprobare, adprobavi, adprobatus *v.* approve, commend, endorse; confirm

adsiduo *adv.* continually, constantly, regularly

adsum/assum, adesse, adfui, adfuturus *v.* be near, be present; appear; aid (w/dat)

adulescens, adulescentis *adj.* young, youthful; n. c. young man/woman

adulescentia, adulescentiae *n.* f. youth, young manhood; youthfulness

adulter, adulteri *n.* m. adulterer; illicit lover

adversarius -a -um *adj.* opposed (to), hostile, adverse; n. c. enemy, rival

adverso, adversare, adversavi, adversatus *v.* apply (the mind), direct (the attention)

adversus *adv.* opposite, against; (w/ire) go to meet; *prep.* w acc. facing, opposite, against

adverto, advertere, adverti, adversus *v.* turn towards; pay attention to; steer

aequalitas, aequalitatis *n.* f. evenness; equality, uniformity, symmetry

aeque, aequius, aequissime *adv.* equally, justly, fairly; just as; likewise, also

aequum, aequi *n.* n. level ground; right/fair/ equitable terms, equity

aer, aeris *n.* c. air; atmosphere, sky; cloud, weather; breeze; odor

aetas, aetatis *n.* f. lifetime, age, generation; time, era

aeternitas, aeternitatis *n.* f. eternity; immortality; permanence

aeternus -a -um, aeternior/-us, aeternissimus -a -um *adj.* eternal; perpetual, forever

aether, aetheris *n.* m. upper air; heaven, sky

affero, afferre, attuli, allatus *v.* bring to; allege, announce; produce, cause

ager, agri *n.* m. field; farm, estate; territory; soil

agnosco, agnoscere, agnovi, agnitus *v.* recognize, realize, discern; acknowledge

ago, agere, egi, actus *v.* drive, urge, do; spend (time); thank (w/gratias)

agricola, agricolae *n.* m. farmer, gardener; plowman, peasant

albus -a -um, albior/-us, albissimus -a -um *adj.* white, pale, gray; bright; favorable, auspicious

ales, alitis *adj.* winged; swift, quick; *n.* c. bird

alias *adv.* at another time/place; elsewhere; otherwise

alienus -a -um, alienior/-us, alienissimus -a -um *adj.* foreign; another's; hostile; *n.* m. foreigner; stranger

alio *adv.* elsewhere; to another place/subject

alioqui *adv.* otherwise; besides; in any case; in general

aliquam *adv.* largely, to a large extent, a lot of

aliquando *adv.* sometime (or other); at length

aliquis, aliquid *pron.* anyone/someone; one or another

aliquot undeclined *adj.* some, several; a few; a number (of)

aliter *adv.* otherwise, differently; (**aliter ac**: otherwise than)

alius, alia, aliud *adj.* other, another; different; (**alii... alii**: some...others)

almus -a -um *adj.* nourishing, kind, propitious; fostering

alo, alere, alui, altus/alitus *v.* nourish, rear, nurse; cherish; maintain, develop

alter, altera, alterum *adj.* one (of two); (**unus et**: one or two); *conj.* the one ... the other (**alter... alter**); otherwise

alternus -a -um *adj.* alternate, by turns, successive; reciprocal

altus -a -um, altior/-us, altissimus -a -um *adj.* high; deep; shrill; lofty; profound

amans, amantis amantior/-us, amantissimus -a -um *adj.* affectionate; beloved; friendly; *n.* c. lover, sweetheart

amator, amatoris *n.* m. lover; friend; admirer; one fond of women

amatus -a -um *adj.* loved, beloved

ambitiosus -a -um, ambitiosior/-us, ambitiosissimus -a -um *adj.* ambitious, eager for advancement; twisting

ambulo, ambulare, ambulavi, ambulatus *v.* walk around; go about; parade, strut

amica, amicae *n.* f. friend; sweetheart; patron; mistress, concubine; courtesan

amicitia, amicitiae *n.* f. friendship; alliance, association

amicus -a -um, amicior/-us, amicissimus -a -um *adj.* friendly, dear, fond of; loyal, devoted; *n.* m. friend

amo, amare, amavi, amatus *v.* love, like; fall in love with; be fond of

amor, amoris *n.* m. love, affection; the beloved; Cupid; passion

amplius *adv.* comp. further, more, beyond; more than

an *conj.* expects a negative answer; whether; or

ancilla, ancillae *n.* f. slave girl; maid servant

animadverto, animadvertere, animadverti, animadversus *v.* pay attention to; notice; punish (in+acc)

animus, animi *n.* m. intellect; soul; feelings; heart; spirit, courage

annus, anni *n.* m. year; age, time of life; circuit, course

ante *adv.* before, previously; *prep.* acc. before; facing

antea *adv.* before this; formerly, in the past

antehac *adv.* before now; previously, earlier; in the past

antequam *conj.* before, sooner than; until

anus, ana, anum *adj.* old (female persons and things), aged

anxius -a -um *adj.* uneasy; concerned; careful; troublesome

appetitus, appetitus *n.* m. appetite, desire

aptus -a -um *adj.* suitable; ready; proper

apud *prep.* acc. at, by, near, among; in the view of

aqua, aquae *n.* f. water; sea, lake; river; rain; spa; urine

arbitror, arbitrari, arbitratus sum *v.* witness; testify; decide; believe, think, imagine

ardor, ardoris *n.* m. fire, flame, heat; brightness, love, intensity

armum, armi *n.* n. arms (pl.), weapons, shield; close fighting; force

ars, artis *n.* f. skill; trick; knowledge; way; character (pl.)

artus -a -um, artior/-us, artissimus -a -um *adj.* firm, tight; thrifty; dense, narrow; strict; scarce

ascendo, ascendere, ascendi, ascensus *v.* climb; go up; mount, scale; embark; rise

assentio, assentire, assensi, assensus *v.* assent, agree; admit the truth of (w/dat)

astrum, astri *n.* n. star, planet, sun/moon; constellation; sky

at *conj.* but, on the other hand; while, whereas; but yet

ater, atra -um, atrior/-us, aterrimus -a -um *adj.* black; gloomy, unlucky; sordid; deadly; poisonous; spiteful

atque *conj.* as well as, as soon as; together with; and even; yet

atqui *conj.* but, yet, however, rather, and yet, still

atrium, atri(i) *n.* n. (reception hall of a Roman house); palace (pl.)

attentus, attenta -um, attentior/-us, attentissimus -a -um *adj.* attentive, heedful; conscientious; frugal

attineo, attinere, attinui, attentus *v.* hold on to; restrain; retain; delay

au *interj.* oh dear! goodness gracious! (used by women)

auctor, auctoris *n.* c. vendor; originator; historian; authority; founder

auctoritas, auctoritatis *n.* f. ownership; power; prestige, reputation; opinion

auctus -a -um, auctior/-us, auctissimus -a -um *adj.* enlarged, abundant (in power/wealth/importance)

audacia, audaciae *n.* f. boldness, courage, confidence; recklessness

audeo, audere, --, ausus sum *v.* intend, be prepared; dare; venture, risk

audio, audire, audivi, auditus *v.* hear, listen, accept; obey; pay attention

augustus -a -um *adj.* sacred, venerable; dignified; August (mensis understood); *n.* m. Augustus

aula, aulae *n.* f. hall, inner court; palace; courtiers; princely power

aura, aurae *n.* f. breeze, wind; gleam; odor; air (pl.), heaven

auratus -a -um *adj.* gilded, golden, gold-embroidered

aureus -a -um *adj.* of gold; gilded; gold-like; beautiful; *n.* m. coin

ausus, ausus *n.* m. daring, initiative; ventures (pl.)

aut *conj.* or, or rather; either...or (aut...aut)

autem *conj.* but, on the other hand; while, however; also

auxilium, auxili(i) *n.* n. help, aid; remedy; resource; auxiliaries (pl.)

averto, avertere, averti, aversus *v.* turn away from, divert, rout; withdraw; steal

B

barbarus -a -um, barbarior/-us, barbarissimus -a -um *adj.* savage; uncivilized; *n.* c. barbarian; foreigner

beatus -a -um, beatior/-us, beatissimus -a -um *adj.* happy, fortunate; wealthy, copious, sumptuous

bellus -a -um, bellior/-us, bellissimus -a -um *adj.* pretty, handsome, agreeable; nice, excellent

bene, melius, optime *adv.* well, very, quite, rightly; better; best

beneficium, benefici(i) *n.* n. kindness, service, help; privilege, right

bis *adv.* twice, double

bonus -a -um, melior/-us, optimus -a -um *adj.* good, honest, brave, noble, kind; valid; healthy

bracchium, bracchi(i) *n.* n. arm; forearm; claw; branch; defensive earthwork

brevis, breve, brevior/-us, brevissimus -a -um *adj.* short, little; concise, quick; small; humble

brutus -a -um *adj.* unwieldy, inert; stupid; irrational, insensitive

C

cado, cadere, cecidi, casusus *v.* fall, sink, drop, topple; be slain, die; end

caedo, caedere, cecidi, caesus *v.* chop, cut down; strike; slaughter; sodomize

caelum, caeli *n.* n. sky, heavens; space; air, weather; universe

calamitas, calamitatis *n.* f. loss, harm; misfortune; military defeat; blight

calor, caloris *n.* m. heat; warmth; fever; passion

campus, campi *n.* m. plain, level field for action/battle/games

candidus -a -um, candidior/-us, candidissimus -a -um *adj.* bright; clean; innocent, pure; pale

candor, candoris *n.* m. radiance, brightness; beauty; purity; kindness

canis, canis *n.* c. dog; subordinate; lowest dice throw

cano, canere, cecini, cantus *v.* sing, celebrate; recite; play music; foretell

canto, cantare, cantavi, cantatus *v.* sing; play; recite; praise, celebrate; enchant

cantus, cantus *n.* m. song, chant; sound; poem, poetry; incantation

capillus, capilli *n.* m. hair; hair of head; fur, wool; hair-like fiber

capio, capere, cepi, captus *v.* take hold, seize; take bribe; capture; occupy

captivus -a -um *adj.* captured (in war); conquered; *n.* c. prisoner

caput, capitis *n.* n. head; person; life; leader; source; punishment

carus -a -um, carior/-us, carissimus -a -um *adj.* dear, beloved; costly, valued; expensive

castrum, castri *n.* n. fort; camp (pl.); army; war service; day's march

casu *adv.* by chance/accident; accidentally; casually

cathedra, cathedrae *n.* f. armchair (for women); cushioned seat; teacher's chair

causa *prep.* gen for the sake of, on account of, with a view to

causa, causae *n.* f. reason; origin; responsibility, blame; occasion; plea, case, trial

cautus -a -um, cautior/-us, cautissimus -a -um *adj.* careful; prudent; wary; safe, secure

caveo, cavere, cavi, cautus *v.* take precaution, beware, avoid; get surety

cavus -a -um *adj.* hollowed out; *n.* m. pit, hole; cave

celeber, celebris, -e, celebrior/-us, celeberrimus -a -um *adj.* famous; notorious; busy, populous; festive

celeriter, celerius, celerrime *adv.* quickly; hastily; soon; in short period

cena, cenae *n.* f. supper (main Roman meal); course; company

centum, centesimus -a -um, centeni -ae -a, centie(n)s *num.* one hundred

cerno, cernere, crevi, cretus *v.* separate, discern, distinguish; examine; decide

certe *adv.* surely, certainly, really; at any rate, in all events

certus -a -um, certior/-us, certissimus -a -um *adj.* fixed, settled, firm; reliable; sure; determined

ceterus -a -um *adj.* the other; the others (pl.). the rest

cibus, cibi *n.* m. food; rations; fuel; a meal; bait

circa *adv.* around, about; near; on either side; *prep.* acc. around; concerning

circulo, circulare, circulavi, circulatus *v.* make round; encircle, encompass

circumeo, circumire, circumivi(ii), circumitus *v.* surround; border; circulate through; go around

circumfero, circumferre, circumtuli, circumlatus *v.* carry around (in a circle); publicize; divulge

circus, circi *n.* m. race course; the Circus in Rome; the games; orbit

cito, citare, citavi, citatus *v.* urge on; promote, excite; set in motion; cite

civilis, civile *adj.* of/affecting fellow citizens; civil; legal; public

civis, civis *n.* c. countryman/woman; citizen, free person

civitas, civitatis *n.* f. community/city/town/state; citizenship

clades, cladis *n.* f. defeat, slaughter; disaster; plague; scourge

clam *adv.* secretly, privately; by fraud; *prep.* acc. secret from; unknown to

clangor, clangoris *n.* m. clang, noise; blare; clamor

clarus -a -um, clarior/-us, clarissimus -a -um *adj.* gleaming; evident, plain; illustrious, famous

classis, classis *n.* f. Roman class distinction; grade; draft; fleet; group

claudo, claudere, clausi, clausus *v.* close; confine; stumble; be weak, fall short; be lame

clausus -a -um *adj.* inaccessible; impervious; shut in, enclosed

clementer, clementius, clementissime *adv.* leniently, mildly; gradually, gently

clivus, clivi *n.* m. slope, incline; street

coactus -a -um *adj.* compressed, forced; unnatural; required

coemptio, coemptionis *n.* f. fictitious marriage to free heiress; mock sale of estate to free it of burdens

coeo, coire, coivi(ii), coitus *v.* fit together; have sexual intercourse; mend; unite; assemble; conspire

coeptum, coepti *n.* n. undertaking, enterprise, scheme; work at hand

coerceo, coercere, coercui, coercitus *v.* confine; check; limit; preserve; punish

cogitatio, cogitationis *n.* f. meditation, reflection; intention; reasoning

cogito, cogitare, cogitavi, cogitatus *v.* think; consider, ponder; imagine, look forward to

cognatus -a -um *adj.* related by birth/position, similar/akin; affinity with; *n.* m. kinsman

cognitus -a -um *adj.* known; acknowledged, recognized

cognomen, cognominis *n.* n. surname, 3rd name; given for a characteristic

cognosco, cognoscere, cognovi, cognitus *v.* become acquainted with; recognize; learn

coitus, coitus *n.* m. meeting, gathering; union, sexual intercourse

collis, collis *n.* m. hill, hill-top; high ground; mountains (pl.)

colo, colere, colui, cultus *v.* inhabit; cultivate; foster; worship; tend; dress, decorate, embellish

colonia, coloniae *n.* f. settlement; land attached to a farm; estate, abode

color, coloris *n.* m. color; pigment; shade; complexion; show; pretext

comis, come, comior/-us, comissimus -a -um *adj.* courteous, gracious; elegant, cultured

comito, comitare, comitavi, comitatus *v.* accompany; attend; follow; grow alongside

commendo, commendare, commendavi, commendatus *v.* entrust, commit; recommend; designate

commode, commodius, commodissime *adv.* conveniently, well; properly; at a good time

commodo *adv.* suitably; seasonably; even now, at this moment

commoror, commorari, commoratus sum *v.* remain; linger; be delayed (menses); dwell on

commotus -a -um, commotior/-us, commotissimus -a -um *adj.* excited, nervous; angry, annoyed

commoveo, commovere, commovi, commotus *v.* agitate; disturb; provoke; produce; cause a war

comparo, comparare, comparavi, comparatus *v.* prepare; compose; collect; unite; compare; arrange

compertus -a -um *adj.* ascertained, proved, verified; (**res**: fact); (**male**: bad character); *n.* m. experience

complecteo, complectere, complexi, complexus *v.* |lay hold of; seize; sum up; include, cover

compono/conpono, componere, composui, compositus *v.* compare; match; hoard; calm; build; arrange, compose; organize, order; settle

comprehendo, comprehendere, comprehendi, comprehensus *v.* arrest; take hold; conceive; include; express

conceptum, concepti *n.* n. fetus; concept; measurement of volume/capacity

conceptus -a -um *adj.* conceived, imagined; understood; (w/ **verba**: solemn utterance); *n.* m. conception; embryo

concessus -a -um *adj.* permitted; lawful; relinquished; conceding

concido, concidere, concidi, concisus *v.* cut to pieces; ruin, kill, destroy; divide; beat

concilio, conciliare, conciliavi, conciliatus *v.* unite; win over; acquire; match; commend; gain

concito, concitare, concitavi, concitatus *v.* stir up, disturb; hurl; rush; enrage; assemble

condo, condere, condidi, conditus *v.* store up; bury/inter; found; hide; make

condono, condonare, condonavi, condonatus *v.* give away; present; forgive; sacrifice to

conduco, conducere, conduxi, conductus *v.* collect, assemble; be profitable; be proper; employ, hire

confidenter, confidentius, confidentissime *adv.* boldly; with assurance; impudently

confido, confidere, confisus sum *v.* have confidence in, rely on, trust; believe

confirmatus -a -um, confirmatior/-us, confirmatissimus -a -um *adj.* assured; proven; resolute; affirmed; credible

congruo, congruere, congrui, -- *v.* agree, correspond, be consistent; fit in; harmonize; be congenial

conicio, conicere, conjeci, conjectus *v.* throw together; conclude; assign; involve; insert

coniugalis, coniugale *adj.* marital, conjugal; faithful; of husband/wife

conor, conari, conatus sum *v.* try, attempt; exert oneself

conpressus, -a -um, conpressio/-us, conpressissimus -a -um *adj.* constricted; constipated, binding

consensus, consensus *n.* m. agreement, consent, unanimity; conspiracy

consequor, consequi, consecutus sum *v.* follow; attend on; pursue; overtake

conservo, conservare, conservavi, conservatus *v.* keep safe; preserve, maintain; spare; observe

considero, considerare, consideravi, consideratus *v.* examine; reflect on; investigate

consido, considere, consedi, consessus *v.* sit down; hold sessions; stay; settle; lodge

consilium, consili(i) *n.* n. consultation; advice; council of state, senate; jury

consolatio, consolationis *n.* f. consolation; comfort; consoling circumstance

conspicio, conspicere, conspexi, conspectus *v.* observe, witness; watch; face; discern

consternatio, consternationis *n.* f. confusion, shock; disturbance; mutiny, sedition

constituo, constituere, constitui, constitutus *v.* set up; resolve; ordain; establish, create; form

constrictus -a -um, constrictior/-us, constrictissimus -a -um *adj.* small in size; compressed, contracted

consueo, consuere, consuevi, consuetus *v.* accustom; inure, habituate; familiarize

consulo, consulere, consului, consultus *v.* take counsel; deliberate; advise; pay attention to; refer to

consulto, consultare, consultavi, consultatus *v.* take counsel; plan; deliberate; weigh, ponder

contemno, contemnere, contempsi, contemptus *v.* disregard, slight; scorn, disdain; despise; avoid

contentus -a -um, contentior/-us, contentissimus -a -um *adj.* content, satisfied (w/abl); eager, serious

contineo, continere, continui, contentus *v.* fasten; retain; hinder, restrain; enclose, limit

continuo, continuare, continuavi, continuatus *v.* put in line, connect; extend, prolong

continuus -a -um *adj.* incessant, recurring; successive; uninterrupted

contra *adv.* facing; towards; opposite; conversely; in reply; *prep.* w/ acc. against, opposite; reply, otherwise than

contumelia, contumeliae *n.* f. indignity, affront, abuse; insult

convalesco, convalescere, convalui, -- *v.* thrive; regain strength, recover; become valid

convenio, convenire, conveni, conventus *v.* fit; assemble; converge; visit; be agreed upon

copia, copiae *n.* f. plenty; troops (pl.), supplies; wealth; resources

cor, cordis *n.* n. heart; soul, spirit; mind; sweetheart; (pl) persons

coram *adv.* in person, face-to-face; publicly; *prep.* abl. in the presence of, before

corpus, corporis *n.* n. body; person; virility; corpse; corporation

correpo, correpere, correpsi, correptus *v.* crawl; slink; creep (of the flesh)

cotidie *adv.* daily; day by day; usually, ordinarily, commonly

creatus -a -um *adj.* sprung from, begotten by, born of

creber, crebra -um, crebrior/-us, creberrimus -a -um *adj.* thick, crowded; frequent; numerous

credo, credere, credidi, creditus *v.* trust; believe; suppose; lend (money); be sure

credulus -a -um *adj.* trusting; prone to believe; full of confidence

creo, creare, creavi, creatus *v.* create; procreate; give birth; institute; conjure up

cresco, crescere, crevi, cretus *v.* arise; be born; become great; grow; multiply

crimen, criminis *n.* n. accusation; blame; sin, guilt; crime, fault

cruentus -a –um, cruentior/-us, cruentissimus -a -um *adj.* bloody; polluted w/blood-guilt; savage

cruor, cruoris *n.* m. blood; murder, slaughter

cubitum, cubiti *n.* n. elbow; forearm; cubit (17-21")

culmen, culminis *n.* n. peak, top; roof, ridge-pole; head, chief

cultum, culti *n.* n. cultivated land (pl.); garden; plantation; crops

cultus -a -um, cultior/-us, cultissimus -a -um *adj.* cultivated; ornamented, neat; polished, elegant

cultus, cultus *n.* m. habitation; cultivation; elegance; style; splendor; worship; cult; training, education

cum *adv.* when; after; since, although; as soon; while

cum *prep.* abl. with

cunctor, cunctari, cunctatus sum *v.* delay; hesitate; be slow to act; doubt

cunctus -a -um *adj.* altogether, in a body; every, all, entire

cupiditas, cupiditatis *n.* f. passion; lust; greed; usury, fraud; ambition

cupido, cupidinis *n.* c. desire, longing; lust; greed, appetite; Cupid

cupidus -a -um, cupidior/-us, cupidissimus -a -um *adj.* eager; desirous of (w gen.); greedy; wanton

cupio, cupere, cupivi, cupitus *v.* be eager for; desire; favor, wish well

cur *adv.* why? for what reason? because

cura, curae *n.* f. concern, trouble; care, pains; cure; office, task

curius -a -um *adj.* grievous; full of sorrow

curo, curare, curavi, curatus *v.* arrange; provide for; heal; take trouble; desire

curriculum, curriculi *n.* n. race; lap, track; chariot; course of action

custodia, custodiae *n.* f. protection, defense; prisoner; watch; prison

D

damno, damnare, damnavi, damnatus *v.* find guilty; sentence; discredit; find fault

dato, datare, datavi, datatus *v.* habitually give; give away, administer

datum, dati *n.* n. present, gift; debit

de *prep.* abl. down from, off; about, concerning; according to

dea, deae *n.* f. goddess

debitus -a -um *adj.* due, owed; appropriate; destined, fated

decedo, decedere, decessi, decessus *v.* depart; relinquish, cease; abandon; die; disappear

decem, decimus -a -um, deni -ae -a, decie(n)s *num.* ten; tenth; ten men; ten times

decerno, decernere, decrevi, decretus *v.* decide, resolve; decree; judge; vote for, contend

decessus, decessus *n.* m. departure; retirement; death; decline, fall

decipio, decipere, decepi, deceptus *v.* deceive, trap; elude; disappoint, frustrate, foil

declaro, declarare, declaravi, declaratus *v.* make known; reveal, prove; mean (word)

decor, decoris *adj.* beautiful; pleasing; *n.* m. beauty; grace

decresco, decrescere, decrevi, decretus *v.* decrease; shrink; decline, weaken, fade

dedecorus -a -um *adj.* dishonorable, shameful; causing disgrace

dedicatio, dedicationis *n.* f. dedication, ceremonial opening; sanctification

dedicatus -a -um, dedicatior/-us, dedicatissimus -a -um *adj.* devoted; dedicated

deduco, deducere, deduxi, deductus *v.* lead off; escort; reduce; describe

deductus -a -um, deductior/-us, deductissimus -a -um *adj.* slender, weak, soft; fine-spun

defectus -a -um, defectior/-us, defectissimus -a -um *adj.* tired, worn out; faulty; smaller

defendo, defendere, defendi, defensus *v.* protect; defend; prosecute; prevent; preserve

defensio, defensionis *n.* f. protection; defense; justification, excuse

defero, deferre, detuli, delatus *v.* convey; denounce; pay; offer; confer; entrust

defessus -a -um *adj.* worn out, weary, exhausted; weakened

defunctus -a -um *adj.* dead, deceased; *n.* m. dead person

deicio, deicere, dejeci, dejectus *v.* throw down; overthrow, depose; kill, destroy

deleo, delere, delevi, deletus *v.* erase; demolish; overthrow; nullify; end

demum *adv.* at last; eventually; (**tum demum**: only then); only

denique *adv.* finally; and then; to sum up; in fact, indeed

denuntio, denuntiare, denuntiavi, denuntiatus *v.* give notice; threaten; intimate; declare; summon

deripio, deripere, deripui, dereptus *v.* snatch away; tear off; remove

derivo, derivare, derivavi, derivatus *v.* draw off

desertus -a -um *adj.* deserted; solitary, lonely; forsaken; desert, waste

desidero, desiderare, desideravi, desideratus *v.* long for, desire; miss, lack, need

desisto, desistere, destiti, destitus *v.* cease, desist from; give up

desolo, desolare, desolavi, desolatus *v.* abandon, desert; empty

despolio, despoliare, despoliavi, despoliatus *v.* rob, plunder

destinatus -a -um *adj.* resolved, resolute, firm

desum, deesse, defui, defuturus *v.* be wanting (w/ dat), fail; neglect; be absent

deterior, deterius *adj.* comp. lower, worse, poorer; weaker; degenerate

detraho, detrahere, detraxi, detractus *v.* drag down; remove; rob; detract; lessen

detrimentum, detrimenti *n.* n. detriment; loss, damage; defeat

deus, dei *n.* m. god; divine being; statue of god

dexter, dextra -um, dexterio/-us, dextimus -a -um *adj.* skillful; favorable, fortunate; on the right hand

dia *adv.* by day; for a long time; **quam diu**: as long as

dico, dicare, dicavi, dicatus *v.* dedicate, consecrate; devote; offer

dico, dicere, dixi, dictus *v.* say, talk; tell, call; name; set; plead; order

dicto, dictare, dictavi, dictatus *v.* say repeatedly; dictate; compose

dictum, dicti *n.* n. saying, word; maxim; witticism; order

dies, diei *n.* c. day; festival; time; age; (**multo**: late in the day)

difficulter *adv.* with difficulty; hardly

digitus, digiti *n.* m. finger; toe; a finger's breadth

digno, dignare, dignavi, dignatus *v.* think worthy, deserving to; deign, condescend

diligenter, diligentius, diligentissime *adv.* carefully; diligently

dimitto, dimittere, dimisi, dimissus *v.* send away; scatter; dismiss; abandon

diripio, diripere, diripui, direptus *v.* tear apart; plunder, pillage

dis, ditis *adj.* rich

discedo, discedere, discessi, discessus *v.* go off, depart; scatter; abandon; lay down (arms)

disciplina, disciplinae *n.* f. instruction; training; discipline, method, science

discipulus, discipuli *n.* m. student, pupil, trainee; follower, disciple

disco, discere, didici, -- *v.* learn; acquire knowledge of

discretus -a -um *adj.* separate; differentiated; discrete, wise

dispareo, disparere, disparui, disparitus *v.* disappear, vanish

diu, diutius, diutissime *adv.* by day, all day; long since; (**quam diu**: as long as)

diuturnus -a -um *adj.* lasting, lasting long

divido, dividere, divisi, divisus *v.* divide, separate; share, distribute

divino, divinare, divinavi, divinatus *v.* divine; prophesy; guess

divinus, -a –um, divinior/-us, divinissimus -a -um *adj.* of a god, godlike; sacred; inspired, prophetic

divitia, divitiae *n.* f. riches (pl.), wealth

divus, divi *n.* m. god

do, dare, dedi, datus *v.* give; dedicate; sell; grant; allow; make; surrender

doceo, docere, docui, doctus *v.* teach, show, point out

docilis, docilis, docile *adj.* teachable, responsive; docile

dolor, doloris *n.* m. anguish, sorrow; resentment, indignation

domesticus, domestica, domesticum *adj.* of the house, familiar, native; civil, personal

domicilium, domicili(i) *n.* n. residence, home, dwelling

domina, dominae *n.* f. mistress of a family, wife; lady, lady-love; owner

domino, dominare, dominavi, dominatus *v.* be in control, rule over; dominate

dominus, domini *n.* m. owner, lord, master; the lord; gentlemen

domus, domus/domi *n.* f. house; home, household; (**domu**: at home)

dono, donare, donavi, donatus *v.* present, grant; forgive; give gift, bestow

donum, doni *n.* n. gift, present; offering

dormio, dormire, dormivi, dormitus *v.* sleep, rest; be idle, do nothing

dubium, dubi(i) *n.* n. doubt; question

dubius -a -um *adj.* doubtful, uncertain; variable, dangerous; critical

dudum *adv.* little while ago; formerly; (**tam dudum**: long ago)

dulcedo/dulcido, dulcedinis *n.* f. sweetness, agreeableness; charm

dulcis, dulce, dulcior/-us, dulcissimus -a -um *adj.* charming; sweet; kind; flattering, delightful

dum *conj.* while, as long as, until; provided that

dummodo *conj.* provided that (+ subj)

dumtaxat *adv.* to this extent, no more than; as long as; only

duo -ae o, secundus -a -um, bini -ae -a, bis *num.* two (pl.)

duodecim, duodecimus -a -um, duodeni -ae -a, duodecie(n)s *num.* twelve

dux, ducis *n.* m. leader, guide; commander, general

E

ecastor *interj.* by Castor! (interjection used by women)

ecquando *adv.* ever

ecquis, ecquid *pron.* anyone? anybody? anything?

edepol *interj.* by Pollux!

edictum, edicti *n.* n. proclamation; edict

edo, edere, edidi, editus *v.* give out, put forth; publish; relate; beget

edo, edere/esse, edi, esus *v.* eat; devour; spend money on food; destroy

educatio, educationis *n.* f. bringing up; rearing

efficio, efficere, effeci, effectus *v.* cause; effect; accomplish; produce; prove

egens, egentis *adj.* needy, poor, in want of; destitute

egeo, egere, egui, -- *v.* need (w/gen/abl), lack, want; require

ego, mei, mihi, me, me *pron.* I; myself

egredior, egredi, egressus sum *v.* go out; set sail; land, disembark; surpass

eheu *interj.* alas! (exclamation of pain or fear)

eicio, eicere, ejeci, ejectus *v.* cast out, extract, discharge, vomit; stick out

electus -a -um *adj.* chosen, select, picked; choice

elegantia, elegantiae *n.* f. elegance; taste; politeness

eloquentia, eloquentiae *n.* f. eloquence

eludo, eludere, elusi, elusus *v.* elude; baffle; cheat; frustrate; mock

eluo, eluere, elui, elutus *v.* wash away, clear of

emancipo, emancipare, emancipavi, emancipatus *v.* emancipate (son from father's authority); alienate

emendo, emendare, emendavi, emendatus *v.* correct, emend, repair; improve

emeritus -a -um *adj.* worn out, unfit; veteran; finished work

emitto, emittere, emisi, emissus *v.* hurl; utter; send out; drive; discharge; publish

emo, emere, emi, emptus *v.* buy; gain, acquire, obtain

enim *conj.* namely; indeed; for; that is to say

eo *adv.* to that place; on this account, to that degree

eo, ire, ivi(ii), itus *v.* go, advance; (pass) flow; pass (time); ride; sail

epistula, epistulae *n.* f. letter, dispatch

eques, equitis *n.* m. knight; equestrian order; cavalryman

equus, equi *n.* m. horse

erga *prep.* acc. towards, opposite (friendly)

ergo *adv.* therefore; well, then, now

erro, errare, erravi, erratus *v.* wander, go astray; err; vacillate

error, erroris *n.* m. wandering; error; uncertainty; deception

erudio, erudire, erudivi, eruditus *v.* educate, teach, instruct

et *conj.* and, and even; also; (**et...et:** both...and);

etiam *conj.* now too, as yet, still; and also, besides; actually

etsi *conj.* although, though, even if

eueho, euehere, euexi, euectus *v.* carry away; exalt; jut out, project

evenio, evenire, eveni, eventus *v.* come out; happen; turn out

eventus, eventus *n.* m. result, success; event; chance, fate, accident

evoco, evocare, evocavi, evocatus *v.* call forth; lure; summon, evoke

ex/e *prep.* abl. out of, from; according to; because of

exanimo, exanimare, exanimavi, exanimatus *v.* kill; scare; exhaust; be out of breath

exanimus -a -um *adj.* dead; lifeless

excedo, excedere, excessi, excessus *v.* pass, withdraw, exceed; go away; die

excelsus -a -um, excelsior/-us, excelsissimus -a -um *adj.* lofty; tall; exalted; noble

excerpo, excerpere, excerpsi, excerptus *v.* pick out; select

excludo, excludere, exclusi, exclusus *v.* shut out; remove; exclude; hinder, prevent

excuso, excusare, excusavi, excusatus *v.* excuse, plead as an excuse; absolve

exemplum, exempli *n.* n. specimen; precedent, case; model; warning

exeo, exire, exivi(ii), exitus *v.* come out; go; die; escape, leave; emerge

exerceo, exercere, exercui, exercitus *v.* exercise, drill, practice; administer; cultivate

exercitus, exercitus *n.* m. army, infantry; swarm, flock

exhibeo, exhibere, exhibui, exhibitus *v.* present; furnish; exhibit; produce

exiguus -a -um *adj.* meager; dreary; a little; scanty, petty, poor

eximius -a -um *adj.* select; excellent; extraordinary

exitialis, exitiale *adj.* destructive, deadly

expecto, expectare, expectavi, expectatus *v.* await, expect; anticipate; hope for

expello, expellere, expuli, expulsus *v.* drive out, banish; disown, reject

experientia, experientiae *n.* f. trial, experiment; experience

experior, experiri, expertus sum *v.* test, find out; attempt; prove, experience

expers, expertis *adj.* free from (w/gen); without; lacking experience

explico, explicare, explicavi, explicatus *v.* unfold, extend; display; explain, disentangle

exploro, explorare, exploravi, exploratus *v.* search out, explore; test, investigate

exsanguis, exsangue *adj.* bloodless, pale, feeble; frightened

exsilio, exsilire, exsilui, -- *v.* spring forth, start up; emerge into existence

exspecto, exspectare, exspectavi, exspectatus *v.* look for, await; expect, anticipate, hope for

exsul/exul, exsulis *n.* c. exile; banished person; wanderer

extemplo *adv.* immediately, forthwith

extendo, extendere, extendi, extentus *v.* stretch out; enlarge; continue, prolong

externus -a -um *adj.* external; foreign, strange

extremus -a -um *adj.* outer; outward; far; foreign; strange

F

fabula, fabulae *n.* f. story, fable; play, drama; (**fabulae!**: nonsense!)

facies, faciei *n.* f. shape, face; appearance; beauty; achievement

facilitas, facilitatis *n.* f. readiness; good nature; levity; courteousness

facinus, facinoris *n.* n. deed; crime; outrage

facio, facere, feci, factus *v.* do, make; create; acquire; cause; compose

factum, facti *n.* n. fact, deed, act; achievement;

fallo, fallere, fefelli, falsus *v.* deceive; disappoint; mistake; cheat

falsus -a -um *adj.* wrong, lying, fictitious, deceptive

fama, famae *n.* f. rumor; reputation; tradition; report, news

familiaritas, familiaritatis *n.* f. intimacy; close friendship; familiarity

famula, famulae *n.* f. female slave, maid-servant; temple attendant

famulor, famulari, famulatus sum *v.* be a servant, attend

fatalis, fatale *adj.* destined; fatal, deadly

faustus -a -um *adj.* favorable; auspicious; lucky, prosperous

fautor, fautoris *n.* m. patron, protector; admirer; supporter

faveo, favere, favi, fautus *v.* favor (w/dat), befriend, support

fax, facis *n.* f. torch, firebrand, fire; torment

femina, feminae *n.* f. woman; female

femineus -a -um *adj.* woman's; female, feminine; effeminate, cowardly

femininus -a -um *adj.* woman's; female, feminine

fenestra, fenestrae *n.* f. window; loophole; orifice; inlet; opportunity

fere *adv.* almost; nearly; generally; (w/neg.) hardly ever

fero, ferre, tuli, latus *v.* bring, bear; tell; win, receive, produce; get

ferox, ferocis *adj.* wild, bold; cruel; defiant, arrogant

ferus, fera, ferum *adj.* wild, savage; uncivilized; untamed

fervens, ferventis *adj.* burning; inflamed, impetuous; zealous

fervidus -a -um *adj.* glowing; boiling hot; fiery

fessus -a -um *adj.* tired, exhausted; feeble, sick

festinus -a -um *adj.* swift; impatient, in a hurry; premature

festum, festi *n.* n. holiday; festival

fidelis, fidele, fidelior/-us, fidelissimus -a -um *adj.* faithful, devoted; trustworthy; constant

fides, fidei *n.* f. loyalty; honesty; credit; trust; good faith

fido, fidere, --, fisus sum *v.* trust (in), have confidence (in) (w/dat or abl.)

fidus -a –um *adj.* loyal; trusting, confident

figo, figere, fixi, fixus *v.* fasten; pierce, transfix; establish

filia, filiae *n.* f. daughter

filius, fili *n.* m. son

filum, fili *n.* n. thread; fiber; texture; style; nature

fio, fieri, factus sum *v.* be made, become; happen

firmus -a -um, firmior/-us, firmissimus -a -um *adj.* steady; strong; loyal; mature; valid

fixus -a -um *adj.* immovable; fitted with

flamen, flaminis *n.* n. breeze, wind, gale; blast

flamma, flammae *n.* f. flame; ardor; object of love

flavus -a -um *adj.* yellow, golden; flaxen, blonde

flecto, flectere, flexi, flexus *v.* bend; turn; persuade, prevail on

fleo, flere, flevi, fletus *v.* cry for; weep

flos, floris *n.* m. flower, blossom; youthful prime

flumen, fluminis *n.* n. river, stream; (**adverso flumine**: against the tide)

fluo, fluere, fluxi, fluxus *v.* flow, stream; proceed from; fall gradually

fons, fontis *n.* m. spring, fountain; source; principal cause

for, fari, fatus sum *v.* speak, talk; say

foras *adv.* out of doors, abroad, out

foris *adv.* out of doors, abroad

foris, foris *n.* f. door, gate; folding door (pl.); entrance

forma, formae *n.* f. figure, appearance; beauty; pattern

formido, formidinis *n.* f. fear; awe; dread; horror

fors, fortis *n.* f. chance; luck, fortune; accident

fortasse *adv.* perhaps, possibly

fortis, forte, fortior/-us, fortissimus -a -um *adj.* strong, mighty, steadfast, brave, bold

fortitudo, fortitudinis *n.* f. strength, courage, valor; firmness

fortuna, fortunae *n.* f. chance, luck, fate; condition, wealth, property

fortunatus -a -um *adj.* lucky, fortunate; rich; happy

forum, fori *n.* n. market; Forum (in Rome); court of justice

frango, frangere, fregi, fractus *v.* break, shatter; subdue; discourage

frater, fratris *n.* m. brother; cousin

fraus, fraudis *n.* f. fraud; trickery, deceit; offense; delusion

freno, frenare, frenavi, frenatus *v.* bridle; curb

frenus, freni *n.* m. harness, reins (pl.); restraint; mastery

frequens, frequentis *adj.* numerous, populous; repeated, constant

frigidus -a -um *adj.* cold, frigid; lifeless, indifferent, dull

frustro, frustrare, frustravi, frustratus *v.* deceive; elude; fail; cheat; refute; corrupt

fugio, fugere, fugi, fugitus *v.* flee; avoid; go into exile

fugo, fugare, fugavi, fugatus *v.* put to flight, chase away; drive into exile

fultus -a -um *adj.* propped up; supported

fundo, fundare, fundavi, fundatus *v.* establish, begin; lay a foundation; confirm

fundo, fundere, fudi, fusus *v.* pour, cast metal; scatter, shed, rout

funebris, funebris, funebre *adj.* of a funeral; deadly, fatal

fungor, fungi, functus sum *v.* perform, execute; be engaged in (w/abl)

furia, furiae *n.* f. frenzy, rage (pl.); furies, avenging spirits

furio, furiare, furiavi, furiatus *v.* madden, enrage

furo, furere, --, -- *v.* rave, rage; be furious; be wild

furtim *adv.* stealthily, secretly

fuscus -a -um *adj.* dark, swarthy; husky; hoarse

fusus -a -um *adj.* spread out, broad, flowing

futurus -a -um *adj.* about to be; future

G

gaudeo, gaudere, --, gavisus sum *v.* be glad, rejoice

gaudium, gaudi(i) *n.* n. joy, delight; source of joy

gemino, geminare, geminavi, geminatus *v.* double; repeat; pair (with)

gemitus, gemitus *n.* m. groan, sigh; roaring

gemma, gemmae *n.* f. bud; jewel; cup; signet; game piece

gena, genae *n.* f. cheeks (pl.); eyes

genetrix, genetricis *n.* f. mother, ancestress

genius, geni(i) *n.* m. guardian spirit; taste; appetite; talent

gens, gentis *n.* f. tribe, clan; nation, people

genus, generis *n.* n. birth; class, rank; mode; race, family; noble birth

gero, gerere, gessi, gestus *v.* bear, carry; manage; (**se gerere**: conduct oneself)

gigno, gignere, genui, genitus *v.* give birth to, bring forth; be born (passive)

gladius, gladi(i) *n.* m. sword

gloria, gloriae *n.* f. fame; ambition; renown; boasting

gracilis, gracile, gracilior/-us, gracillimus -a -um *adj.* slender, slight; unambitious, simple, plain

grandis, grande *adj.* grown; large, tall, lofty; powerful; aged

grates, gratis *n.* f. thanks (pl.); (**grates agere**: to thank)

gravidus -a -um *adj.* filled; pregnant; laden

gravis, grave, gravior/-us, gravissimus -a -um *adj.* heavy; painful; important; serious; pregnant

gravitas, gravitatis *n.* f. dignity; oppressiveness; pregnancy; sickness

graviter *adv.* deeply; severely;(**ferre**: be upset)

gusto, gustare, gustavi, gustatus *v.* taste, sip; experience; enjoy

H

habeo, habere, habui, habitus *v.* have, hold, think, reason; keep; spend time

hac *adv.* here, by this side, this way

haereo, haerere, haesi, haesus *v.* stick, cling to; hesitate; be in difficulty

haudquaquam *adv.* by no means, in no way; not at all

herba, herbae *n.* f. herb, grass

hercle *interj.* by Hercules! indeed

hereditas, hereditatis *n.* f. inheritance, succession; generation; heir

heu *interj.* oh! alas! (expression of dismay or pain)

heus *interj.* ho! listen!

hic *adv.* here, in this place

hic, haec, hoc *pron.* this; these (pl.)

hiems, hiemis *n.* f. winter; rainy season; storm

historia, historiae *n.* f. history; account; story

historicus -a -um *adj.* historical

hodie *adv.* today; at the present time

homo, hominis *n.* m. human being, person; (**novus homo**: new man)

honestas, honestatis *n.* f. honor, integrity, honesty; wealth

honor/honos, honoris *n.* m. honor; esteem; dignity, grace; public office

honoro, honorare, honoravi, honoratus *v.* respect, honor

hora, horae *n.* f. hour; time; season; (**horae**: the seasons)

hortor, hortari, hortatus sum *v.* encourage; urge; exhort

hospita, hospitae *n.* f. female guest; hostess; landlady; stranger

hospitium, hospiti(i) *n.* n. hospitality, entertainment; lodging; inn

hostilis, hostile *adj.* hostile; of an enemy

hostis, hostis *n.* c. enemy of the state; stranger, foreigner

huc *adv.* to this place; to this point

humanus -a -um, humanior/-us, humanissimus -a -um *adj.* human; humane, civilized, refined

humilis, humile, humilior/-us, humillimus -a -um *adj.* lowly, slight; base, mean; obscure, poor

humo, humare, humavi, humatus *v.* inter, bury

I

iaceo, iacere, iacui, iacitus *v.* lie; lie down; be dead, asleep, situated

iacto, iactare, iactavi, iactatus *v.* throw away; disturb; boast, discuss

iam *adv.* already, now; (**non**: no longer; **pridem**: long ago)

ianua, ianuae *n.* f. door, entrance

ibi *adv.* there, in that place; then

idem, eadem, idem *pron.* same, the very same, also

ideo *adv.* therefore, for that reason

idoneus -a -um *adj.* suitable; sufficient for, able

idus, idus *n.* f. Ides (15th of March, May, July, Oct, 13th others)

igitur *adv. conj.* therefore; consequently

ignauia, ignauiae *n.* f. idleness, laziness; faintheartedness

ignis, ignis *n.* m. fire, brightness; passion

ignominia, ignominiae *n.* f. disgrace, dishonor

ignoro, ignorare, ignoravi, ignoratus *v.* not know; be ignorant of; disregard; ignore

ilico *adv.* on the spot; immediately

ille, illa, illud *pron.* that; those; that one; the well known; the former

illic *adv.* in that place, over there

illuc *adv.* to that place; there

illustre, illustrius, illustrissime *adv.* clearly, distinctly

imago, imaginis *n.* f. likeness, image; statue; idea; echo; ghost

imbecillus -a -um, imbecillior/-us, imbecillissimus -a -um *adj.* weak; delicate; fragile; powerless

im/nbuo, imbuere, imbui, imbutus *v.* wet, soak, dip; give initial instruction

imitatio, imitationis *n.* f. imitation, copy

immaturus -a -um *adj.* unripe, immature, untimely

immitis, immite, immitior/-us, immitissimus -a -um *adj.* cruel, rough, harsh, rude, stern; savage

immo *adv.* on the contrary; rather

immortalis, immortale *adj.* immortal; eternal; imperishable

immortalitas, immortalitatis *n.* f. immortality; divinity; permanence

immundus -a -um *adj.* dirty, foul; impure; squalid; evil

impar, imparis *adj.* uneven, unequal; inferior

imperator, imperatoris *n.* m. emperor; general; ruler

imperium, imperi(i) *n.* n. authority; supreme power; the state, the empire

impero, imperare, imperavi, imperatus *v.* order, command; rule (w/dat)

impetro, impetrare, impetravi, impetratus *v.* obtain by asking; succeed, be granted

impetus, impetus *n.* m. attack, assault, charge; vigor; fury

implico, implicare, implicui, implicitus *v.* involve, implicate; be connected

impluvium, impluvi(i) *n.* n. pool in atrium receiving rain from the roof

improbus/inprobus -a -um *adj.* wicked; greedy; immoderate; disloyal; shameless

impudentia, impudentiae *n.* f. shamelessness; effrontery

imus -a -um *adj.* super. deepest, last

in *prep.* w/abl: in, on, at; in regard to; w/ acc: into; about, in the mist of; according to; for; to, among

incedo, incedere, incessi, incessus *v.* advance; approach; walk, march

incendo, incendere, incendi, incensus *v.* set fire to, burn; excite, aggravate

incido, incidere, incidi, incasus *v.* happen; fall into, meet; fall upon, assail

incido, incidere, incidi, incisus *v.* cut into; inscribe, engrave; break off

inclino, inclinare, inclinavi, inclinatus *v.* bend; incline; decay; sun set; deject

incredibilis, incredibile *adj.* incredible; extraordinary

indecens, indecentis *adj.* unbecoming, unseemly, unsightly

indico, indicare, indicavi, indicatus *v.* show, accuse, expose, betray, inform against

indignitas, indignitatis *n.* f. vileness; shamelessness; humiliation

indignus -a -um *adj.* unworthy, undeserving, shameful; unbecoming

indivisus -a -um *adj.* undivided, in common

indoles, indolis *n.* f. innate character; inborn quality

industria, industriae *n.* f. diligence, industry

ineptus -a -um *adj.* silly, foolish

infans, infantis *adj.* speechless, inarticulate; *n.* c. infant; child

infelicitas, infelicitatis *n.* f. misfortune

infelix, infelicis infelicior/-us, infelicissimus -a -um *adj.* unfortunate, wretched; inauspicious; unproductive

infernus -a -um *adj.* infernal; *n.* m. (pl.) those below, the shades

inferus -a -um, inferior/-us, infimmus -a -um *adj.* of hell; vile; low; *n.* m. (pl.) those below, the dead

infimus -a -um *adj.* super. lowest, deepest; humblest; vilest, meanest

infinitus -a -um *adj.* boundless, unlimited, endless; infinite

infirmitas, infirmitatis *n.* f. weakness; sickness

infirmus -a –um, infirmior/-us, infirmissimus -a -um *adj.* frail; sick; powerless; untrustworthy; *n.* m. patient

infra *adv.* below, underneath; *prep.* w/acc. lower, later than

ingens, ingentis ingentior/-us, ingentissimus -a -um *adj.* immoderate; huge; mighty; remarkable

ingenuus -a -um *adj.* natural; free-born; noble, generous, frank

ingredior, ingredi, ingressus sum *v.* advance, walk; enter; undertake, begin

ingressus, ingressus *n.* m. entry; approach; steps

inhibeo, inhibere, inhibui, inhibitus *v.* restrain, curb; prevent

inhumanus -a -um, inhumanior/-us, inhumanissimus -a -um *adj.* rude; unfeeling, inhuman; uncultured

inimicus, -a, -um *adj.* unfriendly, hostile, harmful; *n.* m. enemy

initio, initiare, initiavi, initiatus *v.* initiate

initium, initi(i) *n.* n. beginning; entry; (**ab initio**: from the beginning)

iniuria, iniuriae *n.* f. injury; injustice, offense; insult, abuse

inlustris, inlustre, inlustrior/-us, inlustrissimus -a -um *adj.* bright, shining; clear; illustrious

inmensus -a -um *adj.* immeasurable, vast; great; innumerable

inmoderatus -a -um *adj.* unlimited, immoderate, disorderly

innumerabilis, innumerabile *adj.* countless; without number; immense

inops, inopis *adj.* weak, poor, needy, helpless; destitute, meager

inpatientia, inpatientiae *n.* f. impatience

inpotentia, inpotentiae *n.* f. weakness; violence

inquietus -a -um, inquietior/-us, inquietissimus -a -um *adj.* restless, sleepless; constantly active; unquiet

inquino, inquinare, inquinavi, inquinatus *v.* stain, pollute; soil

inquiro, inquirere, inquisivi, inquisitus *v.* examine, investigate; search, seek

insanio, insanire, insanivi, insanitus *v.* be mad, act crazily

insideo, insidere, insidi, insessus *v.* sit at; lie in ambush; be troublesome

inspecto, inspectare, inspectavi, inspectatus *v.* look at, observe; look on, watch

instinctus -a -um *adj.* roused, fired; infuriated

instrumentum, instrumenti *n.* n. equipment, tools; means; document, deed

insula, insulae *n.* f. island; apartment house

insulto, insultare, insultavi, insultatus *v.* trample on, behave insultingly to, mock

insum, inesse, infui, infuturus *v.* be in; belong to; be involved in

intellego, intellegere, intellexi, intellectus *v.* understand; realize

intentus -a -um, intentior/-us, intentissimus -a -um *adj.* eager, intent, strict

inter *prep.* acc. between, among; during; (**inter se**: mutually)

interdum *adv.* sometimes, now and then

interemo, interemere, interemi, interemptus *v.* do away with; kill, extinguish; destroy

interficio, interficere, interfeci, interfectus *v.* kill; destroy

interim *adv.* meanwhile; at the same time; however

interior, interius *adj.* inner, middle; more intimate

interrogo, interrogare, interrogavi, interrogatus *v.* question, examine; indict; sue

interrumpo, interrumpere, interrupi, interruptus *v.* break into; cut short, interrupt

intersum, interesse, interfui, interfuturus *v.* be in the midst; take part in; be different

intervenio, intervenire, interveni, interventus *v.* come between, intervene; occur

intra, interius, intime *adv.* within, inside; during; also *prep.* w/acc. within

intro, intrare, intravi, intratus *v.* enter; go into, penetrate; reach

introduco, introducere, introduxi, introductus *v.* introduce, lead in

inueho, inuehere, inuexi, inuectus *v.* carry in, import; ride (pass), drive, sail, attack

inuidia, inuidiae *n.* f. hatred, dislike; envy, ill will

invicem *adv.* in turn; mutually (**ab invicem**: from one another)

invoco, invocare, invocavi, invocatus *v.* call upon, invoke; pray for

iocus, ioci *n.* m. joke, jest; sport

ipse, ipsa, ipsum *pron.* himself/herself/itself

ira, irae *n.* f. anger; resentment; rage; wrath

irascor, irasci, iratus sum *v.* get angry, rage; be angry at (with dat.)

irremediabilis, irremediabile *adj.* incurable, irremediable

is, ea, id *pron.* he, she, it, they

iste, ista, istud *pron.* that, that of yours; such

istic *adv.* in that place; in this affair

istuc *adv.* in that direction; to that subject/point

ita *adv.* thus, so; therefore

itaque *conj. adv.* and so, therefore; thus, consequently

iter, itineris *n.* n. journey; road; passage; march

iubeo, iubere, iussi, iussus *v.* order, command, decree; appoint

iucundus -a -um, iucundior/-us, iucundissimus -a -um *adj.* delightful; pleasing; congenial; delicious

iudex, iudicis *n.* m. judge; juror

iudicium, iudici(i) *n.* n. trial; opinion; verdict; court, judicial investigation

iudico, iudicare, iudicavi, iudicatus *v.* judge; sentence; decide; appraise

iugo, iugare, iugavi, iugatus *v.* marry; join to

iunctus -a -um, iunctior/-us, iunctissimus -a -um *adj.* connected, adjoining; related, associated

iunior, iunius *adj.* comp. younger (comp. of iuvenis)

iuro, iurare, iuravi, iuratus *v.* swear; call to witness; (**ius iurandum**: oath)

ius, iuris *n.* n. law, right; duty; justice; oath

iussus, iussus *n.* m. order, decree, (**iussu**: by decree)

iustitia, iustitiae *n.* f. justice; equality

iustus -a -um, iustior/-us, iustissimus -a -um *adj.* just, fair, equitable; lawful, justified

iuventas, iuventatis *n.* f. youth

iuvo, iuvare, iuvi, iutus *v.* help, aid, support, serve; please, delight, gratify

iuxta *adv.* nearly; near, just as, equally; *prep.* w/acc. near

L

labor, laboris *n.* m. effort, labor, work; distress, hardship

lac, lactis *n.* n. milk; milky juice

lacertus, lacerti *n.* m. upper arm, (pl.) strength, vigor

lacrima, lacrimae *n.* f. tear; weeping (pl.); dirge

lacrimo, lacrimare, lacrimavi, lacrimatus *v.* shed tears, weep

laetitia, laetitiae *n.* f. gladness, happiness, joy

laetus -a -um *adj.* happy, joyful; fortunate; luxuriant, lush

lampas, lampadis *n.* f. torch; lamp, lantern; light of the planets

lar, laris *n.* m. tutelary household god; home

largior, largiri, largitus sum *v.* grant; give bribes; give generously

largitio, largitionis *n.* f. generosity; bribery; distribution of dole/land

latus, lateris *n.* n. side; flank

laudatio, laudationis *n.* f. commendation; eulogy

laudo, laudare, laudavi, laudatus *v.* commend; praise; name; deliver eulogy

laus, laudis *n.* f. praise, approval, merit; glory; renown

laxus -a -um *adj.* wide, loose, open, lax

lectus, lecti *n.* m. bed, couch, lounge, bridal bed

legitimus -a –um *adj.* lawful; real, genuine; just; proper

lego, legare, legavi, legatus *v.* bequeath; entrust; send an envoy; choose a deputy

lego, legere, legi, lectus *v.* gather, collect; read; select

lenis, lene *adj.* gentle, kind; smooth, mild, easy, calm

lentus, -a, -um *adj.* clinging, tough; sluggish, lazy; easy, pliant

levis, leve, levior/-us, levissimus -a -um *adj.* light, trivial; gentle; fickle; polished, plain

levitas, levitatis *n.* f. levity; mildness; fickleness; shallowness

libenter, libentius, libentissime *adv.* willingly; gladly, with pleasure

liber, libera, liberum *adj.* free, unimpeded; frank; licentious

liberalis, liberale *adj.* honorable; gentlemanly; liberal; generous

liberalitas, liberalitatis *n.* f. courtesy; generosity

liberi, liberorum *n.* m. pl. children

libero, liberare, liberavi, liberatus *v.* free; absolve; manumit; liberate, release

liberta, libertae *n.* f. freedwoman; ex-slave

libertina, libertinae *n.* f. freedwoman; ex-slave

libertus, liberti *n.* m. freedman; ex-slave

libido, libidinis *n.* f. desire; lust, passion; pleasure

licenter *adv.* boldly; impudently; licentiously; extravagantly

licentia, licentiae *n.* f. freedom, liberty; license, disorderliness

licitus -a -um *adj.* lawful, permitted

lingua, linguae *n.* f. tongue; speech, language; dialect

liqueo, liquere, licui, -- *v.* be in liquid state; (impersonal) be clear, evident

liquor, liquoris *n.* m. fluid, liquid

litus, litoris *n.* n. shore, beach, coast, river bank

loco *adv.* for, in place of, instead of

locuples, locupletis locupletior/-us, locupletissimus -a -um *adj.* opulent, wealthy; trusty

longe, longius, longissime *adv.* distant; by far; for a long while, far (future, past)

longus -a -um, longior/-us, longissimus -a -um *adj.* long; tall; tedious; boundless; far

loquor, loqui, locutus sum *v.* speak, tell; talk; say, utter

lucerna, lucernae *n.* f. oil lamp; midnight oil

lugeo, lugere, luxi, -- *v.* mourn, lament; be in mourning

lugubris, lugubre *adj.* mourning; mournful; grievous

lumen, luminis *n.* n. light; lamp, torch; eye; life; daylight

luna, lunae *n.* f. moon; month

luridus, lurida, luridum *adj.* sallow, wan, ghastly

lux, lucis *n.* f. light; (**prima luce**: at daybreak); life; world; day

luxuria, luxuriae *n.* f. luxury; extravagance

luxuriosus -a -um *adj.* luxuriant; wanton, self-indulgent

lyra, lyrae *n.* f. lyre; lyric poetry

M

macies, maciei *n.* f. leanness, meagerness; poverty

madidus, madida, madidum *adj.* wet, moist; drenched; drunk; steeped in

maereo, maerere, --, -- *v.* grieve, be sad; bewail; utter mournfully

magis *adv.* comp. more nearly; rather, instead

magister, magistri *n.* m. teacher, tutor, master, expert, chief; pilot

magnus -a -um, maior/-us, maximus -a -um *adj.* large, great; powerful; big; extensive; spacious

maiestas, maiestatis *n.* f. dignity, majesty; authority; treason

maior, maioris *n.* m. ancestors (pl.)

male, peius, pessime *adv.* badly, ill, wrongly, wickedly, unfortunately

maledictum, maledicti *n.* n. insult, reproach, taunt

malignus, maligna, malignum *adj.* spiteful; niggardly

malo, malle, malui, -- *v.* prefer; incline toward

malus -a –um, peior/-us, pessimus -a -um *adj.* bad, evil, wicked; ugly; unlucky

mando, mandare, mandavi, mandatus *v.* entrust; commission; order, command

mane *adv.* in the morning; early morning

manifestus -a -um, manifestior/-us, manifestissimus -a -um *adj.* evident; conspicious; guilty; flagrant; undoubted

manumitto, manumittere, manumisi, manumissus *v.* release, free, set free, emancipate

manus, manus *n.* f. hand, fist; gang, band of soldiers; handwriting

masculinus -a -um *adj.* masculine, of the male sex or gender

mater, matris *n.* f. mother; lady; origin, motherland, mother city

materia, materiae *n.* f. matter; topic; means; potential; wood

maternus -a -um *adj.* maternal, motherly, of a mother

matrimonium, matrimoni(i) *n.* n. marriage; matrimony

matrona, matronae *n.* f. wife; married or adult woman

maturus -a -um, maturior/-us, maturissimus -a -um *adj.* early, speedy; mature; timely, seasonable

maxime *adv.* super. chiefly; certainly; most, very much

maximus -a -um *adj.* super. greatest, largest; longest; oldest; utmost; chief

medicus, medici *n.* m. doctor, physician; fourth finger of the hand

meditor, meditari, meditatus sum *v.* consider; ponder; plan, devise, practice

medius -a -um *adj.* middle; common, ordinary, moderate; ambiguous

melior, melius *adj.* comp. better (see bonus)

memini, meminisse *v.* remember (perf); be sure; recall

memor, memoris *adj.* mindful (of w/gen); memorable

memoria, memoriae *n.* f. memory, history; (w/ **tenere**: remember)

memoro, memorare, memoravi, memoratus *v.* mention, relate, remind; speak of (w/gen)

mendacium, mendaci(i) *n.* n. lie; counterfeit, fraud

mens, mentis *n.* f. mind; reason, judgment; intention; courage

mensis, mensis *n.* m. month

mentio, mentionis *n.* f. mention; call to mind; naming

meretrix, meretricis *n.* f. courtesan; public prostitute

meritus -a -um *adj.* deserved, due

merx, mercis *n.* f. commodity; merchandise (pl.), goods

metuo, metuere, metui, -- *v.* fear; be afraid; be apprehensive, dread

metus, metus *n.* m. fear; dread, awe; object of awe or dread

meus -a -um *adj.* my; mine; my own

migro, migrare, migravi, migratus *v.* go away; change residence; depart; remove

miles, militis *n.* m. soldier; foot soldier

mille, milia *n.* n. a thousand; thousands (pl.) (**passuum**: a mile)

minaciter, minacius, minacissime *adv.* menacingly; threatening

minimus -a -um *adj.* super. smallest, least (see parvus)

minor, minoris *n.* m. inferior in rank, grade, age; descendants (pl.)

minus *adv.* comp. less; not so well; not quite

mirabilis, mirabile *adj.* wonderful, astonishing, extraordinary

miror, mirari, miratus sum *v.* admire; wonder; marvel

mirus, mira, mirum *adj.* wonderful, strange, remarkable, surprising

misceo, miscere, miscui, mixtus *v.* mix; involve; confound; stir up

misellus -a -um *adj.* poor, wretched

miser, misera -um, miserior/-us, miserrimus -a -um *adj.* poor, unfortunate, unhappy; *n.* m. wretch

miserabilis, miserabile *adj.* wretched, miserable, pitiable

miseria, miseriae *n.* f. distress, woe, wretchedness

mitis, mite *adj.* mild, meek, gentle; ripe, sweet and juicy

mitto, mittere, misi, missus *v.* send, throw, hurl, cast; release, dismiss; disregard

modestia, modestiae *n.* f. restraint, temperance; discipline; modesty

modestus -a -um *adj.* restrained; modest; reserved; disciplined

modus, modi *n.* m. manner, way, method; measure, size; limit

moene, moenis *n.* n. town walls (pl.); fortifications

moles, molis *n.* f. mass; bulk; monster; difficulty, trouble, danger

molesto, molestare, molestavi, molestatus *v.*
disturb, annoy, worry, trouble
mollio, mollire, mollivi, mollitus *v.* soften, make
easier; civilize, tame, enfeeble
mollis, molle *adj.* soft; calm; pliant, tender; weak;
effeminate
mollitia, mollitiae *n.* f. softness, tenderness;
weakness, effeminacy
momentum, momenti *n.* n. moment, importance;
motion
moneo, monere, monui, monitus *v.* remind, advise,
warn; teach; admonish; foretell
monstro, monstrare, monstravi, monstratus *v.*
show; reveal; advise, teach
monumentum, monumenti *n.* n. memorial,
monument, tomb; record
mora, morae *n.* f. delay, obstacle; pause
morbus, morbi *n.* m. sickness, weakness; disease;
distress; vice
mors, mortis *n.* f. death; corpse; annihilation
mortuus -a -um *adj.* dead, deceased; limp; *n.* m.
corpse
motus, motus *n.* m. movement; riot, disturbance;
gesture; emotion
moveo, movere, movi, motus *v.* move, stir, agitate,
affect, disturb
muliebris, muliebre *adj.* feminine, womanly,
female; effeminate
mulier, mulieris *n.* f. woman; wife; mistress
multitudo, multitudinis *n.* f. multitude; crowd;
rabble, mob
multus -a -um, --, plurimus -a -um *adj.* much,
many, great; large; tedious
munus, muneris *n.* n. service; office; gift; tribute,
offering; bribes (pl.)
musa, musae *n.* f. muse (goddess of arts); sciences,
poetry (pl.)

N

nam *conj.* for; for instance
namque *conj.* for on the other hand (emphatic nam)
nanciscor, nancisci, nactus sum *v.* obtain, find;
meet with, receive, stumble on
narro, narrare, narravi, narratus *v.* tell, relate,
narrate, describe
nativus-a –um *adj.* original; innate; natural; born
natura, naturae *n.* f. nature; birth; character
naturalis, naturale *adj.* natural; normal,
characteristic; innate; physical
natus, natus *n.* m. birth; age, years
navigium, navigi(i) *n.* n. ship
navigo, navigare, navigavi, navigatus *v.* sail;
navigate
navis, navis *n.* f. ship; (**longa**: galley, battleship;
oneraria: cargo)
ne *adv.* not; (**quidem**: not even); truly; *conj.* that not,
lest
necessarium, necessarii *n.* n. necessities (pl.)
necesse *adj.* essential; inevitable; natural law; true
necessitas, necessitatis *n.* f. need; inevitability;
poverty; obligation; bond
neco, necare, necavi, necatus *v.* murder; suppress,
destroy; kill; quench fire
necto, nectere, nexui, nexus *v.* tie, bind
nefas *n.* n. sin, violation of divine law, impious act
neglegentia, neglegentiae *n.* f. heedlessness;
carelessness; coldness; disrespect
neglego, neglegere, neglexi, neglectus *v.* disregard,
neglect; do nothing about; despise
nego, negare, negavi, negatus *v.* deny, refuse; say
... not
nemo, neminis *n.* c. no one, nobody
nequam *adj.* wicked, depraved; naughty; worthless
neque/nec *adv.* nor; and not, neither; *conj.* (neither...
nor; **neque solum...sed etiam**: not only...but
also)
nequior, nequius *adj.* comp. rather wicked,
licentious, worthless
nescio, nescire, nescivi, -- *v.* not know, be ignorant;
(**nescio quis**: someone)
neuter, neutra, neutrum *adj.* neither
nex, necis *n.* f. death; murder;
ni *conj. adv.* if...not; unless; (**quid ni**?: why not?)
niger, nigra, nigrum *adj.* black, dark; unlucky
nihil/nil *n.* n. nothing
nihilominus *adv.* none the less, notwithstanding;
likewise, as well
nimium *adv.* too much; very, excessive, too great
nisi *conj.* if not; except, unless
niveus-a –um *adj.* snowy; white
nobilis, nobile, nobilior/-us, nobilissimus -a -um
adj. noble, respected
nobilitas, nobilitatis *n.* f. nobility; noble birth; fame,
aristocracy; rank
nomen, nominis *n.* n. name; noun; account; sake;
title, heading
nomino, nominare, nominavi, nominatus *v.* name,
call
non *adv.* not, no; (**non modo...sed etiam**: not only..
but also)
nonae, nonarum *n.* f. pl Nones (7th March, May,
July, Oct; 5th of others)
nonne *adv.* not? (expects the answer 'yes')
nonnumquam *adv.* sometimes
nos, nostri, nobis, nos, nobis *pron.* we; ourselves
nosco, noscere, novi, notus *v.* learn, find out;
recognize; study, inspect
noster, nostra, nostrum *adj.* our
nota, notae *n.* f. mark, sign, writing, brand
noto, notare, notavi, notatus *v.* observe; record;
mark; write, inscribe
notus-a –um, notior/-us, notissimus -a -um *adj.*

known, familiar, famous, esteemed; notorious

novitas, novitatis *n.* f. newness; strangeness, rarity; freshness

noxia, noxiae *n.* f. crime, fault

nubo, nubere, nupsi, nuptus *v.* marry, be married to

nudo, nudare, nudavi, nudatus *v.* lay bare, strip; leave unprotected

nudus-a –um *adj.* nude, bare, stripped

nuga, nugae *n.* f. trifles (pl.), nonsense

nullus-a –um (gen --ius) *adj.* no, none, not any; *pron.* no one

num *adv.* whether; now, really (expects negative answer)

numerus, numeri *n.* m. number, sum; strength; category; rhythm, cadence

numquam *adv.* never

numquid *adv.* now (emphatic *num;* expects negative answer)

nunc *adv.* now, today, at present

nuntio, nuntiare, nuntiavi, nuntiatus *v.* announce, report, relate

nuntium, nunti(i) *n.* n. message; notice of divorce or annulment

nuper, --, nuperrime *adv.* recently, not long ago (in our own time)

nutricius, nutrici(i) *n.* m. tutor; foster-father

O

o *interj.* oh!

ob *prep.* acc. on account of, for; instead of; right before

obeo, obire, obivi(ii), obitus *v.* go to meet; attend to; fall; die

obliviscor, oblivisci, oblitus sum *v.* forget; w/ gen

obscurus-a –um *adj.* dark, secret; vague, obscure

obsequium, obsequi(i) *n.* n. compliance; subservience, obsequiousness

obsero, obserare, obseravi, obseratus *v.* bolt, fasten; prohibit access; enclose

observo, observare, observavi, observatus *v.* watch, observe; heed

obsidium, obsidi(i) *n.* n. siege, blockade

obsisto, obsistere, obstiti, obstitus *v.* oppose, resist; withstand

obstetrix/opstetrix, obstetricis *n.* f. midwife

obsum, obesse, obfui, obfuturus *v.* hurt; be a nuisance to, tell against

obtineo, obtinere, obtinui, obtentus *v.* maintain; obtain; hold fast, occupy; prevail

obvius-a –um *adj.* in the way, easy; hostile; exposed (to)

occasio, occasionis *n.* f. opportunity; chance; pretext

occido, occidere, occidi, occisus *v.* slaughter; cut down; weary, be the ruin of

occupo, occupare, occupavi, occupatus *v.* seize; overtake; capture; attack

occurro, occurrere, occurri, occursus *v.* run to meet; oppose; occur (with dat)

oculus, oculi *n.* m. eye

odi, odisse *v.* hate, dislike; be reluctant or averse to

odium, odi(i) *n.* n. hatred, dislike

odor, odoris *n.* m. scent, odor, aroma, smell; hint, suggestion

offensus, offensus *n.* m. collision, knock

offero, offerre, obtuli, oblatus *v.* offer; present; cause; bestow

olim *adv.* formerly; once; in the future

omnino *adv.* entirely, altogether; w/ negative: at all; w/ **num**: in all

omnis, omne *adj.* every; all (pl.); each; the whole of

onero, onerare, oneravi, oneratus *v.* load, burden; oppress

onus, oneris *n.* n. load, burden; cargo

opera, operae *n.* f. work, care; service, effort; (w/ **dare**: pay attention)

operio, operire, operui, opertus *v.* cover; bury; conceal; clothe, cover the head

opinio, opinionis *n.* f. belief, idea, rumor

opinor, opinari, opinatus sum *v.* suppose, imagine

oppidum, oppidi *n.* n. town

oppono, opponere, opposui, oppositus *v.* place opposite, oppose

oppugno, oppugnare, oppugnavi, oppugnatus *v.* attack, storm, besiege

ops, opis *n.* f. power, might; help; resources, wealth

optimus, optima, optimum *adj.* best (see bonus)

opus, operis *n.* n. need; work; (w/ **est**: useful, beneficial); works

ora, orae *n.* f. shore, coast

oratio, orationis *n.* f. speech, oration; eloquence; prayer

orbo, orbare, orbavi, orbatus *v.* bereave (of parents, children), deprive (of)

orbus -a -um *adj.* bereft, deprived, childless

ordo, ordinis *n.* m. row, order, rank; series

origo, originis *n.* f. origin; birth, family; race

ornatus -a -um, ornatior/-us, ornatissimus -a -um *adj.* well equipped, adorned; honored

orno, ornare, ornavi, ornatus *v.* equip; dress; decorate; furnish, adorn

oro, orare, oravi, oratus *v.* beg, ask for, pray; entreat; worship, adore

orsus, orsus *n.* m. web; beginning, start; undertaking, initiative

ortus, ortus *n.* m. sunrise; origin; birth; source; growth

os, oris *n.* n. mouth, speech, expression; face

os, ossis *n.* n. bone; kernel (nut); heartwood (tree); stone (fruit)

ostendo, ostendere, ostendi, ostentus *v.* show; reveal; make clear, exhibit

otium, oti(i) *n.* n. leisure; holiday; peace; tranquility
ovum, ovi *n.* n. egg

P

paene *adv.* nearly, almost; mostly
paeniteo, paenitere, paenitui, -- *v.* displease; regret; repent (**me paenitet:** I am sorry)
palla, pallae *n.* f. lady's outer garment
pallium, palli(i) *n.* n. cover, coverlet; Greek cloak
palma, palmae *n.* f. width of hand; hand; palm tree; date; award
paratus -a -um *adj.* prepared; ready; equipped
parco, parcere, peperci, parsus *v.* spare; economize (with dat); forbear, refrain
parcus -a -um *adj.* sparing, frugal; scanty, slight
parens, parentis *n.* c. parent, father, mother
pareo, parere, parui, paritus *v.* appear, be seen; obey; yield; pay attention
paries, parietis *n.* m. wall, house wall
paro, parare, paravi, paratus *v.* prepare; furnish; obtain; buy; raise; plan
pars, partis *n.* f. part, region; direction; role; piece; party, faction
partitio, partitionis *n.* f. distribution, share; classification
parum, minus, minime *adv.* too little, insufficient; less; (super.) not at all
parvus -a -um, minor/-us, minimus -a -um *adj.* small, little, cheap; unimportant
pateo, patere, patui, -- *v.* stand open; extend; be well known; be accessible
pater, patris *n.* m. father; (**paterfamilias:** head of household)
paternus -a -um *adj.* father's, paternal; ancestral
patesco, patescere, patui, -- *v.* be revealed; become known; open; extend, spread
patiens, patientis *adj.* patient, enduring
patientia, patientiae *n.* f. endurance, patience; suffering
patria, patriae *n.* f. native land; home, native city
patrimonium, patrimoni(i) *n.* n. inheritance
patrona, patronae *n.* f. protectress, patroness
patronus, patroni *n.* m. patron; advocate; protector
patruus, patrui *n.* m. paternal uncle; type of stern discipline
paucus -a -um, paucior/-us, paucissimus -a -um *adj.* little; few (pl.); just a few; small number of
paullum, paulli *n.* n. little bit; small amount; trifle
paullus -a -um *adj.* little; small
paulo *adv.* by a little; somewhat
paveo, pavere, pavi, -- *v.* be frightened or terrified at
pavidus -a -um *adj.* fearful, terrified
pavor, pavoris *n.* m. fear, panic
pax, pacis *n.* f. peace; harmony

peccatum, peccati *n.* n. error, sin
pecco, peccare, peccavi, peccatus *v.* sin, do wrong
pecunia, pecuniae *n.* f. money; property
peior, peius *adj.* comp. worse (see malus)
pello, pellere, pepuli, pulsus *v.* beat; push; banish, strike, drive away, rout
penates, penatis *n.* m. household gods, gods of the family.
pendo, pendere, pependi, pensus *v.* weigh out; pay, pay out
per *prep.* acc. through; during; by, by means of
perago, peragere, peregi, peractus *v.* disturb; finish; kill; complete
percipio, percipere, percepi, perceptus *v.* secure, gain; perceive, learn, feel
perdo, perdere, perdidi, perditus *v.* ruin, destroy; lose; waste
perfectus -a -um *adj.* perfect, complete; excellent
perfundo, perfundere, perfudi, perfusus *v.* pour over, wet; coat, overlay; imbue
perfungor, perfungi, perfunctus sum *v.* perform, discharge, have done with (w/abl)
periculum, periculi *n.* n. danger; attempt; risk; liability
peritia, peritiae *n.* f. practical knowledge, skill, expertise
peritus -a -um *adj.* skilled; experienced, expert (w/ gen
permaneo, permanere, permansi, permansus *v.* last, continue; remain; endure
permissus, permissus *n.* m. permission, authorization
permitto, permittere, permisi, permissus *v.* let through; relinquish; allow; entrust; hurl
perpetuus -a -um *adj.* continuous; everlasting
persaepe *adv.* very often
persona, personae *n.* f. mask; character; personality
persuadeo, persuadere, persuasi, persuasus *v.* persuade, convince (with dat.)
pertenuis, pertenue *adj.* very thin, very fine, slender, slight
pessimus -a -um *adj.* super. worst (see malus)
peto, petere, petivi, petitus *v.* aim at; seek, ask for
philosophia, philosophiae *n.* f. philosophy, love of wisdom
pictor, pictoris *n.* m. painter
pictura, picturae *n.* f. painting, picture
pingo, pingere, pinxi, pictus *v.* paint, draw; depict, portray
pius -a -um *adj.* conscientious; patriotic, dutiful, godly
plane *adv.* clearly, distinctly; completely
planus -a -um *adj.* level, flat
plaudo, plaudere, plausi, plausus *v.* clap, pat; express (dis)approval
plebs, plebis *n.* f. commoners; folk; lower ranks;

masses

ploro, plorare, ploravi, ploratus *v.* cry over, cry aloud; lament; deplore

plurimus -a -um *adj.* most, greatest; very many; highest value

plus, pluris *adj.* more (see multus); several; many

pluvia, pluviae *n.* f. rain, shower

pol *interj.* by Pollux; truly; really

polliceor, polliceri, pollicitus sum *v.* promise

pono, ponere, posui, positus *v.* put, place, set; station

pons, pontis *n.* m. bridge

populus, populi *n.* m. people, nation, state; crowd; following

porrigo, porrigere, porrexi, porrectus *v.* stretch out, extend

porta, portae *n.* f. gate, entrance; city gate; door; avenue

porticus, porticus *n.* c. colonnade, covered gallery

porto, portare, portavi, portatus *v.* carry, bring

positus, positus *n.* m. situation, position; arrangement

possessio, possessionis *n.* f. possession, property

possideo, possidere, possedi, possessus *v.* seize, be master of; occupy; inherit

possum, posse, potui, -- *v.* be able, can; (w/ **multum**: have much power)

post *adv.* behind, after; *prep.* w/ acc. behind, after

postea *adv.* afterwards

posthac *adv.* after this; thereafter, from then on

postmodo *adv.* afterwards, presently, later

postquam *conj.* after

postremo *adv.* at last, finally

postridie *adv.* on the following day

postulo, postulare, postulavi, postulatus *v.* demand, claim; require; ask for

potens, potentis potentior/-us, potentissimus -a -um *adj.* powerful, strong; capable; mighty

potentia, potentiae *n.* f. force, power, political power

potis *adj.* able, capable; possible

prae *adv.* before; forward; *prep.* w/abl. before, because of

praeceps, praecipitis *adj.* head first, headlong; steep, precipitous

praecipue *adv.* especially; chiefly

praeclarus -a -um *adj.* splendid; famous; bright; noble, distinguished

praefero, praeferre, praetuli, praelatus *v.* carry in front; prefer; display

praelego, praelegere, praelegi, praelectus *v.* sail along

praemium, praemi(i) *n.* n. prize, reward; gift; recompense

praeparo, praeparare, praeparavi, praeparatus *v.* prepare

praesens, praesentis *adj.* present; at hand; prompt

praesertim *adv.* especially; particularly

praeter *prep.* acc. besides, except; beyond; more than

praeteritus -a -um *adj.* past

praeterquam *adv.* except, besides; *prep.* w/ acc. except, contrary to

prenso, prensare, prensavi, prensatus *v.* grasp; lay hold of; accost; solicit

presso, pressare, pressavi, pressatus *v.* press, squeeze

pressus, pressa, pressum *adj.* firmly planted, deliberate

pretium, preti(i) *n.* n. price; reward; worth; pay

pridem *adv.* some time ago, previously

pridie *adv.* the day before

primo *adv.* at first; at the beginning

primus -a -um *adj.* first, best; chief; nearest; (**in primis**: especially)

principium, principi(i) *n.* n. beginning

prior, prius *adj.* comp. prior, earlier; *n.* m. (pl.) ancestors; forefathers

priscus -a -um *adj.* ancient, early, former

prius *adv.* earlier, before, previously, first

priusquam *conj.* before; until; sooner than

privatim *adv.* in private; as a private citizen

privatus -a -um *adj.* private; personal; ordinary

pro *prep.* abl. on behalf of; before; instead of; for; according to

probe *adv.* properly, rightly

probo, probare, probavi, probatus *v.* approve, esteem; sanction; examine, test, prove

procedo, procedere, processi, processus *v.* proceed; advance; appear

proclamo, proclamare, proclamavi, proclamatus *v.* raise an outcry; appeal noisily; proclaim

produco, producere, produxi, productus *v.* lead forward; promote; prolong; bury

proelium, proeli(i) *n.* n. battle

profero, proferre, protuli, prolatus *v.* bring forward; advance; defer; discover; mention

profugio, profugere, profugi, -- *v.* escape; run away from

prohibeo, prohibere, prohibui, prohibitus *v.* hinder, restrain; forbid, prevent

proiectus -a -um *adj.* projecting; precipitate; abject, groveling

proiicio, proiicere, proieci, proiectus *v.* throw down; abandon; throw away

promereo, promerere, promerui, promeritus *v.* deserve, merit; deserve well; earn; gain

promitto, promittere, promisi, promissus *v.* promise

promo, promere, prompsi, promptus *v.* bring forth; bring out, display on the stage

pronuntio, pronuntiare, pronuntiavi, pronuntiatus *v.* announce; proclaim; relate; recite; utter

prope, propius, proxime *adv.* near, nearly; close by; almost; *prep.* w/ acc. near

propediem *adv.* before long, shortly

propinquus -a -um *adj.* near, neighboring; *n. m.* relative

proprietas, proprietatis *n.* f. quality; special character; ownership

proprius -a -um *adj.* very own; individual; special, particular, characteristic

propter *prep.* acc. near; on account of; by means of; because of

propterea *adv.* therefore, for this reason; (w/ **quod**: because)

prorsus *adv.* forward; utterly, by all means; in short

prorumpo, prorumpere, prorupi, proruptus *v.* rush forth, break out

proscriptus, proscripti *n.* m. proscribed person, outlaw

prosequor, prosequi, prosecutus sum *v.* escort; pursue; describe in detail

prosperus -a –um, prosperior/-us, prosperrimus -a -um *adj.* successful; lucky, favorable (omens/prospects)

prosum, prodesse, profui, profuturus *v.* be useful, benefit, profit (with dat)

protinus *adv.* forward; immediately; at once

provideo, providere, providi, provisus *v.* foresee; provide for, make provision (w/ dat)

provincia, provinciae *n.* f. province; office; duty; command

proximo *adv.* very lately

proximus -a -um *adj.* super. closest, next; most recent; most like

prudentia, prudentiae *n.* f. discretion; good sense; foresight

pubertas, pubertatis *n.* f. puberty; virility

publice *adv.* publicly; at public expense

publico, publicare, publicavi, publicatus *v.* confiscate; make public property; publish

publicus -a -um *adj.* public; of the people; (w/ **res**: the state)

pudeo, pudere, pudui/puditum est *v.* shame, be ashamed; (**me pudet**: I am ashamed)

pudicitia, pudicitiae *n.* f. chastity; modesty; purity

pudor, pudoris *n.* m. decency, shame; sense of honor

puella, puellae *n.* f. girl; maiden; young woman; sweetheart; slave-girl

puer, pueri *n.* m. boy, child, young man; servant

pugio, pugionis *n.* m. dagger

pulcher, pulchra -um, pulchrior/-us, pulcherrimus -a -um *adj.* pretty; beautiful; handsome; noble, illustrious

pulchritudo, pulchritudinis *n.* f. beauty, excellence

purus -a -um, purior/-us, purissimus -a -um *adj.* pure, clean; blameless; chaste; genuine

puto, putare, putavi, putatus *v.* think, believe, suppose, value

Q

quacumque *adv.* wherever; however; by whatever route

quaero, quaerere, quaesivi, quaesitus *v.* seek, strive for; ask, inquire, demand

qualis, quale *adj.* what kind of, what sort of

quam *conj., adv.* how, than; as (w/ **super**: as ... as possible)

quamdiu *adv., conj.* how long; as long as, until

quamlibet *adv.* however, however much

quamquam *conj.* although; yet; nevertheless

quamvis *conj., adv.* however much; although

quando *adv., conj.* when? at what time? at any time; when, since, because; (w/ **si**: if ever)

quanto *adv.* (by) how much

quantum *adv.* so much as; how much; how far

quantus -a -um *adj.* how great; how much

quasi *conj. adv.* as if; as it were; about

**quattuor, quartus -a -um, quaterni -ae -a, -- ** *num.* four; fourth; four men

querella, querellae *n.* f. complaint; illness; difference; blame

qui, quae, quod *pron.* who?, which?, what?; who, which

quia *conj.* because

quidam, quaedam, quoddam/quiddam *indef. pron.* a certain, a certain one, someone

quidem *adv.* indeed, certainly, at least; (w/ **ne**: not even)

quidnam *adv.* what? how?

quies, quietis *n.* f. quiet, calm, rest, peace; sleep

quiesco, quiescere, quievi, quietus *v.* rest, be at peace; be inactive; permit; sleep

quietus -a -um, quietior/-us, quietissimus -a -um *adj.* tranquil, calm, peaceful; orderly; still; idle

quin *adv., conj.* in fact; but that; (w/ **etiam**: moreover)

quinque, quintus -a -um, quini -ae -a, quinquie(n)s *num.* five; fifth; five men; five times

quis, quid *pron.* any; some; (w/ **si, nisi, numque, ne**: some/anyone)

quisquam, quaequam, quicquam/quidquam *pron.* anyone, any, anything

quisque, quaeque, quodque/quicque/quidque *indef. pron.* whoever, whatever; each, every

quisquis, quaequae, quodquod/quidquid/quicquid *pron.* who/whatever, everyone who, all that

quoad *conj.* as long as, until

quominus *conj.* that not, from

quomodo *adv.* how, in what way; just as

quoniam *conj.* because, since, seeing that

quoque *adv.* likewise, also; not only; even, actually

quotidie *adv.* daily; day by day; usually, commonly
quotiens *adv.* how often; as often as

R

raptim *adv.* hurriedly, suddenly
raptum, rapti *n.* n. plunder; prey
rarus -a -um, rarior/-us, rarissimus -a -um *adj.* thin, scattered; few, infrequent; rare
recedo, recedere, recessi, recessus *v.* withdraw; retreat; retire; move away
recens, recentis *adj.* fresh, recent; rested
recido, recidere, recidi, -- *v.* fall back
recipio, recipere, recepi, receptus *v.* keep back; recover; guarantee; accept
recondo, recondere, recondidi, reconditus *v.* hide, conceal; put away
rectus -a -um, rectior/-us, rectissimus -a -um *adj.* right, proper; straight; honest
recumbo, recumbere, recubui, -- *v.* recline, lie at ease; recline at table
recupero, recuperare, recuperavi, recuperatus *v.* regain, restore; refresh, recuperate
reditus, reditus *n.* m. return; revenue, income; produce
reductus -a -um *adj.* set back
refero, referre, rettuli, relatus *v.* renew; report; return (w/ **gratiam**: return thanks)
refugio, refugere, refugi, -- *v.* flee back; run away, escape
regalis, regale *adj.* royal, regal
regia, regiae *n.* f. palace, court; residence
regina, reginae *n.* f. queen
regio, regionis *n.* f. area, region; district, country; direction
regius -a -um *adj.* of a king, royal, regal
regno, regnare, regnavi, regnatus *v.* reign, rule; be king, lord, master
regnum, regni *n.* n. royal power; control; kingdom
rego, regere, rexi, rectus *v.* rule, guide; manage, direct
relego, relegare, relegavi, relegatus *v.* banish, remove; relegate
relictus -a –um, relictior/-us, relictissimus -a -um *adj.* forsaken, abandoned; left untouched
religio, religionis *n.* f. obligation; sanction; worship; rite; sanctity; reverence; religion
relinquo, relinquere, reliqui, relictus *v.* leave behind, abandon; be left, remain; bequeath
reliquus -a -um *adj.* remaining; surviving
remaneo, remanere, remansi, remansus *v.* stay behind; continue, remain
remedium, remedi(i) *n.* n. remedy, cure; medicine
remitto, remittere, remisi, remissus *v.* send back, remit; relax, diminish

remotus -a -um *adj.* remote
removeo, removere, removi, remotus *v.* move back; withdraw; remove
repente *adv.* suddenly, unexpectedly
reperio, reperire, repperi, repertus *v.* discover; find; get to know; invent
repono, reponere, reposui, repositus *v.* put back; restore; store; repeat
reposco, reposcere, --, -- *v.* demand back; claim as one's due
reputo, reputare, reputavi, reputatus *v.* think over, reflect
requiro, requirere, requisivi, requisitus *v.* require, seek, ask for; need; miss
res, rei *n.* f. thing; event, business; fact; cause; property
rescindo, rescindere, rescidi, rescissus *v.* cut out; cut down, destroy
reservo, reservare, reservavi, reservatus *v.* reserve; spare; hold on to
respicio, respicere, respexi, respectus *v.* look back at; consider; respect; care for
respondeo, respondere, respondi, responsus *v.* answer
responso, responsare, responsavi, responsatus *v.* answer, reply (to); re-echo
retro *adv.* back; behind; formerly
reverentia, reverentiae *n.* f. respect, reverence
revereor, revereri, reveritus sum *v.* respect, honor, fear; reverence
revoco, revocare, revocavi, revocatus *v.* call back, recall; revive; regain
rex, regis *n.* m. king
rhetor, rhetoris *n.* m. teacher of public speaking, rhetorician
rideo, ridere, risi, risus *v.* laugh at (with dat.), ridicule
rigidus -a -um *adj.* stiff, hard; stern; rough
rogo, rogare, rogavi, rogatus *v.* ask, ask for; invite; introduce
rubeo, rubere, --, -- *v.* be red, become red
ruber, rubra, rubrum *adj.* red, ruddy (w/ **mare**: Red Sea)
rumor, rumoris *n.* m. hearsay, rumor, gossip; reputation; shouting
rumpo, rumpere, rupi, ruptus *v.* break; destroy
ruo, ruere, rui, rutus *v.* destroy; overthrow; rush; fall; be ruined
rus, ruris *n.* n. country, farm
rusticus -a -um *adj.* country, rural; plain, rustic

S

saeculum, saeculi *n.* n. age; generation; breed, race; century

saepe, saepius, saepissime *adv.* often, many times, frequently

sagitta, sagittae *n.* f. arrow

salto, saltare, saltavi, saltatus *v.* dance, jump

saluber, salubris, salubre *adj.* healthful; wholesome; healthy

salutaris, salutare, salutarior/-us, salutarissimus -a -um *adj.* healthful, wholesome, beneficial

salutatio, salutationis *n.* f. greeting; formal morning call of client on patron

sanguis, sanguinis *n.* m. blood; family

sanus -a -um *adj.* sound; healthy; sensible; sober

sapientia, sapientiae *n.* f. good taste; prudence, wisdom

sapor, saporis *n.* m. taste, flavor

satio, satiare, satiavi, satiatus *v.* satisfy; nourish

satis/sat *adj.* sufficient; satisfactory; (*adv.*) adequately; quite

saucio, sauciare, sauciavi, sauciatus *v.* wound; stab

saxum, saxi *n.* n. stone

scelus, sceleris *n.* n. crime; wickedness, evil deed

sciens, scientis *adj.* knowing, understanding; skilled, expert

scientia, scientiae *n.* f. knowledge, science; skill

scio, scire, scivi, scitus *v.* know, understand

scitus, -a, -um *adj.* neat, ingenious; nice, excellent

scribo, scribere, scripsi, scriptus *v.* write; compose

scriptor, scriptoris *n.* m. writer, author; scribe

scriptum, scripti *n.* n. written; communication; literary work

secretum, secreti *n.* n. secret, mystic rite, haunt

secundo, secundare, --, -- *v.* favor; adjust, adapt; prosper

secundus -a -um, secundior/-us, secundissimus -a -um *adj.* following, next; second; favorable

securus -a -um *adj.* secure, safe, untroubled

secus *adv.* otherwise; *prep.* w/ acc. by, beside, in accord with

sed *conj.* but; yet; however; yes, but

sedatus -a -um *adj.* calm, untroubled

sedes, sedis *n.* f. seat; home; settlement

seductus -a -um *adj.* distant; retired, secluded

sedulus -a -um *adj.* attentive, painstaking, sedulous

selectio, selectionis *n.* f. selection

sella, sellae *n.* f. seat, chair

semel *adv.* once

semen, seminis *n.* n. seed

semper *adv.* always

senator, senatoris *n.* m. senator

senatus, senatus *n.* m. senate

senectus, senectutis *n.* f. old age

senior, senius *adj.* older, elderly; (comparative of **senex**: man over 45)

sensus, sensus *n.* m. feeling, sense

sententia, sententiae *n.* f. opinion, feeling; sentence, thought; vote

sentio, sentire, sensi, sensus *v.* feel, experience; think, understand

separatio, separationis *n.* f. separation; division

separo, separare, separavi, separatus *v.* divide, distinguish; separate

septem, septimus -a -um, septeni -ae -a, septie(n)s *num.* seven; seventh; seven men; seven times

septemviri, septemvirorum *n.* m. board or college of seven men

septeni, septenai, septena *adj.* seven each

sepulchrum, sepulchri *n.* n. grave, tomb

series, seriei *n.* f. row, succession, sequence, order

sero, serere, sevi, satus *v.* sow, plant; cultivate; beget, bring forth

sero, serius, serissime *adv.* late, tardily; too late (comp.)

serpo, serpere, serpsi, serptus *v.* crawl; glide; creep on

serus -a -um, serior/-us, serissimus -a -um *adj.* late; slow; at a late hour

servilis, servile *adj.* servile, of slaves

servitium, serviti(i) *n.* n. slavery, servitude; slaves; the slave class

servo, servare, servavi, servatus *v.* protect, store, guard, preserve, save

servus, servi *n.* m. slave; servant

seu *conj.* or if; or; (**sive...sive**: whether ... or, either ... or)

severitas, severitatis *n.* f. strictness, severity

severus -a -um, severior/-us, severissimus -a -um *adj.* stern, strict; austere; weighty; unadorned, plain

sex, sextus -a -um, seni -ae -a, sexie(n)s *num.* six; sixth; six men; six times

sexus, sexus *n.* m. sex

si *conj.* if, if only; whether; (**quod si**: but if)

sic *adv.* thus, so; as follows; in such a way

sidus, sideris *n.* n. star; constellation

signo, signare, signavi, signatus *v.* mark, stamp, designate; seal

signum, signi *n.* n. seal; sign, proof; signal, standard; image, statue

silens, silentis *adj.* silent, still

similis, simile, similior/-us, simillimus -a -um *adj.* like, similar, resembling

similitudo, similitudinis *n.* f. likeness, imitation; resemblance

simplex, simplicis *adj.* single; simple, unaffected

simulacrum, simulacri *n.* n. likeness, image, statue

simulo, simulare, simulavi, simulatus *v.* imitate; pretend; counterfeit

sin *conj.* but if; if on the contrary

sine *prep.* without (w/ abl.)

singularis, singulare *adj.* alone, unique; single; remarkable

singulus -a -um *adj.* apiece (pl.); every; individual; several

sino, sinere, sivi, situs *v.* allow, permit

siquidem *conj.* accordingly; if indeed

siquis/siqui, siqua, siquid/siquod indef. *pron.* if any, if anyone

situs -a -um *adj.* stored; situated; centered

sive *conj.* or if; or; (**sive...sive**: whether ...or)

socius, soci(i) *n.* m. associate, companion; ally

sol, solis *n.* m. the sun

solitudo, solitudinis *n.* f. solitude, loneliness; deprivation; wilderness

solitus, solita, solitum *adj.* usual, customary

sollemnis, sollemne *adj.* solemn, sacred; appointed; joyful

solum *adv.* only, merely, alone

solum, soli *n.* n. bottom, ground, floor; soil, land

solus -a -um (gen --ius) *adj.* single; lonely; alone; unique

solvo, solvere, solvi, solutus *v.* loosen, untie, free; set sail; pay back

somnium, somni(i) *n.* n. dream, vision; fantasy

somnus, somni *n.* m. sleep

sono, sonare, sonui, sonitus *v.* make a sound; speak; resound

sopor, soporis *n.* m. deep sleep

sordes, sordis *n.* f. filth, squalor; meanness; baseness

sordidus -a -um, sordidior/-us, sordidissimus -a -um *adj.* dirty; vulgar; base, mean; vile

soror, sororis *n.* f. sister; half-sister, sister-in-law; mistress

sortitus, sortitus *n.* m. lottery

specto, spectare, spectavi, spectatus *v.* observe, look at; test; consider

sperno, spernere, sprevi, spretus *v.* scorn, despise, spurn

spero, sperare, speravi, speratus *v.* hope for; trust; look forward to

spes, spei *n.* f. hope, anticipation; expectation

spiritus, spiritus *n.* m. breath, breathing, air, soul, life

spiro, spirare, spiravi, spiratus *v.* breathe; blow; live; exhale

splendidus -a -um *adj.* splendid, glittering

sponte *adv.* voluntarily; for one's own sake

squalor, squaloris *n.* m. squalor, filth

stabilis, stabile *adj.* stable; steadfast

statuo, statuere, statui, statutus *v.* establish, build; decide, think

sterno, sternere, stravi, stratus *v.* spread, strew; lay out

stimulo, stimulare, stimulavi, stimulatus *v.* goad, torment; incite, rouse to frenzy

sto, stare, steti, status *v.* stand, stand firm; remain, rest

strenuus -a -um *adj.* active, vigorous, strenuous

studiose, studiosius, studiosissime *adv.* eagerly, studiously, ardently, attentively

stultus -a -um *adj.* foolish, stupid; *n.* m. fool

suavitas, suavitatis *n.* f. charm, attractiveness; sweetness

sub *prep.* w/ abl: under, beneath; within; during; w/ acc: under; up to; until, before, up to, about

subditus -a -um *adj.* subordinate; submissive

subicio, subicere, subjeci, subjectus *v.* throw under, place under; make subject; expose

subito *adv.* suddenly, unexpectedly; at once

subitus -a -um *adj.* sudden; rash, unexpected

sublevo, sublevare, sublevavi, sublevatus *v.* raise; support; assist; lighten

sublimis, sublime, sublimior/-us, sublimissimus -a -um *adj.* high, exalted, elevated

subripio/surripio, subripere, subripui, subreptus *v.* snatch away, steal

subsum, subesse, subfui, subfuturus *v.* support, be at hand, be near

successor, successoris *n.* m. successor

sui, sibi, se, se *pron.* him/her/it-self; them; each other, one another

sum, esse, fui, futurum *v.* be, exist

summissus -a -um *adj.* stooping; quiet, humble

summ -a -um *adj.* super. highest, the top of; greatest; last

sumptus, sumptus *n.* m. cost, charge, expense

super *adv.* moreover, besides; *prep.* w/ abl. over, above; during; w/ acc: upon; above, about; besides; during; beyond

superbe, superbius, superbissime *adv.* arrogantly, proudly, haughtily

superbia, superbiae *n.* f. arrogance, pride, haughtiness

superbus -a -um *adj.* arrogant, overbearing, proud

superpono, superponere, superposui, superpositus *v.* place over; put in charge

superstitio, superstitionis *n.* f. superstition; irrational religious awe

supersum, superesse, superfui, -- *v.* be left; survive; be superfluous; remain

superus -a --um, superior/-us, supremus -a -um *adj.* above, high; of this world; greatest, last, highest; *n.* m. (pl.) gods

supplicium, supplici(i) *n.* n. punishment, suffering; supplication; torture

suppono, supponere, supposui, suppositus *v.* place under; substitute; suppose

supra *adv.* more; above; before. formerly; *prep.* w/ acc: over; beyond; more than; in charge of, in authority over

surdus -a -um *adj.* deaf; unresponsive; muffled, muted

surgo, surgere, surrexi, surrectus *v.* rise, lift; grow

suscipio/succipio, suscipere, suscepi, susceptus *v.*

undertake; accept, receive, support

suspendo, suspendere, suspendi, suspensus *v.* hang up, suspend

suspensus -a -um *adj.* uncertain, anxious; light

suspicio, suspicionis *n.* f. suspicion; mistrust

sustineo, sustinere, sustinui, sustentus *v.* check; put up with; sustain; hold back

suus, sua, suum *adj.* one's own; (pl.) their own

T

tabula, tabulae *n.* f. writing tablet; picture, painting; (pl.) records

tacitus -a -um *adj.* silent, secret

taedium, taedi(i) *n.* n. weariness; tedium

tam *adv.* so; nevertheless, all the same

tamen *adv.* yet, nevertheless, still

tamquam *conj.* as, just as if; so to speak; as much as; so as

tandem *adv.* at last, finally

tango, tangere, tetigi, tactus *v.* touch, strike; influence; mention

tantum *adv.* so much, so far; hardly, only

tantus -a -um *adj.* so great, so much; (w/ **quantus**: as much ... as)

tardus -a -um *adj.* slow, limping; deliberate; late

tego, tegere, texi, tectus *v.* cover, protect; defend; hide

temere *adv.* rashly, blindly

temeritas, temeritatis *n.* f. rashness; boldness

templum, templi *n.* n. temple; shrine; holy place

tempto, temptare, temptavi, temptatus *v.* test, try; urge; worry; bribe

tempus, temporis *n.* n. time; season, occasion; necessity

tenax, tenacis tenacior/-us, tenacissimus -a -um *adj.* clinging; steadfast, persistent; stubborn

teneo, tenere, tenui, tentus *v.* hold; comprehend; possess; master; preserve

tenuis, tenue *adj.* fine; delicate; weak, feeble

ter *adv.* three times

tergeo, tergere, tersi, tersus *v.* rub, wipe; clean, cleanse

tergum, tergi *n.* n. back; reverse; rear; (w/ **vertere**: flee)

terra, terrae *n.* f. earth, land, ground; country, region

terreo, terrere, terrui, territus *v.* frighten, scare, terrify, deter

testamentum, testamenti *n.* n. will, testament; covenant

testis, testis *n.* c. witness

theatrum, theatri *n.* n. theater

timeo, timere, timui, -- *v.* fear, dread (**ne** + subj: lest; **ut** + subj: that)

timidus -a -um, timidior/-us, timidissimus -a -um *adj.* cowardly; fearful, apprehensive

timor, timoris *n.* m. fear; dread

titulus, tituli *n.* m. title; inscription; monument

toga, togae *n.* f. outer draped garment of male Roman citizen

tolero, tolerare, toleravi, toleratus *v.* bear, endure, tolerate

tollo, tollere, sustuli, sublatus *v.* lift, raise; destroy; steal

totus -a -um (gen --ius) *adj.* whole, all, entire; every part; all together

tracto, tractare, tractavi, tractatus *v.* draw, haul; manage, treat, discuss

trado, tradere, tradidi, traditus *v.* hand over, surrender; deliver; bequeath; relate

tragicus -a -um *adj.* tragic; of tragedy, *n.* m.: tragic poet, actor

tranquillitas, tranquillitatis *n.* f. stillness; tranquility

transfero, transferre, transtuli, translatus *v.* transport; transplant; translate; transform

transgredior, transgredi, transgressus sum *v.* cross; change allegiance, side, policy

trepidus -a -um *adj.* nervous; alarming, frightened; boiling

tres, tria; tertius -a -um, terni -ae -a, ter *num.* three; third; three men; three times

tricesimus -a --um *num.* thirtieth

tristitia, tristitiae *n.* f. sadness

triumpho, triumphare, triumphavi, triumphatus *v.* celebrate a triumph; conquer

triumphus, triumphi *n.* m. victory parade; triumph

triumvir, triumviri *n.* m. commissioner; a three-man board; triumvirate

tropaeum, tropaei *n.* n. trophy; monument of captured armor; victory

tu, tui, tibi, te, te *pron.* you; yourself

tum *adv.* then, next; besides; (w/ **cum**: not only... but also)

tumultus, tumultus *n.* m. confusion, uproar; rebellion

tunc *adv.* then, thereupon

turbo, turbare, turbavi, turbatus *v.* disturb, agitate, throw into confusion

turpis, turpe, turpior/-us, turpissimus -a -um *adj.* ugly; disgraceful; base, disgusting

turpiter *adv.* repulsively, disgracefully, basely

tussis, tussis *n.* f. cough

tute *adv.* without risk, safely, securely

tutela, tutelae *n.* f. tutelage, guardianship

tutor, tutari, tutatus sum *v.* guard, protect, defend; avert

tutor, tutoris *n.* m. protector, defender; guardian

tutus -a --um, tutior/-us, tutissimus -a -um *adj.* safe, prudent; secure; protected

tuus -a -um *adj.* your (sing.)

U

uber, uberis uberior/-us, uberrimus -a -um *adj.* fertile, rich, fruitful, copious; *n.* n. breast; udder

ubi *conj., adv.* where, when; as soon as

ullus -a -um (gen --ius) *adj.* any

ultimus -a -um *adj.* farthest, latest; last; highest, greatest

ultor, ultoris *n.* m. avenger, revenger

ultra, ulterius, ultimum *adv.* beyond, further; besides; *prep.* w/ acc. on the other side; more than, besides

umbra, umbrae *n.* f. shade; ghost; shadow

umbrosus -a -um *adj.* shady

umerus, umeri *n.* m. upper arm, shoulder

umquam *adv.* ever, at any time

una *adv.* together, along with; at the same time

unda, undae *n.* f. wave

unde *adv.* from which place; from whom

unicus -a -um *adj.* only, singular, unique; uncommon

universus -a -um *adj.* whole, entire; universal

unus, una, unum *adj.* alone, sole; single; only (pl.)

urbanus -a -um *adj.* of the city; courteous; witty, sophisticated

urbs, urbis *n.* f. city; city of Rome

urna, urnae *n.* f. jar for ashes, drawing lots, voting, water

uro, urere, ussi, ustus *v.* burn

usus, usus *n.* m. use; experience, skill, advantage; custom

ut *conj.* in order that; how, as, when, while; even if

uter, utra, utrum *adj.* which of two; either; *pron.* w/ -que: each; both

utilis, utile *adj.* useful, profitable, practical, advantageous

utique *adv.* certainly, by all means; at any rate

utor, uti, usus sum *v.* use, enjoy (w/ abl.)

utrum *adv., conj.* whether; (**utrum...an**: whether... or)

uva, uvae *n.* f. grape

uxor, uxoris *n.* f. wife

V

vacuus -a -um *adj.* empty, vacant, unoccupied; free of

validus, valida, validum *adj.* strong, powerful; valid

valles, vallis *n.* f. valley, vale, hollow

varietas, varietatis *n.* f. variety, difference

vario, variare, variavi, variatus *v.* variegate; waver; fluctuate, change

varius -a -um *adj.* different; various; changing; colored

vehemens, vehementis vehementior/-us,

vehementissimus -a -um *adj.* violent, severe, vigorous

vehiculum, vehiculi *n.* n. carriage, vehicle

veho, vehere, vexi, vectus *v.* bear, carry, convey; pass, ride, sail

vel *adv. conj.* even; or; (**vel...vel**: either ... or)

vello, vellere, velli/vulsi, vulsus *v.* pluck, tear out

velo, velare, velavi, velatus *v.* veil, cover; wrap; conceal; clothe in

velox, velocis velocior/-us, velocissimus -a -um *adj.* swift, quick, rapid

velut *adv.* just as, as if

vendo, vendere, vendidi, venditus *v.* sell

veneror, venerari, veneratus sum *v.* adore, revere, honor, worship; pray, entreat

venio, venire, veni, ventus *v.* come

ventus, venti *n.* m. wind

ver, veris *n.* n. spring; youth

verbum, verbi *n.* n. word; proverb; (w/ **dare**: cheat, deceive)

vere, verius, verissime *adv.* really, truly; rightly, exactly; truthfully

vereor, vereri, veritus sum *v.* revere, respect; fear; dread

veritas, veritatis *n.* f. truth, honesty

vernus -a -um *adj.* of the spring

vero *adv.* yes; certainly; to be sure; however

verto, vertere, verti, versus *v.* turn; change; overthrow, destroy

verus -a -um, verior/-us, verissimus -a -um *adj.* true, genuine, actual; right, fair, proper

vester, vestra, vestrum *adj.* your (pl.)

vestibulum, vestibuli *n.* n. entrance, court

vestigium, vestigi(i) *n.* n. step, track; trace; footstep

vestio, vestire, vestivi, vestitus *v.* clothe

vestitus, vestitus *n.* m. clothing

vetus, veteris veterior/-us, veterrimus -a -um *adj.* old, ancient; veteran, chronic; *n.* n. antiquity

vexo, vexare, vexavi, vexatus *v.* shake, jolt; annoy, harass, disturb

via, viae *n.* f. way, road, street; journey

vicinus -a -um *adj.* nearby, neighboring; *n.* m. neighbor

--, vicis *n.* f. turn, change, succession; repayment; plight, lot

victima, victimae *n.* f. victim; animal for sacrifice

video, videre, vidi, visus *v.* see, look at; (pass) seem, seem good, be seen

viduus -a -um *adj.* widowed, deprived of (w/ gen.); bereft; unmarried

viginti, vicesimus -a -um, viceni -ae -a, vicie(n)s *num.* twenty; twentieth, twenty men; twenty times

vilica, vilicae *n.* f. wife of a farm overseer

villa, villae *n.* f. estate ; country residence; village

vindico, vindicare, vindicavi, vindicatus *v.* claim,

vindicate; punish, avenge

vinum, vini *n.* n. wine

violens, violentis *adj.* violent

violentia, violentiae *n.* f. violence, aggressiveness

vir, viri *n.* m. man; husband; hero

virginalis, virginale *adj.* of a maiden, maidenly, virginal

virginitas, virginitatis *n.* f. maidenhood, virginity

virgo, virginis *n.* f. maiden, young woman

viritim *adv.* man by man; individually

virtus, virtutis *n.* f. strength; bravery; worth, character, excellence

visus, visus *n.* m. sight, appearance; vision

vita, vitae *n.* f. life, career, livelihood; mode of life

vitalis, vitale *adj.* vital

vitiosus -a -um *adj.* full of vice, vicious

vito, vitare, vitavi, vitatus *v.* avoid, shun; evade

vivo, vivere, vixi, victus *v.* be alive, live; survive; reside

vivus -a -um *adj.* alive, fresh; living

vix *adv.* hardly, scarcely, with difficulty

voco, vocare, vocavi, vocatus *v.* call, summon; name

volo, velle, volui, -- *v.* wish, want, prefer; be willing

voluptas, voluptatis *n.* f. pleasure, delight, enjoyment

vos, vestrum/vestri, vobis, vos, vobis *pron.* you (pl.)

votivus -a -um *adj.* in fulfillment of a vow

votum, voti *n.* n. vow, religious pledge; prayer; votive offering

vox, vocis *n.* f. voice, tone, expression

vulnus, vulneris *n.* n. wound; injury

vultus, vultus *n.* m. face, expression; looks